WILLIAM NOWLAND

THE SQUATTER WHO SHOWED THE WAY

Lucie Crawford

Copyright © 2025 Lucie Crawford
This work is copyright. Apart from any fair dealing for the purposes of private study, research, criticism or review, as permitted by the Copyright Act 1968, no part may be reproduced by any process without prior written permission. Enquiries should be addressed to the publisher.

Lucie Crawford – William Nowland: the squatter who showed the way

ISBN 978-1-7641269-3-9 (Paperback)

 A catalogue record for this book is available from the National Library of Australia

The author wishes to acknowledge the Traditional Owners of the lands on which the events in this book took place, and to pay her respects to their Elders, past, present and emerging.
First Nations readers are advised that the book contains material relating to deceased people, and to acts of colonial violence and dispossession. The book quotes from sources that sometimes use language that is inappropriate and offensive today.

Original drawings on front cover, back cover and p. viii
by Stewart Crawford

Cover & internal design: Ronald Proft
Delphian Books
+61 2 8625 5530
www.delphianbooks.com.au

Printed in Australia

Life is a journey – it is how we live it that matters.

*Thank you Stewart,
for your inspiring and exceptional drawings and all your
thoughts, time and energy on this story, your meticulous
commentary and editorial skills, while reading and re-reading
the many draft copies and listening to my endless stories about
William Nowland.*

CONTENTS

Preface ix

PART ONE

William Nowland's Early Life at Wilberforce, as a Pastoralist at Rosedale and a Squatter on the Liverpool Plains

1 The Formative Years 2
2 Venturing into the Hunter Valley 15
3 A Squatter on the Liverpool Plains 28
4 The Kamilaroi Nation 34
5 A Pastoralist and Squatter 44
6 The Nowland Brothers and The Farlow Sisters 51
7 William Nowland – the Furthest North 54
8 Governor Bourke's Proclamation 58
9 Governor Gipps' Response to the Slaughterhouse Creek Massacre and the Myall Creek Massacre 61

PART TWO

William Expands his Interests as a Pastoralist and Squatter

10 Legal Disputes, Claims and Counter Claims 64
11 A Pastoralist at Rosedale 72
12 Moving Further North as a Squatter 77
13 Why 'Ward's Mistake'? 87
14 The Challenges and Tragedies in the 1840s 89
15 Governor Gipps' Proposed New Regulations For Land Tenure 93
16 Camberwell in the Mid to Late 1840s 98
17 Governor FitzRoy's Tenure 101

PART THREE

William Constantly in Court

18	William Enters the 1850s Insolvent	112
19	William, the Courts and Wallalla Station	124
20	Camberwell in the 1850s	137
21	William Back in Court	143
22	More Family Tragedy Followed by Grit and Determination	182

PART FOUR

The Changes in Land Tenure

23	John Robertson's Proposed Changes to Land Tenure Policy	192
24	The Privy Council's Decision on Wallalla Station	196
25	William and His Boys Purchase Allotments at Warrah Ridge	202
26	Changing Family Dynamics in the 1860s	207

PART FIVE

Changes in Transport and Family Life

27	The Roads the Nowlands Travelled & The Paddle Steamers They Took South	212
28	The Steam Trains	218
29	Rosedale and the Dispersal of Family	224
30	Camberwell in 1869	230

PART SIX

The Dynasty William Believed He Had Created

31	The Nowland Family and Their Farms	234
32	The Nowland Voices in the Papers	247
33	William Still an Advocate for Camberwell	264
34	William's Last Will and Testimony	278

Epilogue	292
Endnotes	301
Figures	333
Bibliography	335
About the Author	344

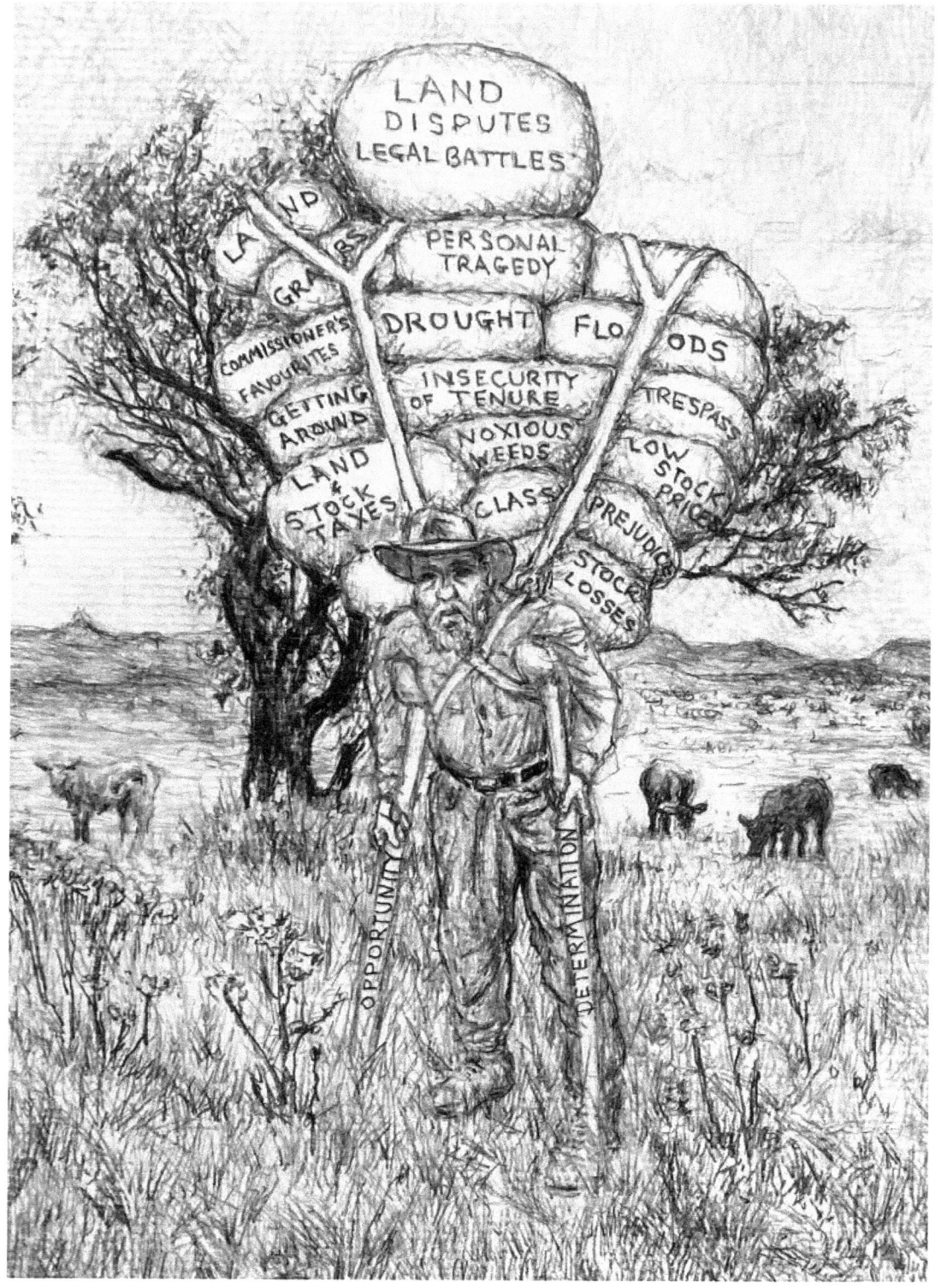

Figure 1: An Indomitable Spirit

Preface

Genealogy is not an exact science – it is full of misinformation, disinformation, bias and innuendo. Facts are often contested and need to be evaluated with diligent appraisal. In this research the propensity for inconsistencies in genealogical data surfaced right at the start of the investigation. William Nowland's birthplace and year varied and what was discovered in one reputable source differed in another source of the same standing. To find a solution, every interpretation of William's birth year was recorded and scrutinised until a credible and uncontested answer emerged. William's story is based on this approach; resolute and where possible, repetitive findings are utilised to tell his story.

This literary journey started during COVID when Sydney was in lockdown and the only library a virtual one: the internet. This stood in strong contrast to my PhD research in the 1990s, when investigation involved a lot of time in the State Library of New South Wales either reading academic articles, books and documents, or in the basement of the library alone amongst rows of printed Federal Hansard and House Papers. Since then, the internet, when used judiciously (with care and discretion), has evolved into a sophisticated tool that provides a wealth of informed knowledge, first-hand accounts, academic articles, historical documents and e-books. The websites in this journey of discovery (many cited) were interesting, insightful and informative and provided a substantial, rich and comprehensive data set for William Nowland's story.

Once the COVID lockdown was over, the historical societies were a valuable source of primary data. One can only admire the volunteer researchers and their generous contribution in collating the data required, making suggestions and exploring new sources of information, once you arrive. The Societies in my study included: Royal Australian Historical Society, Hawkesbury Historical Society, Singleton Historical Society, Scone & Upper Hunter Historical Society, Quirindi & District Historical Society and Glen Innes & District Historical Society.

This story about William Nowland places his life within a period of profound and rapid change, as the colony of NSW moved from a convict settlement to a self-governing colony. Each thread of evidence is drawn together sequentially in 'the imagining' of what it was like to be William as a first-generation colonial Australian.

William's life occurred in conjunction with the dispossession of Country for First Nations people, in all the places he settled. At each stage of his journey first-hand accounts, learned publications and academic articles describe the impact of William and his fellow settlers on each of the First Nations they invaded.

The profound insights I have gained from the story are invaluable and cannot be understated. Though educated and an academic, my knowledge of British colonial expansion in NSW was generic and I knew little about the impact of the settlers on First Nations people who had lived in harmony with Country for tens of thousands of years. In contrast, I was highly aware of the key players in the colonial story, such as Cook, Phillip, Macquarie and Macarthur and as a secondary school teacher had naively taught (as part of the NSW syllabus in the 1970s) Years 7 and 8 about the so called 'nomadic' Aboriginals. My generation and the one that followed were misinformed, and the depth of knowledge and analysis that should have been mandatory in ours and their studies was missing.

With all this in mind I invite you to read this story of mine and possibly your ancestor, William Nowland.

Lucie Crawford
Sydney, 31st October 2025

PART ONE

William Nowland's Early Life at Wilberforce, as a Pastoralist at Rosedale and a Squatter on the Liverpool Plains

William seized every opportunity and was determined to be successful in everything he pursued.

CHAPTER 1

THE FORMATIVE YEARS

William Nowland was born on the 28th September 1804,[1] probably at home, in the Superintendent of Convicts Cottage, Castle Hill Public Agricultural Settlement.[2]

When William was born, his father, Michael Nowland had been the Superintendent of Convicts at Castle Hill for two years, and his mother, Elizabeth Nowland (née Richards) had been married to Michael for 13 years and given birth to five of their children; four surviving. With the birth of 'our' William (their sixth child) Michael and Elizabeth decided on the same name as their first child, who only lived for five weeks and two days.[3]

Fourteen years earlier, William's parents had arrived separately as part of the Second Fleet, after spending many years imprisoned in appalling conditions in England. Each had been found guilty of a petty crime at their local Assizes (courts) and sentenced to transportation to Britain's latest penal colony.[4]

Michael was transported for life and Elizabeth for seven years. Like many of the convicts in the colony, their punishment far outweighed their crime. This was because it was in the interest of the British Government to quickly reduce the number of petty criminals in England's grossly overcrowded gaols and at the same time, conveniently provide an 'indentured labour force' to facilitate the consolidation, expansion and development of the NSW penal colony.[5]

Michael was transported for stealing a horse in 1783, on the King's Highway, London,[6] and Elizabeth, for break and entry into William Field's house, Birmingham, in 1787.[7] Elizabeth came to the colony first on the 3rd June 1790, at the age of 15, under her maiden name Elizabeth Richards on the notorious Second Fleet ship the *Lady Juliana*. While William's father, Michael Nowland arrived, on the 28th June 1790, at the age of 29, on the most reprehensible convict ship of all, the *Scarborough*.[8]

Michael and Elizabeth were married in a mass ceremony of convicts on Norfolk Island in November 1791.[9] A few years later, both received their ticket of freedom (Elizabeth in 1794 and Michael on the 22nd February 1796).[10] They lived as convicts and later as farmers on Norfolk Island for nearly 10 years between 1790 and circa 1800, and with the 'favour' (regard) of Governor King, had started to establish themselves on Norfolk Island, in the newly emerging colony of NSW, before moving to the mainland (The Rocks, Sydney) in 1801 and then to Castle Hill in 1802.

When William was born in Castle Hill in 1804, his father Michael was 43 and his mother Elizabeth was 29. William (as told earlier) had five older siblings, four surviving: William (1792–1792) Norfolk Island; Michael jr. (1794) Norfolk Island; Henry (1796) Norfolk Island; Elizabeth jr. (1798) Norfolk Island; and Ann (1801) The Rocks, Sydney. Three younger siblings followed: Edward (1806) Wilberforce, Mary (1809) Wilberforce; and Sarah Jane (1814) Wilberforce.[11]

Two years after William was born, the family left Castle Hill and moved to the Hawkesbury. William's father was no longer Superintendent of Convicts, and the family had relocated to a leased farm at Wilberforce.

Prior to the move, William's father, Michael, leased 37½ acres of land in the Lower Wilberforce from William Burgess in December 1805, as detailed next.[12]

Lease of 37 ½ acres of land from Wm Burgess to Mic Knowland 20 acres for 3 years at £40 pr. Annum and 17½ A [acres] for 6 years, he, clearing 10 A [acres] of Forrest [sic] Land.[13]

Michael added into this land, and by the time the family had moved to Wilberforce, Michael had expanded his lease to include an extra 14½ acres. See below.

By 1806, Michael and Elizabeth had started to make their own way in the colony. They lived on a leased farm of 52 acres, were raising six children, providing rations and keep for four farm workers and owned cattle, goats and nearly 300 sheep.[14]

The four workers on the family farm were probably indentured convicts who were mustered and assigned on application to Michael Nowland; a practice that was common throughout the colony.

Parts of the original cottage the family lived in on this leased farm still stands today at 87 King Road Wilberforce. See the transcription that follows.

NOWLAND COTTAGE (c.1810–1816)
87 KING ROAD WILBERFORCE

Nowland's Cottage consists of two free-standing cottages and a slab barn. The oldest cottage at the rear is built of vertical adzed timber slabs. It contains three original rooms, wide floorboards, and an attic door. The front cottage constructed of brick is larger and built at a later, date. The slab barn made of timbers is the oldest building on the site. The original buildings are thought to be built by Michael Nowland, Chief Constable of Wilberforce [part of Michael's story] who lived here with his family of nine children.[15] [Based on the known children, there were 'eight'].[16]

It was on this farm that William and his siblings were most likely socialised into the settlers' ominous and shared colonial view of the Dharug people who had been settled on Dharug Country for around 50,000 years. The Dharug were conveniently and righteously challenged, compromised, forced away from the river system wherever the settlers congregated, and expected to be subservient.

> *Between 1794 and 1816, Dyarubbin [the Hawkesbury River] was the site of one of the longest frontier wars in Australian history. Invasion and colonisation kicked off a slow and cumulative process of violence, theft of aboriginal children, dispossession and the ongoing annexation of the river lands.*
>
> *Yet despite this sorry history, Dyarubbin's people managed to remain on their Country and they still live on the river today.*[17]

Michael and Elizabeth's children also learnt the British way of settlement and farming which through its practices obstructed the Dharug way of life. The rapid expansion of colonial settlements stood in stark contrast to the 50,000 years of sustained existence between the Dharug people and Dharug Country. All around them the settlers were denuding the land and rapidly destroying their food supply. The Dharug could not compete with the permanent dwellings, herd animals and fields of crops, where once trees stood, surrounded by edible wild grasses, native animals, and indigenous foods. To add to this devastation, the Dharug waterways were also invaded and taken over by the settlers. Michael and Elizabeth's family farm sat adjacent to the Hawkesbury River at Wilberforce and by the time the family had arrived, the Dharug had already been expelled. While the farmers took advantage of the river and all it offered, the Dharug could not return to their fishing and settlement spots, along the Hawkesbury, in fear of being shot.[18]

It was along this appropriated river that Michael and Elizabeth's children learned to survive the floods and droughts that consistently inundated and threatened their farm and those of the other settlers.

Each of these facets of William's world: the settlers' attitudes and behaviours towards the Dharug people; the British way of settlement and farming; and, the learnt skills of survival during floods and droughts, were informative and influential in shaping William's perceptions and attitude to life in his boyhood and youth. Each is explored in more detail next to ascertain some understanding of William the man who ventured out beyond Wilberforce in circa 1823 (with his brothers), into the northern interior in search of his own land to settle on; initially at Falbrook (now known as Camberwell), and then later, as a squatter on the Liverpool Plains and the New England Tablelands.

The Dharug People

In starting this journey, how William and his siblings viewed the Dharug people can only be inferred based on informed knowledge, research and publications on this time and place in history, along with the British publications of the day.

By the time William was born in 1804 colonial attitudes and behaviours towards the Dharug people were already well entrenched. With the encouragement and support of each successive Governor and the NSW Corps, settlers had successfully challenged and destroyed the livelihood of the Dharug people on Dharug Country along the Dyarubbin (Hawkesbury River). The horrendous impact farmers like William's father, Michael, had on the lands and food supply of the Dharug people, just through their sheer presence, cannot be understated. There are many accounts in the newspapers of the time that clearly demonstrate the settlers' righteousness and sense of a power position – armed with their guns. The one that follows is illuminating and indicative.

The Sydney Gazette and New South Wales Advertiser,
17 June 1804, page 2.
Natives

Last week in consequence of His Excellency's dispatches to T. Arndel Esq. Magistrate for Hawkesbury, a body of Settlers, fourteen in number were in pursuit of the Natives that had committed numerous outrages at Portland Head [Hawkesbury River]; and separated into two divisions, one party, seven in number, lead forwarded by I. Phillips, who was best acquainted by the travel through the brush, proceeded towards the Mountains, and at length came up with forty or fifty of the hostile savages, who had a quantity of property of which they had stripped the Settlers; these retreating towards a cluster of Rocks forms a junction with another group much more formidable, compleating (sic) in all about 300.

The few Settlers, agreeable to their instructions, endeavoured to ascertain their motives for the acts of depredation and cruelty they had committed; to which end they offered a parley and interrogated them whether they had been ill treated; but all they offered in their justification was an ironical declaration that they wanted corn, wearing apparel, and whatever else the Settlers had, then throwing down a flight of spears compelled the pursuers, in their own defense, to commence firing, in hopes to intimidate their assailants, but without the desired effect; and thou' several must have been wounded, yet the body hovered round the Settlers party, three of them [the settlers] laden with the most valuable part of the spoil which they had retaken from the forty at first fallen in with, and undercover of the fire of the other four [settlers], got into Richmond Hill without receiving a spear wound.

Late accounts state that they still continue their ravages, and that another European had been speared at the beginning of the week. Two of the most violent and ferocious were shot at the Green Hills [Windsor] by the Military detachment sent to the relief of the Settlers, whose self preservation requires that they should ever be on the alert to counteract the mischievous designs of the savage and unfeeling enemy.

Etched into the above account is the typical response from both groups. The Dharug men were determined to dissuade the settlers from permanent settlement in Dharug Country. They used guerrilla warfare tactics to deter the settlers, such as, being friendly when needed, observing the settlers without their knowledge, doing the required reconnaissance, lying in wait, raiding homesteads, stealing crops, killing livestock, and threatening isolated settlers, by confronting them, stealing their food and burning their huts. The Dharug were resilient and stood their ground despite the communicable diseases the settlers carried (such as smallpox) and the threatening behaviour they experienced from the settlers, sometimes with their muskets as evident in the deaths, murders and massacres of the Dharug people.[19]

Some 237 years later (in 2025), the Dharug clans share their inherited knowledge of these colonial times, embrace their culture, and continue to impart the rich traditions they sustain.[20]

William was brought up in this British colonial imperialistic environment where the Dharug people were largely treated with indifference, marginalised, murdered, and sometimes massacred.[21] William would have known that the Dharug Nation had engaged in retaliative raids and in some cases, settlers had been killed. Yet he probably largely felt safe, knowing the limited power of the Dharug warrior's spears against the settlers' guns and the military garrison.

By 1816, when William was 12, Governor Macquarie placed a garrison of the NSW Corps in Windsor with instructions to shoot any member of the Dharug people who entered the settlement. Shooting First Nations people on sight, a deplorable act that could only be classed as murder, was seen as legitimate and justifiable behaviour by the settlers. There was no recognition of the Dharug people and their rightful inhabitance of Dharug Country.

William or his family's personal interaction with or response to the Dharug people in the Hawkesbury is unknown and later accounts, from William as a squatter on the Liverpool Plains are brief and generic (as detailed later in the story). One can reasonably assume, based on the literature of the time, that when William left Wilberforce circa 1823, he had been socialised into a commonly held view, that can be summarised as, the settlers were the ones with the rights, and the 'Aboriginals' needed to vacate the land as required and become accustomed to the settlers' presence.

Recurring Floods and Droughts Along the Hawkesbury

William, during his boyhood and youth, also learnt how to survive the endemic cycle of floods and drought in the Hawkesbury. The family farm was adjacent to the river and highly susceptible in times of flood. One can image, as told in the following account, the inundation and the loss of soil, stock and farming equipment with each flood.

> *...the downside of living on the fertile plains [of the Hawkesbury] ... was having to endure the problems of frequent, unexpected floods. Not only did the water rise in the river, isolating the settlements, and destroying both stock and crops, but houses, equipment and belongings were swept away, and farmers were left in financial ruin. The constant destruction of crops led various Government officials to note the impracticality of depending on the district as the main food supply. Inundations...recorded 1799, 1801 [and when Michael and his family were there] 1806, 1809, 1816, 1817 and 1819.*[22]

The family also faced at least three severe droughts between 1813 and 1815. As told in the following extracts from the *Sydney and New South Wales Advertiser*.

On the 28th August 1813
The prevailing droughts have proved very destructive to the flocks and herds...

On the 1st January 1814
The severe distress suffered by the Settlers in general ... from the late long continued drought.

On the 23rd December 1815
...The repeated droughts for the last three Seasons induce the GOVERNOR to recommend to the Settlers to sink large Reservoirs or Tanks for the Reception of the occasional Rains, whereby he is assured that much of the Injury now sustained by the Cattle for Want of Water would be happily avoided...

Farming wasn't easy in the harsh Australian environment – one needed to be resilient as William's parents well knew. When they arrived at Port Jackson in June, 1790 the penal colony was going through a period of severe drought and was on the verge of famine. A few months later on the 1st August 1790, they were both sent to Norfolk Island with 183 other convicts on the *Surprize* where they lived under strict rules and regulations and in harsh living conditions, clearing and tilling the soil and cultivating crops and produce (including a piggery) for the purpose (along with the other convicts) of boosting the colony's food supply. It was on Norfolk Island that Michael and Elizabeth learned the hard lessons of how to live and farm in the virgin soils of Australia, which their children in turn learned from them. William and his brothers, as young men took this knowledge with them when they ventured out on their own into the Hunter Valley (c.1823). Later, in 1827 to 1828, when faced once again with severe drought the lessons and experiences they had had in the

Hawkesbury held them in good stead on their own allotments at Falbrook and for William also at Warrah on the Liverpool Plains.[23]

Carpentry was also a key skill required if one was to successfully build a dwelling in a remote location, house stock, mend the dray, and provide all the wooden tools, fencing and equipment necessary to survive. William's father and his older brothers had honed these skills and willingly passed them on to him. William's father's expertise in carpentry were especially evident in the wooden punt he built in 1812 to carry passengers, wagons and stock across the Hawkesbury from Wilberforce to Pitt Town, for a fee. See the ad in the *Sydney Gazette* that follows.

The Sydney Gazette and New South Wales Advertiser, 25th April 1812, page 1

Whereas Michael Nowland has lately constructed a boat or Punt for the Conveyance of Persons, Cattle, Carriages, Carts &c as a regular Ferry Boat across the river Hawkesbury between the Districts of Wilberforce and Pitt Town, and laid before the bench of assembled at Windsor a list of Schedule of the Tolls which he proposed demanding for the Accommodation thus offered to the Public; and those magistrates having considered the same, and made some Alterations therein, and submitted the amended Schedule to his Excellency the Governor, for His Sanction and Approval, his Excellency is Pleased to give His Sanction and Approval thereto, and directs that all Persons who shall, on or after, the first day of May next, ensuing employ said Ferry boat for the conveyance of themselves, their Servants, Cattle, Carriages, Carts &c. across the river Hawkesbury shall Pay Toll for the same of the Rate specified in the subjoined Schedule.

Schedule of Tolls to be demanded and Paid at Nowland's Punt Ferry, between Wilberforce and Pitt Town:

For each

- *Foot Passenger 3d*
- *Saddle-Horse 1s 6d*
- *Foal 6d*
- *Horse and Chaise 2s 6d*
- *Cart with 1 Horse or 2 Bullocks 2s 6d*
- *Ditto with 2 Horses or 3 Bullocks 3s*
- *Waggon (sic) with 4 Horses or 6 Bullocks 4s*
- *For Horned Cattle 1s per head*
- *For Ditto of more than 1 and not exceeding 20 ... 9d per head*

- *For Ditto of if upward of 20 ... 6d per head*
- *For Sheep 2s per Score, or 7s 6d. per Hundred*
- *For Hogs and Goats 2d. each, or 2s per Score*

Passengers are not to pay Toll more than once in the same day, and all Officers, Civil and Military, and other Persons in the employment of the Government on the Public Service, are to have the Advantage of said Ferry at all times Toll free.

By Command of his Excellency the Governor,

J.T. CAMPBELL; Secretary

The Nowland Punt was a successful business venture for Michael sr. and his family for the next 10 years (1812–1822). William would also learn the necessary crafts a young man needed to be a successful pastoralist and squatter in the interior, from his older brothers; Michael jr., a blacksmith and Henry, a wheelwright.

William also grew up on a reasonably prosperous farm. Going back to 1806, when William was two, the General Muster (the Census) on the 12th August 1806 paints a picture of the family farm.

[Michael listed with] 52 acres of which 18 sown to wheat, 2 to barley and ¼ to orchard ... 34¾ annual pastures, 7 lying fallow. The animals consisting of 150 male sheep, 133 ewes, 1 bull, 9 cows, 2 oxen, 1 male goat and 5 female goats. One bushel each of wheat and maize in hand.

Self, wife and six children not victualled from Government stores. 2 convicts and 2 freemen employed not victualled from Gov't stores. Rents from Burges.[24]

Based on the above account, William's father's farm of 52 acres consisted of an extensive mix of crops and livestock, with enough to get by, as well as give to the Government stores. Even in times of drought and flood, William's parents were able to provide for their family and give surplus produce to the Government stores in exchange for credits.[25]

In particular, the flood on the 30th July 1809, took six lives in the district, destroyed vital crops and provided a real prospect of starvation.[26] In response, Michael delivered 167 pounds of pork to the Hawkesbury Store. See the account that follows.

26th August 1809 Michael delivers 167lbs of pork to Hawkesbury store.

The goods delivered to 'prisoners for their rations, to women and children without support and those affected by floods'.[27]

Based on the above entry, William's father Michael also had pigs on the family farm; the farming practice of having pigs and running a piggery is part of Michael's story in London, and later, on Norfolk Island.[28]

Michael sr. was also one of the earliest settlers to own sheep,[29] most likely, fat-tailed sheep used for their meat, given that his son, William, later as a squatter on the Liverpool Plains, showed no interest in the Merino sheep grazed for their wool by the Australian Agriculture Company, circa 1832 (told later in the story).

William, like his Father, Pursued Every Opportunity

As soon as the family settled on the farm at Wilberforce, Michael sr. employed carpenters to build a granary (1806),[30] he then raised funds to expand his assets on the farm (1806–1810)[31] and found creditors to back the wooden punt he built and operated across the Hawkesbury (from 1812).[32] This sense of drive and ambition was shared by William and his siblings, and shown over and over again once the Nowland siblings (Henry, William, Edward and Mary) ventured out of Wilberforce into 'the interior': Falbrook (later known as Camberwell), Scone, Muswellbrook, the Liverpool Plains and the New England Tablelands; all detailed later in the story.

William's father was opportunistic, always looking for a way to gain more income and status in the growing community of Wilberforce. This was a trait mirrored in William's adult life as he secured and expanded the family farm Rosedale at Camberwell, found and showed others the easiest route onto the Liverpool Plains, and established several runs (later known as stations) beyond the boundaries of settlement.

Yet, before all this could happen, William had a lot of other learning to do. From the age of five or six, William and his siblings, especially the boys, probably went to school at Green Hills (later, known as Windsor); the only school in the Hawkesbury, until 1820.[33]

The Schoolhouse at Green Hills

William's schoolhouse at Green Hills opened in 1804, the year William was born in Castle Hill.[34] Five years later William and his siblings (c.1809) probably went to school by horse or horse and dray (unless they walked) given the school was 4.9 miles (8 km) away from their farm at Wilberforce.

The *Sydney Gazette* describes the appearance of the schoolhouse at Green Hills soon after it was opened in 1804. It was quite a substantial building. See the account that follows.

The Sydney Gazette – 26th Aug. 1804, page 3.

Sydney

The Brickwork of the Church and School-house at the Green Hills [Windsor], Hawkesbury is now finished and the building newly covered. The dimensions are 101 Feet in length, 24 broad and the walls 24 Feet high, comprising the base of an upper story, an end of which is partitioned off for the residence of the instructor. Its situation is such as to form a street behind the New Store. The design of the edifice must interest every person in its speedy accomplishment, as while it promotes Christianity by the benefits that accrue by Public Worship, it also illuminates the infant mind by the inculcation of moral principles and the help of such branches of useful instruction as are absolutely necessary to rescue the rising generation from the morbid glooms of interest.[35]

A photo of the Windsor Schoolhouse (post-1841) is shown in Figure 2.[36]

Figure 2: Thompson Square and Windsor's First School

The teachers at the school (like William's parents) were emancipated convicts who now had some status and position within the colony, as was the case for William's father when he became the Superintendent of Convicts at Castle Hill (in 1802).[37] Later in William's father's life (in 1819) he would once again gain some status in the local Wilberforce community through his position as District Constable and Pound-Keeper, Lower Wilberforce.[38]

William's teachers, Mathew Hughes and later, Joseph Harpur, were both Irish: just like William's father. Mathew Hughes, a soldier, came to the colony as a convict on the *Britannia* in 1797, and Joseph Harpur (previous occupation unknown) on the *Royal Admiral* in 1800. Mathew Hughes taught at the school from 1810 to 1813, after which he was transferred to the schoolhouse at Richmond and replaced by Mr. Joseph Harpur who taught at Windsor from 1813 to 1826 while also acting as the Parish Clerk.[39]

William's Mother, Elizabeth Richards

The impact William's mother Elizabeth had on his life can only be inferred because there is very little data for Elizabeth after William was born. For me, Elizabeth's lived experiences prior to coming to the colony and her early years as a very young mother on Norfolk Island (that are documented) would have required a strong woman who from a very young age rose to the challenges of life in a gutsy and forthright manner.

Elizabeth was born in Warwickshire, in 1775,[40] and based on inference, baptised at St. Martin's Birmingham.[41] Her documentary story starts with her crime at the age of 12 with accomplice Hannah Bolton, 18. The type of crime (break and enter), and the ages of the two girls, are suggestive of a scene from Charles Dickens's *Oliver Twist*: Elizabeth probably small enough to enter and unlock the door or window, with Hannah following behind, both possibly living on the street or employed for scarcely any money, at the local workhouse.[42]

Once caught, Elizabeth and Hannah were taken to Warwick Country Goal, and then at the Warwick Assizes (courts) in August 1787, found guilty and sentenced to seven years transportation. They were then held in Warwick County Goal and fettered in a cold, dark and damp cell,[43] where for just under two years,[44] they worked daily for long hours picking apart tarred rope (picking oakum), making shoes and stitching mail bags.[45] Then, sometime in the spring or possibly, in the early summer of 1789, they were taken by horse and dray 119 miles (191.5 km) to the *Lady Juliana* docked at Woolwich on the Thames, and set sail for Port Jackson on the 29th July 1789.[46]

Elizabeth, now 14 and Hannah 20 found themselves on a female convict ship portrayed in Sian Rees' book as the 'Floating Brothel',[47] because many of the 226 convicts on board were 'street walkers' (prostitutes) who took advantage of their 'profession' to 'gain favour' amongst the crew and officers.

In a journey that took just over 10 months, Elizabeth, Hannah and the other women were set to work making shirts and apparel for the ship merchants to sell on arrival.[48] The women were well fed, the ship was regularly cleaned, and fumigated, and the conditions on board ensured a relatively low death toll; only five women died during the journey.[49]

When the *Lady Juliana* entered Port Jackson on the 6th June 1790,[50] they were greeted with mixed feelings: excitement about the supplies the *Lady Juliana* had retrieved, though limited, from the storeship *Guardian* that they had come across beached and abandoned at the Cape of Good Hope; jubilation on receiving news from home, after three years of isolation; and, concern over the 220 extra convicts that needed to be fed in a colony that was on the brink of starvation.[51]

Initially, Elizabeth 15, and Hannah 21, remained in Sydney for two months as indentured servants. Then, as told earlier they set sail on the *Surprize* for Norfolk Island (1st August 1790). There were 185 convicts on board; 35 male convicts (including Michael Nowland), and 150 female convicts (including Elizabeth and Hannah).[52] The purpose of the journey was to provide indentured labour to clear land, grow crops and provide food for the starving colony. The journey of 1040.7 miles (1,675 km) took six days, and on arrival the convicts were set to work. They were required to live off the land, grow their own food, and provide produce for the colony. Their Commander Major Robert Ross was hard, cruel, and uncaring, and their living conditions and provisions were challenging and inadequate.[53]

It is here Elizabeth met her husband to be, Michael, nearly twice her age. At first, they probably co-habited and as told earlier, later married in a mass ceremony on Norfolk Island, in 1791. Then, in the following year (1792), also told earlier, Elizabeth (16), gave birth to their first child 'William' whom they lost, five weeks later. Though the loss of a child was common, after all Elizabeth had gone through, this must have been the ultimate challenge.

Elizabeth also landed on her feet. Michael was an ambitious man who through his farming practice would turn their life around, gain acknowledgment and success in the colony, but this was not without the support of Elizabeth, both on the farm and in the household. Throughout their life together, Elizabeth had her work cut out for her, raising seven children, and losing two (one soon after birth and one at the age of 18).[54] Elizabeth also lost her close friend (her only family prior to Michael) Hannah Bolton in 1801 (14 years after their conviction in 1787).

Elizabeth was also audacious; family stories tell us when the Battle of Vinegar Hill occurred in 1804, Elizabeth (at least a couple of months pregnant with 'our' William) was there with the Irish convict rebels. Maybe this defiant streak in Elizabeth is mythology, but it is part of my impression of Elizabeth as a person who (for me) was courageous, steadfast, and took all the challenges of life in her stride.

These character traits of William's mother, and the determination and ambition of his father, would have enhanced William's and his siblings' lives. By the time William was 10, his parents, through their daily approach to life (striving and achieving) would have already provided the foundation stones for William's own life experiences.

The Ups and Downs of Family Life

William's tenth year was an eventful year. His last sibling 'Sarah Jane' was born in 1814,[55] his older sibling, Elizabeth jr., 16, married Henry Richardson, in Windsor,[56] and they had their first child, the following year (1815); William was now an uncle.[57]

Two years later (1817) when William was 13, his father Michael sold his Punt because he was asked to pay back the monies he owed to George Howe, a major creditor.[58] This would have been a difficult time for the family, given all the effort they had put into the Punt over the previous five years; especially, their father, Michael, who continued to manage and operate the services across the Hawkesbury. Yet worse was to come in 1819, when William's older sister, Ann 18 died on the 25th November 1819.[59]

In the following year (1820) when William was 16, family life started to improve. William's father was appointed to the position of District Constable and Poundkeeper Lower Wilberforce.[60]

CHAPTER 2

Venturing into the Hunter Valley

The family farm at Wilberforce, though productive, had its challenges. The Hawkesbury district (that included Wilberforce) was described by John Thomas Bigge in his Report to the British government in 1820, as 'exhausted and inundated with small ill-built allotments'.[61] As outlined below.

> *At the early periods of the colony, great dependence was always placed upon the produce of the Hawkesbury districts; at present, although the fertility of the land is not exhausted, yet the admixture of weeds and wild vetches, the foul state of the land, and the continued cultivation of it for a long series of years in the same grain, has greatly deteriorated the quality of both. In maize, however, these lands continue to be still very productive, as well as in the more common kinds of vegetables. The farms, or rather allotments, in these districts are small; the houses generally ill-built and exhibiting the traces of former inundations. The fields are without fences but the vigorous and thriving condition of the horses and cattle, even in the confined state in which they are necessarily kept, bears testimony to the richness of the vegetation and pasturage.[62]*

Exploration of the Interior

Based on Bigge's descriptors, William's childhood and youth was probably rough and ready. One can understand why many of the settlers (including William and his brothers) were keen to leave and try their luck elsewhere. For William, at the age of nine, in 1813, all the gossip, rumours, excitement and expectation in this ill-formed community was most likely about the latest exploration into the interior; in this year, Blaxland, Wentworth and Lawson successfully crossed the Blue Mountains to the west and discovered the Bathurst Plains.

Then, when William was 13, Governor Macquarie turned his attention to finding a route north from Windsor. On the 30th October 1817,[63] William Parr, a mineralogist, under the instruction of Macquarie,[64] headed north-west from Windsor but 'soon became disoriented in the steep valley and mountains around the Putty area. His way blocked by thick brush and bushfires which, coupled with a shortage of rations, saw him abandon his expedition' and return to Windsor.[65]

In the following year, April to May 1818, Benjamin Singleton tried once again to find a route north along what is now known as the Putty Road. Hampered by the thick brush, and more importantly, by 200 Darkinjung men, Singleton also decided to return to Windsor. The extract that follows from Singleton's journal, tells us of the party's encounter with these warriors.

> *About 8 o'clock Disturbed by the Voices of Natives Cracking of Sticks and Rolling big rocks, stones down towards us every man of us arose and fled from the fire secreting ourselves behind trees with our guns and ammunition where we could have a view of the fire Doubting if we staid by the fire every Man was lost spent the Whole of the Night in that Condition Raining very Hard the Native whom we had with us was timid than any of us saying he was sure we should be killed.*[66]

In the same year, 1818, when 'our' William was 14, the Surveyor General, John Oxley, discovered the Liverpool Plains while returning from an aborted exploration of the Macquarie River west of the Blue Mountains. This discovery would have sparked the interest of the settlers in the Hawkesbury; especially amongst the families of first-generation colonial Australians (such as the Nowland boys) who were old enough and ready for a life of their own beyond the confines of Sydney town and the Hawkesbury. Talk of the possibilities, coupled with their awareness of a penal colony in Newcastle, would have honed their interest in the interior.[67]

In concert with Governor Macquarie, the settlers recognised that the colony could no longer rely on the Hawkesbury as the main source of food. In agreement and spurred on by Oxley's discovery, Governor Macquarie tried once more, and commissioned John Howe the Chief Constable of Windsor to build on the work of Parr and Singleton and investigate afresh an overland route from Windsor to the Hunter.

John Howe left Windsor with a party of eight men, including two Aboriginal guides on the 24th October 1819. In part, he followed Parr and Singleton's route, and when hampered by the dense and rugged bush, he sent his lead Aboriginal guide, Mioram (also known as Myles) on to see if he could persuade the local Indigenous people, the Darkinjung, to help.

Mioram came across a local Darkinjung man who was willing to show the party a way through. Howe named this new guide Murphy who took Howe and his men through some 100 miles of difficult and rugged country to the Hunter near Doyle's Creek.[68]

On the return journey south, Howe and his party came across another local Darkinjung man (that Howe named Whirle) who told Murphy he had not shown Howe the easiest route. Armed with this knowledge, Howe returned to Windsor and informed Governor Macquarie and they decided to send Mioram and their other Aboriginal guides back up the track to find Whirle, and persuade him to show them the other less strenuous route. Whirle agreed, and on the successful return of the

Aboriginal guides to Windsor, the expedition set out once again, and Mioram and the other Dharug guides led Howe and 15 men including Benjamin Singleton back up the track to the Hunter Valley along Whirle's route.

Why did the Aboriginal guides help John Howe?

The discovery of an easier route north into the Hunter had a significant impact on William's life journey but one cannot go on with William's story without first asking the above question.

The Aboriginal guides from the Richmond clan of the Dharug people were Mioram (known to the settlers as Myles), 'Woolaboy', 'Jelmarey' and 'Lazy Jack'.[69] Then, once the expedition entered Darkinjung Country the Aboriginal guides included Murphy, Whirle and Bandagran.[70] The reasons why these seven Aboriginal men helped Howe (based on my readings) are complex and nuanced.

Mioram may have helped because he felt threatened. In 1816, towards the end of the Hawkesbury Nepean Wars (1794–1816) John Howe was the District Constable at Windsor and involved in the suppression of the Dharug people and Mioram was at the top of the list of 10 Dharug men who Governor Macquarie had ordered to be apprehended by anyone who came across them with the right to shoot if apprehension proved to be too difficult. Subsequently, by November 1816, several 'on the list' had been apprehended or shot. Macquarie then issued a second proclamation that those of the 10 still at large, including Mioram, would be pardoned if they surrendered. With possibly nowhere to hide, Mioram took this option. Howe then through his acquaintance with Mioram learned of his bush skills and coaxed him to help find a way up what is now known as the Putty Road.[71]

As Mark Dunn tells us:

Three weeks after their return to Windsor, in what appears to be a first for the colony, Myles, his brother Mullaboy and 'a small number of natives' were provisioned, equipped and armed with muskets by order of Governor Macquarie, and sent back out to meet Whirle and another man, Bandagran, and follow their track to the river. Nineteen days later the all-Aboriginal exploring party returned and reported to Howe that they had followed an easier path through the mountains to the river. This was the path that Howe took on his second expedition in 1820, following Myles back through the ranges along the Aboriginal pathway of Whirle.[72]

In essence, the Aboriginal guides showed Howe Whirle's easiest route to the Hunter and in return they were given gifts; for Mioram, a breast plate from Governor Macquarie and a musket from John Howe.[73]

Mark Dunn also speculates on why these Aboriginal guides assisted Howe. Dunn surmises: for guides like Mioram, the expedition would provide 'new knowledge of new country and new people' and on return to Dharug Country this valuable information would benefit Mioram's kin and be useful when trading with other clans and/or the settlers; secondly, all of the Aboriginal guides who participated in the expedition knew they would receive gifts, such as, clothes, tobacco, food and possibly, a musket, in return for their services; and, in the case of Murphy, Whirle and Bangagran, they knew that if they acted as guides through Darkinjung Country it would facilitate the rapid movement of the intruders through and out of Country and steer these interlopers[74] away from the sacred sites.[75]

The Bulga Track

The better route disclosed by the Aboriginal guides to John Howe and his men was initially known as the Bulga Track, or the Parson's Road and later as the Putty Road.[76] It is along this route that William and his brothers made their way to Falbrook (Glennies Creek), sometime before 1824, and most likely, circa 1823. This notorious track was described in the following terms, in an 1827 article in *The Australian*.

> *The Australian, 10th August 1827, page 2 [no title]*
>
> *The road to Hunter's River, by way of the Bulga from Richmond through Curryjong (sic), Colo and Putty, and across which there is constant traffic, is described to be so bad in many places, that it is with extreme difficulty that cattle can be driven along. Thirty or forty head are supposed to have perished this year by falling off rocks and precipices and being dashed to pieces. We hope that this important and fertile country will soon have a good road by Williams through the Wollombi.*

The next part of this story logically leads to the Nowland brothers' allotments at Glennies Creek, Falbrook but before we move on, we need to fill in the intervening years (1821–1823). What was happening in the life of William and his brothers during these earlier years?

A Sliding Door Moment

In 1821, William's eldest brother Michael jr. (27) was running a blacksmith shop with his brother-in-law Henry Richardson (Elizabeth jr.'s husband) when family relationships started to unravel. Elizabeth jr. and Henry Richardson separated, Michael jr. and Henry Richardson's business partnership was dissolved, and the two men sold their blacksmith shop in George Street, Windsor.[77]

This probably was a 'sliding door moment' for Michael jr. given all the talk of the expanse of grazing land in the Hunter Valley. Michael jr. most likely encouraged by his brother Henry (the second eldest) moved on from his blacksmith shop and turned his attention to farming.

Urged on by the drought in the Hawkesbury in the following year (1822),[78] the discussion around the dinner table, in the paddocks and at the local inns, amongst the Nowland boys, must have been all about the opportunities in the Hunter Valley. The Rev. G. A. Middleton had travelled on the newly discovered Bulga Track in 1821, with 173 head of cattle followed by Benjamin Singleton and Philip Thorley and their families in 1822.[79]

In 1823, Allan Cunningham found a way onto the Liverpool Plains through a pass that he named 'Pandora Pass'; located (today) in Coolah Tops National Park, NSW.[80] This Pass did not attract attention from those in the Hawkesbury because it was too far west, while the Bulga Track with its ready access to the Hunter Valley had everyone talking.[81] Settlers from the Hawkesbury, soon followed Benjamin Singleton and Philip Thorley along this track, circa 1822.[82] Whether the Nowland brothers were amongst this initial group is unknown, but they would have needed to be on the Bulga Track by 1823. Any later and they would have missed out on their land grants in the following year (1824), when new claims in the Hunter Valley were converted into grants (detailed soon).

A Steady Stream of Settlers

One can image the steady stream of settlers who went up the Bulga Track with their cattle, in 1823, to claim land in the Lower Hunter and around Patrick Plains.[83] In February 1823, the track was officially opened and an authorised pass signed on behalf of the governor was required to take stock up to the Hunter and claim a space.[84] The four Nowland brothers, Michael jr. 30, Henry 28, William 20, and Edward 18, headed north along this treacherous route with their cattle, and travelled 120 miles, for at least four days.

On arrival at Falbrook (based on custom and practice) each of the four Nowland brothers occupied a suitable place to graze their stock (on adjoining allotments where they could) and once decided, each built a hut on their own allotment as part of their claim.[85] The Nowland brothers (most likely) also brought at least four indentured convict labourers (one for each hut and allotment) who stayed on to supervise the cattle once the Nowland brothers decided to return to Wilberforce.[86]

The Nowland Land Grants

On the 27th May 1824, the Nowland brothers' allotments of 160 acres each were secured as land grants. Henry's, William's, and Edward's grants are included in Henry Dangar's Report (1828),[87] while Michael jr.'s grant (on the same day) is included elsewhere.[88]

Prior to receiving their grants, the four Nowland brothers needed to secure a character reference which they did from three local JPs: William Cox (JP), J. Brabyn (JP) and Arch Bell (JP).

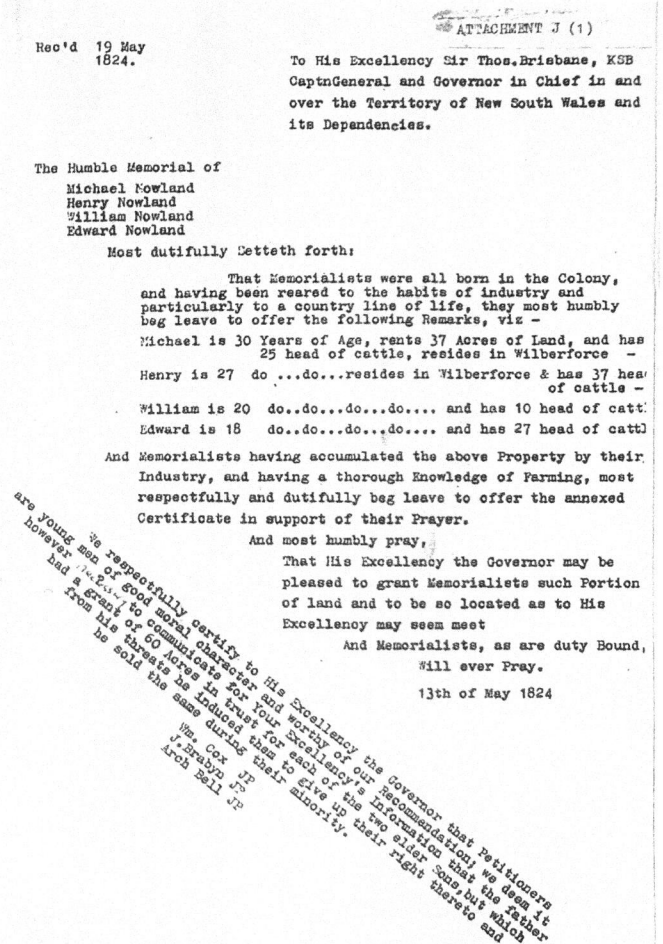

Figure 3: Transcript of Character References

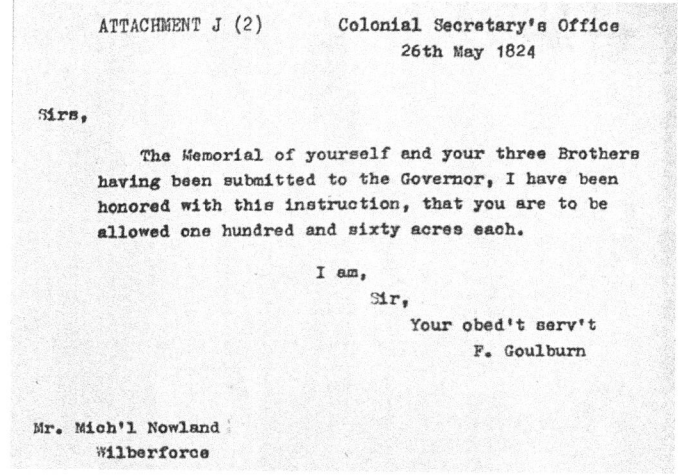

Figure 4: Transcript of Reply

An invaluable transcript of the letter that reports on their character and a subsequent letter of reply are included here to demonstrate the customs and language of the day (see Figure 3 & 4).

William's and his brothers' grants (each of 160 acres) were more than three times the size of the allotment they were brought up on (52 acres, in Wilberforce) and between them they now had an expanse of 640 acres at Glennies Creek, Falbrook where they could graze their cattle.

The location of the Nowland brothers' grants at Glennies Creek (in 1824) are shown on the following map: Henry 129, William 130, Edward 131, and Michael 132 (See Figure 5).

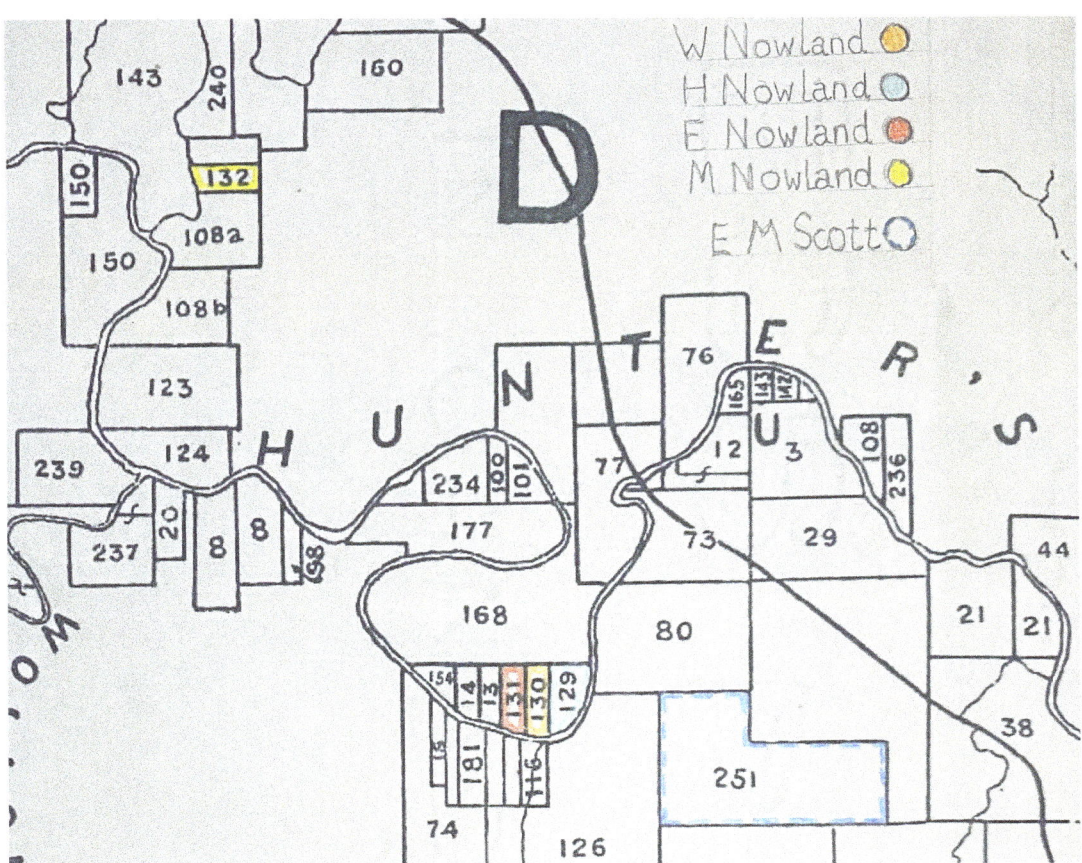

Figure 5: The Nowland Family Allotments at Glennies Creek

As shown above, the allotment sizes vary across the map. William's and his brother's allotments are small compared to the ones that surround them: for example, allotment 251 was a grant from Governor Darling to Ellis Martyn Scott of 2000 acres circa 1825.[89]

In the same year (1824) William also secured an additional land grant of 200 acres promised to Ralph Turnbull and an adjoining allotment of 160 acres. Where these allotments are on the above map is unknown, they are recorded in the land purchases for the year as 'No 311' and 'No 312' and respectively dated 3rd May 1824 and 31st December 1824.[90] Given these pre-emptive leases[91] William now had 520 acres in the Hunter.

Making Changes

A year later (1825) the Nowland brothers were already making changes. William and Edward transferred their allotments (130 and 131 respectively) to Henry, and Henry consolidated his run (along the riverbank) into an area of 720 acres through negotiating the transfer of allotments 13, 14 and 154 from Andrew Biggin, Thomas Biggin and Edward Doyle, respectively.[92] While Michael jr. transferred his allotment 132 to William, and William maintained 520 acres at Falbrook.[93]

This was the end of both Michael jr.'s and Edward's grants at Glennies Creek Falbrook, and for Michael jr., a return permanently to Wilberforce.[94] Their father, Michael Nowland had faced financial difficulty since 1821 and by 1824, his life was starting to unravel.[95] It could be for this reason alone, the Nowland boys decided on a new plan; Michael jr. and Edward would return to farming in Wilberforce and Henry and William would expand their runs in the Hunter.

All the boys still lived in Wilberforce and Henry's and William's runs at Glennies Creek provided extra grazing land. Henry and William (and possibly Michael jr. and Edward) continued to travel along the treacherous Bulga Track (today's Putty Road) regularly with their stock, taking cattle to Glennies Creek to be fattened and returning with stock that was ready for the local markets in Windsor and Sydney town.

As mentioned earlier, the Nowland boys did not need to stay at Glennies Creek for long, because their stockman (most likely indentured convict labour) looked after the cattle when they were away.

Too Many Settlers in the Hunter

By this time (1825), the Singleton area (then known as Patrick Plains) was already overflowing with settlers along the lower part of the Hunter River and its tributaries (See Figure 6).

The Wonnarua Koori

One can only imagine the devastating impact of all this settlement on the local Wonnarua Koori[96] who had lived in harmony with nature on Country, for at least

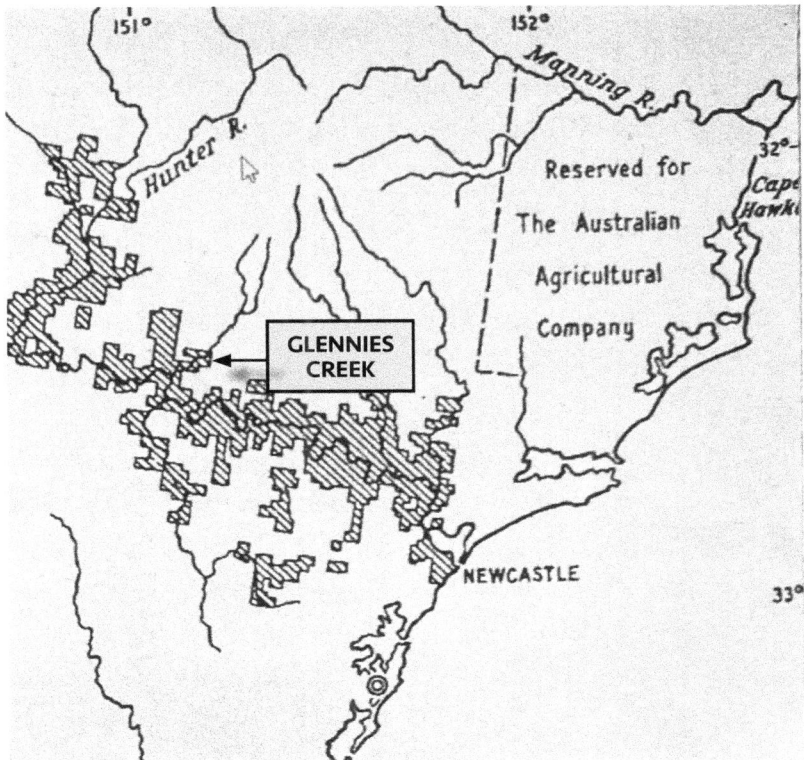

Figure 6: Spread of Settlement – Lower Hunter Valley 1825

30,000 years.[97] It would only take the settlers three years to disrupt the lives and lifestyle of the Wonnarua Koori forever. Between 1822 and 1825, the settlers steadily took over the rich alluvial flats of the Hunter River, and its tributaries, with their huts, herds, and fields of maize, and progressively forced the Wonnarua Koori off large parts of their traditional lands.[98]

Before the settlers came to the Hunter Valley, the Wonnarua Koori moved uninterrupted across Country. As James Wilson-Miller tells us.[99]

In the more mundane aspects of Wonnarua life the quest for food consumed a significant part of the waking hours. Like all tribes in Koori Australia, the Wonnarua followed a hunting and gathering lifestyle. Each kinship group moved in a cyclical pattern through their allotted lands. Men were responsible for hunting the larger game, such as the womboin (kangaroo), murrin (emu), ukae (dingo) and the baninbellang (wallaby). Their skills were also applied to fishing.

Women, on the other hand, gathered bush fruits, yams, grubs, roots, waterlilies and the many species of smaller game such as the wirraman (lizard), mouse and possum. Thus sex roles were clearly defined in the daily round. Although food supplies fluctuated with the seasons and the vagaries of nature, the diet of the

Wonnarua Koori was varied and rich in protein, as was necessary for a physically active people. The land provided everything that was needed to survive. It gave the Wonnarua Koori his implements for hunting and gathering. It provided materials for bark shelters (mia-mias).

Boomerangs were fashioned from selected trees as were spears and throwing sticks (werrewies). Stone implements, such as cleavers, knives, scrapers and bondi points (sharpened stone flakes), were readily available—the patient grinding of the edge producing an effective tool. Most furbearing animals provided skins that were used for body-covering in the cold seasons.

The Wonnarua hunters combined a knowledge of their environment with a knowledge of animal behaviour to effectively hunt their prey. For example, when hunting the womboin (kangaroo) they burnt off the grass and, predictably, about three or four weeks later the animals returned to feed on the young grass shoots. In the early morning the men formed a circle around the unsuspecting game and gradually closed in. They confused their prey with shouts, and when the womboin tried to break the circle they were clubbed by the hunters. Nets (kurrila) strung between trees and suitably camouflaged were also used to capture womboin. A carefully planned and executed encircling movement trapped the prey, leaving only one escape route—in the direction of the nets. A general commotion was made and the panic-stricken animals hurled themselves into the nets where they were clubbed by waiting hunters.

Nets were also used for catching emu and makroo (fish). Women, girls and uninitiated boys gathered their roots, berries and smaller game in the kokas (coolamons) and buakuls (string bags). They dug for yams and other taproots with their yamsticks and waded into creeks for waterlilies. In these instances an intimate knowledge of the seasonal cycle of plant life combined with a knowledge of plant localities were essential.

The Wonnarua Koori's synchronicity with nature was compromised and contained when settlers, like the Nowlands, started to claim the rich alluvial soils along Glennies Creek. The settlers' actions and the Wonnarua Koori's response followed the same pattern of behaviour as in the Hawkesbury: invasion, raids and counter offensives.

In an attempt to make the invaders move on the Woonarau Koori raided the settlers' huts and pastures and the settlers retaliated with the support of the Mounted Police. The conflict with a bias towards the settlers was reported in the newspapers. As shown in the following examples.[100]

The Monitor, 1st September 1826, page 4 [no title]

'The Mountain Blacks in the neighbourhood of Glenny's (sic) Creek, in one of the more remote districts of Hunter's River, have again not only been troublesome, but also evinced a spirit of revenge, and have murdered two shepherds belonging to Captain Lethbridge, at his station. On Monday, the 28th of August last, at the farm of Captain Lethbridge, an unexpected visit was paid to the house by four black men entering, having spears, &c. and bearing the appearance of hostility.'

The Australian, 9th September 1826, page 2 [no title]

'The Native Blacks in the District of Hunter's River are more outrageous than ever. Hundreds of them have lately collected together; and disastrous, indeed, has been the first results of their renewed hostilities. About the latter end, of last month they made their appearance on Mr. Ogilvie's premises, in his absence'.

The means of reprisal suggested in the following articles is abhorrent.

The Australian, 9th September 1826, page 2 [no title]

'For every man they murder, hunt them down and drop ten of them. They will soon find it in their interest to be friendly. It will not be necessary then to coax them into amity and good will towards even the stray and lonely and distant settler, or hut keeper. This is our specific — try it. In six months, we shall neither hear of murders on the one side, nor shootings on the other; and yet all will be peace — peace obtained with little bloodshed.'

The Australian, 16th September 1826, page 2 [no title]

'The Blacks will have more sense than to continue their provocations and out rages (sic) as soon as they experience the determined resistance of our soldiers and of the armed settlers. Bayonet law is the most humane law for them; and will produce the most humane effects. For after two or three conflicts the Blacks will retire; the stock-men (sic) and others will remain, in future, unmolested, and further loss of life saved.'

The Australian, 30 June 1827, page 3 [no title]

'The Aboriginal Natives.' Whether they be true or false reports, they are current. It is said that the natives have become so very troublesome, that many persons have resolved to poison them; and that corrosive sublimate, as one mode of destruction, has in several instances been provided for the purpose.[101]

The Mounted Police

As was the case in the Hawkesbury, the settlers were supported by the establishment; this time in the form of the Mounted Police.[102] Between the 1st August and 1st September 1826, the Mounted Police led by Lieutenant Lowe engaged in the following atrocities:

- *1 August: The execution of Jacky Jacky and the following acquittal of Lieutenant Lowe*
- *12 August: The capture and execution of seven Aboriginal men by the Mounted Police*
- *30 August: Mounted Police reinforced with 'Aboriginal Trackers' are dispatched to hunt for Aboriginal men believed responsible for a retaliatory attack on a farm [Captain Lethbridge's Bridgman Estate, Falbrook]*
- *1 September: Mounted police massacre of 18 Wonnarua people*[103]
- *[The violence continued and] 'in September 1826 eleven men with landholdings in the Upper Hunter, including James Bowman of "Ravensworth", William Ogilvie of "Merton" and John Gaggin of "Sydenham", wrote to Governor Darling highlighting their view of the "very disturbed state of the Country by the incursions of numerous Tribes of Black Natives"; and seeking the continued protection of the Mounted Police'.*[104]

The takeover of Wonnarua Koori Country in this horrendous way was entrenched and progressively over the next two years (1825–1827), the Wonnarua Koori were forcefully alienated from large sections of Country.[105] James Wilson-Miller, a direct descendant from the Wonnarua Koori, provides us with an informed insight.[106]

> *After 1826, the Wonnarua were left to come to terms with the British occupation of their country. This was when the real holocaust began. Firstly, diseases swept through the remaining population. Deaths were common from introduced diseases such as measles and pulmonary complaints. Syphilis spread at an alarming rate causing death or infertility among the Wonnarua remnants who had no resistance to the disease…*
>
> *The invasion of the Wonnarua tribal lands by the British was a total disaster not only in the physical sense but also in the social sense. Traditional methods of hunting and gathering were no longer viable and the tight social and religious fabric of the Wonnarua began to fall apart under the appalling death rate. What is important is that many more Kooris died in the post frontier years from disease and starvation than were killed in actual fighting with whites…*[107]

The Nowland brothers would have been very aware of the catastrophic impact of the settlers and the Mounted Police on the Wonnarua Koori. They may have taken part in some of the skirmishes between the settlers and the Wonnarau Koori people when they returned to check on and turn over the stock on their allotments (though no data was found on their behaviour). At the very least, they would have known about the atrocities especially the Massacre at Glennies Creek 1st September 1826 where 18 Wonnarau Koori were killed.[108] The Nowlands' opinions would have been informed by their upbringing in Wilberforce, personal experience and the newspaper articles they read all laced with bias, self-righteousness and bigoted attitudes. One can hear all the talk at Glennies Creek and at Wilberforce, around the kitchen table, and in the pubs and fields, all about the settlers' rights and how they should respond to the raids on their allotments at Glennies Creek. Whether there was any empathy for the Wonnarua Koori from the individuals amongst them is unknown.

Divergence in the Lives of the Wonnarua Koori and the Nowland Brothers

These years (1824–1827) were totally different for the Wonnarua Koori and the Nowland brothers; the Wonnarua Koori faced on-going threats, challenges and potential genocide while the Nowland brothers looked to Glennies Creek as a means of hope and aspiration given their initial land grants and the potential for prosperity as pastoralists.

In contrast to the devastating impact on the Wonnarua Koori, William's and his brothers' world was full of opportunity and change as they claimed and expanded their allotments and took more and more of their cattle from Wilberforce up the Bulga Track to Glennies Creek.

In January 1824, the Hawkesbury Benevolent Society (HBS) decided to join the settlers and move some of their cattle up to the Hunter.[109] This decision did not have an immediate impact on William's and his brothers' lives, but it would be significant for William and Edward eight years later. In 1832, Edward (with the assistance of William) gained the tender to find a run for the HBS's cattle on the Liverpool Plains, with the tender given to Edward in 'preference to several others.'[110]

CHAPTER 3

A Squatter on the Liverpool Plains

This part of William Nowland's story occurred soon after the seeds of change in land acquisition fostered by John Thomas Bigge were starting to come to fruition. Five years earlier, in 1821, John Thomas Bigge (Judge and Royal Commissioner) who had been sent to the colony, in 1819, to report on its progress, returned to Britain. On arrival in London, Bigge advocated (amongst other things) for significant change in how land should be allotted within the colony between the various participants, most notably, the emancipated convicts, first-generation colonial Australians and the two groups of free settlers, those of small means and those with money. He fostered an interest in his proposals and made several recommendations to the House of Commons in London, between 1822 and 1823 in three Reports he presented to the British Government.[111] Bigge also openly proclaimed his condemnation of Governor Macquarie's approach to the colony between 1810 and 1821 that enabled opportunity for emancipated convicts (such as William's father Michael) and their descendants (such as William).

For Bigge, convicts should be indentured for the whole of their sentence, and emancipated convicts (and first-generation descendants) should not receive land grants so readily. Bigge championed instead, large land holdings to well-heeled free settlers (emigrants) and entrepreneurial companies, based on the view it was these two groups that would deliver surplus produce and trade for the colony.

Governor Brisbane (1821–1825) responded immediately to Bigge's recommendations, followed by Governor Darling (1825–1831). Both Governors favoured and encouraged England's entrepreneurs and the wealthy sons of aristocrats to come to the colony and stake their claim on land of their choosing with an offer of a large land grant on arrival for any amongst them who were prepared to take up the offer and invest in the settlement. Of note at this stage of William's story is the establishment of the Australian Agricultural Company (AACo) in London on the 1st November 1824, and the subsequent land grant of one million acres to the AACo by Governor Darling (in 1826) for the purpose of advancing the Australian Wool Industry.[112]

William, his brothers and the other settlers of limited means were conscious of the pending competition for land from wealthy free settlers, entrepreneurial businessmen and companies such as the AACo. It was there for everyone to read in the papers and the rumours and gossip was compelling. As early as 1823, the

Nowland brothers and their fellow settlers were determined to get in first and well before their competitors, especially, the AACo.

Once the route from Windsor to the Hunter was discovered they made their way up the Bulga Track in droves and flooded into the Hunter (1823–26) to each claim a small grant of land for themselves and their families, under the existing government policy, still in place and inherited from Macquarie. First-generation colonial Australians, like William and his brothers, were driven to make a life for themselves beyond the margins of Sydney. In their everyday life they focused on this pursuit and like all young men and women they aspired to a better life beyond the confines of Sydney.

William's older brother Henry and his wife Harriet is a case in point. Henry (29) and Harriet Farlow (20) married in Windsor in 1825 and planned to move north as soon as they could; though it did take them just over 10 years.[113] Once married, Henry continued to travel the Bulga Track to manage his land grants at Glennies Creek (probably often with William). He also spent a lot of time in Wilberforce. Henry was a wheelwright and William his apprentice. Between the two of them, they had plenty of local work mending and constructing wheels for the drays that carried the families and their household goods up the Bulga Track to a new life in the Hunter Valley.[114] Then circa 1834, Henry took on the opportunity to run the general store in Muswellbrook. Whether Harriet and the children (Ann 9, Sarah 7 and James 5) went with Henry at this time is unknown. Though by 1837, the family most likely were together in Muswellbrook, given that the birth of the fourth child of Henry (41) and Harriet (32) – Henry jr. – is registered in the Hunter in that year.[115]

William also looked for opportunities and in his life journey appears to be even more adventurous. He was constantly in the forefront of each new discovery and moving further and further north whenever he was given the chance.

By 1822/1823, free settlers from wealthy families started to arrive in the colony and many took up the offer of a large land grant whenever they wished on the margins of settlement, including William's Glennies Creek. Then, three years later (in 1826) the combination of these new landholders and the deluge of small free settlers from the Hawkesbury began to crowd out settlers like William from any further opportunities in the Hunter Valley.

Governor Brisbane, a keen advocate of Bigge's plan for the colony had already instructed Henry Dangar (Assistant Surveyor) in 1822 to survey the Hunter Valley, mark out all the claims, villages, reserves, church lands and opportunities for roads and further settlement.

Dangar meticulously drew the maps and did all the surveying over a two-year period (1822–1824) and found a way onto the Liverpool Plains (Kamilaroi Country) through what he called the Dartbrook Pass in October 1824 (situated north-west of present-day Scone).[116] During this expedition Henry Dangar and his men were successfully challenged by 150 Kamilaroi warriors who forced them to retreat without their pack horses, provisions, clothes and implements along a much smaller horse track that Dangar named the 'Cedar Brush Track'.[117]

Despite the Kamilaroi's success, and Dangar's retreat, the discovery of the Dartbrook Pass enticed emancipated convicts and first-generation colonial Australians, like William, to venture into Kamilaroi Country. It was not long before they took the trek with their stock up Dangar's very steep path to claim land on these very fertile plains. As William tells us in his letter to the Editor of the *Sydney Morning Herald* in 1861.

> *The Sydney Morning Herald, 23rd Jan. 1861, page 3*
> *A SQUATTER*
> *To the Editor of the Herald*
>
> *In April 1827 [1826],[118] I formed a station on the borders of the Liverpool Plains, on a creek named "Warrah", in the northern districts, beyond the main range of the colony. There were two stations formed before mine – one by Messrs. Singleton and Baldwin, at Yarramunba, and the other by Messrs. Onus and Williams, on a creek now called Onus's. Singleton's track over the main range was at the head of Dartbrook, and nearly impassable by man or beast, it being so difficult to cross that the drovers had been so exhausted by endeavouring to drive cattle up the mountains, that they had to rest themselves by holding a tree while they caught their breath...*

William – a Squatter at Warrah

When William went onto the Liverpool Plains up the precipitous Dartbrook track, circa 1826, to form a station at Warrah, his run was not claimed, surveyed, and turned into a land grant (as was the case in 1824 at Glennies Creek, Falbrook). Instead, Warrah (by September 1826) was officially designated as being outside the boundaries of settlement and William and all those who established runs outside these boundaries were classified as 'squatters' who had no legal rights over the land they were on.[119]

This change occurred because the Governor of the day (Governor Darling) believed the squatters were anarchical and a new approach to settlement would enable a more orderly development of the colony. Darling and others within the establishment (including Henry Dangar) were cognisant of how quickly settlers had moved in the past, with each new discovery. As detailed earlier, once the Bulga Track was discovered (1820) settlers started to flood into the Lower Hunter (c.1823) and by 1825 the Hunter River was overstocked with cattle and sheep.[120] Now once again, with Dangar's discovery of the Dartbrook Pass, the settlers were keen to expand their horizons and move onto the Liverpool Plains, but the steepness of this Pass, held them back. Only a few took on the challenge: Singleton and Baldwin; Onus and Williams, and 'our' William Nowland (now 22).

William Finds the Easier Route onto the Liverpool Plains

After traversing such a steep gradient for some time 'our' William Nowland decided to look for an easier route. As he tells us below in the continuation of his story.

The Sydney Morning Herald, 23rd Jan. 1861, page 3 [continued]

… Many people went out to find a better road to cross the mountains with their stock, but all failed to do so. I was determined to find a better road if possible and started from the Liverpool Plains with my stockman, taking with me a pack horse and rations. We travelled the mountains, endangering our lives, with the blacks for the space of three months and found at last the Gap in the main range, between Doughboy Hollow and the town called Murrurundi.

We saw the valley of a river before us, now called the Page and Murrurundi. We went down to that river, and followed it for three miles, thinking it was one of the tributaries of the river Hunter, and seeing a large mountain on the south side, now called the Murlow Mountain, we ascended it to see if we could find any place to the southward of it that we knew, and fortunately saw a place called the Downs, on Mr. Little's farm near Scone, and we could see the valley of Kingdon Ponds up to the range now called Walden's Range; we then descended it, and went to the range, after a few days we found a road to Kingdon Ponds. I marked the trees over the Liverpool and Walden Ranges. We not only found a better road for cattle, but one that a team could take two tons over the whole ranges, with one-shilling expense to the government.

I then loaded a tray at Patrick's Plains [Camberwell] and took up the first dray that ever went over the new road to Liverpool Plains. It being wet weather, the ground was soft, left a plain, dray-track behind us from Kingdon Ponds to Liverpool Plains. When we arrived at the west side of the range we stopped and camped at a small creek, which I named Doughboy Hollow. I then proceeded to my station at Warrah.

According to Dr. John Atchison, the entrance to this easier route onto the Liverpool Plains (just north of Murrurundi) had already been discovered by Henry Dangar in 1825, and disclosed by Dangar to the AACo, on an undated map that Dangar drew for the company.[121]

Given this map, I wondered why the sign on the New England Highway near Murrurundi and the headwaters of the Pages River, says, 'Nowlands Gap'. In delving further, the more I researched this anomaly, the more I understood why the gap was 'Nowland's'. The first question that needs to be considered is the philosophical question: 'If you discover something and you keep it secret, and only disclose it to the AACo on an undated map, is it a discovery'? Secondly, what was Henry Dangar's motivation for not disclosing the 'Pages River Gap'? Was it because he agreed with Bigge and the establishment and wanted to avoid a flood of emancipated convicts and first-generation colonial Australians onto the Liverpool Plains? Did Dangar already have a vested interest in the AACo and saw the potential for this company, and himself, on the Liverpool Plains?

We can digress here and answer all these questions and put a case for William. Or we can acknowledge the fact that it was William for three months prior to May 1827 who navigated his way from Warrah (northwest of Murrurundi) on the Liverpool Plains, through the wilderness, until he found the route from Warrah, to Doughboy Hollow, then over the Liverpool Range, to the headwaters of the Pages River, from where he descended via the Pages River, to the valley below, just north of Murrurundi.

It was William (now 23) who disclosed this easier route, and 'blazed the trail' for the settlers.[122] As soon as William came over the 'Pages River Gap' (c. April 1827) he immediately returned to Patrick Plains (Glennies Creek, Falbrook), told as many as he could about his discovery, took his horse and dray back up to the Pass, and then, given the wet weather, the wheels of William's dray, marked out this easier route onto the Liverpool Plains for all the settlers to see.[123]

In essence, it was William Nowland who declared his find and showed the settlers the way; and it is for this reason that the 'Pages River Gap' is known as 'Nowlands Gap'.

In William's article in the SMH, 1861, he continues:

> *The Sydney Morning Herald, 23rd Jan. 1861, page 3 [continued]*
> *… Immediately after the squatters travelled over the track that I had made across the ranges, and commenced farming stations on all parts of the Liverpool Plains, and, in a short-time, they travelled hundreds of miles to the north and north-west, the Mooki, Namoi, Big River, McIntyre, Barwin and the Balloon; the north-east to New England, Clarence, and Richmond Rivers, Darling Downs and Moreton Bay &c. All travelling by degrees over the new road I had discovered, which was used for twenty years without any expense to the Government. Although the Government had been yearly receiving a large revenue from the aforesaid squatter, I have not received any remuneration for my arduous and perilous undertaking.*

For William, finding this easier route onto the Liverpool Plains (in hindsight, some 34 years later) was an 'arduous and perilous undertaking', while for the Kamilaroi people, it was the start of destruction and devastation as more and more squatters moved up onto the Liverpool Plains.

CHAPTER 4

THE KAMILAROI NATION

The way of life of the Kamilaroi people who had lived on the Liverpool Plains for at least 40,000 years was threatened by the flood of settlers who invaded Kamilaroi Country, post 1826.[124] The Kamilaroi faced the same peril as the Wonnarua Koori (in the Hunter Valley), the Darkinjung (along the Bulga Track, and its surrounds) and the Dharug (in the Hawkesbury) before them.[125]

The Kamilaroi Nation extends from the Hunter Valley (NSW) in the south, to Nindigully in Queensland in the north and as far west as the Warrumbungle Mountains (with the Liverpool Plains forming only part of this vast nation). As Greg Griffiths, a proud Kamilaroi man, tells us in 'The Kamilaroi – Short Documentary NITV', 2019:

> *It is where the hills meet the plains, the red soil meets the black soil, the burr meets the spinifex, the rainforest meets the bush.*

A map of the Kamilaroi Nation taken from the above documentary follows.

Figure 7: Map of Kamilaroi Country

A comprehensive account of the Kamilaroi Nation is provided online by the Dhiiyaan Aboriginal Centre, at Moree and detailed below.

> *The Kamilaroi are the second largest nation on the eastern coast of Australia, with Wiradjuri being the largest*[126] *Their nation [Kamilaroi] covers 30,000 square miles of fertile soil, running rivers and streams. Their language is Gamilaraay and their lifestyle is to co-exist with, and maintain a balance with nature. Kamilaroi Aboriginal people lived in harmony with the environment.*
>
> *The Kamilaroi believe in a large number of supernatural beings. Among them, the most important are: Baiame, Dharramulan and Garriya. Baiame, pronounced BYE-umme, is believed to have the greatest of Powers. Dharramulan is the one-legged son of Baiame. Legend says that Garriya, the Rainbow Serpent, a fabulous monster which appeared in a snake-like form, is now believed to be resting deep within Boobera Lagoon, 13.5 km west of Boggabilla, NSW.*
>
> *The Kamilaroi used kinship norms to regulate the behaviour of all people who had dealings with one another. This system of classes or skins governed everyday behaviour including marriage, ceremonies, camp layout, hunting parties and so forth. It brought with it a set of obligations that were performed when relating to others, and these obligations formed part of Aboriginal Lore/Law.*
>
> *Totems handed down through the mother's line differentiate people into groups, for example ringtail possum (kurrawir), porcupine (bigibila), pademelon or wallaby (wang-uy), brown kangaroo (bundar), and so on.*
>
> *Totemism expanded across tribes, and a person with the same totems are regarded as kin, regardless of what clan they belong to. A person's (sic) not allowed to marry their own totem, no matter how distant the connection. The smaller clans mostly stayed within their own hunting area (taurai) but there were times when neighbouring groups came together for purposes such as settling disputes, marriages, trading, festivals, feasts, funerals and for help in bad times.*
>
> *Messengers carrying message sticks (dhulu) were allowed to enter other sub-tribe's and tribe's lands to communicate with each group and would often let other tribes know where and when a ceremony would be held. A special, significant and respected ceremony known as the Bora (buurra) initiated boys into manhood. Other ceremonies that have religious connotations or are simply attended for entertainment are known as 'corroborees'. Today, descendants of the traditional people of the Kamilaroi Nation continue to occupy these lands. They are known as 'Murri' people.*[127]

For tens of thousands of years before the settlers invaded (c.1826) the Kamalaroi had lived in harmony with nature, and engaged in ceremonial ties and trade with bordering nations; especially with the Bigambul people in the north and the Wonnarua in the

Hunter.[128] In this Indigenous world, kinship norms regulated behaviour, within and between the Aboriginal Nations, and the Kamilaroi Nation were known for their warrior skills when challenged.[129]

The Kamilaroi would have been aware of the impact of the settlers on the Wonnarua between 1824 and 1827, and were probably gathering and discussing the pending threat to their own nation prior to the invasion.

John Oxley's Expedition

The earliest documented contact between the Kamilaroi Nation and the British intruders is recorded in John Oxley's 1818 expedition north of Bathurst along the Macquarie River to Port Macquarie, that skirted the northern margins of the Kamilaroi Nation. See the map (Figure 8) that follows.

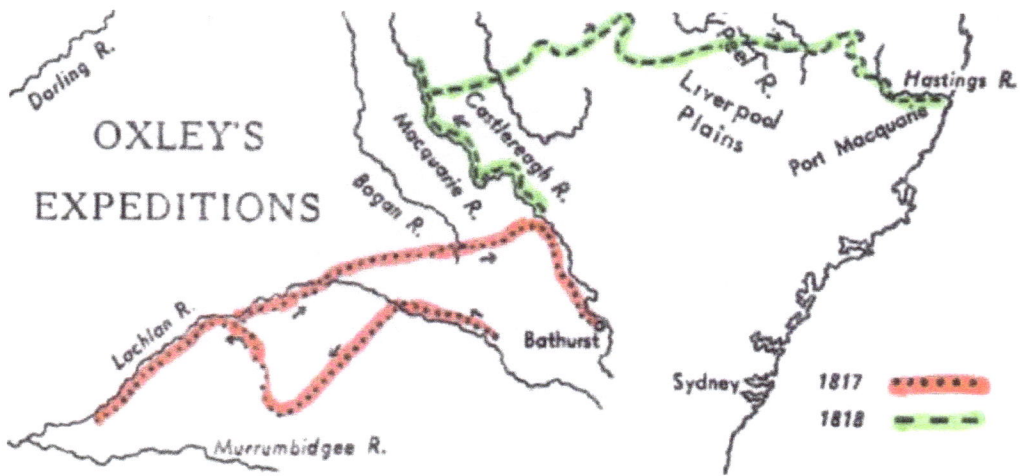

Figure 8: Map of Oxley's Expedition

On the 3rd August 1818, John Oxley, and his party, were in the vicinity of the Warrumbungles; which Oxley named the Arbuthnot Range.[130] The Warrunbungles are part of Kamilaroi Country, and on the following day (4th August 1818) Oxley described the 'natives' in his journal and as he tells us, one of the warriors from the Kamilaroi Nation let Oxley and his party know in no uncertain terms this was Kamilaroi Country.[131] See below.

> The natives appear pretty numerous: one was very daring, maintaining his ground at a distance armed with a formidable, jagged spear and club, which he kept beating against each other, making the most singular gestures and noises that can be imagined: he followed us upwards of a mile, when he left us, joining several companions to the right of us.

Oxley and his party then travelled further east along the northern range of the Warrumbungles and, on the 26th August 1818, came across the plains below which Oxley named the Liverpool Plains. Oxley was still within Kamilaroi Country, and the sketch in his journal (Figure 9) of the Liverpool Plains (August 1818) illustrates Kamilaroi Country before the settlers arrived in large numbers nearly nine years later and claimed their runs.[132]

Figure 9: Liverpool Plains. West Prospect from View Hill

Allan Cunningham's Expeditions

In contrast to John Oxley, Allan Cunningham (botanist and explorer) had limited, transient and incidental contact with the Kamilaroi people (whom he called 'Indian') as told in the following extracts from Cunningham's Paper to the Royal Geographical Society of London in 1832.

> *11th May: Traces of the natives were frequent, although not of recent date. We met, however, with neither the wandering Indian nor any description of animal, for the parched state of vegetation and the distressed condition of the country generally, had evidently driven both to other parts of the interior, where the means of sustaining life.*[133]

Henry Dangar's Expedition

Henry Dangar, who crossed the Liverpool Plains from the east and discovered the Dartbrook Pass, in October 1824, had a totally different experience. As told earlier, the small clans of the Kamilaroi Nation who lived on the Liverpool Plains had grouped together into a band of 150 warriors, and confronted Dangar and his party, while they were camped near Coulson Creek, and forced them to retreat:

The Australian 23 December 1824, page 3 [No title]

Two gentlemen who are attached to the Surveyor General's department, [Henry Dangar and John Richards] lately made an attempt, after they had completed the survey of some townships on the upper banks of Hunter's River, to trace that river to its source. They found that the river divided into several branches; and they succeeded in reaching the source of one branch, to which they gave the name of Dart-Brook...

From Dart-Brook they proceeded on to Liverpool Plains, across the dividing range which separates the waters of Hunter's River from the waters of the Western country. On the borders of these they met with a large body of natives, in number, as they suppose, about one hundred and fifty, by whom they were attacked unawares: — one of their party (which only consisted of four) having been struck by a spear in the head, before they knew that the natives were near them.

They, however, rallied and made front for about three hours, when they were obliged to decamp, leaving their pack horse with all their provisions, clothes and cooking implements in the hands of the enemy, who being content with their booty, allowed the party to proceed without further molestation. Some shots were fired, but without effect.

Our travellers fortunately had about twenty-five pounds of flour slung on one of their saddles, and also their blankets. At the moment of this rencontre they had just reached the eminence which overlooks Liverpool Plains, into which they descended and rode about four miles. They then encamped for the night, and from the loss of their provisions and the proximity of so large a body of hostile natives, they commenced their return on the following day.

Baldwin and Singleton

The Kamilaroi were challenged again, in 1827, when Baldwin and Singleton went onto the Liverpool Plains with their stock. The account that follows provides a window into the detestable behaviour of squatters like Baldwin and Singleton (who were known as settlers inside the boundaries of settlement), and the response of the Kamilaroi warriors in defence of Country.

The Monitor (Sydney, Thursday 8 November 1827, page 8
(DOMESTIC INTELLIGENCE CONTINUED)

Liverpool Plains. Young Baldwin and Singleton, with others and their servants, in all 17, lately started from Patrick's Plains, Upper Hunter's River, with 860 head of Cattle, and a dray, carrying twelve hundred weight. And after a journey of about 90 miles, arrived on the borders of Liverpool plains (sic). They built a hut ten miles on the plains, near some trees. Four natives came one and day (sic) and were very audacious, contrary to their former behaviour. The same day our people discerned a multitude at a great distance; but whether natives or cattle, they could not at first tell. At length they discovered them to be natives. As the latter drew near, they slipped from tree to tree, as though they wished to hide their numbers. At length they came within spearing distance, and threw their heavy wooden spears at our people, casting them out of their hands.

Having but six muskets among the 15 (two had gone out with the cattle) six of our people stood in front, and after firing, gave their pieces to the other nine behind them to load, themselves shifting in the mean time, to avoid the spears. The enemy, though numbers fell, stood to the contest with great bravery. At length, after six had been killed, and still more wounded, they retired slowly and sullenly, leaving their dead behind them. One of our people had his arm broken by a wooden womara, [boomerang] which the Natives threw in great numbers. It is sharpened at both ends. No other damage was received by us.

Three of their number sneaked round to the hut during the contest, and began to pilfer. The four first blacks told our people, that a cart, loaded, with two men, had come to the plains from Bathurst some time ago. That they had murdered the men and plundered the cart, which contained provisions. Nine out of our 17 people, returned to Hunters River, leaving eight men and six muskets, with which they felt competent to repel any fresh attack. We could almost have wished the party could have pursued, and made a more complete discomfiture [discomposure] of the Natives. Their murder of the two men, and their present unprovoked hostility, justifying a very severe retaliation; and the effects of a complete slaughter would perhaps have so terrified the invaders, as to cause them to desire to live on good terms with us hereafter.

They seemed the best knowing, bold, determined race yet met with. The plentifulness of food at the Plains, doubtless, is the cause of this. The hostile party consisted of about 200 young picked men. Two working bullocks joined the cattle on the Plains, supposed to have belonged to the unfortunate men whom the natives had murdered. The presence of these bullocks is strongly indicative of the truth of the story told by the Blacks. Mr. Baldwin narrowly escaped one of their spears in the contest.

Another account in 1828 is appalling and I have debated about including it in full given that it includes gruesome details of the deaths of Kamilaroi people at the hands of the squatters. In the end, and with respect, I have decided to include the account in full. We can only move towards a true account of what happened on the Liverpool Plains with knowledge of narrations like the one below.

> *The Monitor 4 August 1828, page, 8*
> *DOMESTIC INTELLIGENCE (CONTINUED)*
> *Dr Little, of Upper Hunters River, crossed the Liverpool Range and, on coming to a hut, found, to his horror and astonishment, the bodies of some half dozen of black natives, stretched along the earth. From the putrid state of the corpses, it was evident they had been slaughtered a long time. He pursued his journey till he fell in with the white people, stock-keepers and others. He learnt from them, that a large body of blacks had suddenly made their appearance, but whether they paid their visit hostilely, or merely came in great numbers for self-protection, the stock-keepers admitted they could not tell. However, acting in concert, our people commenced a destructive fire of musquetry (sic 'musketry') upon them, and the blacks presently fled. Such were the circumstances of the fight, that some of the black fugitives on being pursued, ascended the trees in hopes of escaping, whence they were brought down by the balls of the assailants.*

Just as in the past, this despicable behaviour occurred in concert with other skirmishes between the squatters and the Kamilaroi people, though little was found in Trove, with a preference in the newspaper articles, for reporting on the Kamilaroi warriors killing the squatters on their runs, and in their huts.[134]

Within 10 years (1827–1837), the squatters along with the settlers (who had obtained grants from the Governor) had occupied large areas of Kamilaroi Country, destroyed large sections of the Kamilaroi's food supply and introduced diseases; in particular, in 1831 smallpox spread through the clans.[135]

Despite the challenges, the Kamilaroi people persisted in the defence of Country. They started to kill a significant amount of the squatters' and settlers' sheep and cattle (including William Nowland's cattle, as detailed later) and in response, some of the squatters and settlers wrote to the papers, and requested the assistance of the Mounted Police. See the newspaper article that follows.

> *Bent's News and Tasmanian Register Saturday 25 November 1837, p.2*
> *Sydney News*
> *Intelligence has reached Sydney of a variety of outrages committed lately by the aborigines among the stock-stations at the outskirts of the Liverpool Plains. Several tribes of the blacks, it appears, have for some time been congregated together in*

that vicinity and have speared a considerable number of cattle, the property of various persons. Two Stockmen, assigned servants of Mr. Bowman of Richmond, have fallen victims to their ferocity. We trust the Government will lose no time in dispatching some of the military to aid the residents in that vicinity in reducing the savages to order.

The Mounted Police came onto the Liverpool Plains and the Kamilaroi warriors were waiting for them; as Raymond Weatherall, a proud Kamilaroi man, tells us in 'The Kamilaroi – Short Documentary NITV', 2019.

We had heard word they were coming so we sent out people to go and tell every other clan group and everybody came. They sent their best warriors. When Major Nunn and Thomas Mitchell were coming, they thought that it was rain, but it was actually our people, waiting, stomping on the ground. They thought they had seen thunder, but it was actually our fires and our camps waiting for them, while bashing on possum skin drums, and hitting their shields on the white box gum tree. That scared them away. Then the 500 people dispersed back to their clan groups and families. They, [Major Nunn and the Mounted Police] actually, came back.[136]

They came to kill. I am a direct descendant of the Waterloo Massacre. They took our people from there to Terry Hie Hie Reserve. They moved them on to that reserve. We certainly did show the responsibility of standing up against it. The 500 is an inspirational story today. We tell our children about that. Our people have always fought for their land and will never stop fighting for it. That's for sure.

The Waterloo Massacre Followed by the Myall Creek Massacre

The Waterloo Massacre occurred at Waterloo Creek near Moree on the 26th January 1838.[137] Six months later the Myall Creek Massacre occurred at Henry Dangar's station, on the Liverpool Plains. There are several accounts in Trove and on the internet that tell of this atrocity; the grim details are deplorable.[138] 'Friends of Myall Creek' (an association of the descendants and other interested parties aimed at reconciliation) provides an informative view.[139]

On Sunday 10 June 1838, a group of 10 convict stockmen, lead by a squatter, rode onto Myall Creek Station (near what is now Bingara in Northern New South Wales) and brutally massacred about 28 Aboriginals, mostly older men, women and children in an unprovoked and premeditated attempt to remove them from what had become pastoral land. This event has become known as the Myall Creek Massacre and, whilst only one of many such outrages committed across Australia over a 100 year period, is notable now for the fact that it was the first time that the perpetrators of such crimes were brought to justice.

Following a second trial, seven men were executed. This did not however herald an end to the massacres which continued for decades and remain as a stain on Australian history. On the site of the Myall Creek Massacre now stands a simple but poignant granite memorial, acknowledging those who lost their lives, the perpetrators and those who courageously contributed to the pursuit and achievement of justice. Importantly now, it stands as a symbol of the desire for a more equitable Australia and as an emblem for those determined to achieve true and lasting reconciliation between our indigenous and more recent settler populations.[140]

John Fleming and Henry 'Boshey' Nowland

On cannot go on from here without acknowledging the following disturbing statement in James 'Toby' Ryan's (1895) 'Reminiscences of Australia' about 'Boshey Nowlen' (William's brother, Henry Nowland).

The same Boshey Nowlen was instrumental in getting Flemming (sic) away, who made his escape from Myall Creek about 1836 [1838] he [John Fleming] being the ringleader in the slaughter of the blacks about that time. He [Henry Nowland] gave Flemming (sic) a relay of horses, which took him to Newcastle, in such a short time, he [Henry Nowland] being a mail contractor.[141]

In delving further, I came across Patricia Withcombe's thesis on John Fleming and his role in the Myall Creek Massacre.[142] In the thesis, Withcombe comments on the above quote, and puts forward substantive evidence-based commentary to demonstrate John Fleming's leadership role in the Myall Creek massacre, even though he was never indicted; Fleming disappeared and resurfaced in Wilberforce in 1840 when he married Charlotte Dunston at the Church of England, Wilberforce.[143] In summary, Withcombe notes:

Fleming's saviour was the mail contractor Boshey Nowlen, who was originally from the Hawkesbury and then a Hunter Valley settler. (p.56) According to Ryan, Nowlen supplied 'Fleming with a relay of horses, which took him to Newcastle in such a short time'. (p.58)

And then towards the end of the thesis:

The execution of convicts and emancipates horrified the colony, but the execution of a freeborn squatter would have been unthinkable. To this end it would appear Fleming's whereabouts after 1838 was known, yet those in authority were powerless against the influential colonial squattocracy and their supporters. In short Fleming's status and leadership was pivotal to the massacre on 10 June 1838…and…his role…[should] be acknowledged and fully understood.

…Fleming has never been held to account for his role in the massacre. Rather, his legendary ride from the scene of the crime elevated him to hero status and continues to be embellished to the present day. The dramatic elements of this escape narrative gave him a legendary status which overshadowed the reality of Fleming's leading role in the massacre, including the brutal murder of the defenseless Wirrayaraay people. (p.77)[144]

After the Myall Creek Massacre, the newspapers concentrated on the 'troublesome blacks' and no further accounts of the settlers killing the Kamilaroi people were found.[145] This is the atrocious context in which William and later Edward made a life for themselves on the Liverpool Plains; that began for William Nowland, circa 1826, and for Edward Nowland, circa 1833.

Despite this history, the Kamilaroi nation was not defeated. Today their cultural heritage lives on: As Dolly Talbott, a proud Kamilaroi woman, tells us:

My hope for the future is that my grandchildren maintain their culture and pass it down through their generations. The most important thing is to remember who you are and maintain connection. Connection to each other and connection to country. It is very important and very important to Aboriginal people.[146]

CHAPTER 5

A Pastoralist and Squatter

Life was changing for the Nowlands. Their father, Michael sr. (66) died in Wilberforce, on the 31st October 1828.[147] Their mother, Elizabeth was 51, and the Nowland children were young adults: Michael jr. 34; Henry 32; Elizabeth jr. 30; William 24; Edward 22; Mary 19; and Sarah 14.[148]

In the same year (1828), William's younger sister, Mary, married Alexander Johnston in Sydney.[149] The following year (1829) Edward, now 23, married Christian Farlow, 18 (Henry's wife Harriet's sister), at the St John's Anglican Church, Wilberforce.[150]

Like the rest of his siblings, William was pursuing a life of his own. He had a land grant at Glennies Creek, Falbrook (Camberwell) as a pastoralist and a run as a squatter on the Liverpool Plains, called Warrah.[151]

The Australian Agricultural Company (AACo) Appropriates William's Warrah Station

William had taken his cattle up and down the Bulga Track for at least 10 years (c.1823–1833) and onto the Liverpool Plains for at least six years (c.1826–1832). His life had revolved around this routine until circa 1832 when he returned to Warrah to find the AACo on his run and the AACo's sheep mixed amongst his cattle. William was surprised and annoyed as he tells us below.

The Sydney Morning Herald, 23rd Jan 1861, page 3. [continued]

My station [Warrah] was one of the best on the Liverpool Plains district. When I had been on it about four years I was surprised to see a large number of sheep, brought on to my run and spread over it in all directions.[152] I asked the superintendent in charge what he meant by bringing sheep on to my run.[153] He said that the Australian Agricultural Company [AACo] had purchased a large tract of land in this country from the home [British] Government, and they were going to take part of it there. After that I had great losses by my cattle straying away, in consequence of the sheep being mixed among them. Worse than all, my run was taken away from me by the Company, and no recompense given, after being tormented by the blacks for about three years.

William and the Kamilaroi People

Before we go on with William's story, and why the AACo was on William's run, we need to acknowledge the last statement in this part of William's story:

> *"...after being tormented by the blacks [Kamilaroi warriors] for about three years [c.1829 to c.1832].*

As detailed earlier, the Kamilaroi warriors came together in large groups and used strategies of intimidation, such as raids with their spears and womara (spear throwing device), the stealing of the squatters' rations from their huts, spearing and mostly wounding the squatters (with some deaths) and the spearing and killing of the squatters' cattle and sheep, not just for food, but to try to pressure them to leave.

We also know, the squatters challenged and confronted the Kamilaroi people, inadvertently exposed the Kamilaroi clans to smallpox (from which they had little or no resistance), murdered and massacred them, destroyed the traditional sources of food and cleared large swathes of Country for grazing.

William's commentary of his own experience with the Kamilaroi clans and warriors is limited and general. Later in his Letter to the Editor of the *Sydney Morning Herald* (detailed soon), William tells us he was 'troubled by the aboriginals, with attacks upon the stockman and the killing of cattle' but he does not tell us how he responded. Did William (as was customary amongst the squatters) bribe the Kamilaroi people with tobacco, food and rations and avoid contact as much as possible, or did he brandish or use his muskets to deter the Kamilaroi warriors? The answers to these questions are elusive because there is no account other than William's about his relationship with the Kamilaroi people. His narration is simply full of complaint about these First Nation people interfering with his run. As far as William was concerned, it was his run, and the Kamilaroi people had no right to interfere with his stock. This was the typical and deplorable colonial view that William shared with the other squatters and settlers.

William was Certainly Annoyed About the AACo Putting Sheep Amongst his Cattle

When William chose Warrah he believed all he needed to do was choose a run, stake his claim with a hut, cattle, and indentured stockmen, and then later, once the land had been surveyed, formalise his run into a grant. That's what had happened in the Hunter, and as far as William was concerned nothing had changed. From William's perspective, he had been at Warrah for six years (1826–1832) and it was his run; how dare the AACo put sheep amongst his cattle!

William would have been aware (from the newspapers and in discussion with others) that the AACo (incorporated in London, in 1824) had negotiated, with the 'Home Government', for a grant of 1 million acres of land, in NSW, for the purpose of '[raising] fine woolled sheep and [selling] wool on the London market'.[154] He would have known the AACo had a land grant at Port Stephens, but he would never had imagined the possibility of the AACo taking up residence on his run on the Liverpool Plains.

When William arrived to check on his run (c.1832) the AACo had already settled on Warrah after being given permission by Governor Darling to select land in the interior of the colony for their company's sheep. Then, a year later (c.1833) Governor Darling gave the AACo '249,600 acres on the Liverpool Plains, west of Willow Tree (Warrah)', with William's run consumed (along with several other squatters)[155] within the grant. The relative locations of the AACo's grant and William's run Warrah is shown on the map that follows. (See Figure 10.)

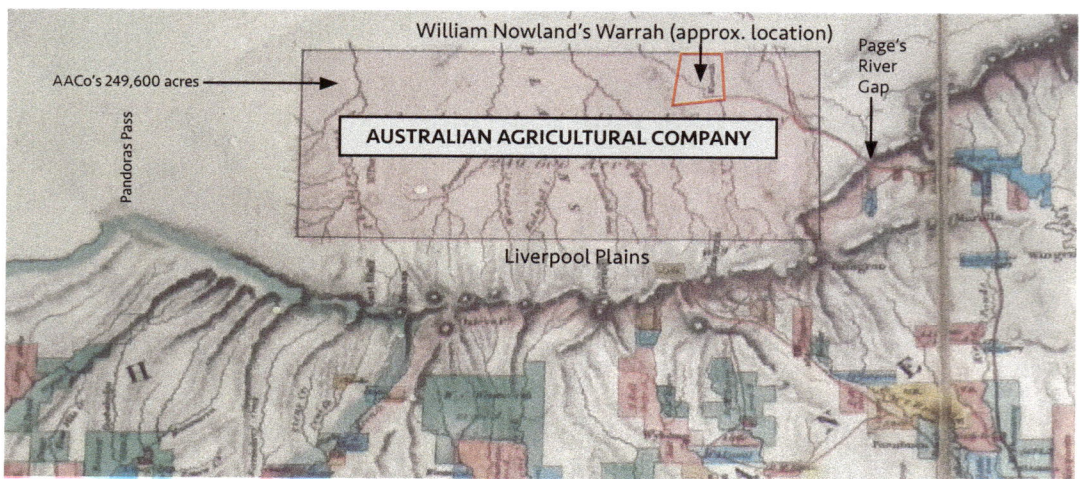

Figure 10: AACo's Land Grant and William Nowland's Run, 'Warrah' (approx. location)

The AACo saw William's cattle on his run (hut and all) and knew this was the land of a squatter. Yet this did not deter them. They knew they could claim land wherever they liked, and the Governor would approve. William was stymied from the start. He challenged the AACo under what he believed were his rights as the first occupant and lost his case on the grounds his run was outside the official boundaries of settlement. From Governor Darling's perspective, the AACo were the ones to be favoured because this company would be instrumental in the advancement of the colony's wool industry in England and Europe. In essence, the size, influence and prestige of the AACo that is, its Directors in London and NSW gave it the power to appropriate land either inside or outside the boundaries of official land settlement and tenure.[156]

There were different rules for those with the right connections, especially if they were London-based and conveniently conversing with and gaining the favour of the Home Government. This level of influence enabled the AACo to secure an exceedingly large land grant from Governor Darling (in 1826) of one million acres on land of their choosing within the boundary of the settlement at Port Stephens. The following year (1827), the settlers moved onto the Liverpool Plains (in number) and claimed their runs outside the boundaries of settlement on the superior and very fertile pastures of the Liverpool Plains. Two years later (in 1829) Sir Edward Parry, the new Commissioner in charge of the AACo's land grant at Port Stephens (from 1829 to 1834) arrived in Sydney and became aware of the difference in quality of the pastures at Port Stephens and on the Liverpool Plains. Parry then sent Henry Dangar (who was now employed by the AACo, 1829 to 1833) to the Liverpool Plains to investigate (c.1831). On Dangar's return, Parry (in 1832) accompanied Dangar and George Boyle White (Assistant Surveyor, Governor General's Department, NSW) up onto the Liverpool Plains where they marked out a claim for the AACo (c.1832). The claim included William's run, the HBS's run at Phillip's Creek (managed by William's brother Edward) and the runs of several other squatters.[157]

Squatters, like William, with their smaller runs and no international agenda didn't stand a chance against friends of the Establishment, as the following newspaper article states (along with a broader rant about the state of the colony, which is not included here).

The Sydney Monitor, Wednesday 18 December 1833, page 2
LIVERPOOL PLAINS

It appears that this choice region, covered for years back with flocks and herds of settlers of all classes, were lately "discovered" by Sir Edw. Parry; and on the recommendation of that gentleman, the present numerous occupiers are to be all dispossessed, and the whole concern given to the million-of-acre Company [AACo] …

William and the Other Squatters Move Further North

The squatters were forced further north. They needed to find somewhere else on the Liverpool Plains to graze their cattle. The Hunter Valley (as told earlier) was no longer an option given it was overcrowded with people, landholdings, and stock.

William and Edward took William's stock (from Warrah) and the HBS's stock (from Phillips Creek) further north to the Mooki River, where they claimed a new 1,000-acre land grant for the HBS; as shown on the map in Figure 11.

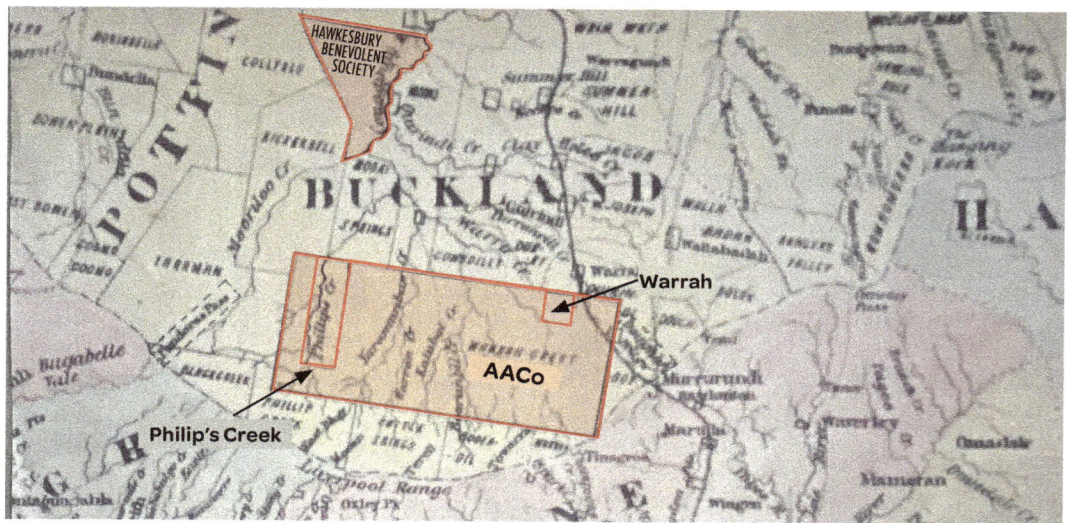

Figure 11: The Squatters Head North

William Marries and Safeguards his Pre-emptive Lease at Falbrook

Just before discovering the AACo was on his run, William (27) married the third Farlow sister, Mary Ann Farlow (18) at St John's Anglican Church, Wilberforce, in 1831; Henry's wife Harriet and Edward's wife Christian were Mary's sisters.[158]

In the same year (1831), William transferred his lease of 160 acres (the lease he gained from his brother Michael jr. in 1824) to Henry and retrieved it in 1834 to maintain his 520 acres of adjoining allotments at Falbrook.[159] It is not known why William transferred this 160 acres to Henry; it is assumed it was for safe keeping, until William found the monies to pay the lease.

In the same year as William's marriage (1831), his youngest sister Sarah Jane (17) married William Adnum at Scots Church, Sydney.[160]

William's Account of the Hawkesbury Benevolent Society's Initial Land Grant at Phillips Creek and then Later Along the Mooki River

Once married, William and Mary initially lived in Wilberforce, with William away from home for long periods of time when he needed to move his stock up the Bulga Track to Falbrook, and then onto Warrah on the Liverpool Plains. Then (as mentioned at the end of Chapter 2) around two years after William (28) married, he set out with his brother, Edward (26) in search of land for HBS's grant. In early 1833 (most likely January or February) the two brothers drove the HBS's cattle up onto the Liverpool Plains and settled on land adjacent to Phillips Creek, as William tells us next.

> **The Sydney Morning Herald – 23rd Jan. 1861, page 3 [continued]**
> *About 1832 [early 1833] my brother Edward and I formed a run at Phillip's Creek, about thirty miles from Warrah, for the Hawkesbury Benevolent Society of Windsor; a short time before that Governor Darling gave the society one thousand acres of land and a run for their stock, but the thousand acres were not (sic) measured. After we formed the society's run the Australian Company [AACo] sent Mr. H. Dangar up to measure the company grant, and he took the society's run into the company's grant, coming a distance, of thirty miles from Warrah.*[161]
>
> *Then the Governor gave the society an order to take another run for their stock, and one thousand acres of land in any part of the Liverpool Plains, instead of the one the company had taken, which they selected on the Mooki River, a station called Mooki, and had their thousand acres of land measured there, and took possession of the run with their stock, in 1836.*[162]

The next map shows once again the Hawkesbury Benevolent Society's new Mooki Station adjacent to the Mooki River. (See Figure 12 overleaf.)[163]

What William tells us in this part of his Letter to the Editor is confirmed by other documentation. The minutes of a meeting of the Hawkesbury Benevolent Society (HBS), in 1833, note Edward and William headed north circa January 1833 to secure a run of 1,000 acres for the Society on the Liverpool Plains.[164]

As we know, Edward and William chose a run at Phillip's Creek; the exact location, unknown. Then months later, they found themselves inside the boundaries of the AACo's 249,600 acres. Edward's initial response (probably ladened with indignation) was to write to the HBS to inform them of what had happened and to advise them he (and William) would head north to find a new run. Edward's initial letter was followed by correspondence between the Society and its first president William Cox. Cox then wrote to the Colonial Secretary and Surveyor-General on behalf of the Society, who both informed Cox, the HBS had no prior claim at Phillip's Creek because nothing had been formalised.[165]

Edward and William did not wait for all this correspondence, instead they headed north and claimed a new run for the Society, along the Mooki River. Then around a year later, in April 1835, Governor Bourke (1831–1837) agreed to the HBS's new run, with its 1,000 acres adjoining the Mooki River at Breeza; with the grant known as Mooki Station and officially leased by the HBS on the 24th June 1835.[166]

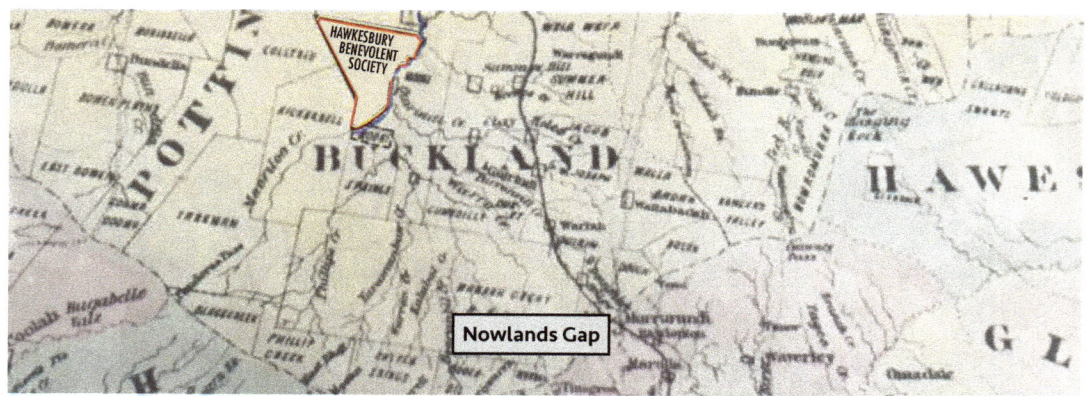

Figure 12: Hawkesbury Benevolent Society's Grant – Mooki Station

CHAPTER 6

THE NOWLAND BROTHERS AND THE FARLOW SISTERS

By 1835, Henry, William and Edward had started to plan for the movement of their respective families north. For Henry and William, into the Hunter, and for Edward, up on the Liverpool Plains. Henry was a storekeeper in Muswellbrook; William a pastoralist at Falbrook and a squatter on the Liverpool Plains; and, Edward the Superintendent of Stock for the HBS's Mooki Station along the Mooki River.

By 1836, Henry had been married for 10 years with three children; William married for four years with two children; and Edward married for six years with three children. Their livelihood was now in the Hunter and on the Liverpool Plains and for Henry, as far away as Guy Fawkes on the New England Tablelands. Yet their connections with Wilberforce, the Hawkesbury and Sydney remained, as they drove their cattle along the Bulga Track to the Windsor and Sydney town markets and most likely stopped in on family along the way.[167]

One can only image what life was like for them; Henry and Harriet in Muswellbrook (with Henry venturing out to Guy Fawkes from time to time); William and Mary at Falbrook (with William, consistently away at Mooki Station attending his own cattle on the station and helping Edward with the HBS's stock); and Edward and Christian, now the most remote, settled at Mooki Station, along the Mooki River, on the Liverpool Plains.

We know by 1837 Harriet lived with Henry, most likely at the back of the general store, at Muswellbrook, with their three children (Ann 11, Sarah 9, and Henry jr., a baby).[168] Life would have been very different given they had moved from the established township of Wilberforce (c.1836) to a general store in the remote settlement of Muswellbrook.[169] Harriet's and her children's connection to the outside world now came from those who stopped in at their general store (pastoralists, squatters and travellers) to replenish their produce, goods and wares. Then when Henry was away (either tending his cattle, and/or taking them to market) Harriet and the children would have busied themselves with stocking and running the store (with the help of indentured convict labour).

Though they were relatively isolated, Harriet and her children lived in an established dwelling in an emerging settlement. While in contrast, Harriet's sisters, Mary and Christian either lived in a hut or log cabin on unfenced grazing land. Mary at Glennies Creek, and Christian at Mooki Station. Hopefully, Mary's and

Christian's hut or log cabin was up to standard given the carpentry skills of William and Edward.

In the 1830s, there was no photography and only descriptors or drawings of the typical settler's hut. In Glennies Creek where Mary lived, Lillian Noble, a resident and descendant of one of the first settlers in Falbrook provides us with some descriptors handed down to her from previous generations.[170]

> *Their huts were made ... mainly from bark, cut in long strips from trees... by overlapping each sheet a little, it made a fairly weather-proof dwelling, fitted onto a strong frame held together by notches and tying. The roof's heavy poles were also tied against bad weather.*
>
> *Strong frames were made for the chimney, the size of a small room. The hearth was filled with stones or rocks and then plastered in with mud to make the floor more level. The back and sides were done the same, fitted with rocks and then plastered in with mud, with a wooden slab outer wall. A big log could be drawn into the hearth and burn for days.*
>
> *With strong poles put across from wall to wall, chains were suspended over the fire for large cast iron fountain boiling pots and kettles. A three-legged, lid covered iron pot usually stood in the hot ashes to cook meat and vegetables or bread [all from the vegetable patch and farm, with pigs, hens, roosters etc.].*
>
> *... The thing missing the most was sufficient crops of grain, to be ground into flour... under the house in the shade, an oblong hole was dug, then thickly lined with charcoal and covered with hessian. On the lid a vessel of water stood with flannel wicks to slowly drip water onto the charcoal, this made a cool container for milk and butter.*
>
> *They made their own ham, bacon and cheese. When the fruit trees were established and bearing fruit they made their own preserves, dried fruit and jams.*
>
> *Settlers also made their own wine... Bull or bullock skin was cleaned of all fat, cured with salt and wattle bark, to tan the hide. From this leather harnesses, reins, halters, bridles, belts and ropes etc. were made. Some ropes having from eight to twelve strands plaited.*
>
> *Whips were often made from kangaroo hide because of its lightness and toughness...*
>
> *Men and women reaped the crops when they were ripe. Sheaves of grain would be put on clean ground for the fowls to scratch out the grain. The straw was then picked up and stored... [for bedding for the pighouse].*

Hopefully, Christian's home at Mooki Station on the Mooki River was as good! In the following account, Sir Edward Parry (Commissioner in Charge of the AACo enterprises in NSW, 1829–1834) describes the rough and ready huts of two of the squatters along the Hunter River, circa 1830.

> *On his first tour of inspection Parry was startled at the way the Hunter River*

settlers lived. Accustomed to servants in England many of them, [obviously the newly arrived free settlers] and lacking the skills of tradesmen, they were making a job of adapting. He stayed a night with one settler, George Graham, and his cousin named Oliver. Mr. Graham's father kept his hunters in England. They now lived in a miserable slab-hut of their own building, open to admit wind and rain in most parts, badly thatched with reeds of which the colour is not to be seen within for the smoke and dirt with which it is covered – no floor – the fire place (sic) a recess made of rafters, and everything giving the idea of filth and wretchedness. They wait entirely on themselves, chop their own wood, boil their kettle, wash their cups and pannikins, plough, reap and everything else themselves. They slept under their cart for three weeks keeping watch with a loaded gun alternately.

Nearby the Maclean's hut was worse, and Mrs Maclean was 'Colonel Snodgrass's sister – a women accustomed in Scotland I understand to all the elegancies and comforts of life!'[171]

Christian's home was most likely more resilient than the ones described above. It is assumed, the Farlow sisters (Harriet, Christian, and Mary, the wives of Henry, Edward and William, respectively) had a much better lifestyle and standard of living. Given, all six were raised on their family allotments and all knew how to be self-sufficient in all the aspects of farm life in a remote part of the colony, including: how to build a substantial dwelling to live in, along with all the farm buildings needed, and of course the stockyards; how to establish and keep a vegetable garden and orchard; how to raise and keep chickens and their rooster; how to keep pigs (especially, given the Nowland brothers' father's knowledge, skill and success in this area); then maybe, some dairy cows and of course the cattle; how to grow a field or more of crops (most likely, wheat, maize and barley) as well as, having the basic medical knowledge; along with the skills of making, mending and caring for clothes; darning socks; and preserving produce for later use, as well as, the myriad of other tasks not mentioned here.

To assist them, all three families brought indentured convict labour into the Hunter and onto the Liverpool Plains. At a minimum each family would have had at least one farm servant, stockman, and overseer.[172] Yet despite this help and the knowledge they possessed, each family was challenged by the environment (especially in times of drought and flood) and most notably, Edward and Christian, who lived in the middle of nowhere on Mooki Station, near the Mooki River, on the Liverpool Plains.

A short while after William and Mary settled in their new home (hopefully at least a log cabin) they had their third son, Robert, in 1836.[173] In the same year, William purchased another adjoining allotment of 142 acres (Lot 14) and expanded their family farm 'Rosedale' to 822 acres.[174]

CHAPTER 7

WILLIAM NOWLAND – THE FURTHEST NORTH

At the beginning of 1837, William and Mary had three boys (William jr. aged 4 Michael 2, and Robert a baby) and just like his father before him (Michael Nowland) William could not wait to get ahead and make as much money as he could for his wife and children.

In March 1837 William claimed a new run on the Liverpool Plains, as he tells us below in the continuation of his story.

> *The Sydney Morning Herald – 23rd Jan. 1861, page 3.*
> *[continued]*
>
> *In March, 1837, I went down the Namoi, about one hundred and fifty miles below the Mooki River, with my drays and cattle, and formed a station called Drildole [sic, Dridool],*[175] *at that time, it was the lowest station on the Namoi River, and was troubled with the aboriginals for two years and a half, continually making attacks upon the men in the huts; [probably, assigned convict labour], and when riding after the cattle, they often made a practice of lying in wait for the men. A stockman of mine was pinned to his saddle by a spear; but fortunately, it went through his clothes, and just at the time they formed a half-moon round him, and then threw spears and boomerangs at him. The man luckily turned his horse and escaped with the spear still sticking in his clothes.*
>
> *Between the drought and the blacks, I lost three hundred head of cattle on the run, and what was worse than all, the commissioner came down and marked my run in the shape of the letter L, by giving one of his favourites, part of a large waterhole that I had in the centre of my run. Through the commissioner acting so arbitrarily I sold my run for a mere trifle.*

There is a lot in this part of William's story that fits with what we already know about the methods the Kamilaroi nation used to dissuade the squatters from settling on the Liverpool Plains; raiding the huts, killing the cattle, lying in wait, coming in number, and spearing the stockman as a deterrent. For two and a half years (March 1837 to circa September, 1839) William's run Dridool (outside the boundaries of settlement and at the forefront of the advancement of settlement) had been raided by the Kamilaroi warriors in this way for the purpose of deterring William and the other squatters from advancement further north.

William was part of an invasion, and at this time, he led the appropriation further into Kamilaroi Country. As Eric Rolls tells us; 'Thomas Arndell, a Hunter River settler, sent some of George Loder's 1,500 head of cattle round to Merah [east of Dridool, on the Namoi] to join William Nowland.'[176]

The map in Figure 13 shows the location of Dridool (today known as Drildool) in the upper reaches of the Namoi River.

Waterloo Creek Massacre

During William's time at Dridool (1837–1839) Major James Nunn and his Mounted Police massacred Kamilaroi people at Waterloo Creek on the 26th January 1838; again, note the date, 50 years after the First Fleet arrived at Sydney Cove, and now known as Australia Day. This massacre occurred approximately 68 km (42.2 miles) north-east of William's run. (See Figure 14.)[177]

Whether William was at Dridool during the Waterloo Massacre (also known as Slaughterhouse Creek Massacre) or on the Liverpool Plains, further south with his brother Edward, and his sister-in-law Christian at Mooki Station or at Rosedale (Falbrook) is unknown.

The NSW Acting Governor, Colonel Snodgrass (from the 5th December 1837 to 23rd February 1838) in an act of self-righteousness sent the notorious Major James Nunn, to the Gwydir and Namoi Rivers, as told next.

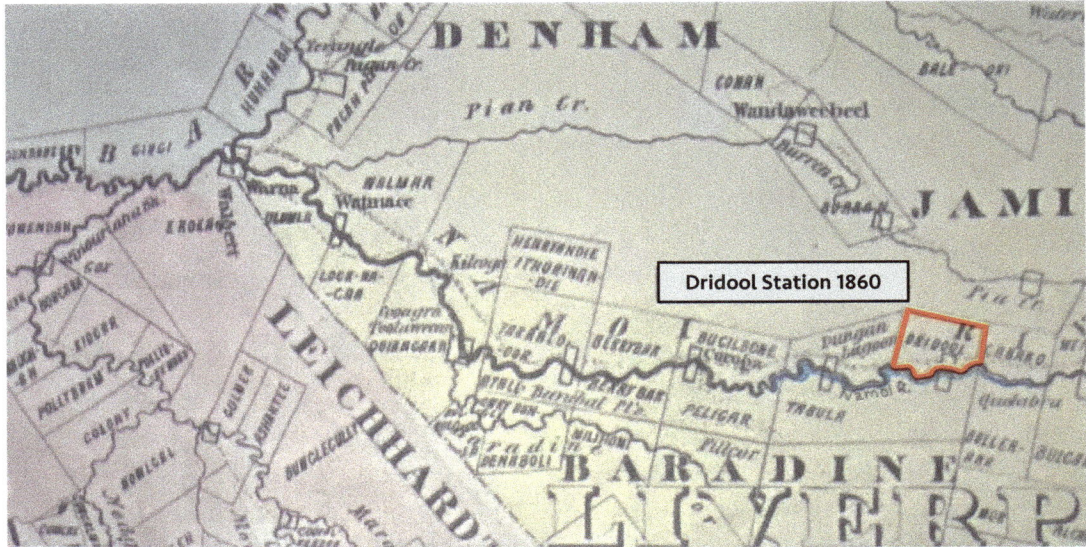

Figure 13: William Nowland's Dridool Run (1837–1839)

Slaughterhouse Creek [Massacre]

As NSW acting governor, Colonel Snodgrass appointed the notorious Major James Nunn commandant of the NSW Mounted Police. Snodgrass ordered Nunn to go out to the Liverpool Plains and deal with the Gamilaraay people's resistance to British occupation.

In late 1837, Major Nunn led the NSW Mounted Police in a two-month sweeping operation along the Gwydir and Namoi Rivers. The operation climaxed on 26 January 1838 with the Waterloo Creek massacre, which saw the wholesale slaughter of Gamilaraay people.[178]

Nunn and his officers continued on with their murderous rampage for a further three days after the slaughter, killing every Aboriginal person they came across. During the course of the operation, its believe that up to 300 Indigenous people were killed by the police on horseback.

A belated inquiry into the murders was carried out by the colonial government, [under Governor Gipps] but there were no prosecutions, and the matter was eventually dropped.[179]

William knew the Waterloo Massacre had occurred and it is likely that his opinion would have not varied from the commonly held view of the squatters as detailed earlier (in Chapter 4) in the article in the 'Bent News' on the 25th November 1837, and noted in part, once again, below.

> …. *We trust the government will lose no time in dispatching some of the military to aid the residents in that vicinity in reducing the savages to order.*

William Sells the Improvements He had Made at Dridool

Like all the other squatters, William on arrival at a new run changed the lay of the land. At a minimum he built a hut and improved the pastures. Then when he decided to move on, he offered the lease to another with an agreed payment for the improvements he had made.

William in the continuation of his Letter to the Editor tells the reader he sold the improvements to Dridool, two-and-a-half years after he claimed the run (c. September 1839). He also informs the reader of the reasons why he decided to sell: the loss of three hundred cattle due to the drought and the Kamilaroi warriors raids, the decision of the Commissioner to mark his run out in the shape of the letter L; and the subsequent loss of a large waterhole in the centre of the run (during a drought) to the Commissioner's favourites.[180]

Who were the Commissioners and the Commissioner's favourites?

Governor Darling left the colony in 1831 and was replaced by Governor Bourke (1831–1837) who in 1836 introduced the Commissioners to survey and mark out the boundaries of each run in their designated jurisdiction. We can only surmise who in William's case were the Commissioner's favourites. In essence, they are assumed to be the Commissioner's friends, associates, and/or the free settlers who secured runs with the added advantage of money, influence and sometimes land grants in contrast to William who was a first-generation New South Welshman and the son of emancipated convicts and who most likely spoke with an Irish accent.

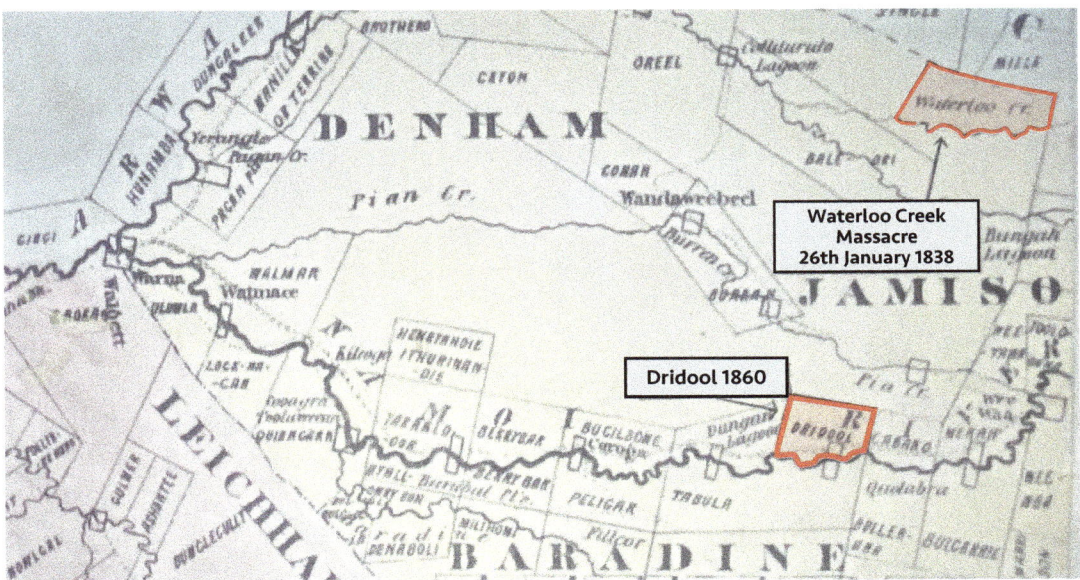

Figure 14: Distance between Waterloo Creek and Dridool

CHAPTER 8

GOVERNOR BOURKE'S PROCLAMATION

Since the start of Britain's occupation of Gadigal Country of the Eora Nation (Sydney) in 1788, the British government had justified their possession of Aboriginal Country on the grounds of *terra nullius* ('nobody's land'); and nothing had changed. William and his fellow settlers were raised to believe the land was theirs for the taking. All they needed to do was get in first, stay ahead of the mob, establish their runs, and formalise them later, through lease, and subsequent purchase.

William wasn't going to miss out, land was a measure of success and prosperity and he had his own magic formula: go out, find a run, claim your space, breed and expand your stock on the expansive fertile Liverpool Plains, sell your well-bred and fattened stock in the Hawkesbury and Sydney markets and then return to Falbrook to reinvest the monies in his and Mary's family farm within the boundaries of settlement; their beloved Rosedale at Glennies Creek.

The commonly held view of settlers and squatters (including William) was that First Nations people had no prior claim on the land. A condescending and self-righteous view formalised on the 10th October 1835, in the following Proclamation from Governor Bourke.[181]

> *The Colonist 10th September 1835, page 2*
> **PROCLAMATION**
>
> *BY His Excellency Major-General Sir Richard Bourke, K. C. B., Captain – General and Governor-in-Chief of the Territory of New South Wales and its Dependencies, and Vice-Admiral of the same, &c., &c., &c.*
>
> WHEREAS *it has been represented to me, that divers of His Majesty's subjects have taken possession of vacant lands of the Crown, within the limits of this colony, under the pretense of a treaty, bargain or contract, for the purchase there of, with the Aboriginal Natives.*[182]
>
> *Now, therefore, I the Governor, in virtue and in exercise of the power and authority in me vested, do hereby proclaim and notify to all His Majesty's subjects, and others whom it may concern, that every such treaty, bargain, and contract with the Aboriginal Natives as aforesaid, for the possession, title, or claim to any lands lying and being within the limits of the Government of the colony of New South*

Wales, as the same are laid down and defined by His Majesty's Commission ; that is to say, extending from the Northern Cape or extremity of the coast called Cape York, in the latitude of ten degrees thirty-seven minutes' south, to the southern extremity of the said territory of New South Wales, or Wilson's Promontory, in the latitude of thirty nine degrees twelve minutes south, and embracing all the country inland to the westward, as far as the one hundred and twenty-ninth degree of east longitude, reckoning from the meridian of Greenwich, including all the islands adjacent in the Pacific Ocean within the latitude aforesaid, and including also Norfolk Island, is void and of no effect against the rights of the Crown ; and that all persons who shall be found in possession of any such lands as aforesaid, without the licence or authority of His Majesty's, Government, for such purpose first had and obtained, shall be considered as trespassers, and liable to be dealt with in like manner as other intruders upon the vacant lands of the Crown within the said colony. Given under my Hand and Seal, at Government House, Sydney, this Twenty-sixth day of August,

One thousand eight hundred and thirty-five.

RICHARD BOURKE.

By His Excellency's Command,

ALEXANDER McLEAY

GOD SAVE THE KING!

William and his Fellow Squatters Required to Have a Licence for Each of Their Runs

To activate the Proclamation, Governor Bourke implemented an Act in 1836, 'to restrain the unauthorised occupation of Crown Lands'.[183] This Act classified all land outside the boundaries of settlement as Crown land, and anyone who occupied these lands required a licence. Unlike the land grants within the boundaries of settlement where settlers could lease and eventually purchase their allotments, squatters like William were required to apply, and gain a licence for each of their runs, annually. William's run on the Liverpool Plains (Dridool) needed a licence (1836 to 1839), then William 'sold' Dridool to the Commissioner's favourites.

To enable the Act, Governor Bourke firstly divided the squatter community into nine distinct areas that incorporated all the squats beyond the Great Dividing Range and outside the boundaries of declared settlement, from Melbourne in the south, to Brisbane in the north, and as far west as the squatters had gone, with each squatter required to hold a licence for each of their runs. It would cost William and his fellow squatters £10 per squat; renewed each year at £5 per annum.[184]

William and his brother Henry are listed (in 1840) amongst those 'who have obtained licences from the Colonial Treasurer for depasturing stock beyond the boundaries of location'; Henry in the New England District at Guy Fawkes and William in the Gwydir District at Boonanga (detailed later in the story).[185]

To enact Governor Bourke's proclamation, a Commissioner was assigned to each of the squatter districts to ensure each run had a licence from the Crown and the person in possession of the run, held a certificate of good character from the nearest Justice of the Peace or the Commissioner himself.

For William, and his fellow squatters on the Liverpool Plains, Alexander Paterson was their first Commissioner (appointed, 9th May 1837) followed soon after by Edward Mayne (appointed, 1st October 1838).[186]

Henry – a Squatter on the New England Tablelands

Of particular interest during this time is Henry's activities. The entry of Henry's lease at Guy Fawkes on the New England Tablelands tells us Henry's pursuits extended beyond the Golden Fleece Inn (c.1836), in Muswellbrook; later known as the Royal Hotel (c.1838). As early as 1840, Henry had moved beyond the Liverpool Plains and established a run on the New England Tablelands (Guy Fawkes). Undoubtedly, William would have visited or helped Henry with this run; a run much further north than William's Dridool (1839) on the Liverpool Plains.

On reflection and towards the end of writing the first draft of this story I wondered whether Henry's interest in Guy Fawkes was in terms of rounding up and domesticating stray horses and possibly also breeding horses on this run given his interest in developing a stage coaching service that starts to emerge in his story in the 1840s.

Henry's Guy Fawkes was on Gambainggir Country.[187] The impact of Henry and his fellow squatters on the Gumbainggir Nation and the other Aboriginal Nations on the New England Tablelands was devastating as detailed later in this story when William leases a run adjacent to Henry's Guy Fawkes, Ward's Mistake, in 1842.

Chapter 9

Governor Gipps' Response to the Slaughterhouse Creek Massacre and the Myall Creek Massacre

Governor Gipps arrived in Sydney on the 24th February 1838, just after the Slaughterhouse Creek Massacre (also known as the Waterloo Massacre) on the 26th January 1838. Knowing this, the first thought that comes to mind is what was Gipps' response to the massacre and then a few months later, the subsequent massacre at Myall Creek?

In the case of the Slaughterhouse Creek Massacre, at Waterloo Creek, Gipps' response was tentative; he ordered an Inquiry with equivocal results and Major Nunn and his troops escaped indictment.[188] Then, six months later (on Gipps's watch) the Myall Creek Massacre occurred on the Liverpool Plains. This time, Gipps order a trial and when 11 stockmen (made up of former and indentured convicts) were acquitted, Gipps ordered a second trial, based on subsequent evidence that linked seven of the stockmen to the murder of one of the Aboriginal children. This time there was a guilty verdict and seven of the convicts were hung while the other four stockman went free.

Gipps Established the Border Police

The following year (1839) Gipps established the Border Police whose primary purposes were to assist the newly appointed Commissioners implement the new licence and leasing requirements for the squatters and settle and minimise the skirmishes between the squatters and First Nations people.

The Border Police were largely made up of 'a force of ex-convicts equipped with a horse, a gun and rations and funded by a tax on squatters'.[189] Their presence consolidated and enforced the commonly held view amongst the squatters and the British establishment (both in NSW and Britain) that the land was there for the taking (*terra nullius*) and as detailed in Governor Bourke's proclamation (1835) all land within the colony was Crown Land.

The Survival of the Kamilaroi People

By the end of the 1830s, the hordes of squatters who had taken over Kamilaroi Country were there to stay. They and the Mounted Police had decimated the Kamilaroi clans (from an estimated 15,000 Kamilaroi people to 1,000). The threat to the Kamilaroi people and Country was imbedded and each clan needed to do everything they could to not only survive but to also hand down the traditional knowledge and lifestyle they had inherited from their ancestors to each new generation. Which they did – an admirable and amazing feat. See the account that follows:

> *The Kamilaroi nation had been inhabited by Aboriginal people speaking the 'Gamilaraay' language for an estimated 40,000 years. During the course of this time, it has been suggested that 15,000 people roamed the nation of north-west NSW. In the 54 years post-colonisation [1788–1842], the population of the Kamilaroi drastically dropped to only 1000 people through displacement, conflict and disease brought about by European occupation.*[190]

Today the Kamilaroi clans continue to maintain their connection to their culture, each other, and their Nation.[191]

PART TWO

William Expands his Interests as a Pastoralist and Squatter

William still very determined in 1840

CHAPTER 10

LEGAL DISPUTES, CLAIMS AND COUNTER CLAIMS

In the latter part of the 1830s, the squatters continued to spread across the Liverpool Plains; William amongst them.[192] 'Cashed up' free settlers also came, lured by Governor Bourke's (1831–1837) offer of a reasonably large land grant and for some, a place in the emerging wool industry.

When they returned to their runs, the squatters challenged each other about exclusive possession: whose run was whose and where did the boundaries of each run start and finish? Surveying began, Commissioners arrived, and boundaries were determined amongst all the squabbling. The steady arrival of cashed up free settlers into the colony added another layer of complaint and debate that eventually ended up in the courts. Many affluent and well connected free settlers (mainly from Britian's aristocratic families) chose land in the best location that suited their needs without any regard for the squatters, their huts or their stock. As far as they were concerned the squatters did not have exclusive possession of the land on which they grazed their stock, while the choices they made were official given they were the ones with the land grants from the Governor. They took over the land, wherever they wished, mainly with their sheep and challenged the original squatter (when they returned to their squat) on the grounds of trespass.

William's Wallalla Station on the Liverpool Plains is a case in point. After selling Dridool for a 'mere trifle to the Commissioner's favourites' (in 1839) William gained a licence for a new run he called Wallalla on the Liverpool Plains (September 1839). William's exclusive possession of this new run (known as Wallalla Station) was consistently challenged by those with money, position and an adjacent land grant, for at least 20 years. As he tells us in the continuation of his Letter to the Editor.

The Sydney Morning Herald, 23rd Jan. 1861, page 3. [continued]

In September 1839, I purchased [paid for improvements made to] a station named Wallalla on the Mooki River, Liverpool Plains, from the first occupants, Messrs. Parrott and Ross, who held it for seven years before any trespass had taken place. Immediately after taking possession, I gave the trespassers notice to quit the run. One of the trespassers left [Edmund Uhr, detailed later in this story], but another came in his place, with whom I have had several lawsuits before the Crown Lands Commissioner [John Eales, in the 1850s, detailed later in this story]. I never could get a written decision, only a verbal one in my favour: the reason, I suppose, was, that I was not so rich a man as the trespasser [John Eales].[193]

Afterwards, boundary commissioners were introduced through unjust commissioners I was at law for up to twenty years, and whenever my cattle were comfortable, the trespassers used to put sheep amongst them and when my cattle went to drink at the river, the trespassers would have the aboriginals in charge of sheep and camped on the banks of the river, and hunted away (sic) my cattle with dogs from the water. The injury was done to my cattle through being disturbed, and the sheep eating their food. I have been drawing cattle out of bogs, with bullocks, for nearly three years at a time, and the losses of my stock were about eight hundred head within three years, and several hundreds, at different times since, which was the cause of my having but very few fat stock for market. And I consider my losses to have amounted to upwards of ten thousand pounds. This is a specimen of "free selection before survey." God help the free selector if he is to be served as I have been, which he most likely be.[194]

William's New Run, Wallalla

When William left Dridool and replaced it with Wallalla (in September 1839) he travelled 145 miles (233.3 km) south with his stock and established this new run just north of the HBS's Mooki Station (which his brother, Edward, managed for the Society). This new run (Wallalla) is listed in the *Government Gazette* in 1848 and at that time, consisted of 87,040 acres with frontage along the Mooki River'. (See Figure 15.)[195]

William most likely leased Wallalla because it was close to the HBS's Mooki Station. Edward needed help; he had struggled through the extreme droughts of the 1837 and 1839 and the HBS's stock had been compromised further by the cattle of others, straying onto, or being put on Mooki Station and competing for whatever grass was left.[196]

William probably thought if he and his brother Edward worked together on Mooki Station and Wallalla, the extra grazing land Wallalla offered would lift the quality of his and the HBS's cattle. There would be plenty of pasture for Edward's, William's and the HBS's cattle. They could also assist each other in rounding up the stock of the trespassers and then when William was ready to go home to Rosedale, he could take the trespassers' stock with him and deposit them in the local Pound.[197]

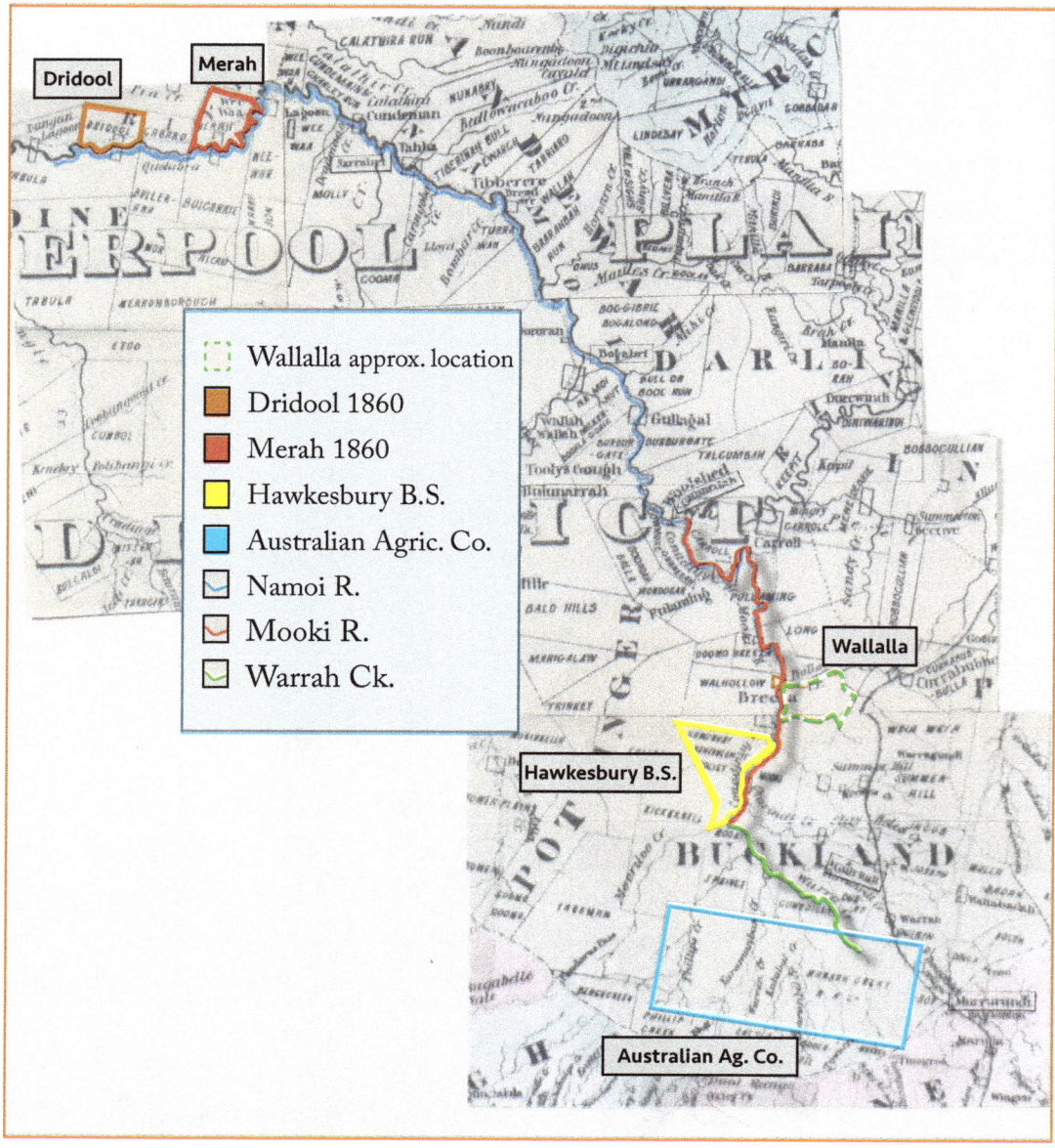

Figure 15: William Nowland's Wallalla Run (approx. location)

Questionable Activities Between the Squatters

The on-going account of Wallalla (all in the newspapers and courts) gives us a glimpse into the challenges William faced against wealthy and well-connected free settlers with land grants. For now, the focus is on the disagreement between the squatters as they expanded beyond the boundaries of settlement. The squatters disrupted the stock of others, caused substantial stock loss and during the 1850s and 60s, brought lawsuits against each other to court with claims and counter claims about the boundaries of their runs. Most of the court cases germinated from Bourke's Proclamation of 1836 and the subsequent disputes, after the Commissioners arrived, surveyed the runs, assessed the stock and determined the boundaries.[198]

There are numerous summarised accounts in the colonial newspapers of lawsuit between the squatters. For 'our' William there are several in the 1850s and 60s that recount William's experience either as the claimant or defendant, and/or a witness. The most pertinent of the cases, in terms of William and his role as a squatter on the Liverpool Plains are highlighted chronologically in the story, at the time they occurred.

From the time that William had shown the squatters the easier route onto the Liverpool Plains through the Pages River Gap (c. April 1827) the squatters had come in large number to settle this land outside the boundaries of official settlement. The runs were hurriedly obtained in an ad hoc fashion with verbal agreements and arrangements between the various squatters. You can hear them now: *'You take the land down to the big white gum and I'll run my cattle from the river edge to the hill in the distance.'*

The boundaries of the runs were ill defined, and unfenced, and the stock of different squatters roamed, grazed and became mixed in with the stock of other squatters across the various runs. The squatters were transient, they came and went as they pleased and left their indentured labour and stockmen (some with a ticket of leave) in charge of their run/s. Then periodically they returned after months of absence to inevitably find (like William) the stock of other squatters on their run/s. They could readily see whose stock they were based on the branding and would immediately confront the different offenders if they were around or if not, their resident indentured labour and stockmen who would be told to remove the cattle, at once! They would then try to deter the culprit/s from any further infringement with a warning of trespass, such as: *'If I see your cattle on my run again, I will round them up and take them to the nearest Pound and you will have to pay to retrieve them.'*

The squatters were forceful in their approach and when satisfied they had sorted things out, they would go away again only to return months later for another round of clashes and disputes with their neighbours, over wandering stock. It will be shown later in the story William often rounded up the stock of others and drove them to the nearest Pound to try and truncate such behaviour.

For those, like Edward, who lived permanently on the Liverpool Plains, things became difficult when the stock of other squatters was found on the HBS's Mooki Station and there was no one to question or challenge, especially if the squatter who owned the stock was elsewhere and there was no resident indentured labour or stockman. The dilemma for superintendents like Edward was what to do with the squatter's stock when they were munching on the Station's grass, especially in times of drought and he had no one to question. It would be time consuming and expensive for Edward, on his own, to round up all the different stock and take them to the nearest Pound. He just didn't have the time or money. Edward's solution instead was to sell the stock to any interested squatter who was willing to pay for the stock and take them away (as documented shortly).

When Bourke appointed and sent a commissioner to each of the nine districts beyond the boundaries of settlement (c.1838) to try and solve the squabbles and disputes and formalise the runs, the squatters became unsettled and difficult to manage. The commissioner's task was riddled with hearsay and innuendo systemic within the makeshift approach of the squatters to claiming and managing their runs. Local disputes festered and eventually found their way to court with squatters seeking official recognition of the exact boundaries of each run, retribution for trespass, and legitimate assessment of their stock.[199]

The first of such court cases relevant to William's story is 'Reynolds versus Nowland' (September 1856); where William is the defendant and a witness, and the Superintendent of the HBS's Mooki Station.[200]

Although this court hearing occurred in 1856, the case is positioned here because it takes us back to when Edward (with the assistance of William) established Mooki Station (in 1835). It gives us an indicative glimpse into the HBS's station and provides explicit examples of the mischief and quarrels that occurred between Edward (William) and the squatters including: Edward's access to the Mooki River; the prevalence of trespass; the sale of other squatters' cattle by Edward when he found them unattended on Mooki Station for a long period of time; William and Edward's use of the station for their own cattle; and, the boundaries of Mooki Station.

The first extract below, from the summary of the case in the *Maitland Mercury*, concerns Edward's access to the Mooki River (c.1835).

> *The Maitland Mercury and Hunter River General Advertiser,*
> *16 September 1856, page 2.*
> **REYNOLDS V. NOWLAND**
>
> *... The main body of the society's cattle [HBS] used to run at Windy [HBS' first station on the Liverpool Plains at Phillips Creek] came to the water-mark on the Mooki run for water. Fawcett had told Edward Nowland, who then had charge of them, to fetch his cattle away from the Mooki. Nowland [Edward] had a hut within the society's boundary line, not far from the hut of Fawcett. ... Nowland [Edward] got possession in 1836 [June 1835][201] and came in 1837 to live at the Mooki [by this time, permanently, with Christian and their three children] on a grant of a thousand acres, herding them at a stockyard and hut he built about a mile from Fawcett's.*

The article then goes on to tell us about the movement of the HBS's cattle between the Mooki and Warrah.

REYNOLDS V. NOWLAND (continued)

Mr. Gaggin a member of the Society was at the Mooki in 1836 or 1837 and saw the Society's cattle running between Mooki river and Warrah.

And then between Phillip's Creek and the Mooki, as detailed next.

REYNOLDS V. NOWLAND (continued)

In January that year (1836 or 1837 when) he saw Fawcett, the society's cattle were then being removed from Phillips's station to the Mooki [given the Society took possession of Mooki station in June 1835, the year is more likely 1836].

The article then provides a first-hand account of the problem of the mixing of cattle owned by different squatters on the one run. As mentioned earlier, this often occurred because there was no fencing and many of the runs were left unsupervised for a long period of time. The cattle just followed the best grass from one run to the next. Then when a squatter returned, they saw the cattle of other squatters, differentiated by brand marks, on their run. In the case of Mooki Station, even though Edward was there all the time, it was difficult to control the cattle of others, and when a squatter didn't return for months on end Edward removed their stock and sold them. As told earlier and detailed below:

REYNOLDS V. NOWLAND (continued)

Richardson (probably a stockman employed by Edward) had charge of some of the 4D cattle [4D was the brand mark on HBS's cattle] and some of Nowland's at Mooki [probably Edward's cattle].

In 1837 they ran all over it [Mooki Station]. There were straggling cattle there of Fawcett's and Burns's [also identified by their brand mark]. Turner came and collected Burns's, and drove them away, only leaving behind those he could not collect, Fawcett and Nowland [Edward] had a conversation, and after it, Fawcett's cattle were sold. Hobler bought Burns's [cattle] and they were taken away.

As mentioned earlier, there were also disputes about the boundaries of the runs: who owned what. See what happened below, as the case continued.

REYNOLDS V. NOWLAND (continued)

When Turner came, he spoke to Edward Nowland about the station. Turner claimed the run as from Fawcett, and Nowland [Edward] objected, saying that he had a letter in disproof of his claim. Witness heard Nowland [Edward] and Fawcett also talking before this. Nowland [Edward] asked Fawcett to go away, he said he would, and proposed taking the fat cattle away first. Nowland [Edward] agreed, provided he did so in reasonable time.

In the next section of the hearing William is denoted as the defendant (given at the time of the case, in 1856, William was the Superintendent of Mooki Station). William elaborates and recalls his time with Edward at Mooki:

REYNOLDS V. NOWLAND (continued)

William Nowland, the defendant, first went to his brother's place [Edward's place] at Windy [Phillips Creek] in 1836,[202] and then took eleven hundred cattle thence to Mooki and took possession of the hut, yards, run, and everything else. His brother Edward took possession in the name of the Society, and went away again, leaving men in charge, who stopped at Burns's hut. [Probably indentured stockman]. [William and Edward Nowland then] returned in 1837. Fawcett was there then. … Fawcett was allowed to build a yard and was allowed six weeks' time to collect his cattle after the building of the yard.

Witness [William Nowland] saw Turner there [at Mooki Station] in 1839 and [noted Turner had] turned out the JB cattle [Burner's cattle] on the run. Fawcett said Turner did it on his own account. Nowland [probably Edward] asked Turner what right he had to do so, and he said he had bought Fawcett's cattle, and he would stop.

From the start (1835), William (and Edward) had an agreement with the Society to run their own cattle at Mooki Station. For Edward, it was part of his contract, and for William, according to him, it was a verbal agreement between him and the HBS. It worked both ways, William was able to use the extra grazing land at Mooki Station and quid pro quo share his run at Wallalla, with Edward, and the HBS's stock. See below, as the informative and lengthy case continued.

REYNOLDS V. NOWLAND (continued)

The Society's cattle, with his own [William's cattle], to the number of 1500 to 2000, were then running over the whole of what had been Burns's run.

Fawcett's cattle varied in number and were often shifted about. Witness [William Nowland] had been there with the cattle from that time to the present [1839–1856]. Witness [William Nowland] had an adjoining run, Walhollow [Wallalla] from 1839. He had a verbal agreement with the Society, that their cattle might go on his run, and his cattle on theirs.

[William Nowland was then cross-examined:] It was on the representation that the Society's cattle should run on Walhollow [Wallalla] that he was allowed to run his cattle on the Society's land. He paid licence and assessment for Walhollow [Wallalla], [since c.1840].[203]

A new stockyard was put up in Turner's time, and a hut also. Witness [William

Nowland] had used this yard during the last 13 years [1843–1856] whenever he liked, without asking plaintiff's permission [Reynolds]. They were on good terms [Nowland and Turner]. Plaintiff [Reynolds] had seen a quantity of his [William's] cattle in the stockyard, and claiming the run [Reynolds claiming the run], witness [William] told him [Reynolds] the whole of it, east and west of the river, belonged to the Society...

The last paragraph of the above summary of the court case exemplifies the issues at hand. The ill-defined nature of the runs, with squatters just laying claim and making verbal agreements with their neighbours, some taking advantage and grazing their cattle across adjoining runs, especially when other squatters were absent for lengthy periods, or staking a claim on another squatter's run because the original squatter had been absent for such a long period of time, that the new arrival, having grazed their cattle there for months became convinced the run was theirs, reinforced by the fact that so far, no one had come to dispute their claim.[204]

Disputes and discourse went on for years. For Mooki Station these types of contentious issues came to court some 21 years after Edward and William had gone north to the Mooki River to establish Mooki Station (c.1835).

William Repositioned Himself on the Liverpool Plains to Maintain and Enhance His Income

Despite the persistent altercations, William gained a steady source of income from his runs. Firstly, at Warrah (1826 to c.1833), Dridool (1837 to 1839), and Wallalla (from September 1839 to c.1860).

As circumstances changed William repositioned himself, initially from Warrah to the HBS's Mooki Station (when the AACo consumed his Warrah as part of their land grant) and later from Dridool to Wallalla (when the Commissioner changed the boundaries of Dridool and left William with a rather small run and a limited water supply).

William also spent time on the Liverpool Plains with Edward, at Phillips Creek (c.1833 to c.1835) and Mooki Station (from c.1835–1842) and later as Superintendent, himself, of Mooki Station (1842–1857). For some 22 years, William took advantage of the verbal agreement between him and the HBS, that allowed him to graze his cattle on the pastures at Mooki Station, for no fee or cost.

CHAPTER 11

A Pastoralist at Rosedale

The returns on William's runs most likely assisted him as a pastoralist at Rosedale. He probably used his earning as a squatter (along with some of the money he made at Rosedale) to progressively purchase adjoining allotments at Glennies Creek, Falbrook.

After William's pre-emptive lease (with the first right to purchase) in 1824 of 160 acres (which William transferred to Henry the following year) the size of Rosedale increased with each new purchase and included: the 200 acres 'promised to' Ralph Turnbull in 1824 and the adjoining allotment of 160 acres; two allotments from his brothers Michael and Edward (each of 160 acres) in 1825 (with Michael's allotment transferred to Henry, in 1831, and then bought back by William, in 1834); and a further 142 acres, in 1836. All these purchases over a 12-year period (1824–1836) increased William and Mary's Rosedale to 822 acres.[205]

William also built a more substantial homestead for Mary and their growing family; positioned two miles back from Glennies Creek.[206] It is not known when the homestead was completed, but it most likely was a sizeable and prominent building in Falbrook in the mid to late 1830s; given William built an inn in the village of Camberwell (quite an impressive building) in 1841 (detailed soon) and, of course, Mary's Rosedale would have come first.

There are no known photos of William's and Mary's original homestead. The photo in Figure 16 (taken in 2023) is of Wendy Bowman's Rosedale, and although this modern homestead is a much larger and extended dwelling, it still incorporates the original building. For me, this photo conjures up an imagined view of what William's and Mary's Rosedale may have looked like; the original dwelling though presumably altered is on the left.

By the beginning of the 1840s, William and Mary had five children to raise: William jr. 8, Michael 6, Robert 4, James 2, and Charles, a baby.[207] All boys! This was incentive enough to build a substantial homestead and grow the 'family farm'.

William also continued with his purchases; on the 30th April 1840, he purchased another 50 acres adjoining Rosedale (the property, now 872 acres).[208]

William's Village 'Camberwell on Falbrook'

William also turned his attention to the development of their village: 'Camberwell on Falbrook'. On the 26th August 1840, William purchased a town allotment of 2 acres, and then a further 2 acres on the 31st December 1840.[209] The latter purchase

Figure 16: Wendy Bowman's Rosedale (2023)

was only seven weeks after the plans for the township of 'Camberwell on Falbrook' were announced in the press. See the Government notice that follows.

Government Gazette Notices – New South Wales Government Gazette, 18 November 1840, page 1216
Colonial Secretary's Office, Sydney, 12th November, 1840.
NOTICE is hereby given, that a Site for a Township has been fixed upon at the undermentioned place, and that a copy of the approved plan may be seen at the Office of the Surveyor General in Sydney; and at the Police Office, Patrick's Plains, viz.:— Camberwell, on Falbrook, in the County of Durham.

By His Excellency's Command,

E. DEAS THOMSON

William had waited 16 years (1824–1840) for this proposal and presumably filled with excitement, busied himself with Camberwell's development. He purchased town allotments, built an inn, and later (in 1845) made another substantial town purchase of 300 acres for a Village Reserve.[210]

Queen Victoria Inn (The Queen)

William knew if a locality was to become a town it needed an inn. So, William set about building one, the Queen Victoria Inn, that soon became colloquially known as The Queen. A description of William's inn follows (most likely, written by William) when the inn was advertised for sale in 1844.

INVESTMENT OF CAPITAL

THE township of CAMBERWELL, lying in the direct line of road to the northern establishments, presents a splendid field for the investment of capital; and being the only place where travellers can refresh between Singleton and Muswellbrook, has advantages which few spots possess.

The Property consists of:-

A first-rate INN, known as "The Queen" containing on the ground floor two parlours, tap, bar, and two bed rooms (sic); two parlours and six bed rooms up stairs (sic); and two cellars below the building, which is of stone on the ground floor, and brick above, being: finished in a most substantial and neat manner, and occupied by a respectable tenant.

A weather-boarded HOUSE, formerly a public house, containing eight rooms, in complete repair, and suitable, from the situation, for a store.

A slab building, containing three rooms, at present let to a respectable tenant, carrying on a lucrative business in the retail line – a general store.

The outbuildings attached to the inn (kitchen, stable, and coach-house) are of the first description; and there is a good substantial stockyard on the ground, which comprises two acres.

Title – A grant from the crown.

Terms – Less than one-half what it cost the proprietor. A purchases (sic) will be dealt with liberally. Part of the purchase money may remain on mortgage for three years at ten per cent.

For further particulars apply (if by letter, post paid) to Mr. Adam, George-street, Sydney; Mr. Johnston, Queen Inn, Falbrook, Hunter River; or Mr. John Rotton, auctioneer, J. Singleton.

The description above of The Queen invokes images of a set of quite substantial buildings. Yet, William is selling The Queen for 'one half of what it cost to build'. Why was William selling The Queen at such a low price and so soon after it had been built?

William was probably short of money. There was a global depression in the 1840s and the colony suffered the consequences with a sharp rise in indebtedness, bankruptcy, insolvency, unemployment, and plenty of unsold goods and produce.[211] William most likely looked for a quick sale at a low price, given the obvious impact of the global depression (c.1840–1845) on his own assets and business concerns.

There was also another interesting factor that probably played into William's decision to sell. William's brother, Henry, had also built an inn, 10.3 miles (16.6

km) further north, at Liddell, in 1842.

Why was this the case, and why didn't the brothers pool their resources together in these difficult economic times and just build the one inn? Were the two inns in competition with each other and did William lose out?

The answers to these questions are based on informed knowledge that emerges later in the story. William wanted to build an inn at Camberwell to enhance and promote his village. Henry probably wanted to build an inn at a reasonable distance from Singleton because he was passionate about establishing his own business as a stagecoach owner who also provided inns for customers to stay at along the way. As a wheelwright Henry had the expertise to build his own coaches and an interest in horses that he could readily breed at Guy Fawkes. He would also need his own inn at a competitive distance from Singleton where paying customers would be willing to stop for the night on their journey to and from the interior. Customers could stop at Singleton for a rest and refreshments, in a quite attractive settlement that was starting to entice the weary traveller and then travel north once again, until they reached Henry's inn and stay there instead overnight.

For Henry, Camberwell was far too close to Singleton to attract patronage. Any inn Henry built needed to be at a good travelling distance from Singleton. Liddell (where Henry built his inn) and Muswellbrook (where Henry already had an inn) were a better distance apart; Singleton to Liddell 17.8 miles (28.8 km) and Liddell to Muswellbrook 11.9 miles (19.3 km). So, the brothers each built their own inn and William missed out on the passing trade; Camberwell was just too close to Singleton (9.3 miles) and many just passed by 'Camberwell on Falbrook'.

Henry's Inn, 'Chain of Ponds'

William's Queen Victoria Inn (The Queen) has been lost to history, while Henry's Chain of Ponds still stands.[212]

A photo of Henry's inn, the Chain of Ponds (Figure 17) is included in the story because it was most likely similar in appearance to William's Queen Victoria Inn.

The Chain of Ponds was placed on the NSW State Heritage Register on the 2nd April 1999. Today it is in a dilapidated state, boarded up and inaccessible.[213]

William Expands Rosedale Once More

In the early 1840s, William also continued to expand Rosedale once more. On the 18th March 1841, he made his biggest and last purchase; 725 acres and the additional purchase expanding the family estate to 1,557 acres.[214]

Figure 17: Henry Nowland's Chain of Ponds Inn, Liddell

Mary and Alexander Johnston Join William and Mary at Camberwell

Once William completed The Queen (in 1842) he needed a publican. His brother-in-law was a publican at the Noah's Ark in Sydney.[215] So William invited his sister Mary, and her husband Alexander Johnston, to join them in Camberwell and run The Queen. Alex and Mary took up the offer and ran the inn from 1842, until William sold it in 1845.[216]

In the early 1840s, William also made another Town Purchase of 2 acres in 'Camberwell on Falbrook' on the 13th April, 1842.[217]

CHAPTER 12

MOVING FURTHER NORTH AS A SQUATTER

The expansion of William's assets in the 1840s was not limited to Camberwell. He also gained a licence for a new run in the Gwydir District in 1840 that he called Boonanga.[218]

The descriptors of the location of William's 'Boonanga' are in the *Government Gazette* in September 1848 (spelt Boonangar). See below.

> *New South Wales Government Gazette, 9 September 1848, page 1165*
>
> CLAIMS TO LEASES OF CROWN LAND,
>
> BEYOND THE SETTLED DISTRICTS.
>
> GWYDIR DISTRICT
>
> …
>
> *No.71*
>
> *Nowland William.*
>
> *Name of Run—Boonangar [Boonanga].*
>
> *Estimated Area—46,080 Acres.*
>
> *Estimated Grazing Capabilities—1,440 Cattle*
>
> *Bounded on the north by the Barwin River by a line of about 12 miles west to the junction of Gnowra Gnowra Creek; on the west by Doyle, by a line bearing south of about 6 miles to the Boomi Creek; on the south by the Boomi Creek, by a line bearing east of about 12 miles to Pringle's lower north and south boundary line; and on the east by Pringle, by a line bearing north of about 6 miles to the Barwin River.*

The squatters' runs were large; William's Boonanga was 48,080 acres and was still in existence in 1860 – around 10 years after William sold the improvements he had made (c.1850). (See Figure 18.)

William's account of Boonanga (as detailed below) is informative. William tells us of the Commissioner's role in determining the boundaries of Boonanga (most likely Edward Mayne), the tentative nature of a verbal agreement between William

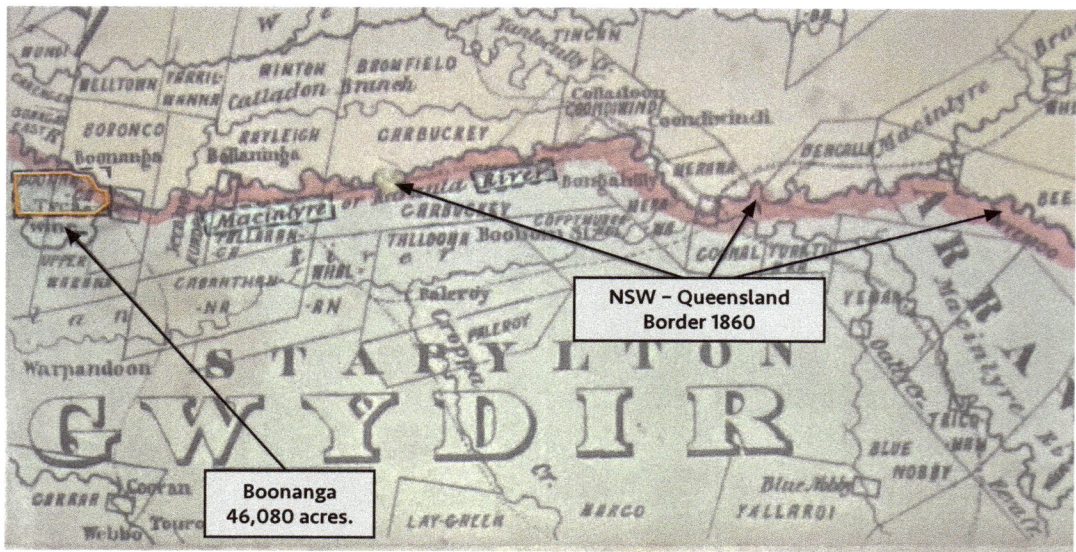

Figure 18: William Nowland's Boonanga Run (1840–c.1850)

and the other squatters about the borders between their runs and the tactics the First Nations people used to dissuade him and the other squatters from permanently grazing their stock on Country.

The Sydney Morning Herald – 23rd Jan 1861, page 3. [continued]

In 1845 or 1846, [in the public records, 1840] I formed another station, named Boonanga, on the McIntyre River, near Wayland; my neighbour and I agreed to a boundary that would start from a certain hole of water in the river, and we also marked a tree with the first two letters of our names, on the bank of the river, and were satisfied with our boundaries. About eighteen months after, a commissioner came down and arbitrarily gave my neighbour two miles frontage, by seven miles back, of the very best run, and also gave another squatter the south-west corner of my run. He had then left me a piece of land in a triangular shape that was no use to me, being so small. The blacks slaughtered about three hundred head of my cattle, and I had one man killed. Being disgusted with the usage I had received I then sold my station for twenty-five pounds. [Date unknown, William still had a licence for Boonanga in 1849].[219]

Boonanga was on Bigambul Country

William's run of Boonanga was on the border between two Aboriginal Nations: the Kamilaroi and Bigambul.[220] The Bigambul people, like the Kamilaroi were not going away. They were survivors and they too engaged in guerrilla warfare against the squatters in defence of Country.

The Bigambul people actively opposed European colonisation [invasion] of their territory. From the early 1840s they mounted a 14-year guerrilla campaign to expel the [squatters] and settlers. The Bigambul leadership understood the importance of economics in warfare and they specifically targeted horses and cattle rather than just the settlers themselves. The campaign was initially successful with 17 selections being abandoned in Macintyre region in 1843, of which only 13 were re-occupied when Europeans returned 3 years later [William obviously amongst them]. The economic war was so successful that it is recorded that one selection was making a loss of £150 per year until 1849. The tide of the campaign turned in 1848 when the Governor set aside £1000 to form the Native Police and appointed Frederick Walker to command them [detailed soon in this story]. Walker took the battle to the Bigambul, attacking them in their camps with his stated objective being their annihilation. By 1851 the economic war was effectively over, land values in the area doubled and the wages paid by settlers to employees were halved. Most of the work done on selections in the area was performed by Aborigines in return for food rations. By 1854 only 100 of the Bigambul people were left alive.[221]

As told earlier by William, when the Kamilaroi and the Bigambul saw the opportunity, they disrupted and killed 300 of his cattle at Boonanga. Whether William retaliated is unknown. All we know from this, and William's other accounts, detailed later in the story, William and the other squatters saw the land as theirs for the taking and if needed the Mounted Police (post-1825), the Border Police (post-1836) and the Native Police (post-1848) would protect them from potential raids and guerrilla warfare.[222]

Yet Another Run – 'Ward's Mistake'

William experienced similar guerrilla warfare tactics (c.1842 to c.1862) on his next run on the New England Tablelands – Ward's Mistake; as told next by William, in the continuation of his Letter to the Editor.[223]

The Sydney Morning Herald – 23rd Jan 1861, page 3. [continued]

In April 1842, I formed a station on the table lands (sic) of New England, called Ward's Mistake. For the ten years I held it[224] *the aboriginals were slaughtering my cattle right and left, and disturbing them off their run, and, to this day, slaughtering a few of them whenever they want them, I am convinced that from 1842 to this date [23rd January 1861] I have lost five hundred head of cattle by the aboriginals. My station is bounded by the waterfall of the tributaries of the Clarence River, where there is a great shelter for blacks, and the border police have never visited my station for the whole time.*

William on Bānbay Country

The Bānbay (most likely in conjunction with the Anēwan, and the Gumbaynggirr) were able to engage in guerrilla warfare to deter William (and the other squatters) for at least 20 years because of their intimate connection to Country and their deep knowledge of the lay of the land. In William's case, the caverns, gorges, and gullies, adjacent to Ward's Mistake aided them in their efforts to deter him (and the other squatters) from staying. The Bānbay and other supportive Nations, came out from the caves and gullies (especially at night) to unsettle, dislocate and kill the squatters' stock. They then returned to their hiding places and came out once again when the time was right, to disrupt and kill more stock.[225]

The map in Figure 19 shows the gullies and gorges which are evident to the east and north of Ward's Mistake. The next map (Figure 20) is also useful as it shows the location of Ward's Mistake within the New England Tablelands. (See Figure 20.)

Another account in Trove (from 1842) informs us of a particular raid on a Mr. Nowlan's (sic) station on the New England Tablelands (most likely either, Henry's Guy Fawkes or William's Ward's Mistake) by First Nations people who *'took several muskets from Nowlan's hut (while he was absent), killed three of his men, took possession of the horses of the Mounted Police and speared the cattle'*. As told in the article that follows.

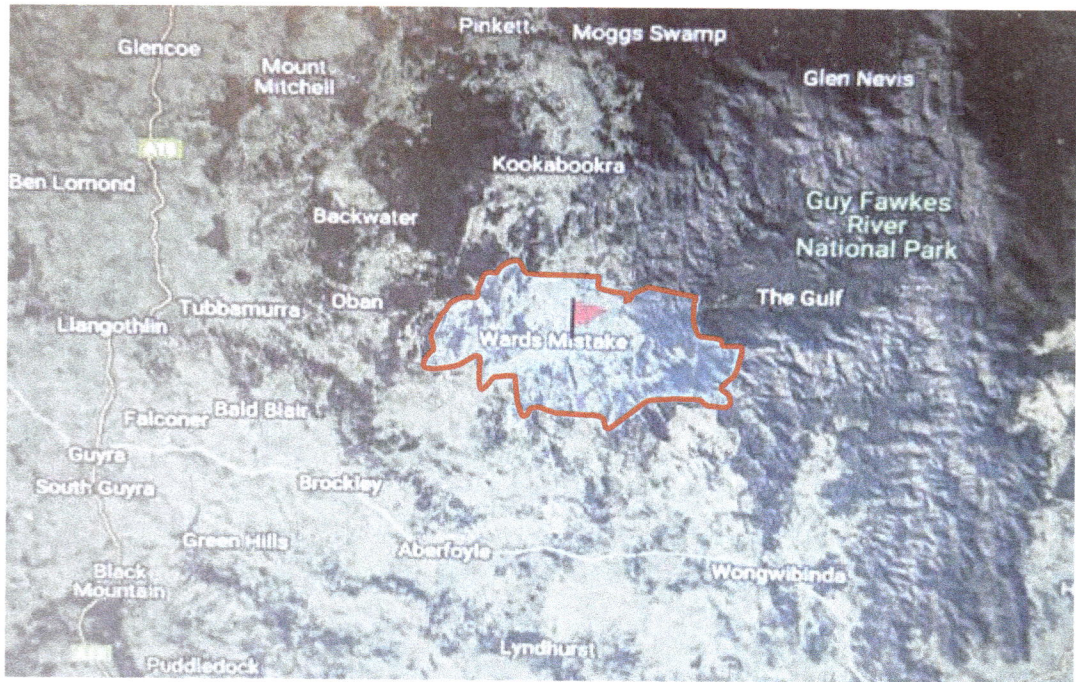

Figure 19: Location of Ward's Mistake and the Gullies and Gorges

The Hunter River Gazette and Journal of Agriculture, Commerce, Politics, and News, 16 April 1842, page 3
NEW ENGLAND

Intelligence has just reached town of the perpetration of various outrages by the blacks in this district. About a week ago they ransacked a hut on the station of Mr. Nowlan, [sic] during the absence of its occupiers, who were at work in the neighbourhood, from which they took several stand of arms. They afterwards made a rush on the men, killing no less than three outright, and wounding desperately a fourth, who, however, contrived by great exertions, to make his escape into the bush. The savages were in large force and carried a number of muskets. They also took possession of the horses belonging to the mounted police under the orders of Mr. Commissioner Fry, and drove them off, and have, besides, speared and dispersed various herds of cattle. None of the perpetrators of these disorders had been apprehended, according to the last intelligence but as the police were after them, it was not expected they would long escape.

Aboriginal Guerrilla Warfare was Also Recorded More Broadly Across the New England Tablelands

Callum Clayton-Dixon, an Ambēyang man (author and academic) whose people come from the southern part of the New England Tableland, provides us with an informative account of the defence of Country by First Nations people on the New England Tablelands for over 30 years between 1832 to circa 1865, as detailed next in the following quote from Callum Clayton-Dixon.

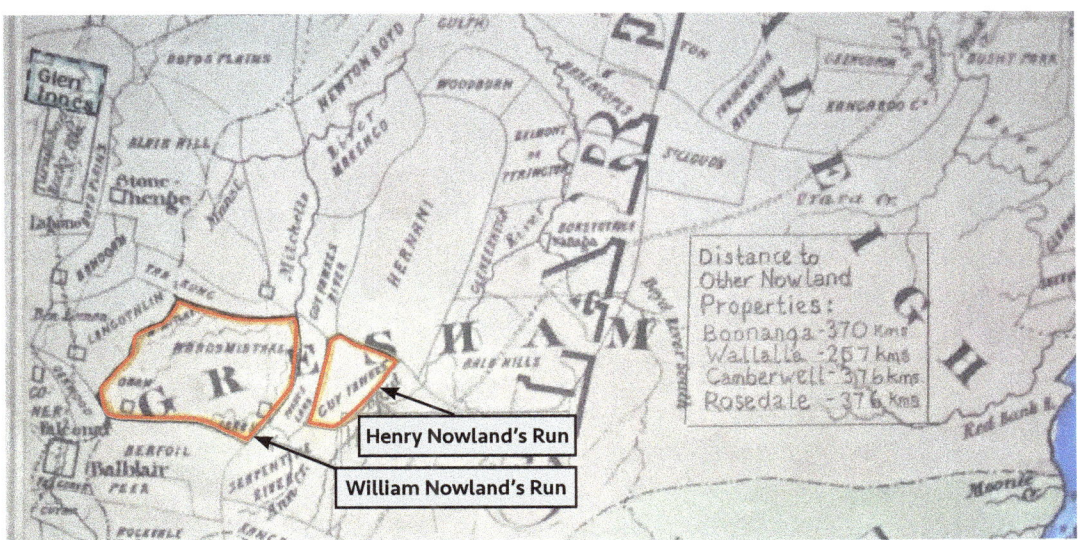

Figure 20: Ward's Mistake (1860)

Where neither white man nor horse could follow –
rough country & the Aboriginal resistance

The rough country on New England's fringes was once the Aboriginal guerrilla fighter's stronghold. From the gorges and ravines, our people were able to maintain their war of resistance for over 30 years. … their fierce war of resistance against the belligerent colonial occupation…

…Archival records documenting conflict on the Tableland reveal that it was primarily from the rough country that our warriors launched raids on the district's pastoral enterprises, the lifeblood of the New England colonial project. They took advantage of favorable terrain — a common tactic employed in guerrilla warfare — and I would argue that this allowed our warriors to continue sabotaging the pastoral industry for an extended period of time, seizing and destroying thousands of livestock, killing and wounding numerous laborers, and ransacking stations of supplies. While the squatters were able to quickly entrench themselves in the mostly undulating and lightly-wooded landscape of the Tableland, the region's more rugged fringes would, as H.G. Hamilton predicted in the early 1840s, "be left for many years to come in the hands of the blacks".

In fact, it wasn't until the mid-1860s, more than three decades after the squatting invasion began, that the armed Aboriginal resistance was finally crushed. And it took a Native Police unit brought down from Queensland to drive the rebels — a coalition of gun-wielding warriors from the Macleay and Bellinger Rivers, and the Tableland — from their rough country strongholds.[226]

The colonial archive contains a number of accounts which illustrate how, in effect, gorges and ravines largely remained Aboriginal controlled zones well after runs had been taken up in the surrounding areas. In February of 1839 near Ingleba, Ambēyang warriors ambushed an outstation, killed a shepherd, and seized almost a hundred sheep. Australian Agricultural Company overseer Patrick Brennan went out in pursuit:

> *"…about six miles from the station [Ingleba], on the banks of a ravine, they discovered the smoke of a black camp. They approached the spot very cautiously, and perceived nearly one hundred of these savages, men, women, and children, busy round several fires…Brennan told his mate to do as he did, and sticking spurs into his horse, he galloped up to the camp, shouting as loud as he could… the blacks taken by surprise rushed from the camp down the ravine, where none could follow them but blacks and kangaroos." — Sydney Herald, 12th of April 1839, page 3*

Similarly, in March 1840 on the Tiara run, when warriors drove off sheep and killed a shepherd, the station superintendent organised a search party:

On the shepherd not making his appearance as usual at sundown, my younger brother and I with all the men we could muster went in search the whole night, and at sunrise the following morning we came on an encampment of blacks on the falls of the M'Leay River, into which they made their escape, leaving the heads and skins of fourteen sheep. – Sydney Herald, 1st of May 1840, p.2

G.J. Macdonald, New England's first Commissioner of Crown Lands, observed that 'on the eastern falls of the Table Land, the precipitous and profound ravines... afford them safe harbour and secure retreat, where neither [white] man nor horse can follow' (Macdonald to Colonial Secretary, 1st of January 1845). And it's abundantly clear that Aboriginal raiders intentionally targeted runs which backed onto the eastern escarpment.

Take Ward's Mistake Station for instance, formed by William Nowland in 1842 [William's account in the SMH in 1861 also noted by Clayton-Dixon]:

> WILLIAM NOWLAND: "For the first ten years I held it the aboriginals were slaughtering my cattle right and left, and disturbing them off their run, and, to this day, slaughter a few of them whenever they want them, I am well convinced that from 1842 to this date [21/02/1861] I have lost five hundred head of cattle by the aboriginals. My station is bounded by the waterfall of the tributaries of the Clarence River, where there is a great shelter for blacks..." – Sydney Morning Herald, 23rd of January 1861, page 3

William Gardner, annalist and resident of New England in the 1840s and 1850s, discussed the nexus between the location of runs and the frequency of raiding, and I would suggest that his comments seem also to hint at a strategy of economic sabotage:

> "Everywhere in New England the blacks take too much liberty with the cattle belonging to the settlers, sometimes killing eight bullocks out of a herd at a time...it is galling for the stock keepers to find eight speared and dead, without even answering the purposes of the blacks, and merely to show what injury they can inflict...Those settlers who hold stations near the falls, and in sequestrated situations, must be content to lose their cattle by the inroads of the blacks, and to part with their runs at an undervalue, in comparison with those who hold runs where the blacks are afraid to use such liberties." – William Gardner (Volume 1, page 78)

Colonists were well aware that Aboriginal people more or less had the upper hand in the rough country, so they feared descending into the gorges and took precautions when skirting the edges. John Connal of Surveyor's Creek Station wrote the following in his diary about when he and number of others visited Apsley Falls in November 1843:

> "We were told the Blacks were about here but we did not see any. I had my gun ready for action if necessary — they are always wild about the falls as they can disappear in a moment amongst the rocks from the whites."

> But it wasn't only the eastern escarpment which served as an Aboriginal stronghold. Connal's diary also details his ventures into the rough country on the Tableland's southwest, namely the Back Creek:

>> The Back Creek is one of the wildest places in the country so mountainous and rocky, I think the blacks must have heard me and escaped. I camped beside their gunnies and fully expected them down upon me through the night, but I had a pistol with me and a couple of kangaroo dogs so I was pretty well off and my horse short-hobbled beside me all night in case of accident. — Diary of John Connal, entry for 8th of August 1842

> It was there that Connal found evidence of some of his cattle having been killed and cooked by members of the Ambēyang tribe:

>> …on examining their gunnies I observed the bones of a bullock or cow which induced me to examine their fires, I found about ½ dozen large ovens built round with stones, I saw pieces of bone, the hoof and teeth of a fullgrown bullock or cow which they had speared at the waterhole close by, but they had burned almost everything so that no vestige of the remains might be seen by the white people.

> Much of the land around New England now designated as 'wilderness areas', as well as other patches deemed unfit for the purposes of economic exploitation, were bastions of strength and survival for our people during the early decades of the colonial apocalypse. It was from these places on the fringe that they were able to sustain the war of resistance for so long. These places were a refuge for the warriors hunted by police and vigilante settlers alike, a refuge for those who were holding out against the mounting pressures to 'come in' to the stations. When out in the bush, I often find myself wondering what lessons might be gleaned from the resistance tactics and strategies of old. What role does the so-called 'rough country' now play?[227]

Callum Clayton-Dixon's narration above, and the more extensive coverage, in his book *Surviving New England*,[228] enables an appreciation and understanding of the extent and nature of the resistance and resilience of the Aboriginal people against the squatters on the New England Tablelands. The Ambēyang, Anēwan and Bānbay (also cited as Bānbai) were determined for decades, to deter the increasing numbers of squatters who flooded into Country, along with the Mounted Police and later, the Border Police in 1836, and the Native Police, post-1849.[229]

Darkie Point Massacre

The horrendous impact of the squatters, in conjunction with the Mounted, Border, and Native Police, on the Aboriginal people of the New England Tablelands is self evident. The following account of the Darkie Point Massacre at Ebor, reaffirms the injustices First Nations people faced.

Massacre Darkies Point, Ebor, New England Plateau
May 1841

[Finney Eldershaw was the first to write of the dark secret of 'Darkies Point' in 'Australia as it really is. …'; published in 1854. The following account is a precis based on Eldershaw's book] [230]

… an attack in May 1841 on an out-station that left three shepherds dead and a flock of sheep carried off as spoils. A revenge party is assembled, and the chase begins leading to a tremendous battle that takes place over a wild landscape, for a night and day, until their "butchered comrades blood was fearfully avenged" and the sheep recovered. At least 10 members of the Baanbay [Bānbay] people died, [30 in other accounts] driven off the cliffs by gunfire to fall to their death in a "horrid carnage".

There is no memorial here, no sign. Rocks cold to the touch, a shifty early morning breeze. I eat my muesli, the trees watching over me, while I struggle to make sense of this traumascape. Walking is a way I understand place and come to belong, but there is nothing to help me here.

Others have written more eloquently of this tragic story. Australian poet Judith Wright was raised near here and published Niggers Leap, New England in 1946.[231] *Local poet Chris Armstrong published the beautiful poem The Watershed and a blog 'awildland' about her walk along this escarpment. Callum Clayton-Dixon's award winning 2020 book Surviving New England reclaims the story of settler violence as one of resistance and survival of the Anaiwan people of New England Tablelands…*[232]

First Nations People on the New England Tablelands in 2025

Today, the Aboriginal people of the New England Tablelands are revitalising their culture inheritance, through their local Indigenous social groups and organisations. Through the work of researchers, such as Callum Clayton-Dixon and the Nēwara Aboriginal Corporation, the First Nations people on the New England Tablelands are reviving each Nation's 'history, language, traditional lifeways, and the lands to which they belong' for theirs, and future generations.[233] Theirs is a remarkable story of survival, given that at the start of the squatters' occupation of the New England Tablelands, in 1832, each Nation was relatively small; for example, the Ambēyang, numbered around 500 people and by the time their resistance was quelled in the mid-1860s, the number of First Nations people on the Tablelands was roughly halved.[234]

The warfare between the squatters and the Aboriginal peoples was well entrenched when William gained a licence for his new run, Ward's Mistake on 'Bānbay Country', in 1842. The hostilities likely started in 1832, when the first squatter Hamilton Collins Sempill entered the Tablelands with a flock of sheep, and set up a run that he called, Wolka, along the Apsley River, at present day Walcha.[235] Then others followed, including William's brother Henry who gained a licence, in 1836, for his run, Guy Fawkes. William probably came as well, in the late 1830s to inspect his brother's run and find one for himself.

William's story sits within this reality. In essence, William consolidated and expanded his run Ward's Mistake while the local Aboriginal people, the Bānbay people, confronted warfare, dispossession, marked loss of clan, and uncertainty.

Once again, William and his fellow squatters saw the land as theirs: all they needed to do was find a suitable site, leave their stock there and register their claim. William did just that and called his run on the New England Tablelands Ward's Mistake.

CHAPTER 13

Why 'Ward's Mistake'?

Who was 'Ward'? What was the 'Mistake'?

In searching for answers to these questions, I came across seven newspaper articles, all written in the 1949, in the *Guyra Argus* and all with differing opinions. Three of the articles are included next, while others are excluded because they are either not factually correct or ramble on and tell us very little. Let's start with: 'Ward's Mistake – Now We Know Why'.

Guyra Argus, 20 Jan 1949, page 1
WARD'S MISTAKE
Now We Know Why

Mr. N. C. J. Heagney, of Wyoming, Guyra, provided us with an interesting explanation of how Ward's Mistake received its quaint and intriguing name: Many years ago, when selecting was easy and fashionable, he related, two men named Ward and Nowland chose adjoining selections out of Guyra. However, for some reason, when formalities were completed, Ward was allotted the selection chosen by Nowland, and Nowland received Ward's.

Apparently, each blamed the other for the mistake, for Ward named his newly acquired property, 'Nowland's Folly', and Nowland retaliated by giving his, the title of 'Ward's Mistake.'

Mr. Heagney has lived over 60 years in this district, and we thoroughly enjoyed our yarn with him on Tuesday.

And then, the second account, 'More Light On Mystery'.

Guyra Argus, 3 March 1949, page 6
WARD'S MISTAKE
More Light On Mystery

Mr. R. J. Roberts, of Llangothlin, gives the following version as to how Ward's Mistake acquired its name… Here is my theory. The man, Ward, was looking for a property to settle on and he decided on the place known as Ward's Mistake. At that time, the nearest lands office was at Maitland; As Ward was returning to Maitland to put in his application for the land, a lands office was opened at, Armidale and Nowland applied for the same land at that office. Maitland lands office granted the land to Ward, Armidale granted the same land to Nowland. Both parties became eligible and claimed the lease for the same land. Ward took possession and claimed the land and so did Nowland. After a fight of three years through the Court, it went in Nowland's favour and Ward had to get out. Nowland named it Ward's Mistake. After some years, things went wrong for Nowland so he said Ward's Mistake was Nowland's 'Folly.'

And a third account (most likely the most factual) from the stepson of William Nowland jr.: 'How Ward's Mistake Was Named'.[236]

> *Guyra Argus 31 March 1949 page 4*
> *HOW WARD'S MISTAKE WAS NAMED*
> *More Light On Problem*
>
> *Mr. H. J. Clark, of "Raeburn" Guyra, gives the following version of the naming of Ward's Mistake. William Nowland Senior came from Singleton about the year 1839 and took up the land known later as Ward's Mistake the area being 40,960 acres. In 1850 William Nowland Junior took over the management of the property and it remained in his possession until it was sold to Messrs. White brothers in 1900–1901… William, [jr.] … died at Oban [Guyra] in 1907.*
>
> *With reference to the mysterious Mr. Ward who came, saw, and vanished. He camped on a gully half a mile west of where the station homestead was later built, the gully being called then as now Ward's gully. Mr. Ward made application, to the nearest Lands Office for a lease but as the land was already occupied there was nothing for him to do but take himself elsewhere, which he did, and Nowland called the place Ward's Mistake. To my knowledge there was never any fight in court, never any Jim Nowland and certainly 'I Owned' was never the name of 'Ward's Mistake' as stated by Mr. R. J. Betts. William Nowland [jr.] was my stepfather and this is the story as told to me by him.*

If the above account is true, Ward had been camped at the gully for so long it became known as Ward's Gully; a name the gully retains today. Then, when Ward eventually got around to applying for a licence (because that was the 'law' from October 1836) William sr. had already staked his claim, gained a licence and called the run Ward's Mistake. Interestingly, William sr. did not tell Ward of his intention to gain a licence and build a homestead near Ward's Gully. Obviously, the unwritten rules between the squatters had changed. Now it was every man for himself and the first one to acquire a licence was entitled to the run.

CHAPTER 14

THE CHALLENGES AND TRAGEDIES IN THE 1840S

For around the first 10 years (c. 1826 to c. October 1836) the squatters on the Liverpool Plains secured their run/s through declaring their exclusive possession of a designated section of land based on verbal agreements between them and their neighbours. You can still hear them now, the conversations, arguments and righteous cries of entitlement: *'I was here first and I can prove it, given my brand is on the cattle grazing here'* (for William, branded on the hip WN, and on the ribs N). Then as we know, in October 1836, Governor Bourke proclaimed all the land of the squatters north, south and west of the boundaries of settlement as Crown land with each squatter required to pay the colonial government an annual licence and stock fee, for each run. This was a prerequisite that tested the squatters, especially those (like William) who had very few assets, little or no capital and more than one run.

Finding the money to finance the runs for William and his fellow squatters became more and more difficult in the 1840s; initially due to the loss of income while going through a period of severe drought, followed by the steady decline and eventual loss of cheap indentured convict labour (who only worked for rations), an international depression, and finally, Governor Gipps' proposed changes to land tenure (in the mid-1840s) that recommended even more fees and requirements.

These unexpected challenges came in quick succession, along with significant personal tragedy, for William and his family; starting with the drought.

Two Years of Severe Drought (1837–39)

A long period of severe drought between 1837–39 continued into the early 1840s. The HBS's Mooki Station, managed by Edward, and William's Wallalla on the Liverpool Plains, suffered badly: as outlined in the following account.

> *The Sydney Herald, 10 December 1841, page 2.*
> *ORIGINAL CORRESPONDENCE,*
> *LIVERPOOL PLAINS.*
>
> *…This place has not been visited with any beneficial rain since November, 1840, and the destruction which has occurred among the stock from the long drought is very great. I can safely assert, that no less than five hundred head of cattle have*

died from want in the immediate vicinity of the Mooki; the banks of the water holes are literally covered with dead carcasses, which have been taken out of bog by the stock-keepers, being unable to again rise. By the brands the principal sufferers are Messrs. Allan, Reynolds, Nowland [Edward's or William's], and the A.D. Cattle [HBS cattle at Mooki Station], &c…

J. S. W. Mooki, Liverpool Plains, November 27.

In 1841, Edward wrote to Hawkesbury Benevolent Society to inform them of the difficulties he faced at Mooki Station due to 'the long continued dry weather', as told below.

The Sydney Morning Herald, 26 November 1841, page 3.
NEWS FROM THE INTERIOR
(From our various Correspondents)

HAWKESBURY BENEVOLENT SOCIETY. – On Monday, the 22nd instant, a special general meeting of the committee and members of the above society was held at the Asylum, Windsor, for the purpose of taking into consideration a statement relative to the funds of the Institution, furnished by the Treasurer, S. North, Esq, ; by which it appeared that, owing to the long continued dry weather in the part of the country where the society's herds are at present depasturing, a great number of valuable cattle have been lost in the waterholes, and others have died from starvation. Two letters received from the superintendent of stock, Mr. Edward Nowland were read to the meeting, in which it was stated that the cattle were in a most deplorable condition, and that even if the late rains had extended to that part of the country, there is no chance of the committee getting any fat cattle down for at least six months. – From these and other circumstances it appeared that there was a serious deficiency of money in the hands of the treasurer to meet the expenses of the current quarter…

Personal Tragedies

In the early 1840s, William, Mary and their children also confronted the deaths of a son (a brother) and an uncle. William and Mary's fourth child James died on the 10th November 1841, at the age of three years and five months.[237] What James died of is unknown. It may have been scarlet fever given there was an outbreak of scarlet fever amongst children in Sydney, and the surrounding regions (including Maitland), in 1841. There are several family notices and accounts in Trove of the death of children and young teenagers from this disease during this year, but none for James.

In the following year (1842) William and Mary had their sixth child (five surviving) who they named John.[238] In the same year, William's brother, Edward who had lingering consumption, decided to make his way from Mooki Station to Rosedale (probably with Christian and their children, assisted by William). Maybe William, when returning from Ward's Mistake stopped in at Mooki Station and discovered Edward was ill and advised the family to come to Rosedale. According to Ian Nowland (a direct descendant of Edward) the plan was to rest up at Rosedale, and when Edward was feeling up to it, to travel to Wilberforce.[239]

Edward's mother Elizabeth ('our' Elizabeth Richards, now 67) was probably anxiously waiting for Edward's return to Wilberforce, but it was not to be. Edward died, at Rosedale, on the 24th August 1842, at the age of 37. The notice in the *Australasian Chronicle* read:

Australasian Chronicle, 1 Sep 1842, page 3.
Family Notices

On the 24th instant, at Singleton, Hunter River, Mr. Edward Nowland, of Liverpool Plains, after a lingering consumption. [Bacterial infection of the lungs]

James and Edward were Buried at Rosedale

William and Mary decided to bury their son, James and his uncle, Edward, at Rosedale, as told below.

Singleton Argus 23 Dec 1948 – page 3

Two tombstones each over 100 years old were discovered on the Rosedale (Glennies Creek) property…one of the stones bears the name of Edward Nowland who died on August 24, 1842, aged 37 years. The other stone bears the name of James Nowland who died on November 10, 1841, aged three years and five months. The tombstones were found on the banks of the creeks.[240]

Where Did Life Take Edward's Wife Christian After Edward's Death?

Edward's wife Christian (now 31) was left to raise their five children: Edward jr. 12, James 11, Christian jr. 9, Matilda 6 and Robert, a baby. Initially, Christian continued to manage the HBS's run at Mooki Station for nearly a year and until mid-1843, presumably with William's help.[241]

It is assumed Christian then went back to family in Wilberforce because her daughter's birth (Matilda) was registered there in 1843; as detailed earlier. A few years later, Christian started a new relationship with Edwin Baldwin, who she lived with for the rest of his life.[242]

Financial Hardship Continued For William

William faced several challenges of his own when he helped Christian, at Mooki Station: between circa August 1842 after Edward's death, to circa July 1843 when William became the Superintendent of Mooki Station. The loss of William's young son (James, 3) and his brother (Edward, 37) would have been difficult enough without the drought and financial hardships he faced. William's stock was still recovering from the drought and there were fewer fat cattle for market: on the HBS's Mooki Station; William's runs (Wallalla, Boonanga, and Ward's Mistake); and, on the family farm (Rosedale).[243] The transportation of convicts to NSW ceased in 1841 and the cheap indentured convict labour William employed was coming to an end; William would have to give more than a hut and rations to his future employees.[244] The international depression was also starting to have a profound impact on the colony (c.1842–43). Pastoralists and squatters like William were confronted with falling prices for wool, wheat, stock, and any goods destined for trade; a decline in land values; the closure of some colonial banks due to insolvency, and a rush on others; creditors calling in debt; and for some colonists, bankruptcy.[245] To top it off William was also confronted with an ad in the newspaper in September 1842 where the improvements on his run of Wallalla were being advertised for sale by Edmund Uhr without William's knowledge or approval. William immediately responded with the following advertisement.

The Sydney Morning Herald, 10 September 1842, page 3
Caution to the Public.

IT having been represented to me that Mr. Edmund B. Uhr of Balwanna, near Maitland, has been offering for sale the station known by the name of "Wallalla," Mooki River, Liverpool Plains, and having in my possession ample documentary evidence to show that the said station is mine, for recovery of which an action is now pending in the Supreme Court,—all parties are hereby warned against purchasing the abovementioned station from Mr. Uhr.

WILLIAM NOWLAND

Falbrook, Hunter River, September

William's warning worked and for the moment the threat of the Supreme Court was enough. Though this would not be the last time William's exclusive possession of Wallalla, as detailed in his lease, would be before the courts.[246]

Another notable uncertainty, William and his fellow squatters faced in the 1840s was Gipp's proposed changes to land tenure as detailed in the next chapter.

Chapter 15

Governor Gipps' Proposed New Regulations For Land Tenure

Like his fellow squatters, William would have been highly aware of all the rumours and innuendo that surrounded Governor Gipps' intended changes to land tenure. If the rumours were right, the financial strain would be too great, and William would have to give up some, if not all his runs.

Gipps' Proposed Regulations

On the 2nd April 1844, Gipps issued the first of his suggested regulations, which in essence redefined a run, as 'an area of no more than 20 sq. miles [12,800 acres] capable of carrying no more than 4,000 sheep or 500 head of cattle'. Followed, by a second proposal in May 1844, where Gipps recommended each squatter would be granted the right to buy 320 acres of his run at a minimum price of £1 an acre (£320 in total), after five years occupation, for the purpose of establishing a homestead. The squatter would also be required to pay the annual licence fee for the rest of his run (at least £10), for a further eight years, after which the squatter would be eligible to purchase another 320 acres of his land for £320 and gain a licence for the rest of his run again, until such time through this process, he had purchased the whole of his run. The proviso being, if the squatter did not take up the initial offer of the purchase of 320 acres for his homestead, he would face the risk of losing the whole of the run, to another, who was willing to purchase the initial 320 acres, at auction. This was because after purchasing the initial 320 acres, the highest bidder (most likely, at a higher price per acre) would automatically be entitled to the rest of the run if they were prepared to pay the annual licence fee and provide monetary compensation to the squatter for the improvements the squatter had made to the run. Then eight years later, the new lessee would need to demonstrate an on-going commitment to purchase, with a pre-emptive requirement of purchasing another 320 acres of the run at £1 an acre. With this second purchase, guaranteeing the new lessee retention of the run and negating, the risk of an auction and subsequently, a new purchaser and a new lessee.

The article that follows from the *Sydney Morning Herald* outlines Governor Gipps' proposed regulations based on what the journalists knew about the despatches to London on the 3rd April 1844. Of particular interest (at the beginning of the article) is the suggested covert approach taken by Governor Gipps regarding his proposals; Gipps obviously 'played his cards close to his chest'.

The Sydney Morning Herald – 13th May 1844, page 2.
Squatting Regulations

FOR several days past, there have been rumours that the GOVERNOR denied that the recently promulgated regulations had been construed correctly, and we have now much pleasure in informing our readers, despatches dated 3rd April, and sent home by the General Hewett, before the Royal Hotel Meeting had been held, gave a very different version of His EXCELLENCY'S views, to what he has been generally supposed to hold respecting the squatters. In the despatches referred to, His EXCELLENCY went at great length into the general question, and we have reason to believe that the following is the substance of His EXCELLENCY'S recommendations.

1. Every squatter, after an occupation of five years, shall have an opportunity afforded to him of purchasing a portion of his run, not less than 320 acres, for a homestead.

2. The value of any permanent and useful improvements which he may have made on the land, shall be allowed to him; but the land itself (exclusive of improvements) cannot be sold for less than the established minimum price of £1 per acre.

3. Any person who may have purchased a homestead shall not be disturbed in the possession of his run during the following eight years. He must, however, continue to take out for the unpurchased parts of it, the usual licence, and pay on it the usual fee of £10 per annum.

4. A second purchase of not less than 320 acres shall be attended with the similar advantage of being undisturbed for the next eight years; so that each successive purchase of 320 acres will act virtually as a renewal of an eight years lease.

5. The right of the Crown must, however, remain absolute, as it at present is, over all lands which have not been sold or granted, it being well understood, that the Crown will not act capriciously, or unequally, and will not depart from established practice, except for the attainment of some public benefit.

6. Persons who may not avail themselves within a certain period, to be hereafter fixed, of the advantage offered to them of purchasing a homestead, will be exposed to the danger of having any part of their run offered for sale, either at the pleasure of the Crown, or on the demand of an individual. The value of any useful and permanent improvements which they may have made on their lands will be secured to them, should a stranger become the purchaser.

7. The person, whoever he may be, who purchases the homestead, is to have the remainder of the run.

8. All sales to be as at present by auction—the appraised value of permanent and useful improvements (which will be considered as the property of the former occupant), being added to the upset price of the land.

9. As stated in the notice of 2nd April, a licence is not to cover more than 12,800 acres of land, unless it be certified by the Commissioner that the 12,800 acres are not sufficient to keep in ordinary seasons 4000 sheep. No existing run is, however, to be reduced below 12,800, on account of its being capable of feeding more than 4000 sheep. But, if any licenced person have (sic) on his run more than 4000 sheep, he is to pay £1 for every 1000 above 4000. A person therefore, having on a run of twenty square miles, 5000 sheep will not, as has been supposed, be required to take out two licences, but will be charged an extra £1 for his licence, or £1 instead of £10. If he have (sic) 8000 sheep, he will be charged £4 extra, or £14 in all. This is not stated in the notice of the 2nd April, but it forms a part of the proposals which were sent home, as before referred to.

There is a great deal in this which is equitable; but it must not cause us to relax our exertions for the repeal of the Crown Lands Act, and then the squatter can have the right of pre-emption [first right of purchase], instead of the land being put up to competition.

The Squatters Were Infuriated

The squatters could ill afford to pay the monies required in Gipps' proposed regulations. Very few of their runs were 12,800 acres or less, and most of the squatters would be required to pay (at a minimum) an extra £1 for their licence, and more on top of this for their stock.[247] Then, based on the second proposal, five years later they would be required to pay a further £320 to purchase a further 320 acres for each of their runs, plus the licence fee, and this would be on-going until they had purchased all of each of their runs. If you do the sums, the expenditure for each squatter was exorbitant (given that many of the squatters had more than one run) and at a payment of £320 every eight years, the squatters' contribution to the government coffers, would be on-going and last for decades, and for many given the size of their runs, into the next generation.

Take for example William's runs; he had 40,960 acres at Ward's Mistake, 87,040 acres at Wallalla and 46,080 acres at Boonanga and the cost for him alone would be unmanageable.[248] William would need to purchase 960 acres (320 x 3) at the cost £960, pay £30 in licence fees each year, built a homestead at Wallalla and Boonanga and pay the on-going costs required annually for the privilege of grazing his cattle on Crown land. No wonder the squatters were concerned.

Governor Gipps Dines at Henry's Royal Hotel Muswellbrook

Six months after Gipps' proposed changes to land tenure (November 1844) he decided to go on a tour of the colony. Gipps headed north and after a few days, became ill. On reaching Muswellbrook, he could go no further, and decided to spend the night at the Royal Hotel. William's brother Henry, as 'the respectful publican' knew just what to do. According to the *Maitland Mercury* '[Henry] deserved great credit for the superior manner in which he was able to entertain his Excellency'.[249]

Gipps' Regulations Approved by Lord Stanley, London

Seven months later, in June 1845, Governor Gipps, sent his proposed regulations for the lessees of Crown land (mainly the squatters) to the Colonial Secretary in London, Lord Stanley, and a month later they were approved.[250]

The Pastoralists and Squatters Retaliated Against the Proposals and Won

The pastoralists and squatters retaliated.[251] In NSW they formed the Pastoral Association of NSW and sent a petition to the House of Commons in London.[252] This along with the increased representation of landholders (affluent pastoralists) on the Legislative Council in NSW raised doubts in Downing Street as to whether Gipps' proposal would be accepted in the colony.[253]

The pressure on the establishment was significant enough for Sir Robert Peel (Prime Minister) and his Government in London to have second thoughts and five months later, in December 1845, Sir Robert Peel postponed Gipps' proposed regulations.[254]

One can imagine the conversations, around the dinner table, amongst the squatters, and at the local inns; they must have been elated.

William's Tenure Renewed at Mooki Station

In the same year (1845) William's tenure as the Superintendent for the HBS's Mooki Station was renewed. See the newspaper article that follows.

> *The Sydney Morning Herald, 19 November 1845, page 2*
> *WINDSOR.*
> *HAWKESBURY BENEVOLENT SOCIETY.*
>
> *A special meeting of the members of this Society was held at the Asylum, on Monday, the 10th of November instant, at two o'clock P.M. The Vice-Président, Thomas Tebbutt, Esq., in the chair. The first matter the meeting took up was the duty of appointing a Superintendent for the station and stock of the Society, running at Mooki, Liverpool Plains, for which post several tenders had been received by the Secretary. On the motion of Mr. F. Beddek, the Committee retired to consider the lenders made, when, by a majority of seven to one (Mr. J. Odell), they resolved on re-appointing the late Superintendent, Mr. William Nowland, of Liverpool Plains, to the situation, at a considerably reduced salary however. The resolution of the Committee was submitted to the meeting by the Chairman, when it was unanimously agreed to and confirmed by them. Mr. J. Odell suggested, and the meeting agreed, that, immediately on Mr. Nowland taking the charge, the stock should be mustered and branded, which operation he (Mr. Odell) lamented had been seriously neglected by the late Superintendent [William Nowland] for the last three years… [1842–1845]*

William Improves the Quality of the Stock on Mooki Station

The HBS's concerns about the quality of the stock sent William searching for answers, as told below.

> *On the death of Edward, his brother, William took charge of the Society's stock about the 1st July 1843.*
>
> *… Writing from Falbrook [now Camberwell] on the 27th June 1856, William referred to the Society's cattle being badly bred when he took charge in 1843.*
>
> *He [William] purchased a pure-bred bull from Mr. Bowman and he bred 20 to 30 fine bulls which he turned amongst the Society's herd. He afterwards purchased from the A.A.Co. 50 cows, which he had 20 bull calves. "These were three parts bred," then he turned them among the Society's herd, together with one pure bull that cost £20.*
>
> *"The consequence is the Society's cattle are now well bred which I consider has put at least one Pound (£1) per Head on their Herd of 2002.*[255]

By the end of 1845, all the uncertainty of the earlier years of the decade had dissipated. The pastoralists and squatters were more settled, especially given the deferment and possible annulment of Governor Gipps' proposed changes to land tenure. For William and his fellow squatters on the Liverpool Plains and New England Tablelands this was a reprieve, and they looked once more to their own futures, laced with inherent drive and ambitions.

CHAPTER 16

CAMBERWELL IN THE MID TO LATE 1840S

Besides an inn, the other essential ingredient for a town was a grand local church. So, the locals (presumably, including William) got together and St Clement's Anglican Church, Camberwell was erected. In the beginning it was a very basic church and took ten years to complete. The first service in 1844 was on an earthen floor.[256] In the end, it was a relatively grand provincial church perched on a rise on the eastern side of the Great Northern Road that travellers would see as they passed by on their way into the interior. See the extract below from a retrospective article written in 1927.

> *Singleton Argus – 5th April 1927, page 2.*
> **ST. CLEMENT'S CAMBERWELL**
>
> …*The Registrar of the Diocese of Newcastle has kindly forwarded us the following information concerning the early days of St. Clement's Church…*
>
> "On January 1st, 1844, Bishop Broughton licenced Rev. J. Cooper as minister in the 'United Parochial District of Falbrook and Jerry's Plains.' The church at Falbrook, St. Clement's, had had quite a long history in the early period of which the Bishop of Australia and then the Bishop of Newcastle had taken a very close interest. The building of the church was in hand in 1842, but next year was delayed through lack of funds, [obviously, due to the depression] and indeed, the Bishop (Australia) felt that he, would never see it finished, but in 1845 the work was again in progress, and then he thought it would be ready for consecration within twelve months.
>
> 'The Tower,' he wrote, 'will be a striking object, especially as the church is situated so beautifully.' However, two years later he was still looking forward to its completion, but wrote that only gradual and preserving efforts would bring this about. In the meantime the Incumbent of 'Jerry's Plains' was preaching in the School House just across the Brook to a regular and numerous congregation. The early fifties with the gold rush and scarcity of labour delayed the work further, and indeed what had been done got into a quite ruinous condition, but Bishop Tyrrell, who had arrived in Newcastle in January 1848, urged, encouraged and assisted the church people, and in March, 1855, he had the pleasure of consecrating it. The pulpit, the font, the hangings, and the carpets were the gifts of different individuals who

> *thus greatly encouraged the Incumbent, the Reverend Joseph Cooper, so wrote the Bishop, in his unwearied efforts to complete this House of God…*

After the consecration of St Clement's in 1855 it was progressive and significantly changed and modified over the next 72 years (1855–1927); as told in the rest of the above article and not included here. Then for another 90 years (1927–c.2017) St Clement's continued to service the Anglican community, before it was unfortunately vandalised and locked up.

Today, St Clement's still stands in all its historic grandeur on the eastern side of the New England Highway going north just past the Camberwell sign on the highway. See Figure 21 for a recent photo of the church taken within the church grounds.

An earlier photo of St Clement's closer to the original (© Nov 1920) can be found at University of Newcastle, 'Plans for St Clement's Church, situated in Camberwell NSW' The University Library Special Collectionshttps://livinghistories.newcastle.edu.au.

Like most towns in the colony, Camberwell also established itself as a one of the local meeting places for annual horse races and associated festivities. Descriptors (in the local paper) of the festivities surrounding the Camberwell Races at Glennies Creek in June 1849, follows.

Figure 21: St Clement's Anglican Church Camberwell

The Maitland Mercury and Hunter River General Advertiser
2nd June 1849, page 3
THE CAMBERWELL RACES GLENNIES CREEK

These races came off, as advertised, on Monday last [despite the rain]. The meet was not so numerous as on a former occasion, but all things went off pleasantly and well. The course was in good order, and much improved, and the worthy host took good care to provide amply for his guests, who were greeted on their arrival with a tremendous round of beef, which we consider far more welcome to a traveller than a round of applause. Among the visitors we noticed a large majority of Singletonians, who apparently had made up their mind to have a day's enjoyment. Some of our punters were there also, and were continually cracking their jokes, and passing, because they said it was Whit Monday... Previous to the last race being run a general invitation was given to the assembled guests to meet at the dinner table, where a good spread of poultry, hams, tongues, &c. was prepared; the tables were soon crowded by all classes of sporting characters, who stowed away the "witness" with good appetites, though we can't say they were as liberally washed down.

Henry Starts his Mail Service

While William continued his work developing and promoting Camberwell, his brother Henry ventured into the conveyance of mail and supplies throughout the region.[257]

William's and Mary's Sixth Surviving Child

Soon after Henry established his conveyancing business, William and Mary had their sixth surviving son, Alexander (mine and possibly your direct ancestor).[258] Alex was born in 1846 and had five surviving older brothers; William jr. 14, Michael 12, Robert 10, Charles 6, and John 4.

William's Three Eldest Sons Now Old Enough to Help Around the Family Farm

Alex's eldest brothers (William jr., Michael and Robert) were now old enough (in 1846) to independently help their parents around the family farm: Rosedale. They probably also ventured out with their father when William sr. travelled inland to check on his runs, especially Wallalla on the Liverpool Plains, that was not too far away. They probably also stayed awhile at Mooki Station. They may have also travelled by horse as far as Ward's Mistake on the New England Tablelands and Boonanga in the Gywdir Shire. An incredible distance by horse and remarkable today as one travels by car up and down the New England Highway across the same vast expanse.

CHAPTER 17

GOVERNOR FITZROY'S TENURE

In the same year Alex was born (1846) the Governor for NSW changed from Sir George Gipps (February 1838 to July 1846) to Sir Charles Augustus FitzRoy (August 1846 to January 1855).

From the start, the governance of Governor FitzRoy stood in stark contrast to Governor Gipps. Squatters (like William) soon discovered they had a like-minded and collegial benefactor in FitzRoy. A year after Gipps left the colony his proposed regulations were replaced from London with an Order in Council on the 9th March 1847.[259] This enacted regulation did away with all the fees and charges Gipps had proposed and pleased both the pastoralists and squatters. Each lessee was guaranteed the exclusive lease of their run/s for at least the next 14 years, at a similar price to the one they had paid before: a stock fee determined by the Commissioner and £10 annual licensing fee.

Comments within the article that follows outline the positive impact the Order in Council had on the squatters.

> *Geelong Advertiser – 29th October 1847, page 2.*
> *Squatting*
>
> *In our fourth page will be found the whole of the Order in Council, with the proclamations declaring the introduction of the new system and explaining the routine to be followed in making applications for leases. The new system, taken as a whole, is, in our opinion, and we have devoted considerable attention to the subject, an admirable one; with fewer defects in the details than might reasonably have been expected from any plan concocted in Downing-street. The regulations will give peace of mind to the settlers, will urge them to the improvement of their runs, and in the same degree promote the welfare of the whole community; while they will afford ample protection to the owners of purchased lands, in their agricultural operations, and will open a market for their produce; for we consider the restrictions on growing grain will act as a prohibition in all places within a reasonable distance of farming districts. Since the promulgation of the Order in Council, the office of "Squatter's Advocate" has been a sinecure, and as judgment has been pronounced in favor (sic) of our clients, (nothing remaining to be done but the details of investing them with their rights) it is time for us to get down from the rostrum.*

When, in the month of June, 1845, we first directed our special attention to the Squatting question, the colony was divided into two extreme parties—those who utterly denied the claims of the squatters to any consideration, and the "pastoral association" clique, who aimed at nothing short of fixity of tenure free and for ever (sic). The former we reasoned with—the latter we held up to scorn. Throughout the discussion which followed, and which agitated the colony from end to end, our constant endeavor was to keep in view all the interests likely to be affected by the settlement of the question, to mete (sic) out justice to all, and to endeavor to reconcile conflicting pretensions. In so doing, we flatter ourselves that we were instrumental in giving such a "tone" to public opinion in this district, as was calculated to smooth the way for an amicable and rational adjustment of the question. Beyond this, we claim no praise.

When, two years ago, we expressed-a-hope that the day was not far distant when squatters would cease to be squatters, and become settlers, we must confess that, in our most sanguine expectations that their just claims would be speedily recognised, we did not anticipate that a final settlement of the question on so equitable a foundation, would have been realised at so early a period. It is, therefore, with a feeling of satisfaction rather than regret, that we must now exclaim—

"Othello's occupation's gone."

More Border Police and the Establishment of the Native Police

Governor FitzRoy's more settled and supportive approach to the squatters and pastoralists through the Order in Council was questionably at odds with his approach to First Nations people. FitzRoy's arrival was accompanied by his approval of the increased presence of the Border Police, and the establishment of the Native Police, in 1849. As told earlier:

> *"The main purpose of the native police was to kill Aboriginal people in sufficient numbers, to terrorise them into submission, and to prevent them from attacking the colonists and their property."* [260]

The murderous destruction caused by the Native Police became more and more prevalent as the squatters and pastoralists occupied Country to the north in even greater numbers and moved into areas such as, the New England Tablelands, the Darling Downs and even further north into other parts of Queensland. The article that follows provides some informative descriptors of this migration.

The Sydney Morning Herald, 1 June 1847, page 3.
LIVERPOOL PLAINS AND NEW ENGLAND
(from the Correspondent of the Maitland Mercury)

We have gathered some information of interest from a gentleman who has just come down from the squatting districts. The migration of cattle, horses, and sheep, and we presume men, appears to be still steadily going on from the older districts, northwards, and at the present time there are about 100,000 sheep crossing the Liverpool Plains, on their way to the districts west and north of Moreton Bay [today's Brisbane]. A week or two back, 1800 brood mares, the property of Mr. Boyd, were observed wending their way in the same direction.

A rapid and very beneficial change is taking place in the state of society in the older squatting districts, more particularly in New England. Scarcely a week passes that families are not seen on their way to join their husbands or fathers, and the consequence is, that comfortable houses and gardens are often to be met with, where formerly the bark or slab hut was considered all-sufficient. Vegetables, formerly all but unknown in these districts, are now getting abundant, and prove in general easy to raise and of excellent quality. But, as a consequence also, another want is felt more and more urgently, and that is, the presence of clergymen. Visits are occasionally paid to the districts nearest the boundary by zealous clergymen of different denominations, but even here the want of more frequent ministrations is often severely felt; while in the more remote portions the year passes over, without a clergyman being able to visit the people. Our informant gave us, many instances of the eagerness with which the ministrations of a clergyman were taken advantage of whenever they were fortunate enough to receive a visit from one!

The squatting stations are also now being rapidly extended in the direction, of the Balonne River [Murray-Darling Basin, South-West Queensland]; and we may presume no long time will elapse before stations are found on the road to the Victoria [Victoria Point, Queensland], so clearly traced out by Sir Thomas Mitchell on his last journey. It is indeed a direction, for under the system that has hitherto been generally followed, of allowing flocks and herds to go on increasing ad libitum [as much or as often as necessary] in any given district must soon be stocked to the full extent of its capability.

At the present time the Liverpool Plains is estimated by our informant to be stocked to its full extent for an average season, while a season of drought would necessarily cause serious loss to the owners of stock. The system of yearly culling flocks and herds is, however, gradually superseding the old plan, and necessity will probably force this system more and more on the attention of squatters.

With respect to the attention paid to the improvement of breeds, our informant's opinion was less cheering than on any other point; he thinks that sheep, cattle, and horses, are all neglected on this head by very many, horses more particularly so.

The flood of squatters onto Country was now well north of William's runs and in the lands of the Yuggera Nation (Moreton Bay and Victoria Point, today's Brisbane) and further west in the lands of the Mandandanji Nation (along the Balonne River).[261]

As before, the squatters and pastoralists threatened and devastated Country and the lives of First Nations people. While the Native Police in the guise of protecting the settlers forced Indigenous clans further north and progressively murdered and massacred them.[262]

The Juxtaposition Between the Lives of the Squatters and Pastoralists (like William) and the Lives of First Nations People

The Hunter Valley was full of farms, villages and towns and the Liverpool Plains was no longer outside the boundaries of settlement, given it was declared a district in 1847.[263] Squatters like William on the Liverpool Plains were now recognised as living within the boundaries of settlement and had the option (like the original squatters elsewhere) of leasing their run/s for up to 14 years. Life for them came with some certainty and was mostly settled and stable.

Their lives contrasted inconceivably with those of the various clans, within the Indigenous Nations, they now occupied. Within a few years (c.1822–1827) the Hunter Valley had been taken over by settlers and 20 years later (in 1847) squatters, pastoralists and settlement had also consumed Country on the Liverpool Plains. The clans within the Wonnarua and Kamilaroi Nations had been decimated and those who had survived were completely compromised and confronted with unimageable hardship. While on the New England Tablelands the First Nations people were still engaged in guerrilla warfare in defence of Country. Though ultimately (by c.1865) Country here would also be destroyed, and these Nations would also be decimated, compromised and finally they too would face unconscionable challenges.

Yet all these Nations were not defeated. Each progressively (within the Hunter Valley, Liverpool Plains and the New England Tablelands) refused to give up their heritage (as was the case elsewhere). The people from each Nation who survived, continued to nurture and foster their legacy and traditions amongst themselves and their children. The children in turn passed on their cultural knowledge to the next generation, and then on down the generations, until today. Though some knowledge has been lost over the last 175 years or so, each Nation has conserved their culture beliefs, ideology and values and today they continue to foster, celebrate and where needed revive their cultural heritage.

In contrast to First Nations people, William's life with Mary and their children was secure and assured. In 1847, their seventh surviving child George was born at Rosedale; another boy.[264] William was 43, Mary 34 and their surviving children were: William jr. 15, Michael 13, Robert 11, Charles 7, John 5, Alex 1, and George, a baby.

William's and Mary's children were growing up and the eldest two were obviously quite capable. Within two years of George's birth (1849) William's and Mary's two eldest boys (William jr. (17) and Michael (15)) were old enough to have a run of their own. So, William sr. transferred the lease of Ward's Mistake to them and placed the lease for Wallalla (now 87,040 acres) in his and William jr.'s names.[265]

For William's and Mary's two eldest boys, this was the start of a life of their own on the land.[266] In today's world it is hard to imagine two young men of William jr.'s and Michael's ages venturing out on their own, but the world was very different then: no teenage years.

In essence, from this time on (1849), William's story is a tale of ambition and relative prosperity until his death in 1884. In contrast, the history of this time for the lives of First Nations people and Country is one of challenge and compromise. As detailed next, starting with the Wonnarua Nation on Wonnarua Country.

The Wonnarua Nation

As told earlier, the Wonnarua people were decimated by the invasion of the squatters (c.1826) and from that time on they battled against European diseases, dislocation, and starvation. Dr James Wilson-Miller, a Wonnarua Koori man, academic historian, researcher and author provides us with the following precis of the life of the Wonnarua people between the 1840s and the 1920s.[267]

Death by Disease

... The death figures [from disease] in this post-frontier period were horrendous. One Hunter Valley magistrate wrote in 1845 about the rapidly decreasing population of three kinship groups of the Wonnarua. "Of the first there are 14 men and 10 women, two male children and one little girl. The Elalong people, 18 men, eight women, one boy eleven years and one girl 5 years old. The Macdonald River people, 12 old men, three women aged 40, 35 and 25 years old, two boys about 11 years old and no children. This latter tribe in my memory exceeded 300."

Death by Starvation

... [the] *main cause of death was starvation due to the total disruption of the Koori traditional economy. One sometimes hears the disruption of the Koori traditional economy. One sometimes hears the claim that European settlement did not disrupt the numbers of native food plants and game in Australia. This nonsense should be put to rest once and for all. Let us look at what some European observers in the Hunter Valley in the 1830's wrote of the impact of white settlement on the native ecology. The explorer, Major Thomas Mitchell, while travelling near Falbrook just north of present-day Singleton in 1831, stated that, "the Kangaroos and wallabies had become very scarce." In 1845, the Dungog magistrate, E.M. McKinley claimed that, "the ordinary means of subsistence had diminished on account of the brushes having been cleared, which native game and vegetables formerly abounded in and were easily obtained." In the same year, David Dunlop, the magistrate at Wollombi, south of Singleton, wrote that, "the black swan, the wild duck, the wonga-wonga pigeon and the kangaroo were daily decreasing." The invasion of the Wonnarua tribal lands by the British was a total disaster not only in the physical sense but also in the social sense. Traditional methods of hunting and gathering were no longer viable and the tight social and religious fabric of the Wonnarua began to fall apart under the appalling death rate. There are mountains of primary source evidence to attest that this pattern was repeated right across Australia ...*

The Wonnarua's New Reality

... *it is clear from the records that many Wonnarua died in the early years of European settlement in the Hunter Valley. What is important is that many more Kooris died in the post frontier years from disease and starvation than were killed in actual fighting with whites. But this is the very period that has largely been ignored by historians. It is undoubtedly one of the most important periods in Koori history. Inevitably, there was a period of adjustment. The Wonnarua had to come to terms with the new reality. They clung to the old ways as much as they could, no doubt believing that their old ways, were best. But most Wonnarua Kooris adopted those white ways that were necessary for survival in a new world, which they were losing control of. As with every people who find their lands occupied by foreign invaders, there was an element in Wonnarua society that tried to keep up violent resistance. Their efforts were futile but were to last for almost twenty years. As late as 1843 two Wonnaua Kooris named Harry and Melville went on a killing rampage north of Singleton. ... Some weeks later, Harry and Melville were caught and hanged. Most Wonnarua Kooris came to more peaceful terms with the dominant culture. But the expectation of compensation for land loss was widespread.* One old Koori man near Singleton knew he would not get much out of the white people but he at least expected a blanket a year from the government as compensation for the loss of his land. When the blankets did not arrive on time in 1845 the old man uttered a pathetic lament to the local white court official. "What we do bad, not fight like New Zealand Fellow, No! I gave land and have cold, and very hunger. No, did no bad, we get no blanket! What for?"

Not only was the land no longer theirs but Wonnarua Kooris of the postcontact period soon found that their own tribal laws had been circumscribed. In 1835 a Koori named Charlie killed a white man near Dungog. He was arrested and stood trial for the offence. The trial was of course conducted in the foreign language and format of the English but there was on this rare occasion an interpreter present, to record Charlie's point of view. It seems that the dead white man had been living with a Koori woman of Charlie's clan. The white man had stolen a sacred stone from the Kooris and had committed the capital offence of showing that stone to the woman. Charlie, who was responsible for the safe-keeping of the stone, had the duty of killing the white lawbreaker. Of course, Charlie's evidence was not admissible in the English court and he was hanged in front of a forced gathering of his people just outside of Dungog. Koori law was no longer viable. It had been superseded by the "superior" laws of the British. After all, Kooris were British subjects with the full protection of British law, even though their evidence was not admissible either as defendants or prosecutors. Certain Koori ceremonies did survive this period and the intense Koori belief in a spirit world was to last for many generations despite the efforts of later Christian missionaries. Initiation ceremonies, for instance were still being practised by Wonnarua Kooris as late as the end of the nineteenth century. Corroborees were still held in the early years of last century. Other forms of tribal behaviour were altered by the presence of the white people. Inter-tribal fighting took on a new and savage form.

One incident in 1843 near Maitland was well recorded. Kooris of the Wonnarua and Worimi tribes met outside the town to settle an old difference. But local white "sporting gentlemen" had given the Kooris a few guns and some generous quantities of rum and sat back to watch the entertainment. The result was a bloody battle in which two Kooris were left dead and others were seriously wounded. With the coming of the white man inter-tribal fights had changed in violence and intensity. …

As the years moved on towards the middle of the 19th century, Wonnarua Kooris learned, or were forced to adopt certain European ways. European morality abhorred nakedness and so the Kooris donned the prickly clothes of the dominant society. They were arrested if they did not. A form of English became necessary for communication. White settlers for reasons best known to themselves, taught *the Koori a typical frontier Pidgin. This pidgin became the lingua franca in inter-racial communication, and slowly over the years merged into that dialect of English spoken by most Koori people today. As the generations passed the Wonnarua language died out to the extent that only a very few Wonnarua can speak today. Quite importantly, the Wonnarua Kooris adopted, as much as necessary, the obsessive European attitude to work. Their efforts were occasionally recognised especially when settlers had to rely on Koori labour to get their work done. But rarely was the Koori treated equally. As the Maitland Mercury commented in 1848.*

"There are few who would deem it expedient or proper to give an equivalent for his labour to a blackfellow. A check shirt or two, a pair of duck trousers, and a daily supply of broken victuals are generally deemed satisfaction in full for a twelve months work, although similar services – perhaps less efficiently rendered by a white man would cost an additional fifteen or twenty pounds in hard cash."

It must be remembered that these enormous adaptations to white society were mastered by that generation of Wonnarua Kooris born in tribal days, who knew the hostility and hatred of the frontier, who had seen the collapse of their traditional society, and had experienced and survived the holocaust of death by disease and starvation. This was a remarkable achievement matched by few other people in the world. More importantly that same generation geared themselves for the survival of their race. The remnants of the clan groups, which had once been the economic unit of Wonnarua society, were no longer viable as separate groups. Gradually the groups merged for companionship and so that the young could marry. By the middle of the last century the main Wonnarua groups were concentrated around Gresford, Scone and Singleton.

By the end of the 19th century these three groups had merged into one, living as a separate community on reserved called St Clair, 20 kilometres north of present day Singleton in the Hunter Valley. In the 1920s the Aborigines Protection Board destroyed this community, gave the already cleared virgin land to returned white servicemen from World War 1 and dispersed the families. But there are still many people today, like myself, who can trace their ancestry directly to the Wonnarua and find very few white ancestors in the family tree.

The Kamilaroi Nation

The Kamilaroi people demonstrated their resilience, despite the Myall Creek Massacre, the reshaping of their lands by the squatters, and the subsequent on-going devastation and destruction of Country by the pastoralists. See the narrative that follows.[268]

RECONCILIATION TRAIL
Moree to Myall Creek – Kamilaroi Country

As we start off in Willow Tree and Gunnedah on the way to Moree and then travel to Terry Hie Hie, Gravesend, Cranky Rock and Myall Creek we are making a long curving path that joins onto the one at the Memorial site which for Aboriginal people speak of the path of the Rainbow Serpent moving through the land and creating the features of the landscape.

Who belongs to this country?

The traditional custodians of the Liverpool Plains are the Kamilaroi nation which is the second largest in Eastern Australia after the Waradjuri land that lies further south and west of the Blue Mountains. The Kamilaroi (pronounced Gamilaroi) inhabited a large country, stretching from as far as the Hunter Valley in NSW through to Nindigully in Qld and as far west as the Warrumbungle Mountains near Coonabarabran. They maintained fertile soil, running rivers and streams, and plentiful fish supplies. Today, descendants of the traditional people of the Kamilaroi Nation continue to occupy these lands. They are known as 'Murri' people. The towns in their country include Moree, Inverell, Narrabri and Gunnedah.

… As early as 1855 the missionary William Ridley found that the Kamilaroi were "much reduced" through introduced diseases, massacre, and deprivation of traditional tribal lands and foods. Those Aborigines left were settled in small groups at almost every pastoral station. Aboriginal women were exploited by white station workers, and many children were born to these liaisons. Because of the rush to the goldfields by the white stockmen, Aboriginals were indispensable in stock keeping, droving (men and women), helping in domestic work for the free settlers and other occupations. These changes led to the destruction of the Aboriginal social order and a significant loss of Aboriginal culture. This loss of culture can be seen in the ending of the great religious festivals such as the Bora ceremonies.[269]

How would you feel if the place you lived in was taken over by someone else?

Government Reserves

By the 1880s Crown land was gazetted as 'Reserved for the use of Aborigines' and in 1883 the Aboriginal Protection Board was set up by the NSW government to monitor the church missions and reserve activities and to give out rations. There were 114 reserves by 1895 including Terry Hie Hie.[270]

The First Nations People of the New England Tablelands

The First Nations people of the New England Tablelands (in this story, the Ambēyang, Anēwan, Bānbay) also survived the advance of the squatters, though the number in each were at least halved through loss of Country, starvation, introduced diseases, skirmishes, killings and massacres.[271]

As Callum Clayton-Dixon tells us, although the resistance of these First Nations people lasted for at least 30 years (circa mid-1830s to circa mid-1860s) it could not be sustained. In the end, the only action these Indigenous people could take, if they were going to survive, was to work on the sheep and cattle stations for rations.[272] Government Reserves were also established by the colonial government in the 1850s, around Armidale and Walcha. The response of these First Nations people to this shallow and highly questionable tactic quickly became apparent when the clans did not use the reserves and continued to maintain their traditional lives as best they could on Country and to gather where they always had for traditional meetings and ceremonies. Although they were confronted and challenged, their ceremonial sites taken and their traditional food decimated, their resilience prevailed, and today they continue to maintain and foster, their culture, language and heritage.[273]

William lived out his dream (not withstanding his legal battles), raised his family, and became reasonably well off. Meanwhile, the First Nations people at Glennies Creek (Camberwell), on the Liverpool Plains, and the New England Tablelands (as elsewhere throughout the colony) faced devastating destruction of Country, murder, starvation, disease, and an inexcusable and appalling loss of clan. Indigenous Australians learned how to survive and worked on cattle and sheep stations for rations and/or lived along the river courses (on the stations) in their clans in small pockets of Country where they maintained their cultural heritage. Later, they were forced to live within Government Reserves under rigid and controlled conditions on small, altered parts of Country.[274] These reserves were established across First Nations Country by the colonial government, predominately in the early 1880s.[275]

PART THREE

William Constantly in Court

William refuses to give in or give up

CHAPTER 18

WILLIAM ENTERS THE 1850S INSOLVENT

In 1849, William became insolvent; at least in the eyes of the law. William's journey down this pathway started with a hearing in the Supreme Court between John Booth and William Nowland on the 3rd August 1849; *Booth v Nowland*.

John Booth a licensed publican, lived in Sydney at the Windsor Hotel on George Street [276] and was one of the Executors for the Will of Patrick White.[277]

Patrick White was a drover who had taken his cattle up on the Liverpool Plains (in 1837) and arranged with Robert Roberts (maybe a stockman) to graze his cattle on Ross' and Parrott's run; just below Breeza and next to the Mooki River.

Then William (as told earlier) took over the arrangements with Patrick White when he purchased the improvements to the run from Ross and Parrott, in 1839. William then registered the run as Wallalla, in 1840. As part of the 'sale' William agreed to continue the management and care of White's cattle in return for William's ownership of 'a third of the increase in the stock, and five shillings a head for every fat bullock from the herd that William bought to Richmond'; as told in the summary of the court hearing *Booth v Nowland* (3rd August 1849) detailed soon.

Two years later, Patrick White died (in November 1842), and then five years passed, before John Booth requested in writing (in 1847) for William to bring Patrick White's cattle to Richmond, so they could be sold, or alternatively, if William wanted to keep the stock, he would need to pay for them, as part of the probate.

By this time, Patrick White's cattle had been on Wallalla for at least 10 years (1837–1847). The matters in dispute, included: which cattle were Patrick White's; how big was the herd; had the amount of White's cattle been reduced during the recurring droughts (1839–42) when William initially took over the station; and, whether William had slaughtered any of White's cattle for meat.

A large part of the summary of the court hearing in the SMH is provided next and included almost in full, because it outlines the extent and nature of the dispute between William and John Booth and provides some notable insights into William's life as a squatter including: how the cattle were arranged on the station, the various prices of the cattle depending on their age and condition; the quality of the pasture and conditions of the cattle in times of drought; and the slaughter and butchering of cattle as sustenance while staying on a run (the runs were now known as stations).

The Sydney Morning Herald – 3 August 1849, page 3.
LAW INTELLIGENCE.
SUPREME COURT. – THURSDAY.
NISI PRIUS. [Original Trial]
BEFORE His Honor Mr. Justice DICKINSON,
and a Jury of four special jurymen.
JOHN BOOTH v. W. NOWLAND.

Mr. MICHIE (with whom was Mr. FISHER), stated the case for the plaintiff [John Booth]. He said, the action was one of drover [Patrick White], brought to recover the value of a lot of cattle, being a mixed herd, and was brought by the plaintiff [John Booth] as executor to one Patrick White ; the declaration contained but one count, which laid the cattle as the property of the plaintiff [John Booth], as executor; the defendant [William Nowland] has pleaded that he was not guilty of the conversion alleged [slaughtering Patrick White's cattle for meat], and that the cattle was not the cattle of the plaintiff [John Booth], as executor; On these pleas issues were joined. [In dispute].

The deceased [Patrick White] was entitled to run cattle over a station on the Liverpool Plains District, in the year 1839, and at that time had a mixed herd running there, in number from three to five hundred head. Prior to 1839, the station known by the name of the " Woolhollow," [Walhollow][278] *and the cattle, had been under the charge of a person of the name of Roberts; he [Roberts] handed them however over to the defendant [William Nowland] at the instance [instruction] of White, upon the terms, as it would seem, that the defendant [William Nowland] should have a third of the increase [in the stock] for his care and management, and further, that he was to have five shillings a-head for every fat bullock brought into Richmond. The defendant [William Nowland] on these terms managed the cattle until the death of White, which took place sometime in the year 1842 or 1843.*

At this time, and since, the original herd had increased greatly; though it may be contended by the other side that they had not so increased, but on the contrary, that they had decreased through casualties arising from a severe drought [c.1839-42]; but on this point, the evidence to be adduced, will show, that the drought, through the station being an exceedingly well watered one, did not cause many, if any deaths.

[The above is contrary to the newspaper article cited earlier in this story from the SMH on 10 December 1841, where cattle branded 'Nowland at the Mooki River' (most likely Edward's cattle) have fared badly].

Prior to the action, the plaintiff [John Booth] after having obtained probate, made many requests, or demands of possession, of the cattle, but the defendant [William Nowland] always made shuffling answers; they being sometimes to the effect that before they could be delivered up it would be necessary to consult an attorney, and at other times that he was perfectly willing to do so, upon being satisfied who really was entitled to them, as he alleged there were disputed claims made to them. These subterfuges would not, however, avail the defendant [William Nowland], though his learned counsel would doubtless contend, that because he had never absolutely refused to deliver, them, he had never been guilty of a conversion [slaughter of the cattle for meat], and therefore would not be liable to that form of action. This was not the law, however, he was happy to say; for if it were, any unconsciousness and cunning depositee (sic) of property would never absolutely refuse to give up property deposited when asked, but would resort to shuffling answers, as this defendant [William Nowland] did. He would submit that the answers of the defendant [William Nowland], citing Atkin v. Slater, I. C. and K. were to be coupled with his subsequent conduct. And if so, there was a clear conversion [slaughter of the cattle for meat]; the whole evidence indeed would show that there was a clear case, not uncommon, and which is known in colonial slang– as "sticking to the cattle."[279]

The case for the plaintiff [John Booth], said the learned counsel, will be one easily proved; it will involve the proof that the original cattle were those of White; that White was dead, and that the plaintiff [John Booth] was his executor, &c. The plaintiff [John Booth] will claim liberal damages for the value of the maximum number of cattle that the herd would have increased to up to the time of the last demand made. From the evidence 'de bene esse' [for what it's worth], and of persons examined to-day, it appeared that White, many years ago, had acquired through his industry, a middling sized herd of cattle; they were first under the care of a person of the name of Hatton, afterwards they were removed to the Hunter, and thence placed under the care of Robert Roberts, at the station called "Woolhollow," [Walhollow] in the Liverpool Plains. After Robert Roberts gave up the care of them, they seem to have been for some time left on the station under the superintendence of no one; but afterwards they were handed over to the defendant [William Nowland] on the terms mentioned by the learned counsel.

The station was described as an exceedingly good one, even during dry seasons so much so that the drought of 1840 did little or no havoc amongst them [again refer to the article in the SMH, 10 December 1841]. The cattle were always branded P. W., being the initials of the deceased's name. Some of the witnesses said the yearly increase of one hundred ewes would – be about seventy-five head, and that the herd delivered to the defendant [William Nowland] would by this time taking into consideration all casualties, and making allowance for the occasional draughting [the separation into different parts of the run] of the fat cattle, be about six hundred, and which were valued, one with the other, at 25s. [twenty five shillings] per head. It was proved by one witness that he [William Nowland] had offered £1000 to White for six hundred of them, which offer was refused.

It was proved that before the action was commenced, a demand 'vive voce' [oral not written] was made for them, to which the defendant [William Nowland] answered that he would give up the P. W. cattle, meaning those in question, provided he were paid 5s. [5 shillings] per head for all the fat cattle. Other demands were also made, one in particular in writing, and by word of mouth. On the 29th September, 1847, the written demand set forth that the herd was 700 strong. The witness Sheriff, who served the notice, and made the verbal demand, (it seemed to have been made in Windsor) to-day said that he did not get the cattle, the defendant [William Nowland] saying that he would have difficulty in finding them, as they were all scattered; the witness advised the defendant [William Nowland] to settle the matter by arbitration, to which he answered he had always been prepared to go to arbitration, and was so still; the defendant [William Nowland] afterwards said he would never give them up until he were paid 5s. per head for the fat cattle, and that the plaintiff [John Booth] must come and get them how he could.

There seemed to be some doubt as to the exact time when the defendant [William Nowland] took charge, and from the testimony of some of the witnesses, the herd ought to be nearer 1000 head than 700. It was proved that the deceased [Patrick White], who lived near or in Richmond, died in November, 1842. Upon a letter of the defendant [William Nowland] being put in evidence (being in answer to a demand) to the effect that as some one (sic) besides the plaintiff [John Booth] was making a claim to the cattle, he could not deliver them up, until he could understand to whom they belonged – the plaintiff's [John Booth's] case was concluded…

…The SOLICITOR GENERAL, [representing William Nowland] with whom was Mr. BROADHURST, first having made an attempt to move for a nonsuit on the ground that the plaintiff [John Booth] had failed to prove a conversion [slaughter of the cattle for meat] … proceeded to address the Jury for the defendant [William Nowland].

He [the Solicitor-General] said in this case, upon the issues raised by the pleadings, they, the jury, must be satisfied before they could find a verdict for the plaintiff [John Booth], that the defendant [William Nowland] had converted [slaughtered for meat] the cattle to his own use. Upon the evidence adduced, he would submit, the Jury could not, find that fact against the defendant [William Nowland] … It was true other demands were also made by letter, but even from the nature of *the property demanded, it was an utter impossibility for the defendant [William Nowland] to comply with the request, the cattle were wild, and running at large on the station…*

…They proved he [William Nowland] offered that, if he would pay him (the defendant) according to the original agreement, which, by-the-by, the plaintiff [John Booth] had not put into evidence; but which the defendant [William Nowland] would also make part of his case—five shillings per head for the fat cattle. He [William Nowland] would have had them mustered, and actually named two different periods for that purpose, but which were not heeded by the plaintiff [John Booth]; he also offered, that if the plaintiff [John Booth] was unwilling to abide by the agreement on his [William Nowland's] part and provided that the plaintiff [John Booth] was willing to come to the station and take the trouble and nuisance of mustering them himself, he might do so. These were most fair offers, and which no man who was acting prudently would spurn; but it so happens that the plaintiff [John Booth] somewhat litigious, and as the action of trover is a little hard against a defendant [William Nowland], provided the evidence can be screwed up to a certain pitch, and then the sale of cattle at the present moment rather difficult, the plaintiff [John Booth] would rather sell to the defendant [William Nowland] the cattle in question [Patrick White's cattle], by gaining from the defendant [William Nowland] damages equal to the supposed value of them. The action to say the least of it was speculative. As to the number of the cattle, the evidence adduced on that head exaggerated the number exceedingly; they never were equal to any thing (sic) like the number already stated by the witnesses, and evidence will yet be adduced to show that those witnesses have overstated the numbers.

Indeed out of the plaintiffs [John Booth's] own mouth, he will be estopped [prevented] from recovering for so great a number. When probate was granted to him, notwithstanding that the testator [Patrick White] died possessed of other property, besides the cattle in question, the plaintiff [John Booth] actually valued the whole property of the deceased under £200. The defendant [William Nowland] had, on some occasions, when asked to give up possession of the cattle, replied that others were making title to them, and therefore he could not deliver them to the plaintiff [John Booth] until he made his [John Booth's] title apparent. He [William Nowland] had good reason for making this answer, as will be shown, and this evidence will bear upon the issue, viz., as to the property of the plaintiff [John Booth] in them. After commenting upon the testimony of some of the witnesses, the learned counsel concluded a rather long address by calling upon the jury to return a verdict for his client. [William Nowland]

The following is an outline of the evidence then adduced:-The agreement was produced, and proved, under which the defendant [William Nowland] took charge of the cattle in the first instance; the Will of the deceased [Patrick White] was also produced, from which it appeared that half of the cattle in question were bequeathed to the plaintiff [John Booth], the other half to the plaintiffs [John Booth's] brother [brother in law, James White], he [James White] being now represented by the [his] widow [John Booth's sister]…

…Rotton said he had been on the Liverpool Plains, during the drought of 1840 and 1841, White's cattle having been removed there in the mean time (sic); he described, the Plains as being completely bare of grass, though there was plenty of water; indeed the cattle would have to wander from their watering places fifteen miles to feed; at that time he said many of the P. W. cattle [Patrick White cattle] were lying dead, many of them were bogged in the river, and in the waterholes dead, or dying; in 1847, he said a mixed herd of cattle would only have been worth 10s. per head. A man of the name of Ross said he had charge of the cattle before the year of the drought, viz., in 1837 and 1839; he was paid for them 5s. per head: the first year he had them there were only forty, and the second only fifty, head. He also visited the Plains during the drought and saw the same total want of pasture described by the last witness; and added that he saw a great many of the P.W. cattle dead in the water-holes, one on top of the other. After the drought there could not have been more than forty or fifty alive; the greatest havoc was made amongst the females.

This witness [Ross], in cross-examination, admitted that he had been employed by the plaintiff [William Nowland] to collect the cattle; he denied having offered to buy them, or having warned the plaintiff [John Booth] against the defendant [William Nowland], as he might be bit by the latter [William Nowland]. To contradict him [Ross] in the first denial, a letter was produced, written by himself [Ross], wherein he had made an offer to buy Mrs. White's (the widow of James White) share. [Interesting, every man for himself] A person of the name of Richardson said he knew the cattle and station well, and that after the drought the cattle could not have been in number more than forty, that their increase in 1842 was not more than two or three head at the most, and that the plaintiff [William Nowland] in 1846 had made an offer to him to sell the whole herd at £50, which, was declined, because he said he thought £40 would be more than their value, even if brought together in a stock-yard [by William Nowland].

Mr. BROADHURST, [representing William Nowland] in the absence of the Solicitor-General, replied shortly upon the letter deduced, to contradict the witness Ross; and Mr. MICHIE [representing John Booth] replied, generally, upon the whole case, analysing the evidence adduced on either side; showing that the witnesses who spoke to the number of the plaintiff's [John Booth's] cattle, was persons, from their vocation, and from their opportunities of observing that which *they came to speak about, more likely to be uttering the truth than those called on the other side, who, independent of their want of means of knowing the truth, had every inducement to lessen the number.*

As to the affidavit made by the defendant [William Nowland] and so much relied on, by the other side, he [Mr. Michie] said many views might be taken of it. He [William Nowland] might have made it with a view of defrauding the Government of extra probate duty; or he [William Nowland] may have made it in ignorance of the circumstances, thinking perhaps indeed that he [John Booth] should not be able to prevent the defendant [William Nowland] from sticking to the cattle [slaughtering the cattle for meat]; but which ever (sic) way it was, it was no reason why the Jury should take it into consideration in assessing their damages: for if they relied upon it, they would punish an innocent party [John Booth] for the wrong doing of another [William Nowland]; it must be remembered another [James White's widow] was entitled to the half share of the cattle, and of course would be entitled to the half damages they the Jury would give.

His HONOR summed up very carefully, going through the pleadings and the evidence as applicable to such issue; and fully explained the law as to conversion [slaughter of cattle for meat]. He said he was of opinion that the plaintiff [John Booth] might, as executor, not only recover damages for his own half share of the cattle, but also for the half share of Mrs. J. White, [John Booth's sister] and for her in equity would be trustee, and as such would be liable to account for her share of the damages. He said there was a great discrepancy between the witnesses adduced on either side, both as to the number of the cattle, and as to their supposed value when they were demanded; however, this was a question for them [the jury] peculiarly to consider and decide.

Jury retired for half an hour, and found verdict for the plaintiff [John Booth], damages £200; which they said, in answer to His HONOR they found as the value of all the cattle in the defendant's [William Nowland's] charge.

Whilst the Jury were out, Mr. BROADHURST, with, the consent of the other side obtained leave from His Honor to move the Full Court to reduce the damages by one-half, in case, the Court should think the plaintiff [John Booth] could not maintain the action in respect of the half share of Mrs. J. White. [Damages for the plaintiff, £100.]

Attornies (sic) for the plaintiff [John Booth], Messrs. Allen and Son; and for the defendant [William Nowland], Mr. Yeomans.

William lost the case, and his integrity was challenged by those who supported John Booth's position. Booth's attorneys and witnesses claimed William made excuses, avoided giving over Patrick White's cattle, and possibly, William had slaughtered some of Patrick White's cattle for meat. All in the papers and written in detail in the *Sydney Morning Herald*.

William wasn't going to stand for it. He decided to pay John Booth as little as possible up front and delay any further payment as long as he could. He probably proclaimed; '*You will have to wait I can't afford anymore.*'[280]

The above summary of *Booth v Nowland* paints a picture of Wallalla Station and how it was managed with verbal agreements and exchanges between the various parties. An image probably not dissimilar to the experiences of other squatters. The competition was fierce, and the stockman and squatters positioned themselves as best they could.

For me, William's Wallalla Station was left at times to take care of itself (when William and his boys were busy elsewhere) and then active at other times. William and his eldest sons (William Jr. 17, Michael 15, and possibly, Robert 13) probably returned to the station from time to time, to check on the cattle, round them up, rearrange them, slaughter some for food, stay a while, and then take the fat cattle to the local and Sydney markets.

One can visualise the comings and goings as William and his sons tracked north on their horses from Rosedale, through Murrurundi, up the Pages River to the Pages River Gap (today, known as Nowlands Gap) and on to the Liverpool Plains. Their horses laden with supplies, and possible at times, bringing their goods on a dray and then after a while, setting off once again this time south to take the fat cattle to market: with William and/or one or two of his eldest sons taking charge. Sometimes, stopping in on family. Henry and Harriet and their children, at Muswellbrook; Mary and Alex, now at Scone; William's wife, Mary and the other children, at Rosedale; and then on to Wilberforce and Windsor, to William's mother Elizabeth, William's brother (Michael jr.) and sister (Elizabeth jr.) and their partners, and families; and possibly, William's sister, Sarah and her partner, and their family, in George Street Sydney.

From my perspective, William and his sons, led a hard life; on the road for long periods of time, facing recurring droughts (and sometime floods), and living in the open for months on end, or on one of their stations, in a very basic hut.

The summary of the above court case (*Booth v Nowland*) also reflects on the witnesses. Their recollections dependent on their associations (for example, Ross who was wary of taking sides). The case relied on allegations re the character of the plaintiff (John Booth) and defendant (William Nowland). In the end, William lost the case and was ordered to pay John Booth £100 in damages.

Nearly three months later, William had not paid the full amount; he still owed John Booth £67. This was not good enough for John Booth and he took William once again to the Supreme Court. The Court ordered the Sheriff to sell William's 'right, title and interest, and estate' to the amount needed to pay the debt owed to John Booth (£67). The court order below provides an informative summary of William's assets in 1849 and is of particular interest because some of William's assets have already been confirmed in the story.

Government Gazette Private Notices – New South Wales Government Gazette 23 November 1849, page 1748.
In the Supreme Court. Sheriff's Office,
Sydney, 16th November 1849.
Booth v. Nowland

ON Wednesday, the 26th December next, at noon, at the London Tavern, George-street, Sydney, the Sheriff will cause to be sold, all the right, title, and interest, and estate, if any, of the above named defendant [William Nowland], in and to the Equity of Redemption in the following properties, viz :—

All that parcel of land, containing by admeasurement 160 acres more or less, situate in the County of Durham, in the parish of Auckland, at Falbrook, in the Colony of New South Wales.

Also, all that parcel of land, containing by admeasurement 200 acres more or less, situate at Falbrook, in the Colony of New South Wales as aforesaid.

Also, all that parcel, of land, containing by admeasurement 725 acres more or less, situate in the parish of Auckland aforesaid, near Dulwich, in the Colony as aforesaid. [Dulwich part of Falbrook]

Also, all that parcel of land, containing by admeasurement 185 acres more or less, situate near Dulwich in the Colony aforesaid. Also, all that parcel of land, containing by admeasurement 50 acres more or less, situated in the County of Cook, near Roberts' Swamp, Kurrajong, in the Colony aforesaid. [Interesting William also had land at Kurrajong]

Also, that piece or parcel of land, containing by admeasurement 2 acres more or less, in the Town of Falbrook and Colony aforesaid—together with all buildings, &c., erected on the several parcels of land before mentioned, and now under mortgage to William Hall, by deed dated 30th August, 1842.

Also, all that piece or parcel of land, containing 142 acres more or less, situate in the County of Durham, parish of Auckland, on Falbrook, at the western extreme of the south boundary line of the village reserve; and bounded on the north by that boundary line bearing east 60 chains; on the east by 25 chains and 50 links of the west boundary of James Glennies' additional grant bearing south; on the south by 54 chains of the north boundary line of Turnbicks' grant, bearing west to Falbrook; and on the west by Falbrook upwards to the western extreme of the south boundary line of the village reserve.

Also, all that piece or parcel of Land, or building allotment, being allotments 14 and 15, adjoining the road leading from the Long Bridge to the Falls, in the town of West Maitland; bounded on the north by 150 feet of allotment No. 11 : on the north west by the said road from the Long Bridge to the Falls 84 feet; on the south by Bourne Russell's 168 feet; and on the east by allotment, 12 and 13, by a line of 74 feet, more or less; together with all buildings, &c. Mortgaged to Michael Nowland [William's brother] by deed 15th November, 1843. [Interesting William also had land in West Maitland]

After which, all the right and interest, if any, of the abovenamed defendant, in and to the equity of redemption, of about 30 head of cattle, branded on the hip WN, and on the ribs N.—nine being working bullocks; also, twelve horses branded WN on the neck, and N on the shoulder, now at Falbrook, in the County of Durham. Overseer—William Nowland.

Also, about 300 head of cattle, branded WN on the hip, and N on the ribs, others branded J P, others N, others GP, others HP, others MR. J J.

Also, 6 horses, more or less, some branded WN and N on the shoulder," and others, branded NO on the neck; now at Liverpool Plains. Overseer—John Richardson.

Also, about 500 head of cattle, branded MN and N on the ribs, some being working bullocks; 4 horses, branded X and WN; at New England. Overseer—John Duval. Mortgaged to Alexander Johnston, by deed 15th November, 1843.

Also, about 1800 head of cattle, branded WN on the rump, and N on the ribs ; 700 head of which cattle are running at Ward's Mistake in the District of New England; and about 1100 head of the same cattle are running at Wallala, Mooki River, in the District of Liverpool Plains.

Also, about ten head of horses, branded N on near shoulder, and WN on the neck, and also running at the Mooki River, under the superintendence of William Nowland. Mortgaged to Mary Perrett, by deed 1st of June, 1849.

Unless this execution be previously satisfied.

CORNELIUS PROUT,

Under Sheriff. 1388

£1 11s.3d. [It is assumed this is the remittance to the Under Sheriff.]

Whether William couldn't or refused to pay the £67 is unknown; but most likely, William just 'ummed and ahhed' to delay payment. A flawed tactic that facilitated a long and drawn out battle with John Booth in the Insolvency Courts for the next two and a half years (November 1849 to May 1852).[281]

William's Supposed Insolvency

Amongst the hearings on William's supposed insolvency two different newspaper accounts in the *Maitland Mercury* baffled me. The first, on the 8th June 1850 follows; it must be a partial account because the figures are not representative of what we know about William's assets at this stage of his life. See below.

> *The Maitland Mercury and Hunter River General Advertiser –*
> *8 June 1850, page 2.*
> *Sydney News (From our Correspondent)*
> *Sydney, Thursday Evening*
> *Insolvency Proceedings*
>
> *In the estate of William Nowland, a single meeting was held, and the following claims were proved: Michael Nowland, £58 17s. 1d.; John Richardson, £16 4s.; William Hull, £372 16s. The insolvent was examined, and the meeting adjourned. Nowland filed as schedule as follows: – Liabilities, £3031 10s. 10d. Assets-landed property, £20; personal property, £110; debts due to insolvent's estate, £67. Balance deficiency, £2834 10s. 10d.*

In the second account, three more creditors emerge, and an offer is made by William to pay his creditors back at 'five shillings in the pound…'. See below.

> *The Maitland Mercury and Hunter River General Advertiser –*
> *12 June 1850, page 2.*
> *INSOLVENCY PROCEEDINGS. PROOF OF CLAIMS.*
>
> *In the estate of William Nowland, an adjourned single meeting was held in Sydney, on Friday. The following claims were proved: — J. Yeomans, £90; Kemp and Fairfax, £16 2s. 3d.; and Mary Perrott, £207. The insolvent was examined on behalf of the petitioning creditor; after which he made an offer of 5s. in the pound — 2s. 6d. cash, and the remaining 2s.6d. at six months, which was accepted.*

In the first hearing (above), William owed his creditors (including his brother Michael jr.) £446.37s.1d. While, in William's own schedule his liabilities are stated as, £3031.10s.10d, and his assets, £120 (hard to believe) with his debts to insolvent's estate £67 (assumed to be the debt to John Booth), and another figure cited as 'balance deficiency' noted as £2834.10s.10d; which is assumed to mean, William's overall debt. This last figure for me is a bemusing anomaly. If William was insolvent to this level (£2834.10s.10d) one would assume he would have lost all or most of the assets listed in the *Government Gazette* on the 23 November 1849; including Rosedale. Yet we know this was not the case. To add further to the confusion, William, in the early 1850s was also still heavily engaged in purchasing town allotments in Camberwell (as will be detailed in a later chapter). A person insolvent to this level could not possibly afford to purchase land in this way.

Turning to the second hearing on 12 June 1850 three other creditors are cited, with a total debt to these creditors of £341.3d; making William's overall debt to his creditors (based on these two accounts) £787.37s.4d. A rather large amount of money, that William (after several other court hearings, where he puts his case) agreed to pay back progressively to his creditors; the details of how the money was to be paid is unknown, as no further account on the matter was found.

One wonders why William didn't just pay the £67 in the first place to avoid all the claims and counter claims on his finances and reputation. He obviously thought he could engage in delaying tactics for as long as it took for Booth to go away.

Despite the Court Hearings William Just Got On With His Life

While all this 'to-ing and fro-ing' was going on in the Insolvency Court, William was still engaged in his work; droving and selling stock and moving between Rosedale, Wallalla, the HBS's Mooki Station, and Ward's Mistake (maybe sometimes alone) but presumably mostly with one or more of his three eldest sons.[282] The eldest boys would have also managed the family business when William was required to attend the court hearings on his insolvency.

William Declared Solvent

After two and a half years of hearings, William finally convinced the Insolvency Court that he could repay all his debts. William was lucky because his creditors were on his side. He did not lose any of his assets and was declared no longer insolvent, with the case discharged on the 1st May 1852.[283]

Henry also Ambitious Expands his Carrying Services

William's brother Henry also continued to expand on his interests, most notably, his mail conveyancing services: between Singleton, Muswellbrook and Scone, and as far as Tamworth, by three horse and four horse coach.[284]

By the early 1850s, Henry had a stock of horses and had built a number of his own coaches at his coach building and blacksmith business in Hunter Terrace, Muswellbrook.[285]

Another Child for William and Mary

William's wife, Mary was also very busy at Rosedale caring for another baby; Alfred, born in 1851; Mary and William's eighth surviving child, another boy.[286]

CHAPTER 19

WILLIAM, THE COURTS AND WALLALLA STATION

William's and Mary's son Alfred (in 1851) was born into a very different NSW to his parents. NSW was no longer a penal colony. The wealthy and well-connected pastoralists had established themselves well beyond the small colonial settlement of William's youth and become an influential force in the colony of NSW. The *Australian Colonies Government Act* (in 1850) consolidated their position and potentially increased their number in the Legislative Council from 36 to 54 members with (as before) two thirds of the representatives, elected by eligible pastoralists and town residents.[287]

During the 1850s, the colony of NSW moved from a penal colony (c.1840) to responsible government (in 1856) and universal suffrage (for adult males) in 1859. This was a long way from William's Wilberforce when he was a child.

The year 1851 also heralded in the Gold Rush in NSW that brought a flood of prospectors, mostly from the UK and the USA. The impact was significant with the prospectors crowding into settlements and digging up land wherever there was a hint of gold. While other ancestors of mine (in Gulgong and Bathurst) were affected by the Gold Rush, no account was found of the impact of the gold rush on William and his family; though one could speculate given the exponential growth in population and the sea of calico tents that emerged wherever rumours canvassed the possibility of gold.

Besides giving the pastoralist a louder voice in the Legislative Council, the *Australian Colonies Government Act 1850*, created two separate colonies. The colony of New South Wales was separated from the Port Phillip District, and the Port Phillip District was renamed the colony of Victoria on the 1st July 1851.[288]

NSW became a separately governed entity and had plenty to offer those who wanted to get ahead. William was amongst the ambitious New South Welshmen who did just that. His story tells us of an opportunistic, hardworking man who always tried to stay ahead of the game, outsmart his components, and defend his assets and position. As a first-generation colonial Australian (whose parents were emancipated convicts) William had worked as a squatter on the land for over 20 years. Initially, as a young man, he had ventured out from Wilberforce with his brothers (Edward and Henry) and positioned himself to make enough money to get by and offer his future wife Mary a farming lifestyle where they could prosper in their own small way. Twenty-six years later (in 1850) William, Mary and their seven surviving children entered the 1850s (despite William's insolvency) as a part of the Camberwell community, with a farm of their own (Rosedale) and enough assets to make a reasonable living.

William Accused of Trespass

The world William and Mary had created for themselves, and their boys was challenged in 1851 by John Eales; a wealthy pastoralist who had a land grant (Walhollow), adjacent to William's Wallalla Station on the Liverpool Plains.[289]

While in the Insolvency Court (in 1851) William was summoned to the Supreme Court, in June of the same year, on a matter of trespass. John Eales (the Complainant) put the case that William had taken his sheep from where they were depasturing (grazing) on his (Eales') Walhollow Station, and impounded them at the settlement of Mooki, and then refused to give the sheep back, until he (Eales) paid William a fee to retrieve them.[290]

The hearing was not straight forward because the boundaries between John Eales' Walhollow Station and William's Wallalla Station were in dispute. A complication that dominated the hearing as outlined in the summary of the case that follows.

> *The Maitland Mercury and Hunter River General Advertiser,*
> *17 September 1851, page 4*
> *EALES V. NOWLAND AND ANOTHER.*

On the 25th of June last, a rule in this case was obtained by Mr. Fisher, under the Law Simplifying Act, calling upon the respondents [William Nowland and Another] to show cause why two undertakings, given by Charles Humphreys [Eales' superintendent] and acting for and on behalf of the Complainant, [John Eales] to the respondent [William Nowland and Another], for payment of the sum of £115 5s. 8d. for damages and charges on the impounding by respondent, Nowland, of certain sheep belonging to the complainant [John Eales], in February, 1851, should not be delivered up to be cancelled, and for an injunction to restrain the respondents [William Nowland and Another] from taking any proceedings for the purpose of enforcing the same.

It appeared from the affidavit of the complainant [John Eales], upon which the rule was obtained, that he had been the occupier of a station on Liverpool Plains, called Walhalla [Walhollow] since 1842; and that, since that year, respondent Nowland had occupied some land adjoining. [For William, the western side of Wallalla Station along the Mooki River.]

There were disputes between the parties which were still pending.[291]

In February last the respondents, [William Nowland] with some other persons, drove £1,000 or 12,000 sheep belonging to the complainant [John Eales] off the run, and impounded them at the public pound at Mooki. The complainant's superintendent [Charles Humphrey], after an ineffectual attempt to rescue the sheep, entered into the undertaking required by the Act of Council, 4th William IV., No. 3, to pay a certain sum for damages within one month. It was sworn that the undertaking was given to save the sheep from starvation.

[The damages required by William were most likely, due to Eales' sheep depasturing William's Wallalla Station, and/or the sheep unsettling and dispersing William's cattle].

A similar act was sworn to have been committed in the same month, and a similar undertaking given. The amount undertaken to be paid was £115 5s. 8d. A summons for the illegal impounding had been taken out before the Tamworth bench, but the magistrates dismissed the case, on the ground that it was a case of disputed boundaries.

The respondent, Nowland, it appeared, had been insolvent, and had not obtained his certificate… [This is the only comment on William's Insolvency between 1850–53.]

…Mr. Broadhurst [representing William Nowland] showed cause upon an affidavit of the respondent, Nowland, in which he denied the material facts relied upon by the complainant [Eales], and cited the following cases Skeate v. Beale, 11 A. and E.; Lindon v. Hooper, 1 Cows. And Jullian v. Cress, 9 Tur., 666. The Court, stopping Mr. Fisher in the course of his reply, stated that they had no doubt as to the complainant's [John Eales'] right to support the rule upon equitable principles, and made an order to the effect that the complainant [John Eales] should, within a certain time and upon certain specified terms, bring an action of trespass against the respondent, William Nowland, for the purpose of fixing the right to the run mentioned in the affidavits; and that in the event of his failing in such action, or not fulfilling the terms of the order, the rule should be discharged with costs. – S.M. Herald, Sept. 11.

The hearing determined John Eales needed to prove a case of trespass. For William, this was not good enough. As far as he was concerned, John Eales had trespassed on Wallalla Station and there was no way John Eales could prove otherwise. William had a licence for Wallalla and he had held it since 1839 and for the past twelve years!

As told earlier, this wasn't the first time William had been challenged on the boundaries of Wallalla. In 1842, Edmund Urh placed an ad in the SMH for Wallalla declaring it was for sale.[292] In response, William placed his own ad cautioning others that Wallalla Station was his and he had plenty of documentation to prove it.

William didn't just place the ad once. He placed it in a prominent newspaper (SMH) and at least eight times between 10th September and the 27th September. The ad is included again below as a reminder of William's passion and belief in his 'ownership' of Wallalla Station; a property he had leased from the colonial government since 1839.

The Sydney Morning Herald, 10 September 1842 – page 1
Advertising
Caution to the Public.

IT having been represented to me that Mr. Edmund B. Uhr, of Balwanna, near Maitland, has been offering for sale the station known by the name of "Wallalla" Mooki River, Liverpool Plains, and having in my possession ample documentary evidence to show that the said station is mine, for recovery of which an action is now pending in the Supreme Court, – all parties are hereby warned against purchasing the abovementioned station from Mr. Uhr.

WILLIAM NOWLAND.

Falbrook, Hunter River, September 8.

Later in the same decade (1848), William placed another ad warning others not to disperse their sheep amongst his cattle on Wallalla Station; as shown below.

The Sydney Morning Herald, 24 June 1848, page 3
PUBLIC NOTICE

ALL parties, with the exception of the Hawkesbury Benevolent Society, who may have cattle in my charge, depasturing on my station, Wallalla, Mooki River, Liverpool Plains, are hereby required to remove the same on or before the 30th day of September next, and those concerned are to take notice, that all expenses Incurred for keep, &c. are to be paid previous to the removal of the said cattle.

WILLIAM NOWLAND.

June 1.

William continued his defence of Wallalla Station throughout the 1850s with further cautions and public notices in the *Sydney Morning Herald* and the local papers, where he warned others and impounded stock. This unsettled William's neighbours and bade William to court, time and time again; starting with *Eales v Nowland and Another* in September 1851, and ending in May 1862, after William took his case to the Privy Court in London.

There are too many court hearings with William, either as the plaintiff or defendant, for all to be included in the story. The summaries in the newspapers are lengthy and can be readily found in Trove under the keyword 'Nowland' and within the years '1851 to 1862'.

Those selected (between 1851 and 1862) provide an historical account of the evolution of the exchange between William and those who challenged him about the boundaries of Wallalla Station on the western side of the Mooki River; the dispute about the boundaries of Wallalla only concerned the western side of William's station.

William's court hearings were continuous and did not go unnoticed. For more than a decade the summaries of each court hearing appeared in the papers some for days on end. One can imagine the discussion and gossip as interested readers waited for the next instalment of 'William Nowland and Wallalla Station'.

For William, his battle for Wallalla started in 1842 when Edmund Uhr advertised the station was for sale and ended (20 years later) with the judgment of the Privy Council in London in May 1862.

The Confusion About the Boundaries of Walhallow Station and Wallalla Station

As already mentioned, William's court hearings were probably initially instigated by the ad hoc names and boundaries of John Eales' Walhollow Station and William Nowland's Wallalla Station as evident in the *Government Gazette*, in 1849. The descriptors of the boundaries below demonstrate the confusion over possession and entitlement. The use of the name 'west (Walhollow)' on the western side of William's station is vague and ominous and the descriptors of the boundaries of Wallalla Station (though detailed) are too pedestrian to be clear.

Government Gazette Notices – New South Wales Government Gazette, 31 October 1849, page 1621.

No. 182. Nowland William, now Messrs. Nowland. [William Nowland sr. and jr.]

Name of Run—Wallalla east and west (Walhollow)[293]

Estimated Area—87,040 acres.

Estimated Grazing Capabilities—2,720 Cattle.

Wallala (sic) East.—Bounded on the south by the Hawkesbury Benevolent Society's run, by a line bearing west about nine miles through a point of the spring ridge; on the west by Windham's run, by a line bearing north of about eight miles to Lang's south-west corner; on the north by Lang's run by a line bearing east of about nine miles to the Mooki River; and on the east by about eight miles of the Mooki River.

Wallala (sic) west; —Bounded on the south by the Benevolent Society of Windsor now used as John Allen's Run by a line bearing east of about eight miles from the Mooki River to Weary's Mountain ; on the east by Messrs. Single and Vidal's Run by a line bearing north of about eight miles to Lang's south-east corner; on the north by Lang's Run by a line bearing west of about eight miles to the Mooki River; and on the west by about eight miles of the Mooki River.

N.B—This Run has been transferred with the sanction of Government, to Messrs. William Nowland, senior, and William Nowland, junior.

The descriptors for John Eales' Walhollow Station were also vague and ill-defined. See the government notice that follows.

*Government Gazette Notices – New South Wales Government Gazette –
20 September 1848, page 1225
No. 65 Eales John
Name of Run – Walhollow.*

Estimated Area—50,000 Acres.

Estimated Grazing Capabilities—6,000 Sheep.

Bounded on the south by a cattle track adjoining the Hawkesbury Society's Grant, bearing west about 4 miles and by a line from Allen's fence bearing east about 1½ mile; then south-east to the Dury boundary; on the east by the Werries Creek ranges; north by a line from Cuna Gap adjoining. Brezer bearing west about 7 miles to the Mucki (sic) River, then by a gully known as the Dog Trap Gully, adjoining Clift's about 3 miles bearing west.

Wallalla was divided by the Mooki River and adjoined or most likely, overlapped with John Eales' Walhollow Station on the western side of the river; given each were given entitlement without reference to the other. No wonder there were disputes. The map that follows, provides a visual representation of the relative position of the HBS's Mooki Station, John Eales' Walhollow, William's Wallalla Station (approx. location) and the Mooki River. (See Figure 22 overleaf.)[294]

The Court Rules in William's Favour

Seven months after the first court case (September 1851) on whether William had the right to impound Eales' sheep and the associated disputed over the boundaries between their stations, William and John Eales were back in court again, on the 10th April 1852. John Eales was the plaintiff and William Nowland the defendant.

This time, the court ruled in William's favour: John Eales was ordered to pay William £86 9s. 3d. for trespass (as requested by William) on the proviso from the court that

William would not take John Eales to court again to recover any further money.

The courts were starting to settle matters for William. The following month on 1st May 1852 William also gained his certificate from the Insolvency Court and he was declared solvent on condition he started to pay back his debts to his creditors as arranged in the hearing.

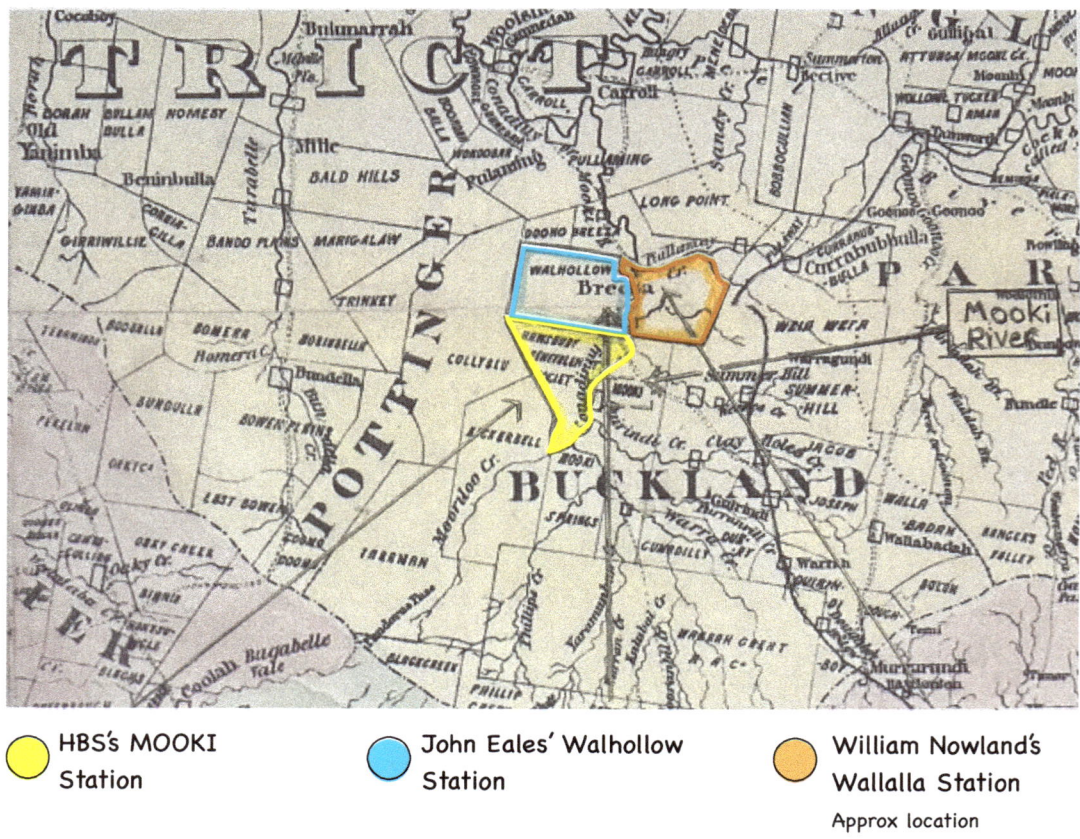

🟡 HBS's MOOKI Station   🔵 John Eales' Walhollow Station   🟠 William Nowland's Wallalla Station
Approx location

Figure 22: Relative Position of Mooki Station, Walhollow Station and Wallalla Station.

Death of William's Mother, 'Elizabeth Richards Nowland'

Three months and one week later after all the success in court, William's mother Elizabeth Richards (77 years) died in Wilberforce, on the 8th August 1852.[295]

Elizabeth is buried near her first husband Michael Nowland, at Wilberforce Cemetery (under the name Elizabeth Richards Nowland). Elizabeth's and Michael's daughter Ann (who died in 1819) is buried between them; three tombstones in a row.[296] There was no family notice for Elizabeth's death; one wonders why.

Death of Mary's Parents Robert and Anne Dyer Farlow

In the same year (1853) William's wife Mary lost both of her parents. The family notice read:

The Maitland Mercury and Hunter River General Advertiser –
25th June 1853, page 3.
Deaths

At his residence, Wilberforce, on the 22nd May, Robert Farlow Esq., aged 75 years; also, on the 13th June, Mrs. Farlow, [Anne Dyer] aged 75 years-much and deservedly regretted by a numerous circle of friends. They were the beloved parents of Mrs. H. Nowland of Muswellbrook, (Harriet) and Mrs. W. Nowland, of Falbrook [Mary]. [They are both buried at Wilberforce cemetery]

The deaths of William's mother and Mary's parents (1852–53) go a long way to explaining why the descriptors of William's location (1852–53) in his Insolvency Case read: 'William Nowland late of Singleton, now of Windsor'.

William's and Mary's Last Child Henry

In the same year (1853) William (49) and Mary (40) had their nineth surviving child (again a boy) Henry registered at Camberwell, and most likely, born at home, at Rosedale.[297]

Many of Henry's siblings were now: either working around Rosedale, when not going to school (John 9, Alex 7 and George 6); or venturing further afield onto the Liverpool Plains and the New England Tablelands, and sometimes taking the cattle down the Bulga Track (the drover's route) to the markets, in the Hawkesbury and possibly, on to Sydney (William jr. 21, Michael 19, Robert 17 and possibly, Charles 13 were most likely, doing all this droving). Only Alfred 2, and Henry, a baby, still needed care from their mother.

William Back in Court

In the same year (1853), and soon after William's mother-in-law's funeral, William was back in the Supreme Court over Wallalla. This time as the plaintiff. The summary of the court hearing published in the SMH on 27th June 1853 (*Nowland v Eales*), provides an insight into the behaviour between the original squatters and the wealthy and well-connected pastoralists who were now grazing their sheep across their large expansive land grants.

John Eales' Superintendent (Charles Humphrey) and what was left of Eales' indentured convict labour, demolished William's hut on the west side of the Mooki River and William took them to court.[298] As told below in the summary of the court case.

> *The Sydney Morning Herald, 27 June 1853, page 2.*
> *LAW INTELLEGIENCE*
> *SUPREME COURT.*
> *NISI PRIUS SITTINGS. [Unless before]*
> *Thursday, FRIDAY, AND SATURDAY.*
> *BEFORE Mr. Justice THERRY, and a Jury of three.*
> *NOWLAND v. EALES.*

This was an action for trespass on plaintiff's run [William's Nowland's run] Walhalla [Walhollow] on the river Mooki, Liverpool Plains. [William's station on the western side of Wallalla Station, next to Eales' Walhollow].[299]

The declaration, besides alleging a trespass by defendants' sheep [Eales' sheep], and the consequent driving away, &c of plaintiff's cattle [William Nowland's cattle], went on to aver [state] that defendant [John Eales], with a number of armed men had pulled down plaintiff's house [William Nowland's hut] and destroyed or damaged his furniture, &c. The pleas were 1 not guilty; 2, that plaintiff [William Nowland] was not legally possessed [of the run]; 3, that the close [the run] being the property of defendant [John Eales], and the house [actually a hut] erected thereon without his [John Eales] permission, he [John Eales] had requested plaintiff [William Nowland] to quit, and the latter having done so he [John Eales] (defendant) had peaceably removed this obstruction to the enjoyment of his rights.

Counsel for plaintiff [William Nowland] Messrs. Broadhurst and Meymott, attorney Mr. A. Little; counsel for defendant, Messrs. Foster and Darvall, attorney Mr. Daintry.

Although the trial of this case occupied three days, its main facts may be very briefly stated. This being one of that class of actions usually termed squatting cases, in which the principle question at issue was the priority of occupancy, there was a great deal of evidence on either side bearing upon this question. This was of a contradictory nature. On the one hand there was evidence that the land had been taken up as a cattle station so far back as 1828, and passed through various hands, without abandonment, until plaintiff [William Nowland] obtained possession in 1839 or 1840 [according to William SMH 1861, 1839] by purchasing the interest of the then occupants [according to William SMH, 1861, Messrs. Parrott and Ross]. The hut in question was built within sight of defendant's [Eales] head station, but on the opposite side of the river, and was erected in the place of a hut, put up by one of the earlier holders. Of the hut, therefore, there had not been continuous occupancy. The question of occupancy consequently rested almost exclusively upon the evidence as to the grazing of cattle on the one hand, and of sheep on the other. The evidence already alluded to, as to the occupancy of plaintiff [William Nowland] and of those through whom he claimed, was met by statements from defendant's [Eales] witnesses that there had been no continuous possession, but a clear abandonment of the run during a part of the time in question; and that it had been taken up as a part of the adjacent sheep station by a Mr. Uhr, from whom defendant [Eales] purchased. And further that the hut, which was destroyed had only been built and occupied since defendant's [William Nowland's] occupancy commenced; there having, when it so commenced, been no more than the frame of a hut standing on the spot.

There has, it seemed, been a long contest between the parties, [William Nowland and John Eales] each of whom pressed his own claim to the run, and treated, or claimed to treat the other as a trespasser. The officers of the Crown Lands department had been appealed to, and the final decision of the Chief Commissioner had been in favour of the defendant, [John Eales]. There was evidence that plaintiff [William Nowland] had in the first instance agreed to abide by this decision, and a letter announcing it was produced to him first before this hut was pulled down, at which time defendant [John Eales] made a formal demand for possession of the hut, or rather for the removal from it of plaintiff [William Nowland] and his effects. But the plaintiff [William Nowland] refused to abandon either the possession of the hut, or his claim to the run, and disputed the justice and impartiality of the decision on account of the defendant's [John Eales] intimacy with the Local Commissioners. [A view, William Nowland reiterates in his 'Letter to the Editor' SMH, 1861].

That the plaintiff's [William Nowland's] hut had been pulled down was an unquestioned fact. The dispute was as to how this was done. According to the plaintiff [William Nowland] the defendant and his men were somewhat the worse for liquor, and went to work in a violent reckless manner to demolish the whole place so soon as he (plaintiff) had refused to abandon possession, and his son [most likely, one of William's eldest sons: William jr.21, Michael 19 or Robert 17] had locked the door behind him to prevent entrance. According to the defendant, [John Eales] and to others who were present, the whole party were perfectly sober, and there was no more violence than was absolutely necessary in fact that the thing was done in a quiet and (so far as such a proceeding could be orderly) in an orderly manner.

There were some collateral points upon which evidence was elicited, such as the capacity of the run, the previous history and actings of the parties, &c. A question, was also raised as to whether, assuming the claim of the defendant [John Eales] to be good, he had not acted with an excess of violence in asserting this claim, and as to whether such excess was not in any event, a trespass, for which a verdict must pass against him [John Eales].

His HONOR told the Jury (after directing them upon the immaterial issues) that the sole question for their determination was as to which party had the priority of possession, coupled with a continuous subsequent occupation. If the plaintiff [William Nowland] had had an exclusive and uninterrupted possession during the time stated, then he was entitled to recover damages for the pulling down, of his hut, the damage to his property, and the trespass of defendant's [John Eales'] sheep. But if there had not been this exclusive and continuous possession; if there had been an abandonment of that possession, and during such abandonment the person through whom defendant [John Eales] claimed had entered upon its occupancy; then the defendant [John Eales] would be entitled to a verdict, having done no more than maintain his rights. There could not, of course, in such cases, be proof of exclusive possession in the strict literal sense of these terms for there were no fences or artificial boundaries, and struggling or wandering cattle might be found probably upon every run. It would be sufficient, therefore, to consider such possession as proved by the party who, in the opinion of the jury, had had prior occupation of this run, and had constantly, after such occupation, continued to deal with such run as part of his property, either by personal residence, or by the occupation of his servants, and by the constant feeding upon it of his cattle or sheep.

The Jury, after a good deal of consideration, found for the plaintiff [William Nowland], with £40 damages, for the destruction of the hut &c, but upon being requested to state how they found as to the possession, the foreman remarked that they could not determine this point. Some consultation ensued between Bench, Bar, and Jury during which the learned Judge reiterated his charge, that upon the question of possession alone must the verdict, in point of law, depend inasmuch (sic) as the plaintiff [William Nowland] would not be entitled to recover damages for the destruction of the hut, unless the Jury should find that he had proved his exclusive possession of the run upon which it was erected.

The Jury consulted still further, and there was also some additional discussion with counsel, in the course of which it was understood that the learned gentlemen who represented the plaintiff [William Nowland] were prepared to dispute the correctness of this part of his Honor's charge, and to maintain the right of the Jury to award damages for the destruction of the house, &c, even without finding that plaintiff [William Nowland] had proved exclusive possession of the run. Finally, the Jury adhered to their verdict, awarding £10 damages to plaintiff

[William Nowland] *for the destruction of his hut, &c; adding their opinion 'that the plaintiff [William Nowland] had exclusive possession of the hut, but not of the run, the latter having been used in common.'*

Court adjourned until ten o'clock on Monday (this) morning.

The Judge (Justice Therry) and a Jury of three, determined 'William had exclusive possession of the hut but not the run'. William was not satisfied with such a verdict. He was determined to gain official recognition, through the courts, of his claim on the land on which the hut stood.

So William went back to court, as the plaintiff. A month later with minimal success, he received greater compensation for the loss of his hut (this time, £40) while the land on which the hut was erected remained contested. See the summary of court hearing that follows.

Empire Sydney, 20 July 1853, page 3.
NOWLAND V. EALES.

This was a motion for a new trial. The action was of tres-pass, (sic) for breaking and entering a run belonging to the plaintiff, [William Nowland] called Walhalla [western side of Wallalla Station], in the Liverpool Plains District, and the plaintiff [William Nowland] claimed special damage for the forcible demolition by the defendant [John Eales] of a hut erected on the ground and of the property contained therein. The defendant [John Eales] pleaded several pleas, in addition to a denial of the trespass, the gist of the defence raised thereby being that the plaintiff [William Nowland] was not possessed of the run, in question. The evidence of possession was conflicting, the plaintiff [William Nowland] proving a devolution of the right thereto, from the party by whom the ground was originally taken up, and showing, that at all events, his possession of the hut had been uninterrupted; the defendant [John Eales] on the other hand, showing that the sheep of the parties through whom he claimed, had always fed over the ground in dispute.

The Jury found a verdict for the plaintiff [William Nowland], with £40 damages, and they found specially that there was no exclusive possession of the run either by the plaintiff [William Nowland] or the defendant [John Eales]. This verdict was impeached by the defendant, [John Eales] on the ground that it was against evidence, and against the weight of evidence.

Mr. BROADHURST and Mr. MEYNOTT appeared for the plaintiff [William Nowland], and Mr. FOSTER and Mr. Darvall for the defendant [John Eales].

The Court after hearing the defendant's [John Eales] council (sic), and without calling on the other side to support their verdict, at once decided that it ought to stand. The evidence was no doubt conflicting, and might be said to preponderate slightly in favour, of the defendant, [John Eales] but still there was sufficient evidence to justify the conclusion at which the jury had arrived, and the Court could not say that their verdict was demonstrably wrong. The motion for a new trial would therefore be refused.

William Decides to Write to Queen Victoria

Again, William failed to gain recognition of his possession of the land, on which his hut once stood. William had had enough, he was really frustrated, annoyed and convinced he was right. To prove his case, he decided to go to the highest authority and write to the Queen (Queen Victoria). You can hear him now *'This is not good enough! I will not stand for such injustice! I will write to the Queen!'*

William waited for an answer to his letter for at least three years. All was silent, until around 1856, when William received an adverse finding from the local authorities without explanation or any knowledge of what was contained in the correspondence between London and the local authorities. So, he approached his local member, Richard Jones a member of the Legislative Assembly who represented Durham (William's County).[300]

What happened next is intriguing and positioned later in William's story in the year that it occurred (1856).

CHAPTER 20

CAMBERWELL IN THE 1850S

When William was before the courts (in the early 1850s) he was still putting a lot of time and energy into the development of Camberwell. Ten years had passed, since Camberwell was declared a site for a township. Camberwell had an inn, a large and impressive church on a hillock (though, still not complete inside), a village reserve (or green), a blacksmith's shop, and most likely, a general store. The Great Northern Road went through the town and coaches stopped at the inn. Horse races and local cricket matches were held periodically on the village green, the congregation at St Clement's was growing, and the blacksmith shop and the assumed general store had adequate patronage.[301]

The Schoolhouse in Camberwell

In the early 1850s, the discussion in Camberwell was all about the need for a larger schoolhouse for the growing number of school-aged children.[302] The first schoolhouse built circa 1840 was a one room timber slab building; a church school probably built by William and his fellow Church of England petitioners.[303] By 1853, this church school was too small for the 34 school-aged children who attended. William (who probably had three of his own children at the school (John 9, Alex 7, and George 6) suggested a building he had, as an alternative larger schoolhouse. The town took up the offer and William's 'iron-house' became the school building. See the article that follows.

Falbrook Public School (1853–1855)[304]

In December 1853, the Falbrook Public School was opened in a building which was made available by William Nowland and "put into a proper state of repair by the united and personal exertion of some of the patrons".[305]

When the children were examined in July 1854 their "clean, smart, orderly appearance" was highly commended, and the school declared to be "an invaluable blessing to the locality". Thirty-four children were enrolled, and it was noted, numbers were "slowly and steadily increasing".[306]

In June, the following year, [1855] the Government acquired two acres of land "as a site for a National School.[307] The intended new school site [located at the] … corner of Glennie and Dawson Streets [Camberwell].

[In August 1855, William advertised the sale of the allotment where 'Falbrook Public School' was located and based on this knowledge it is assumed the National School was built within a couple of months]

The new [National] school was constructed of studs and weatherboard and was unlined.

This new National School system provided the foundations for a uniformed educational system, with a standardised curriculum and monetary encouragement from the Board of National Education (established in January 1848, by Governor FitzRoy) for school-aged children to attend school. Prior to this new system of education, the schooling of children depended upon the initiatives taken by the local community to establish and develop their own local Church school.[308]

Governor FitzRoy departed the colony seven years after the establishment of the National Schools and his replacement Sir William Thomas Denison (20th January 1855 to 22nd January 1861) amongst other endeavours, continued to foster the development of this new system of education.[309]

Under Governor Denison the colony entered a period of stability and progress, and William once again turned his attention to the growth and development of the small community of Camberwell.

William's Town Allotments

In 1855, William purchased a significant number of town allotments in Camberwell; 30 in total, as recorded in the *Government Gazette Notices* that follow.

Government Gazette Notices – New South Wales Government Gazette,
20 March 1855, page 988
Registry of Deeds Office, Supreme Court
Sydney, 27th March, 1855.
TITLE DEEDS.

THE Deeds specified in the annexed list having been enrolled in this Office, under the provision of the Act of the Governor and Legislative Council, 13th Victoria, No. 45, have been transmitted to the Surveyor General to be forwarded to the Colonial Treasurer for delivery to the Grantees.

ALFRED ELYARD,

Registrar of Deeds.

COUNTRY LOTS.

74. William Nowland, Camberwell, 2 roods.

[a rood is one quarter of an acre]

75. Ditto, ditto, 2 roods.

76. Ditto, ditto, 2 roods.

77. Ditto, ditto, 2 roods.

78. Ditto, ditto, 2 roods.

79. Ditto, ditto, 2 roods.

80. Ditto, ditto, 2 roods.

81. Ditto, ditto, 2 roods.

82. Ditto, ditto, 2 roods.

83. Ditto, ditto, 2 roods.

84. William Nowland, Camberwell, 2 roods.

85. Ditto, ditto, 1 rood 36 perches. [a perch is 16.5 feet]

86. Ditto, ditto, 1 rood 36 perches.

87. Ditto, ditto, 1 rood 36 perches.

88. Ditto, ditto, 1 rood 37 perches.

89. Ditto, ditto; 1 rood 39 perches.

90. Ditto, ditto, 1 rood 32 perches.

91. Ditto, ditto, 1 rood 23 perches.

92. Ditto, ditto, 1 rood 11 perches.

93. Ditto, ditto, 1 rood 20 perches.

94. Ditto, ditto, 1 rood 24 perches.

95. Ditto, ditto, 1 rood 38 perches……

And on the 6 April 1855, as follows:

Government Gazette Notices – New South Wales
Government Gazette – 6 April 1855, page 1040.
Registry of Deeds' Office, Supreme Court,
Sydney, 3rd April, 1855.

TITLE DEEDS

TOWN LOTS ...

9. William Nowland, Camberwell, 2 roods.

10. Ditto, ditto, 2 roods.

11. Ditto, ditto, 2 roods.

12. Ditto, ditto, 2 roods.

13. Ditto, ditto, 2 roods.

14. Ditto, ditto, 2 roods.

15. Ditto, ditto, 2 roods.

16. Ditto, ditto, 2 roods.

17. Ditto, ditto, 2 roods.

The next figure provides a street map of William's 30 town allotments. (Figure 23).

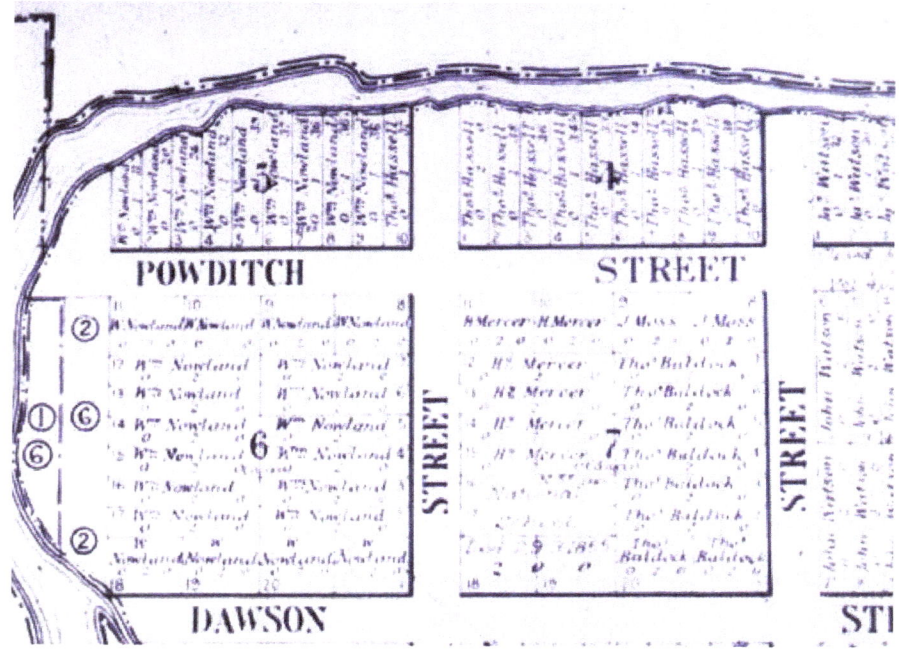

Figure 23: William Nowland's 30 Town Allotments.
Powditch St (10 allots.) and Dawson St (20 allots).

Death of William's Brother Michael jr.

The year before William purchased his 30 town allotments, William (maybe with Mary, and some of the family) most likely, returned to Wilberforce. William's brother Michael jr. (61, on his gravestone) died at Wilberforce on the 27th October 1854.[310] The family notice for Michael jr. read.

The Sydney Morning Herald, 16 November 1854, page 8.

At his late residence, Wilberforce, on the 27th October, 1854, in the 60th year of his age, Mr. Michael Nowland, much respected and deservedly regretted by a numerous circle of relatives and friends, who will long remember his kind and benevolent disposition.[311]

Within two years (1852–1854), William had lost his mother (Elizabeth, in 1852) and his brother (Michael jr., in 1854) and Mary had lost both her parents (Robert and Anne Farlow, both, in 1853).

After Michael jr.'s death (in 1854) William (50) had four surviving siblings: Henry (58) who lived in Musellbrook; Elizabeth jr. (56) who lived in Wilberforce; Mary (45) who lived in Scone; and, Sarah (40) who lived in Sydney.

William's Warning to Those Who Trespass on Walhallow Station or Mooki Station

The following year (1855) William warned others that he would take them to court it they trespassed 'in search of stray horses and cattle on Walhallow Station on the Mooki River and Mooki Station', without first gaining permission from the person in charge. William's ad read:

The Maitland Mercury and Hunter River General Advertiser,
24 February 1855, page 1
[The ad repeated on the 3rd March, 1855,
The Maitland Mercury, page 2]
Ten Pounds Reward.

WHEREAS, two of my STOCK HORSES, on the Mooki Run, were RIDDEN and one of them BROKEN DOWN in the month of January last, in the absence of my sons.[312] *Any one (sic) giving me the information, and prosecuting to conviction the party or parties so riding them, will receive the above reward of Ten Pounds. The names of the horses are the Doctor and Spring, both well known in the district. And I hereby caution all parties, unless the owners of adjacent runs, from TRESPASSING on the WALHOLLOW STATION, on the Mooki River, and the station known as the MOOKI STATION, after stray cattle or horses, without first asking permission from the person in charge, otherwise they will be prosecuted, according to law.*

WILLIAM NOWLAND

Falbrook, February 20.

How curious and confusing. In the above ad, William named the west side of Wallalla, 'Walhollow Station'. No wonder the courts were bemused by where the boundaries were between William's Wallalla Station and John Eales' Walhallow Station, as detailed in the following chapter.

CHAPTER 21

William Back in Court

In June 1855, William was summoned once again to the Supreme Court. This time by Arthur Dight who claimed William had cattle on Wallalla Station that were the property of William White (now deceased).[313]

It had been almost six years since the *Booth v Nowland* case (in 1849) re Patrick White's cattle, where William had to pay £100 in damages to John Booth. Now, Arthur Dight placed a similar claim before the Supreme Court re the cattle of Patrick White's brother William White (also deceased).

Before the court hearing, William paid Arthur Dight £120 in what William thought was a negotiated settlement, but this amount of money was not enough to satisfy Arthur Dight, who took William to the Supreme Court to secure a larger payment. The judgment against William required him to pay another £165 (based on the estimated size of William White's herd); in total William paid £285 for William White's cattle. A summary of these points in the hearing follows; plus the 'shifty case' of another £50.

The Maitland Mercury and Hunter River General Advertiser,
27 June 1855, page 2.
SUPREME COURT.
SATURDAY, June 23, 1855.
(From the S. M. Herald.)
(Before Mr. Justice Dickinson and a jury of four.)
DIGHT V. NOWLAND

This was an action of a drover for cattle: plea the general issue. Messrs. Darvall and Wise appeared for the plaintiff [Arthur Dight]; and Mr. Broadhurst for the defendant [William Nowland]. There was, substantially, no defence (sic) to this action, the only contest being as to the amount which the plaintiff [Dight] was entitled to recover.

The circumstances were these:— A herd of cattle branded WWW, which belonged to the estate of one William White, who had died intestate, were for sale in the hands of the agent of the Curator of Intestate Estates, one Lindsey, who was also clerk to the bench at Murrurundi. They then running on the station of Mr. Nowland [Wallalla Station], the defendant in this suit, their precise number being unknown. The right to the whole herd, or in technical terms the right to the brand was sold by Lindsey to Mr. Herring, who was the agent for Mr. Arthur Dight, the plaintiff within the suit, for £50. But a sum of £120 was offered by Mr. Nowland to the curator [Lindsey] of Intestate Estates for the purchase of the herd, and after some correspondence Lindsey was instructed to accept this offer if he had not already closed with Herring. He had closed with Herring, and had received the money, but he nevertheless took the £120 of Mr. Nowland, who, conceiving that he had purchased the cattle, determined to retain them. The contest was to the number of the animals and their value. There appeared to be under 100 head, but there was a fair proportion of fat cattle, some of which had brought £2 10s per head for boiling down. His honor having told the jury that the only question which remained for their consideration was the amount of damages, they found a verdict for the plaintiff; damages, £165.

William paid what was required, and secured William White's '100 head of cattle' for £285.

William's Management of Mooki Station

The following December (1855), William's management as the Superintendent of Mooki Station was called into question at a special general meeting of the Hawkesbury Benevolent Society. Fifteen members of the Society were present, and William survived the vote: eight for William staying on as superintendent, and seven against. A summary of the views of some of the members that attended the meeting were all in the papers, for everyone to see. See below.

The Sydney Morning Herald, 17 December 1855, page 9.

HAWKESBURY BENEVOLENT SOCIETY. — *A special general meeting of the subscribers to this institution was held at the Asylum in Macquarie-street, on Wednesday last [the 12th December], for the purpose of taking into consideration certain proposed changes with reference to the appointment of a superintendent of stock.*

There were very few numbers present [15]. Mr. James Hale president took the chair and explained the objects of the meeting. The secretary, Mr. Walker, read the minutes of the preceding committee meeting, from which it appeared that, certain alleged delinquencies having come to their ears respecting the management of the Society's cattle, by Mr. Nowland, the superintendent, it was resolved to remove him from his office on the 31st of January next, and to appoint a Mr. Reynolds [Richard Reynolds] in his stead.[314] *The resolutions of the committee, however, required the approbation of a general meeting, as provided by the Act of Incorporation, and hence the present meeting was called.*

Mr. Nowland appeared at the meeting and offered an explanation of his conduct. Certain members, however, did not think it satisfactory, and a motion was proposed by Mr. B. Stewart, seconded by Mr. John Galloway, that the resolutions of the committee of management, passed on the 14th of November ultimo, respecting a change in the appointment of superintendent of stock, be approved and confirmed.

No amendment was proposed, but one of the members present expressed his disapproval of any change, on the ground that Mr. Nowland had been rather suddenly dealt with. Besides the proposed new superintendent [Richard Reynolds] had always acted in an inimical manner respecting the Society's run, at Mooki, Liverpool Plains. The chairmen put the motion to the meeting, when there was found to be seven for, and eight against it. The motion was therefore declared lost; and things remain as they were. Mr. Nowland, however, stated that on the 31st of July, he would be prepared to give up the stock and resign his charge, if requested.

William's place as the Superintendent of the HBS's cattle on Mooki Station (given the vote) was still secure, yet tentative, and his suggested replacement, Richard Reynolds, enters his story.[315]

Another Round in the Courts re Wallalla Station

Fifteen months later (on 16th September 1856) William was back in court. This time, Richard Reynolds (the plaintiff) argued a case re his (Reynold's) ownership and rightful possession of part of the HBS's Mooki Station.

The first hearing in the case (on the 16th September) is detailed and lengthy and has already been cited in part, earlier in William's story, because the hearing provided a retrospective on the HBS's Mooki Station when William's brother Edward was the Superintendent (c.1835–1842, see chapter 10).

The second and final hearing and judgment occurred three days later (on the 19th September 1856) with the final hearing focused on whether Richard Reynolds or the HBS had exclusive possession of the land where William was grazing his cattle.

William's defence in the case was he had permission from the HBS to graze his cattle on Mooki Station and he had been grazing his stock on the Society's land and not on Reynolds' Station. William could not convince the jury; he lost the case and was ordered to pay Richard Reynolds (the plaintiff) £300 in damages.[316]

The summary of the final hearing follows.

The Sydney Morning Herald, 19 September 1856, page 8.
MAITLAND CIRCUIT COURT
(Abridged from the Maitland Mercury)
Tuesday, September 16.
Before the Chief Justice and a Special Jury of four.
Reynolds v Nowland

This case was resumed, and three additional witnesses, Michael Nowland [William's son now 22], William Singleton, and John Single, called for the defence [William Nowland]. Mr. Manning called for the plaintiff [Richard Reynolds], in reply, Thomas Hutchins, Richard Reynolds [most likely, Richard Reynold's son], and David Charles, Frederick Scott, the latter in reference to his belief of the credibility of defendant [William Nowland sr.] as a witness.[317]

Mr. Darvall then addressed the jury for the defendant [William Nowland sr.] on this new evidence. Mr. Manning replied. His Honor told the jury that this, like numerous other squatting cases, was a possessory action, with which the question of title was not connected. The defendant [William Nowland sr.] did not dispute that he had been on the Mooki [with his own cattle] but denied that plaintiff [Richard Reynolds] had been at the time in exclusive possession.

This was the first issue to try. The evidence tracing the possession from one party to another only bore upon the probabilities of the exclusive possession. It was not for the judge to say when continued trespass might acquire the character of mixed possession; but the question was for the jury to determine.[318]

The defendant [William Nowland sr.] said, secondly, that not only was plaintiff [Richard Reynolds] not in exclusive possession, but that the society [HBS] was, and that he acted as their servant and with their permission [to graze his cattle on Mooki Station].

The question was, did the defendant [William Nowland sr.] act on behalf of the society [HBS], at the time having exclusive possession. If the jury did not find that the plaintiff [Richard Reynolds] had exclusive possession, they must find a verdict for the defendant [William Nowland sr.] on the first issue; if they did not find exclusive possession on the part of the society, they must return a verdict for the plaintiff [Richard Reynolds] on the second issue.

In the first case [the HBS had exclusive possession] there would be no damages; the second issue [Richard Reynolds had exclusive possession] would affect the question of costs. If the exclusive possession by plaintiff [Richard Reynolds] were found proved, the jury must find a verdict for him.

His Honor concluded with a reference to the serious nature of the contradictions in the evidence in this case. The jury retired for an hour and a-half, and returned a verdict for the plaintiff [Richard Reynolds]; damages £300.

This court case brought into question the boundaries of Mooki Station. Richard Reynolds had won in the Supreme Court on the grounds that he had exclusive possession of the land where William grazed his cattle. For William the judgment was not just a case in point. It could act as a precedent and undermine his position on Wallalla Station and his call for the courts to recognise the boundaries of Wallalla, as per his lease.

William's Case for Wallalla Station Presented to the Legislative Council

John Eales had already questioned the boundaries of Wallalla on the western side of the Mooki River and William needed to resolve the matter. William's petition to Queen Victoria (re Wallalla Station) had failed, so as told earlier, he approached Richard Jones a member of the Legislative Assembly who represented Durham (William's County).[319]

Jones took up William's case and presented a motion on William's behalf in the Legislative Assembly in October 1856. See below.

Empire – 1 November 1856, page 2.
LEGISLATIVE ASSEMBLY.
Friday, OCTOBER 31, 1856.
The SPEAKER took the chair at half-past three o'clock
… THE CASE OF WILLIAM NOWLAND

Mr. JONES stated that some two or three years ago [1853 or 1854] William Nowland, grazier,[320] believing that he had sustained some injury by the Government authorities, sent a petition to the Queen [Queen Victoria], with an address on the subject of dispute between him and the Government. A direct answer had not been sent out, but certain queries had been sent out to the local authorities for information about the case, with an intimation that the decision of the Home Government would be based on that information. The information had been furnished, and the decision given, which was adverse, to Nowland.

[William] Nowland was under the impression that the information which had been supplied by the local authorities was not altogether a fair representation of the case, and he wished to ascertain the nature of that information; that was the reason he was so anxious that the papers asked for should be made public.

He (Richard Jones) presumed that the Government would not feel any difficulty in the production of the papers. He would now move, – "That an address be presented to his Excellency the Governor-General, praying that his Excellency will cause to be laid on the table of this house, copies of all correspondence between the colonial Government and the Secretary of State for the colonies, with reference to a petition of William Nowland, grazier, of Falbrook, to her Most Gracious Majesty the Queen [Queen Victoria], on the subject of his claim to the station on Liverpool Plains called Wolalla (sic)[Wallalla]"

Mr. HAY [Sir John Hay] [321] *said there could be no objection whatever to the production of the papers asked for by the honorable member. But as they were very voluminous, he trusted that if they were laid upon the table of the house, it would be quite sufficient to answer all purposes, without having them printed.*

The question was then put and passed.

What was in the 'voluminous correspondence' and whether it was ever displayed 'on the tables' in the Legislative Assembly is unknown. William had to wait for almost another two years before he heard any more about the boundaries of Wallalla Station and whether he was entitled to this very rich fertile grazing land. Yet the delay did not dissuade William. He remained emphatic in his approach to 'his' Wallalla Station. William just got on with what he had always done at Wallalla Station for the last 16 years: grazing his stock; impounding the stock of others (cattle, sheep, and horses) when they strayed on to 'his station'; and, when his cattle were fat enough, rounding them up and taking them to market. William's warnings to others continued to appear in the local paper. See below.

The Maitland Mercury and Hunter River General Advertiser,
31 January 1857, page 1
Wallalla Station, Mooki River,
LIVERPOOL PLAINS.

ALL PERSONS are hereby cautioned to REMOVE their CATTLE, SHEEP, and HORSES from the above station, as from and after the first day of February next, I shall Impound (sic) all stock found trespassing thereon.

WILLIAM NOWLAND.

Glennie's (sic) Creek, 15th Jan.

William's Employment with the HBS Terminated

The following February (1857), in the annual meeting of the HBS (which William attended) the Society terminated William's employment as Superintendent of Mooki Station based on the following claims, aired in the meeting: William had over-stocked Mooki Station with his own cattle; involved the Society in disputes and differences with their neighbours (exemplified in the *Reynolds v Nowland* case); been neglectful of the HBS's cattle by allowing them to stray on to the neighbours' stations, with one of the neighbours writing to the HBS and threatening legal action. All these pronouncements were written up in the SMH as detailed in the following account.

The Sydney Morning Herald, 12 February 1857, page 8.
WINDSOR
THE HAWKESBURY BENEVOLENT SOCIETY.
[FROM OUR CORRESPONDENT].

PURSUANT to advertisement, and in accordance with the terms of the Act of Incorporation, the annual meeting of the subscribers to the above institution took place on Monday last, at noon, at the Hospital Buildings, Macquarie-street. There was a numerous and respectable body of subscribers present. Mr. James Hale, of Fairfield, president, took the chair, and having shortly stated the purport of the meeting, called upon the Secretary to read the report of the Committee for the past year.

Mr. WILLIAM WALKER then read and submitted to the meeting the following REPORT.

… Your committee have next to recur with regret to the difficulties and complications so long attendant upon the occupation of the Society's station [Mooki Station]. Mr. Richard Reynolds, one of the parties who has hitherto set up a claim to the whole or part of the Society's run at Mooki, Liverpool Plains, recently [September 1856] commenced and prosecuted an action against your superintendent, Mr. William Nowland, for the trespass of the cattle of the latter upon the alleged run of the former, part of which is said to be Mooki. Mr. Nowland having stated that the Society's right to their run would be to some extent mixed up with the proceedings, he applied to your committee for assistance in the matter; but your committee conceiving that the rights of the Society could not be affected by a dispute between Mr. Reynolds and Mr. Nowland, declined involving the Society in the affair. However, believing that Mr. Reynolds was somewhat actuated by adverse motives to the Society;[322] whilst the committee felt friendly disposed towards their employe (sic), Mr. Nowland, they so far acceded to the wish of the latter for assistance as to grant his solicitor the loan of some of the official documents relating to the run belonging to the Society; but further to this your committee declined to go.

Your committee need scarcely state that the trial resulted unfavourably to Mr. Nowland, the court holding that, whatever superior rights the Society might or might not have over the run, in dispute to Mr. Reynolds, Mr. Nowland individually had no title whatever. These unhappy differences, however, have tended to plunge the position of the Society in regard to then run (in the continued absence of any settlement of the disputes by the Government) into further difficulty and incertitude, and have been a subject of much concern and uneasiness to your committee during the past year. Added to this, complaints have reached your committee of the conduct of Mr. Nowland, as the superintendent, in over-stocking the run with his own cattle, and involving the Society in disputes and differences with the neighbouring proprietors.

In these circumstances your committee, through their secretary, first wrote to Mr. Nowland in July last [before the case against Reynolds], stating that, in accordance with his own proposition at a former general meeting, they would be willing to relieve him of his situation at the end of three months from his then current half-year's engagement.

To this proposal, however, Mr. Nowland paid no attention, and further complaints having reached the committee of irregularities committed by him, and the Society having been threatened with legal proceeding by one of the adjacent graziers, inconsequence of alleged neglect on his part in permitting the Society's cattle to commit trespass, your committee on the 12th of November last, unanimously resolved that it was expedient for the interests of the Society, and in order if possible to terminate all further causes of complaint, to remove Mr. Nowland from his situation on and after the 31st day of January, 1857, when his current half-year expired, and Mr. Nowland was written to accordingly. Your committee further resolved to advertise for a suitable person as superintendent, to supply Mr. Nowland's place, which having been done, a considerable number of tenders were sent in.

These were opened by the committee on the 10th of December last, when it appeared that the several parties tendering, were willing to perform the duties at salaries ranging from £700 to £300 per annum. A tender was also received from Mr. Nowland offering to continue his services at £200 per annum, upon condition of his cattle and the Society's running mutually upon the Mooki run, and a run called Wallala (sic) [Wallalla] said by Mr. Nowland to belong to him. [Again, William's licence for Wallalla and the boundaries of Wallalla were being covertly questioned].

At the same time, a tender was received from Mr. Andrew Loder offering to rent the Society's cattle with the use of the run for three or five years, at the rate of £10 per hundred head, payable half-yearly in advance, for all delivered, and to return the same number (sex and ages) at the expiration of the agreement to the Society at Mooki.

The committee after carefully considering the various offers came to the conclusion that Mr. Loder's (though differing from their original requirements) was the most eligible and satisfactory proposal, inasmuch as they believed, by such a method, a sum would be annually received by the Society equaling, if not exceeding, what they might reasonably expect from personal management, whilst it would no *doubt put an end to differences with superintendents, and probably (at least for some time) obviate all further disputes with the proprietor of contiguous runs…*

…It was as follows:– "That this meeting approves of and confirms the proceedings of the committee as detailed in the report relative to the removal of Mr. Nowland as superintendent of stock, and hereby authorises the successors to complete the arrangements entered into with Mr. Andrew Loder to lease the Society's cattle and run for a term of years, or otherwise in the discretion of the committee to appoint another superintendent in Mr. Nowland's stead [place].[323]

Mr. WILLIAM ABRAHAM seconded the motion, when Mr. NOWLAND, who was present, rose and protested vehemently against it. He said if the arrangement with Mr. Loder were carried out, it would be at the loss of the Society's run, for he believed there was a combination between him and Messrs. Reynolds and Humphries to get possession of it by some means or other [William was right, given the Society's loss of a large portion the station to Richard Reynold's widow in 1862].

He [William Nowland] said he had been shamefully used by the Society and challenged them to prove that he had overstocked their run with his own cattle. He had not more than 600 cattle altogether at Liverpool Plains, [on the Mooki and Wallalla Stations] and he paid £52 a year for a license [for Wallalla]. The committee had been led away by false reports from Mr. Loder and others, who had been uniting against him.

Mr. HALE, the President, said that Mr. Loder had never made the least allusion to, or complaint against Mr. Nowland, in the negotiations that had taken place between him and the committee; and as to the charge of overstocking the Society's run, he (Nowland) acknowledged to having recently put 500 head upon it; besides, it came out in evidence at the trial [Reynolds v Nowland, Sept 1856] that he [William Nowland] had ten of his own to one of the Society's cattle running at Mooki.

Mr. NOWLAND; That was Mr. Loder's evidence; but it was false. [As far as William was concerned, the falsehoods in the 'Reynolds v Nowland' case was being used against him]

Mr. LODER said it was not his evidence; and it was well known that his sheep station was sixteen miles from the Society's hut, and he had no wish whatever to unite his run with the Society's.

The resolution was then put to the meeting and carried – without dissent.

The Potential for Accounts in the Newspaper to Tarnish One's Reputation

The above account provides an insight into how court hearings and the summaries in the local newspapers could potentially tarnish your reputation. Five months after the *Reynolds v Nowland* case, the same matters were raised again at the HBS's annual meeting and the members present at the meeting appear to be influenced by this court case. As far as they were concerned, William had overstocked Mooki Station with his own cattle, and through neglect, allowed the HBS stock to stray onto other stations; with some of the neighbours, threatening litigation. Most likely, given the press and the judgment in the *Reynolds v Nowland* case, William was probably considered to be too much of a liability to continue as the Society's Superintendent.

What was said about a person in the courts and in the papers could undermine their reputation and livelihood. Those with concerns wrote to the editor of the paper of their choice, and then waited (with expectation) for their letter, stating their position and defending their reputation, to appear hopefully in full in the paper.

Following the above meeting of the HBS, Richard Reynolds (not William) wrote to the *Maitland Mercury* and stated his concern about William Walker's statement in the minutes of the meeting that 'his [Richard Reynolds] motives were 'adverse to the society'.[324]

In the letter that follows, Reynolds defends his position, questions the boundaries of Mooki Station and gives us a further insight into the *Reynolds v Nowland* case re Mooki Station. William (according to Richard Reynolds) did not gain any assistance from the HBS in defending their case and was required to pay £300 in damages, from his own pocket.[325]

Richard Reynolds' Letter to the Editor, follows.

The Maitland Mercury and Hunter River General Advertiser,
26 February 1857
To the Editors of the Maitland Mercury.

GENTLEMEN – *Having noticed in your issue of the 14th instant an abridged report of the Hawkesbury Benevolent Society's annual meeting, I trust you will permit me to make a few remarks thereon in your valuable columns.*

After stating to their subscribers that their superintendent, Mr. Nowland [William Nowland] was defeated in the late action of Reynolds v. Nowland, which one ever doubted that knew the whole circumstances of the case, the report goes on to state, that "Believing Mr. Reynolds to be actuated by motives adverse to the society."

Now, how could they entertain any such idea, when the whole of my letters to them for the last twelve or more years have been written in the friendly spirit. From interested motives, they may say. I at once admit the fact; but it was much more their interest, they having so many more cattle. But had my letters been acted on in the spirit in which they were written, the monstrous trespass, by which I have been so seriously injured, would years ago have been put an end to. Had I been actuated by "adverse motives," as they state, they would have been the nominal as well as the real defendants (which I contend they were) in the late notion.

The report states that the committee took "no part in the late action;" if so, why was the defendant's [William Nowland's] attorney allowed to ransack their office and the Government offices for all papers that he thought would aid his case? Why was a certain paper produced which they, in an unwary moment cunningly induced me to sign under the pledge of the word and honor of these gentlemen that it should never go into any court to my prejudice? when lo! and behold! this was about the first paper produced.

It was really pleasing to notice the triumphant smile that passed over the fine features of the opposing counsel when he heard my brother pronounce the signature to be mine. So much for the word and honor of those gentlemen. It is true, they sent no witnesses, having none to send; that portion of the defence being left to Mr. Nowland [William], the whole of whose witnesses came, not to disprove his trespass, but to disprove my right to the run in which they signally failed. So much for their neutrality.

They next state that they have appealed to the Government to define their boundaries. This, indeed, shows the weakness of their case, when they are obliged to appeal to the strong arm of power (assuming for a moment they possess the power) to deprive the weak of his just and proved rights; but the Government know just as much of the late Burns' boundary lines as Mr. Nowland [William] does, which is nothing at all.[326]

It is very easy for the Government surveyor to run the lines as described by Mr. Nowland [William], which includes two entire stations and a very large slice of two others. It is palpably absurd to suppose that any private society or individual can come into a district, every acre of which is taken up and occupied, and quietly sit down with the enormous claim of Eighty Thousand Acres, to the expulsion of those who had risked their lives to obtain it; and I am perfectly satisfied that the Government, if they could act upon irresponsible power, would not be unjust enough to do so in this instance.

To inform the Government that they cannot keep their cattle without this run would be untrue, as I have tendered for them four times, and, I believe, each time lower than any others [at a lower price], as being on my run they would suit me best; and there are impartial persons who are silly enough to think that he who feeds them has the best right to any small emolument arising from their management. But no, any one (sic) but me, because I have dared so far to prevent their wresting my just rights from me.

Apologising for taking up so much of your space, I remain, gentlemen, your obedient servant,

RICHARD REYNOLDS. *Feb. 10, 1857.*

The ill-defined and disputed runs and stations laid the foundations for letters such as the one above. The court hearings were full of witnesses who based their evidence on hearsay and innuendo because the descriptors in the *Government Gazette* (1849) of runs/stations (like William Nowland's Wallalla and John Eales' Walhollow) could not be mapped; then or now.

No wonder there were disputed boundaries and mixed possession. When a dispute came before the court, the judgment was largely based on innuendo, influence, connection and networking.

William Just Got On With His Life

William was not fazed by all the 'argy-bargy'. Shortly after being dismissed as Superintendent of Mooki Station (February 1857) William advertised store cattle for sale.[327] See the ad that follows.

The Maitland Mercury and Hunter River General Advertiser –
10 March 1857, page 3
CATTLE FOR SALE.

On the Mooki Station, Liverpool Plains. A prime lot of STORE CATTLE, bullocks two years old and upwards, at £3 per head; cows, two years old and upwards, £1 10s. If the purchaser is not prepared with cash, good approved bills will be taken for six and twelve months, at six per cent interest. Some of the above mentioned cattle are nearly fit for the butcher. They can be delivered in a week's notice. All applications to be made to the undersigned, at Falbrook, near Singleton.

WILLIAM NOWLAND.

March 9.

Most likely, the store cattle were part of the stock William needed to remove from Mooki Station before Andrew Loder took over as Superintendent. If the buyer did not have the ready cash William was prepared to take 'approved bills' that guaranteed payment at an agreed date at 'six percent interest'.

William had lost the convenience of grazing his stock at Mooki Station and most importantly, the income of £200 p.a. for managing the HBS's stock; a position he had held for nearly fourteen years (circa June 1843 – February 1857).

William most likely moved his stock from Mooki Station to one of his properties or he spread them across all three: Wallalla Station (87,040 acres); Ward's Mistake (now 81,920 acres); and the family estate, Rosedale (1557 acres).

William's and Mary's Boys were Old Enough to Become Pastoralists in Their Own Right

By this time (March 1857), at least four of William's and Mary's boys were old enough to help their father William sr. at Wallalla and Ward's Mistake. Periodically, they probably ventured out alone or together, to check on these two stations; William jr. 25, Michael 23, Robert 21, Charles 17, and possibly, John 15; while Alex, the next in line, now 11, was probably still mastering the common farming tasks around the family farm of Rosedale and maybe, occasionally, going to the family's cattle/sheep stations.

William Back in Court

Seven months after William lost his position as the Superintendent of Mooki Station he was back in court. William's possession of the western side of Wallalla Station was being questioned once more, this time by Samuel Clift.[328]

Samuel Clift was given permission by John Eales to graze his cattle on Walhollow Station and found his cattle mixed in with William Nowland's on what William claimed was the western side of Wallalla Station. A map of the relative location of William's Wallalla Station and Samuel Clift's Doona Station can be found overleaf (see Figure 24).[329]

Whether William had legal possession of the western side of Wallalla Station was challenged once again. This time by Samuel Clift who questioned William, on the matter; Did William have prior possession and/or exclusive possession of Wallalla Station? Had William abandoned the run/station for long periods of time (known as abandonment)? And did William have continuous possession of the area in dispute? Samuel Clift took William to court on this basis and after several court hearings a final judgment was made with £250 in damages awarded to Clift. A summary of the final judgment follows.

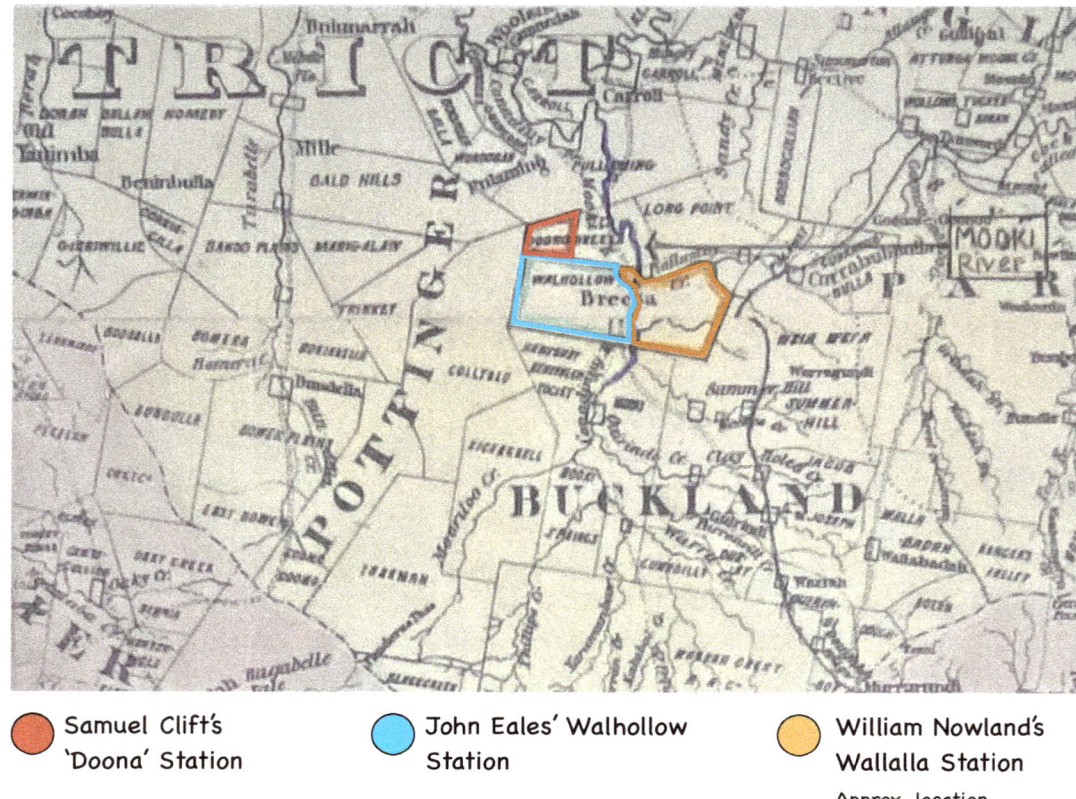

Figure 24: Location of Wallalla Station in Relation to Walhollow Station and Doona Station (spelt Doono on the map)

Northern Times, 26 September 1857, page 1
TUESDAY SEPTEMBER 24TH
CLIFT V NOWLAND

In this case his Honour summed up the evidence and laid down the law to the Jury. The question the jury had to consider was, who first had possession of the run, and whether the right of occupancy had been correctly traced.

He need scarcely state that no attention ought to be paid to the relative social position of the parties before the court.[330]

The comparative wealth of the parties ought not to affect the issue. The rule usually observed in criminal cases did not apply to civil ones. In the former case, if there remained a doubt after the evidence had been properly balanced, the benefit of that doubt was mercifully given to the prisoner, but in civil cases the rule was different. If the jury had nine reasons for giving a verdict for the plaintiff [Samuel Clift], and ten for giving a verdict for the defendant [William Nowland], they were bound to give the defendant [William Nowland] the benefit of that reason, and vice versa.

The smallness of the sum given or alleged to have been given by Mr. Clift for the run, was a circumstance not material to the trial. They all knew that in this colony great bargains were occasionally to be had, and that this had been specially the case in the early days of the colony. As an example, he might allude to ten acres of land in Sydney, which he knew to be now worth £200,000, and which were originally purchased for a puncheon of rum.

His Honour then commented on the evidence. It was conflicting on all the points material to the issue. The alleged boundaries of the run, the right of occupancy, the transfer of right, and in fact all the points mooted, during the trial, have been disputed, and with respect to all of them the evidence is conflicting. His Honour then proceeded to show how and wherein the evidence was contradictory.

The jury then retired, and after a consultation which lasted about two hours, they returned a verdict in favour of the plaintiff [Samuel Clift] — on the first count [possession of the run], damages £50, and on the other counts [whether the right of occupancy had been correctly traced], damages £200.

William was out of pocket (in theory) a further £250. Though he probably never paid the damages because he took Samuel Clift, straight back to court. This time, William was the plaintiff, on exactly the same matter. See below.

Northern Times, 26 September 1857, page 1
NOWLAND V CLIFT
(Before his Honour Mr. Justice Therry and a Special Jury of four.)

This was an action for trespass, in which William Nowland was plaintiff, and Samuel Clift defendant.

The counsel for the plaintiff were, Mr. Darvall and Mr. Isaacs; attorney, Mr. Want; for the defendant, Mr. Faucett and Mr. Dangar; attorney, Mr. Mullen.

The declaration stated that since the year 1839 the defendant's [Samuel Clift's] cattle had broken into the lands of the plaintiff [William Nowland], which said lands were known by the name of the Walhalla Run [western side of Wallalla Station], and had trampled down and other wise (sic) destroyed the grass and effected other injuries to the plaintiff's [William Nowland's] property, to the serious loss and detriment of the said plaintiff [William Nowland].

Against this it was pleaded that the land did not belong to the plaintiff [William Nowland]; that, at the time the trespass was alleged to have been committed, the land was part of the waste lands of the crown; and that it was then rightfully occupied by John Eales, [Walhollow Station] from whom the defendant [Samuel Clift] had obtained permission to run his cattle. On these pleas issue was joined. [Both the plaintiff and defender challenged each other's position]

... [After a lengthy discussion of 'who owned what' via the various witnesses, with conflicting evidence from the witness of the plaintiff and the defendant.] ... It was then suggested by the plaintiff's counsel [William Nowland's counsel] that a special verdict of nominal damages for the trespass committed on that portion of the run southward of the dry creek should be returned and so end the litigation.

... the court adjourned for 20 minutes. When the court resumed its sitting, Mr. Darvall proposed that the jury should return a verdict for the plaintiff [William Nowland], damages 40s, for trespasses committed between the dry creek's junction with the Mooki and the Rocky crossing place, and the country lying east and west between those places. This was accepted by the litigants, and so the matter ended.

Even though William won this second case he didn't get much out of it; 40 shillings in damages and partial recognition of the boundaries of Wallalla Station, west of the Mooki River.

Both William and Samuel would have not been satisfied with this second judgment and Samuel Clift more so; it was his turn to call for a re-trial. Why was this the case?

After reading and re-reading the accounts between Samuel Clift and William Nowland, sequentially in the newspapers of the time, a pattern of behaviour on William's and Samuel's behalf started to emerge. Neither William or Samuel were prepared to accept the judgment of the court when they were the defendant. They both didn't want to pay the damages when they lost the court case (£250 for William, and 40s for Samuel) because if they paid, by default, they agreed with the claim of the plaintiff of trespass, and subsequently, the other's view of the boundary between the two stations: Walhollow and Wallalla.

Supportive commentary of this view is contained in the following extract from a summary of a later court hearing between William and Samuel in December 1857, where the venue for a re-trial requested by Samuel Clift is changed from Sydney to Maitland and William's counsel is pleading a case for the venue to be changed back to Sydney.

The whole summary of this hearing in December 1857 is detailed later in this chapter; for now, the opening remarks are of interest in terms of Samuel's and William's ploy in deferring payment when the judgment was against them. See below.

The Maitland Mercury and Hunter River General Advertiser, 24 December 1857, page 3.
NOWLAND V CLIFT

... That of Clift v. Nowland was first tried [Sept. 1857], and the jury had found a distributive verdict — which, although favourable for the most part to Clift [£250 in damages], was against the claim of the latter [William Nowland] as respected

this suit, wherein he was defendant. [In the second trial, Nowland v Clift, circa September 1857] His [William Nowland's] counsel therefore, consented to a verdict with nominal damages [40s]. But a new trial had been moved for in the case of Clift v. Nowland, and the proceedings therein consequently stayed.

The information contained in the above extract from this hearing tells us both William and Samuel are yet to pay each other the damages required by the judgment of the first two court cases (*Clift v Nowland* and *Nowland v Clift*) because the same matter has been raised once again and 'the proceedings therein of the previous two trials are consequently stayed', that is delayed.

William had already sent a petition to Queen Victoria about the matter of the boundaries of this station (c.1854) and his petition had been rejected. Then in October 1856, Richard Jones put forward a motion to the NSW Legislative Assembly on William's behalf on the boundaries of Wallalla, with very little response. Now on the same matter (in December 1857), William is the plaintiff in court, where William's counsel is requesting the upcoming retrial between William Nowland and Samuel Clift (*Clift v Nowland*) be held in Sydney, based on the argument 'a strictly impartial trial by a Maitland jury was impossible'. See below.

The Maitland Mercury and Hunter River General Advertiser, 24 December 1857, page 3.
NOWLAND V CLIFT

This was a motion to set aside an order by Mr. Justice Milford, in Chambers, rejecting an application for a change of venue from Sydney to Maitland, in an action for trespass upon a squatting run at Liverpool Plains.

Mr. Wise and Mr. Faucott appeared in support of the application [William Nowland], and the Attorney General and Mr. Isaacs in support of the Judge's order [to move the venue for the case from Sydney to Maitland].

The venue had been originally laid in Sydney, and a motion, to change it to Maitland was made in Chambers upon the ground, that being a local action it must be tried in the Court of that district within which the locus in quo was situated. Also, because the witnesses were chiefly resident in that district.

The plaintiff [William Nowland], on the other hand, sought to have the trial at Sydney, because, as he averred, owing to the nature of the question, and local influence of the defendant [Samuel Clift], a strictly impartial trial by a Maitland jury was impossible. Also, that there would be very little difference as to expense between a trial at Maitland and a trial at Sydney…

[The Maitland Mercury, then tells the reader of the other factors discussed in the hearing that included the judgement in the two previous court cases: Clift v

Nowland (September 1857) and Nowland v Clift (circa September 1857) and the direction by the Court for William to claim the 40s owed to him by Samuel and for Samuel to pay this amount 'to abide the result of a new trial motion'.]

William's counsel won their request and four and a half months later, on the 8th May 1858, Samuel Clift's previous request for a retrial (to avoid the consequences of paying 40s to William) was heard in the Banco Court (the Supreme Court), in Sydney.[331]

Samuel lost this case and was denied a retrial mainly on the grounds that William had 'prior possession' although 'there was evidence from which the jury might infer that there had been an abandonment of this right'. See the summary of the hearing that follows.

The Sydney Morning Herald, 8 May 1858, page 7.
LAW.
SUPREME COURT-FRIDAY.
SITTINGS IN BANCO.
Before the Chief Justice, Mr. Justice Dickinson, and Mr. Justice Therry.
CLIFT V. NOWLAND.

This was a motion for new trial of action for trespass, in which the plaintiff [Samuel Clift] had obtained a verdict for £200 [£250] [in Sept 1857]. The grounds of the motion were twofold-that the verdict was against the weight of evidence, and that the learned Judge who tried this case, at the Maitland Assizes (Mr. Justice Therry) had misdirected the jury as to the principle upon which they were to view the conflicting proofs of these claimants, in order to arrive at their decision.

The litigants were the proprietors of adjacent land [Doona Station], and the dispute was as to the possessory right to a particular tract of land. There had been other actions and proceedings involving precisely the same questions and with various results, the evidence was, as is usual in such cases, very lengthy and conflicting. Each party commented upon this evidence as maintaining his own view of the case.

The alleged misdirection was an expression of opinion by his Honor to the effect that the jury must find for the party who proved the longest continuous possession, the rule of law being that the plaintiff [Samuel Clift] must make out His title, and that, failing this, the defendant [William Nowland] ought to succeed without any necessity for proving priority and continuity of possession.

The Attorney-General and Mr. Isaacs appeared in support of the motion, and Mr. Faucett supported the verdict.

The Court sustained the verdict. The evidence clearly pointed, in their Honors' opinion, to the conclusion that the person through whom defendant [William Nowland] claimed had had prior possession, but there was evidence from which the jury might infer that there had been an abandonment of this right. The charge of the judge must be looked at as a whole and although he might have expressed a particular opinion, still, as that opinion was not proved to be erroneous, and as the questions at issue were fairly before the jury, the verdict must stand.

The above judgment did not allow Samuel to claim from William £250 in damages as determined in the original trial (in September 1857) and Samuel had to pay 40 shillings to William as requested by the court in the third 'hearing' in December 1857. William also gained acknowledgement of his 'prior possession' of the land in dispute and recognition of at least part of his station on the western side of the Mooki River; the payment of the 40 shillings in damages by Samuel was for trespassing on William's Wallalla Station 'between the dry creek's junction with the Mooki River and the Rocky crossing place, and the country lying east and west between those places.' The case had enabled payment and more importantly, for William, recognition of Wallalla Station at least within the area in dispute; though today, these descriptors would not suffice and are too vague, to locate this area on a topographic map.

William would have been pleased with the outcome. At last, he was getting somewhere, the matter had been settled and William decided to keep it that way. When 'Charles Humphrey and Another' trespassed on Wallalla Station, just over three months later (August 1858) William took them to court and won again with damages to William of £2150. What a large sum of money! The summary of the final court hearing, after seven long days in court, follows.

The Sydney Morning Herald, 17 August 1858, page 3.
SUPREME COURT-MONDAY.
SITTINGS FOR THE TRIAL OF CAUSES.
JURY COURT.
BEFORE the Chief Justice and a special jury of twelve.
NOWLAND V. HUMPHREY AND ANOTHER.[332]

This case, which, having taken up seven days, now came to a close, was an action for trespass upon a squatting run called Walhollow [the west side of Wallalla], in the district of Liverpool Plains.

The Attorney-General, Mr. Isaacs, and Mr. Wild appeared for the plaintiff [William Nowland] and Mr. Broadhurst, Mr. Wise, and Mr. Stephen for the defendant [Charles Humphrey and Another].

The possessory title in dispute between these parties was one which had formed a subject of repeated litigation in various shapes. As in all cases of the same character, *there was a great mass of conflicting evidence, not only as to the acts and sayings of the litigants and their servants, but as to the acts and sayings of all those parties through whom each of them claimed up to the time that the station was first occupied, many years ago.*

The great bulk of this evidence was such as would be scarcely intelligible without reference to a map of the 'locus in quo', and such also as would be uninteresting to any others than the litigants themselves or their connections.

The question for determination here, and to which this conflicting testimony was to he applied, was – Which of these parties had made out a priority of exclusive possession, and a continuity of such possession to the time of commencing this suit?

His Honor, in his charge to the jury, directed them as to the principles of law by which claims of the nature here in question resting on possessory titles were to be decided upon.

The charge of the learned Judge in this respect was substantially the same as in all cases of this nature the principal questions left to the jury being whether there had been a prior possession in the plaintiff [William Nowland] or the parties through whom he claimed? Whether this possession had been exclusive? Whether there had been any abandonment of those possessory rights, either actual or constructive? Whether there had been trespasses by the defendants [Charles Humphrey and Another], and if so, to what extent? His Honor also left it open to the jury to find a verdict for trespasses on a part of the 'locus in quo' only if they conceived that the evidence made out a title to such part only, and that plaintiff [William Nowland] had no cause of action as to the remainder. The jury found a verdict for the plaintiff [William Nowland] on all the issues, damages £2150.

At last, William's 'exclusive possession' of the areas in dispute (Wallalla Station west of the Mooki River) had been recognised in the Supreme Court.

William Had Won at Last, and Decided to Sell the Improvements he had Made to Wallalla Station

William placed an ad in the *Maitland Mercury* eleven days later. I can hear his advisors (especially Mary); '*Just sell! You have won at last after a failed petition to Queen Victoria and all these years in the courts! Get it settled, once and for all, while you have the chance!*'

William decided to do just that and placed an ad in the local paper less than two weeks after the judgment, with the ad repeated on the 31st August, and the 4th and 7th September.

William's confident and straightforward ad read as follows.

The Maitland Mercury and Hunter River General Advertiser –
28 August 1858, page 3.
SALE, Sheep and Cattle Station, THALLALLA [misspelt WALLALLA]

The above-named station is offered for sale, in three portions, without stock.

As a fattening station the above is unrivalled, and from its proximity to the market, is doubly valuable.

Apply to

WILLIAM NOWLAND

Falbrook.

Then on the 14 September, William placed another ad. This time he only offered the east side of Wallalla Station for sale (the ad repeated on 16th September). The ad follows.

The Maitland Mercury and Hunter River General Advertiser,
14 September 1858, page 3.
WALHOLLOW, LIVERPOOL PLAINS.

THE above RUN, offered FOR SALE by me, will include only the EAST SIDE, having a frontage to the Mooki River of about eight miles, and running back about five miles.

I have altered my plan of selling the west side, and should I receive no offer for the above East Side before the 1st October next, I shall stock it with sheep or cattle

WILLIAM NOWLAND

Why did William change his mind and advertise only the 'EAST SIDE' of Wallalla for sale? Most likely, someone had challenged him (probably verbally) about the actual boundaries of his station on the WEST SIDE of Wallalla.[333]

They probably provoked William in the following way. '*I saw your ad in the paper. The land you describe on the west side of the Mooki, is not all yours! And is not for sale!*'

The matter of the boundaries of Wallalla Station on the west side of the Mooki had been in and out of the courts for years. The case was well known because it had been all over the press. William just couldn't win. He was caught in a bind. Obviously, no one would buy William's improvements to the west side of Wallalla Station until the disputes about the station's boundaries on that side of the Mooki River were settled, once and for all!

William decided to go back to the Supreme Court as the plaintiff to ask for a retrial to clarify the boundaries once again; the case scheduled for the 28th October 1858 (detailed soon).

William would not be intimidated. He continued to impound animals straying on to Wallalla Station in September and October 1858; this time, William impounded horses.[334]

William also had plenty of responsibilities elsewhere. He had a station to run on the New England Tablelands (Ward's Mistake) mostly with his two eldest son's William jr. (26) and Michael (24); a family farm at Rosedale that still had a lot of potential and was still being developed by William and the rest of the family; and, the township of Camberwell to foster, which needed a lot of attention, if it was to be more than a village.

An account of Camberwell (in 1858) tells us the townsfolk were relieved as the rain was now falling after an extensive dry period. The writer (possibly William) invites the passerby to drop in on this very small village with its church, national school and two inns. All written in the article that follows.

Northern Times, 16 October 1858, page 3.
DISTRICT INTELLIGENCE
CAMBERWELL, FALBROOK.
(From a Correspondent.)

At length this locality has been blessed with four days continual rain, and there is every prospect of a continuance. Previously, every thing (sic) in the shape of vegetation was destroyed [with the long dry spell], and the cattle looked as if their most prudent action would be "to lay them down and die." In most instances the rain will be in time to save the wheat crops, and where not so, the farmer will have heart to prepare the ground for corn and other seasonable crops.[335]

This district has lately suffered a severe loss in the departure for Sydney of our late respected but very aged minister, the Rev. J. Cooper. He was always foremost in every good work, and many useful collections would not have been made but for his zeal and indefatigability in hunting up those who would not give out of their "fulness". Pending the appointment of his successor, we believe Theophilus Foote, Esq., of Oakville, will perform Divine service here.

Our township, though so little known, is gradually extending and growing into importance. Our church would be a positive ornament to the metropolis; then we have our National school, which, we regret to say (unexceptionable institution as it is), is very poorly supported. Of its local board, we may remark 'en passant' [by the way] that the most fastidious could not object to the manner in which its members have been appointed; certainly, upon very broad and national grounds, embracing, as it does, various degrees of erudition, from the really well educated person, to him who, like Paddy Malone, can only make a 'bold mark.' Nothing teaches the value of anything better than the want of it; and the Government have, wisely perhaps, trusted to this feeling operating upon the worthies aforesaid, to make them redouble their energies in giving to others what they so lamentably want themselves.

We have two inns, where the promise contained in the old sign of 'good entertainment for man and horse,' is made good; we confidently recommend a trial. In fine, we have all the usual accompaniments of a country village, minus a lock-up and its permanent tenants – her Majesty's subjects of Falbrook being too liege [loyal to the Queen] and orderly to require any such expensive or distasteful appendage.

October 16, 1858.

William Back in Court

Ten days after the above article appeared in the *Northern Times* telling of Camberwell's 'liege and orderly town folk' William took his case, for a retrial, re the boundaries of the west side of Wallalla Station, to the Supreme Court.

The case was widely reported in the press and found in the SMH, two days after the hearing. See the summary that follows.

> *The Sydney Morning Herald, 28 October 1858, page 6.*
> *SUPREME COURT. – WEDNESDAY*
> *SITTINGS AS IN BANCO.*
> *BEFORE the Chief Justice, Mr. Justice Dickinson, and Mr. Justice Therry.*
> *NOWLAND V CLIFT*

This was a motion for new trial of an action for trespass upon a squatting run, in which the plaintiff [William Nowland] had succeeded [c. September 1857]. The run forming the subject matter of the action was one called Walhalla [Wallalla], or Duno [Doona], in the district of Liverpool Plains. The question of possessory right, at issue here, had been repeatedly litigated in various forms, and with various results.

The main grounds of the present motion was, that the verdict was against the weight of evidence, and the arguments were, necessarily, very lengthy, being, in fact, a commentary upon the testimony of the various witnesses examined on either side, during the protracted trial of this case.

Mr. Plunkett, Q.C., Mr. Faucett, and Mr. Stephen, supported the motion; and the Attorney-General and Mr. Isaacs supported the verdict.

The Court granted a new trial ex gratia, upon payment of costs [court costs]. The principal ground for so doing was that, according to the evidence of several witnesses three of whom were unimpeached—a former holder of the run, through which plaintiff [William Nowland] claimed-one Cronan had made a declaration as to his boundary which was antagonistic to plaintiff's claim in this respect.

But in the opinion of a majority of the Court there was not so manifest an error in the decision of the jury as to warrant the granting of a new trial a matter of right. Mr. Justice Dickinson however, thought otherwise, and that a new trial without special terms ought to have been granted.[336]

The last paragraph in the above account (for me) is ambiguous; was a re-trial granted? In searching further, another summary was found, in another paper, where the judgment in the case is clear and to the point. See below.

The Moreton Bay Courier – 10 November 1858, page 3.

In the case of Nowland v. Clifton, in which a disputed claim to part of a squatting run at Liverpool Plains has several times occupied the Supreme Court, a new trial has been granted.

William's re-trail had been granted.

William Approached his Local Member

William also approached Richard Jones once again for assistance. Richard Jones obliged and around 20 days after the October court hearing, Jones put forward a motion to the Legislative Assembly, on William's behalf, about the boundaries of Wallalla Station. See the extract below, from the minutes of this meeting of the Legislative Assembly; all detailed in the SMH.

The Sydney Morning Herald, 17 November 1858, page 3.
LEGISLATIVE ASSEMBLY.
Tuesday

The SPEAKER took the chair at twenty-five minutes after three o'clock…

WALALLA. RUN. (sic)

Mr. JONES [Richard Jones] asked the hon. Secretary for Lands and Works.

1. By what authority has a portion of the run called Walalla (sic), in the district of Liverpool Plains (which by a late decision in the Supreme Court, in the case Nowland v. Christian and Humphreys, has been decided to belong to Nowland, been alienated [sold] to John Eales?

2. Has the sanction of the Government been given to Samuel Clift's claim to purchase 160 acres at Duono [Doona], a portion of the Walalla Run(sic), notwithstanding that in the case sued in the Supreme Court in February last, a verdict adverse to Clift was gained by Nowland?

3. What is the reason that no notice has been taken of the application of William

Nowland for the sale to him, under his right of pre-emption, of several portions of his Run of Walalla? (sic)

Mr. ROBERTSON [John Robertson], in reply stated, that these questions turned upon an assumption which did not appear to be correct.

1. With regard to the first, the alienation [sale] of a lot of 320 acres, reported by the Commissioner of Crown Lands for the district as forming no portion of the disputed land, was sanctioned in August, 1857 by the then Executive Council, to be sold to Mr. Eales, under the right of preemption, the money being paid in the following month.

2. The sanction of the Government to Mr. Clift's application had not been given.

3. A reply was made to Mr. Nowland on the 8th of September, 1856, in reference to one application from him, others were only made on the 8th instant, and would be duly replied to.

He [Mr. Robertson] might also be permitted to state that this was one of a class of cases involving difficulty of a peculiar character, and not easily settled. The Government appeared to be bound, both morally and legally to acknowledge the claims of the lessee of the run; whilst, from the fact that the lease, or license, contained no description of the land intended to be leased, the lessee was not permitted to avail himself of his right in the Supreme Court, but to have the decision of that Court upon an entirely different ground, namely, priority of occupation. That occupation was frequently not only unsanctioned by the Government of the period, but it might be contrary to its expressed decisions. That matter had received from him (Mr. Robertson) much and anxious consideration, and would be carefully dealt with during the recess.

The Ramifications from the Exchange in the Legislative Assembly

The exchange in the Legislative Assembly (November 1858) between Richard Jones and John Robertson on William's Wallalla Station, provides us with a definitive insight into William's predicament. William had advertised the whole of Wallalla Station for sale (August 1858) without knowing part of the land on the western side of the station had been sold to John Eales (with government approval), and another 160 acres purchased by Samuel Clift (without sanction from the government).

These transactions between Eales and the government authorities, and Clift and another (most likely, unknown to William, at the time), were probably the reason why William's application for approval of the sale of the improvement to Wallalla Station was still pending. The transactions also explain why William was challenged and changed his ad for the sale of the improvement to just the 'east side' of Wallalla Station on the 14th September 1858.

In reply to Richard Jones' support of William's claim on Wallalla, John Robertson stated there were many cases like this one, where: a licence was obtained with no description of the land intended to be leased; the decision of the court was based on entirely different grounds ('priority occupation'); the original occupancy was unsanctioned by the Government of the period; and, the taking up of land in this way (as a squatter) was possibly contrary to the Government's expressed decisions.

John Robertson's commentary from William's perspective could be challenged; William bought the improvements to Wallalla Station (on both sides of the Mooki River) from Ross and Parrott in 1839; he had had a licence for Wallalla Station, since 1840 (for 18 years); he had the written descriptors for his station (that can readily be found in the *Government Gazette* (31st October 1849, p.1621) and as far as he was concerned these descriptors included the land sold to John Eales and the land purchased by Samuel Clift; the courts had determined he had possession of Wallalla Station (*Nowland v Humphrey*, August 1858 and *Nowland v Clift*, October 1858) and based on all of this, he had the right to offer his improvements for sale.

While from John Robertson's perspective he was drafting a new land tenure scheme for NSW and any decision that favoured a squatter (like William) re the boundaries of a 78,040-acre station, would act as a precedent. Other squatters would follow, with similar claims, and potentially, derail Robertson's proposals.[337]

William was caught in a bind. If the disputes about the boundaries of Wallalla Station weren't settled soon in his favour he would be forced by Robertson's new land tenure policy to walk away with only the value of his stock. William was conscious of his predicament and he continued to plead his case in court.[338]

Yet there was more to come for William. The views expressed in the papers about the proposed Robertson Act (especially in 1859) didn't help William with his cause and probably heightened William's concern and determination.[339] For squatters, like William, the intended Act (not yet disclosed) had the potential to marginalise and change their life on the land. See the extract from an article in the local paper that follows.

The Maitland Mercury and Hunter River General Advertiser,
Saturday 23 April 1859, page 2.
FREE SELECTION

... "We understand the Convention [and Land League] reading of it to be, the right of any intending purchaser to select a block of country land for purchase, anywhere in the colony, provided it has not been previously sold or granted...[340]

... Even supposing that some compromise was made as respects the squatters, by

which the renting out of the waste lands [Crown land] for grazing was continued, the right of free selection for purchase would be a constant thorn in the side of the grazier…

The Potential Impact of John Robertson's Proposed Changes to Land Tenure

William and his fellow squatters were on leased land. They did not own the land and were vulnerable to any change in land policy that enabled the sale of parts or the whole of their stations. Another matter was also at the forefront of the minds of the squatters who had stations on the New England Tablelands. When William went to check on Ward's Mistake (in the latter part of the 1850s) the discussion amongst the squatters about land tenure would have included the impact on their livelihood of the proposed border between the colony of NSW and the colony of Queensland. If the border was positioned at the southern entrance to the Tablelands their stations would be in another colonial state under another administration. Luckily this didn't happen, and probably in June 1859 a sigh of relief, rang out across the paddocks.[341]

Once the borders were settled, all the talk amongst the squatters on the New England Tablelands (as elsewhere) was focused on the need for a homestead and continuous occupation of their stations if they were to retain their leases under John Robertson's proposed new land tenure policy. If the gossip was right, Robertson's policy, if enacted, would enabled the purchase of Crown land (their stations), by others through 'free-selection'.[342]

William and his sons had a homestead at Ward's Mistake and from circa 1850, William jr. (18) and Michael (16) had lived there, off and on, and now, William jr. lived there permanently and largely managed the station, for his father.[343]

This was not the case with Wallalla Station; there was no homestead; only a hut. For William and his sons, Wallalla Station was different. They frequented Wallalla when needed, and had grazed, managed, and expanded their stock, on the station for nearly 20 years. They had built a hut at Wallalla on the western side of the river in the 1840s, when the boundaries of Wallalla were questioned by their neighbours; but never a homestead. There was no point. Wallalla was conveniently located, next to Mooki Station and William and Edward had built a homestead there (c.1836). William and his sons could go to Mooki Station, if they wanted more comfort, up until the time when William lost his position as Superintendent, in February 1857.

Since August 1858, William had wanted to sell Wallalla Station. There was no point in putting a homestead on Wallalla Station, at this stage, when the boundaries were still in dispute, regardless of any new land tenure policy.

For nine years and since the initial hearing on Wallalla Station, where John Eales was the plaintiff (17th September 1851), William had sought a judgment in his favour about the boundaries of Wallalla Station. The dispute just went on and on. In essence nothing much had happened: no one had paid the damages determined by the court, even William's colossal amount for damages of £2150, in *Nowland v Humphrey and Another* on the 17th August 1858, appeared to be a 'furphy' and to cap it all off, parts of Wallalla Station on the western side of the Mooki River had been sold (without William's knowledge) to John Eales and Samuel Clift. Time was running out. It was the end of the decade, and a new land tenure policy was coming.

William needed to do something; the matter needed to be settled.

William Returned to the Supreme Court

William returned to the Supreme Court again seeking clarification on the boundaries of Wallalla and payment from 'Humphrey and Another' for the damages he had been awarded in the previous judgment (£2150). The lengthy summary of the case that follows (January 1860s) provides a historical perspective on all the comings and goings of the squatters and land grant holders in the vicinity of Wallalla going back to 1828, and then from the time, when William purchased the improvements to Wallalla station, in 1839, and gained a licence for it in 1840.[344]

This 1860 hearing is important to William's story because it provides a precis and comprehensive account of the various views on Wallalla, William's place within these views, and the difficulties William faced in trying to secure recognition of Wallalla Station. All William wanted to do was sell and all he needed was the court's judgment on the exact boundaries of Wallalla Station.

What happened next follows, courtesy of the local newspaper, and provides a very lengthy summary of the case (once again) where William this time is the plaintiff.

The Maitland Mercury and Hunter River General Advertiser,
5 January 1860, page 3
NOWLAND v. HUMPHREY AND ANOTHER.
(From the Herald of Saturday.)
Supreme Court, Friday, December 30.
In Banco. Before the full Court.

Sir Alfred Stephen, C.J., delivered the judgement of the Court, on the remaining points in this case, as follows : This was an action of trespass to land, comprising a very extensive tract of country, lying on both sides east and west of the River Mooki, at Liverpool Plains—the land itself (or the whole, except a very small portion) being the property of the Crown, but having been for many years occupied for grazing purposes, under the name of Walhala (sic) [Wallalla] as a sheep and cattle run. The plaintiff [William Nowland] claims, as against those defendants [Charles

Humphrey and Another], to have been in possession of the whole of that land, at the time of the alleged trespasses by their sheep and cattle; and he complains not only of such trespasses to an enormous extent, but also of the defendants [Charles Humphrey and Another] having pulled down and destroyed a hut, and the fencing of a large paddock, erected by the plaintiff [William Nowland] on the land. The former acts of trespass are complained of as having extended over a long series of years; ... The defendants [Charles Humphrey and Another] pleaded, besides a denial of the trespasses, that the close [run] in question was not the close [run] of the plaintiff [William Nowland]; and, as to the hut and fencing, that the close [run] on which they were erected was the close [run] of the defendants [Charles Humphrey and Another], who accordingly prostrated them for that cause. The action was tried before me in August 1858, when a verdict was returned for the plaintiff [William Nowland]—as to the hut and fencing, with £150 damages, and, as to the trespasses by the sheep and cattle, with £2000 damages. [£2150]

The defendants [Charles Humphery and Another] thereafter moved for a new trial, on various grounds, which are substantially as follows. First, that on the issue as to the plaintiff's possession [William Nowland], the verdict was against the evidence. Secondly and thirdly, that the damages were assessed without evidence, and were excessive. Fourthly and fifthly, that certain evidence received by me (that is to say of conversations between a Mr. Uhr and two individuals, who were afterwards called to contradict him), was not admissible. Sixthly, that I refused to receive in, evidence under the issue as to possession in the plaintiff [William Nowland], a grant said to have been made by the Crown, to one Eales of a certain small portion of the property. Seventhly and eighthly, that all evidence which was received under that issue, of possession in former occupiers, from whom the plaintiff [William Nowland] claimed to have derived his possession, ought to have been rejected. And ninthly, that the jury was misled by certain acts of their foreman, who was said to have exhibited prejudice against the defendants' case [Humphrey and Another] from the outset.

The motion was heard before us in June last; when we disposed of the said ninth objection, in the plaintiff's favour [William Nowland]. And, in the following term (chiefly in a view to other cases then pending, in which the same question was expected to arise), we delivered our opinion, also in his favour [William Nowland], on the seventh and eighth objections. Finally, after much hesitation and doubt on my part, we announced that our judgment was with him [William Nowland] on all the other points – but it has not been possible, owing to the pressure of other business, and the continuing daily sittings of this court in its various jurisdictions, to prepare that judgment in writing for delivery until now.

The dispute as to the possession of Walhala [Wallalla],[345] it may be taken as certain, arose out of the following circumstances. The particular details and facts relied on by each party, will be mentioned presently. The station was originally occupied by one Rotton, as a cattle run (we use the term in its colonial sense, meaning horned cattle only), in the year 1828. At that period, as is well known, grazing land in the remote interior was not so valuable as it has since become, and in 1832 or thereabouts Rotton abandoned the run to two of his servants named Dunn and Cronan. The former went away, and the latter occupied (or at any rate resided on) the station with one Ross, or with him and Parrott, jointly, for some years, during which their cattle, or the cattle of one or more of them, indiscriminately, fed over the property, although it seems pretty clear that the number, compared with that required fully to stock the land, was small. Sheep were never kept there.

In this state of things, that is to say, some time (sic) in the year 1835, a Mr. Uhr came on the property east of the river, with a large number of sheep, and sat himself down upon it. Up to that time, Cronan and Ross, alone or together with Parrott (or the latter and Ross, exclusively of Cronan), had certainly occupied or used the land, or portions of it, more or less, by their cattle. But it has contended for the defendants [Humphery and Another], that those persons (whichever of them held or claimed to hold it), could not in any true or fair sense be taken to have been in "possession" of the property; as the cattle, it was said, were mere occasional stragglers over the run, or over all but a small portion of it; and that, at most, they possessed only the tract of country west of the river, where their hut and homestead were.

This, therefore, was the great point of contest. Cronan, so the plaintiff [William Nowland] asserted, sold his interest in the land (and cattle, if he had any left) to Parrott, in the same year 1835—thereby transferring an actual possession to the latter, jointly with Ross. Then, according to the plaintiff, [William Nowland] Parrott transferred such possession similarly to him (the plaintiff, William Nowland) in 1839; who a few years afterwards purchased, in like manner, the interest of Ross, and thereby obtained the sole possession.[346]

So that the plaintiff's [William Nowland's] case was, an asserted unbroken continuity of possession (though not of legal title in or of this land), by cattle never at any time off it, but always in greater or less numbers there grazing, notwithstanding the continuing intrusion from year to year of the defendants [Charles Humphrey and Another) and their precursors.

On their part, the defendants [Charles Humphery and Another] relied on the possession of Uhr who, they insisted, entered on a property (sic) then derelict or abandoned—but in which nevertheless, he [Uhr] immediately afterwards obtained by purchase from Cronan all the latter's interest, and continuity of possession if any such then remained in any of his [Cronan's] party. Cronan was, at the time (they alleged) the sole remaining resident on the east side of the river, and no one of that set was on the eastern side, either personally or by cattle.

Mr. Uhr transferred his possession, if such it was, with the sheep, or some of them, to Mr. Eales, in the year 1843 and the latter, in like manner, his possession and flocks, to the defendants [Charles Humphrey and Another], as already mentioned, in 1854.

Thus, each party maintained that at the last-mentioned period he was the actual exclusive possessor of the entire run. For the defendants (Charles Humphrey and Another], unquestionably, an actual feeding over the land in all parts of it was shown continuously, by the sheep either of Uhr, or of Eales, of themselves, to the extent of many thousands ever since 1835. On the other hand, there was evidence that cattle of Cronan, Ross, Parrott, or the plaintiff [William Nowland], similarly claiming by a continuous chain of possession, to a greater or less extent, had always been upon the property or portions of it, ever since the year 1832. But the plaintiff's [William Nowland's] case was embarrassed by questions of abandonment, or cessation of enjoyment as occupier, for the reasons already suggested, and also because of his own alleged absence from the land, and his eventual insolvency in the year 1850.

And it was urged, that if the continuance of a few wandering cattle on land, extending over many miles of open country could constitute possession is their owner, there was probably not one settler's sheep or cattle run in the colony, of which such a possession could not be asserted by any one of his neighbours…

According to the plaintiff's [William Nowland's] own testimony, he, in 1830, saw Ross on the station… keeping there his own [Ross'] and Parrott's cattle. It appears from other witnesses, as well as the plaintiff [William Nowland], that the latter [Parrott] then lived in the neighbourhood, in charge of another station; and that he so continued to reside, or occasionally at a township many miles distant… He was often, however, on the run; and in 1834 he says that he saw Cronan, in the presence of Ross, give up his cattle to Parrott. But Cronan remained on the run, minding the cattle (both of Ross, or the two Rosses [brothers], and of Parrott, apparently), until 1836; and from 1834 up to 1839, those cattle and their increase (with some, it would seem, of the plaintiff's [William Nowland's] own) continued grazing on the property. In 1839, the plaintiff [William Nowland] swore that he purchased and took possession of Parrott's cattle; and in 1840 he bought also, and received possession of, those belonging to the Ross family. From the first of those dates hitherto, his cattle and servants have been continually on the land.

On his [William Nowland's] purchase from Parrott, the plaintiff [William

Nowland] and George Ross, as joint occupiers, gave Uhr notice, in writing (which the latter [Urh] admitted that he received), to remove from the property, and, in or about the year 1842, the plaintiff [William Nowland] brought an action of trespass against him [Edmond Uhr].

For some reason, however, that action was discontinued; and the plaintiff [William Nowland] paid the costs of it. He [William Nowland] said on cross examination, that his object was to apply for redress to the Land Commissioners, and that he was too poor to maintain a lawsuit...

In 1852, the plaintiff [William Nowland] sued Eales for the latter's intrusion, and for pulling down a hut there; and, as to the latter, obtained a verdict. He offered Eales, also at that time, to sell the eastern side to him. The entire run will carry about 4000 cattle, or 20,000 sheep. Horned cattle, it is well known, will not graze on spots where sheep are depastured [grazed]. ...

...Ross said, that he placed cattle on the run, and found there about 700 head belonging to the plaintiff [William Nowland], whose men were also there, in 1838 – that Uhr's sheep were then all on the east side... Roberts said... the plaintiff [William Nowland] acquired by purchase all Parrott's cattle, that there were cattle on the run, besides Cronan's, Ross's, and Parrott's, and that the sheep dispersed and drove many away. Parrott, junior, confirmed the fact of this last mentioned purchase, and said that in 1835 Ross and Cronan were jointly in possession. Parrott's widow gave similar evidence and fixed the date of the sale in 1839. Singleton said, that he delivered Parrott's cattle to the plaintiff [William Nowland] in that year on the run; and that he then saw, on different parts of it, both sheep and cattle grazing.

Richardson declared, that Parrott and Ross had cattle on the run in 1836, but that he (the witness) was then the plaintiff's servant [William Nowland], and as such lived with Cronan in the latter's [Cronan's] hut, in that year.

Against that testimony, Mr Uhr, for the defendants [Charles Humphrey's and Another], gave evidence ...

Eales acknowledged, however, that while he was there, he and the plaintiff [William Nowland] had disputes about the place and impounded each other's animals.

Humphrey stated, that he went to the station in 1844, as Eales's superintendent, and remained till 1854 and afterwards; and Nowland [William] never came on the run till 1856, when he put up a hut and paddock, which Bassett and Humphrey pulled down. Humphrey admitted, however, that the plaintiff [William Nowland] had a few stragglers on the east.

During all those years, the run was fully stocked with sheep on both sides of it. With the testimony of those and other persons, there was much evidence therefore for the defendants, that Uhr went up in 1834 and 1835; and then that no one occupied except Cronan, who lived in a hut on the west side;—that Cronan left the run in the latter year, and that Uhr occupied all the place thenceforth for many years, and then sold it and the stock to Eales; and that the latter [Eales], and the defendants [Humphery and Another], had been occupying the whole as sole owners from 1843 till the commencement of this suit.

There was also evidence to show that the plaintiff [William Nowland] for many years prior to 1854 had not been on the land, in such a manner as indicated him to be the possessor, or even a claimant for the occupation of the run. The evidence on the defendants' [Charles Humphrey's and Another's] behalf was very strong, that the plaintiff [William Nowland] and his predecessors exercised comparatively but little, if any, ownership over the west side of the river.

On the other hand, we have Mr. Uhr's admission, that he had seen cattle on the east side, but did not count them, nor observe if they were stragglers; and Mr. Eales's that he had disputes with the plaintiff [William Nowland], at all events as long ago as 1852, and that they severally impounded the sheep or cattle of the other. [Impounding each other's stock]

There was a piece of evidence on the defendants' [Charles Humphery and Another's] part to this effect, that the plaintiff [William Nowland] was declared insolvent in the year 1850, and that although he then made the usual affidavit that his schedule contained a true list of all his effects, nevertheless the place in question was not there inserted as an asset. [As detailed earlier, William appears to be hiding/or transferring his assets to others, to protect them, during this time of insolvency.]

There was, moreover, some evidence, though not of a very distinct character, that the plaintiffs [William Nowland's] cattle had previously been mortgaged; and that under the insolvency the whole, with the equity of redemption in them, were sold…

… But we will assume, that in point of fact there was clear evidence on both sides, of a continuous possession on the one side in the plaintiff [William Nowland] through Cronan, Ross, and Parrott, and on the other side, in the defendants [Charles Humphrey and Another], through Cronan, Uhr, and Eales. There is undoubtedly such evidence. But, as it was conflicting … we are of opinion that we can grant no new trial on the ground that the verdict on this point was against the weight of evidence. [The boundaries of the two stations still a contentious point.]

We proceed next, in connexion (sic) with the same point, to the objection that the plaintiff [William Nowland] could not in 1850 have had (and so that he must at or before that time have lost) his alleged possession of Walhala [Wallalla], because he did not make insertion or mention of it in his schedule. [William did not mention either Ward's Mistake or Wallalla in his schedule when he was declared insolvent; a ploy that would come back to haunt him in this court hearing].

As the plaintiff [William Nowland] stated, that stations were considered at that period to be worth very little, and there was evidence that Cronan's interest in Walhala [Wallalla] was really sold to Uhr for £3 and offered to Clift for the same amount, and it did not appear that the plaintiff [William Nowland] had any license for the place, the jury may have concluded that the plaintiff [William Nowland] thought there was no such interest in the run, as could be beneficial to his creditors, and, on this ground, they may have accounted for the omission.[347]

With regard to an abandonment of the station, or at least a portion of it, either by the plaintiff [William Nowland], or some of those who were there before he was, the question is involved in the continuity of possession, on which, as we have remarked, there is abundant evidence…

The plaintiff's son [Michael, now 26 yrs.] stated that for the last six years (1854–1860) the plaintiff [William Nowland] had from 500 to 1000 cattle on the run, both west and east. The plaintiff's [William Nowland's] own evidence was distinct that cattle grazed on both sides of the river in 1834, and for six years afterwards [1834–1840] when he got possession of the run [a licence]; that he maintained that possession till 1854, by different servants to the number of twenty; and that he always insisted that the run was his, and told the defendants [Charles Humphrey and Another] that he would put them off it[348] *From those instances and others, we are satisfied that the jury had abundant materials, if adopted by them, to enable them to find as a fact that neither the plaintiff [William Nowland] nor any of his predecessors ever abandoned the station.*

From this conclusion I do not dissent I nevertheless feel myself bound to express the opinion that the verdict of the jury (unless, indeed, as to the Western portion of the run), was a mistaken one. The evidence appears to me largely to preponderate, and especially when we consider the probabilities, in favor of the conclusion arrived at by Mr. Uhr, when he took possession, that the Eastern side of the river was unoccupied. Here was an enormous extent of country, capable of feeding 4000 cattle or more. Two men [Cronan and Ross], of obviously very small means uniting afterwards with a third [Parrott] similarly situated (for so I collect from the facts), lived in two huts on the Western side of it. We do not find that they had servants. They could not, therefore, have looked after cattle far from their own homestead, and they had, in 1831, about 700, or at the most 1000, head among them. It is highly improbable that men so circumstanced could possibly have retained possession, even had they desired to do so, of the more distant and unmanageable tract on the opposite side of the stream. There may have been, as there always are with every large herd, stragglers from the station, but that cattle of Parrott, the Rosses, or Cronan, occupied that side, or were intentionally depastured there, either in 1835 or 1836, seems to me to be scarcely credible.

I cannot say, however, that—if any part whatever of the Walhala [Wallalla] run, trespassed on by the defendants, was in the plaintiff's [William Nowland's] possession at the time of such trespass—the verdict on the whole was wrong. It is probable that I might not have returned a verdict for the complainant [William Nowland] even as to the Western side; but the evidence affecting that portion differed very widely from that which respects the other portion.

We come now to the objection that the damages were excessive. The first count of the declaration charged the defendants [Charles Humphrey and Another] with having committed trespasses from the 1st January, 1852—the commencement of the suit being March, 1858. The defendants [Charles Humphrey and Another] were proved to be liable, however, only since the month of June, 1854. For these trespasses the jury awarded £2000 damages.

The second count complained that the defendants [Charles Humphrey and Another] pulled down a paddock, stockyard, and hut, and scattered the plaintiff's [William Nowland's] cattle by turning in sheep there; whereby some of the cattle were lost, and the rest were injured. For these latter trespasses the jury gave £150 damages.

As to the damages first mentioned, Michael Nowland [William's son] proved that the defendants [Charles Humphrey and Another], during the period specified, had always 3000 sheep on the east of the river, and above 1000 on the west, besides 800 or 900 cattle. William Nowland swore that during the same period the defendants [Charles Humphrey and Another] had there from 500 to 1000 cattle, and 5000 or 6000 sheep.

With respect to the smaller damages, the injury proved to have been done was unquestionably great; and, in fact, little, if any, complaint was made as to the verdict on that score. But the damages under the first count, it was urged, were utterly unprecedented and unjustifiable, and must have included the period, evidently, of Eales's occupation—long prior to that of the defendants [Charles Humphrey and Another].

It is doubtless extremely difficult, in this case as in many others, to perceive that the *sums awarded for the trespasses, if reduced to arithmetical calculation, are duly proportioned to the injuries inflicted. And with respect to the £2000 damages, no evidence was given to furnish the jury with any guide, as to the pecuniary loss likely to have been sustained, or even as to the annual money value of the station. It must be obvious, however, that the plaintiff [William Nowland] was seriously damnified (sic) by the knocking down of the hut, and destruction of his fencing; and still more by the continuous intrusion of the defendants' sheep and cattle. The actual damage done to the owner in such cases is not to be estimated, as we conceive, by the mere value of those erections, and of the grass that was eaten or destroyed by the intruding animals; nor even altogether, we think, by the losses arising from the non-increase or the deterioration of his flock or herd. The plaintiff [William Nowland] here sustained considerable annoyance, and was put to much (sic) trouble by the defendants' acts and they moreover inflicted on him the more serious injury, of thereby furnishing evidence against the plaintiff [William Nowland] in their own favour.*

For every act of entrance, and especially of continued depasturing [grazing] by the defendants' sheep and cattle, as also of their pulling down huts, and the like, is itself evidentiary of ownership and possession in those individuals. The amount of money, which may be adequate for the compensation of such injuries, is not susceptible of minute pecuniary computation. By the verdict, the defendants [Charles Humphrey and Another] have been shown to be wrongdoers; and when a wrong has been committed, the wrongdoer must suffer from the impossibility, which will often occur, of accurately estimating the amount of damages. In actions of tort, moreover, the court will not interfere with the damages, unless they are grossly disproportionate to the injury. William v. Currie, C. B. 841.

Now the damages founded on the first count, we find, will give the plaintiff [William Nowland] rather more than £500 a year, for the time indicated. Can we see that such an amount is grossly disproportionate to the injury here inflicted on the plaintiff [William Nowland]. If we consider the number of sheep and cattle, actually depastured [grazed] on the ground yearly by the defendants [Charles Humphrey and Another], or the number which the plaintiff [William Nowland] might have fed on it, as sworn to on the trial, a very small annual sum for each animal would alone make the aggregate amount. But to this we may add something, for the annoyance and trouble sustained by the plaintiff [William Nowland], and also the injury done by the furnishing of evidence, in and by the mere act of occupying the land.

On the whole, therefore, we are of opinion that the amount awarded for damages on the first count, will not justify the grant of a new trial. As to the sum given for the damage alleged in the second count, the same or similar observations arise. On neither do we think that, under the circumstances stated, we ought to disturb the verdict. It is possible that we might ourselves have given less damages; but we cannot see that the jury were influenced by any improper motive, or that they proceeded on any erroneous principle. Creed v. Fisher, 9 Exchequer, 472.

On the assumption that the verdict is unimpeachable, as to the continuous possession in the plaintiff of the entire run, I concur in the conclusion just announced; although it would have been more satisfactory to me, had a new inquiry as to the damages been awarded…

… I have already expressed the opinion, that—as to all the Eastern portion of the property—no continuous possession in the plaintiff [William Nowland] was established. It is quite possible that the jury may have thought so too; although they have omitted to distinguish, by their verdict, between the two portions. The legitimate and probable conclusion is, however, the other way; and if the jury have, in fact, assessed damages for the entire station, it follows that according to my view of the matter the damages are assessed wrongly. On the other hand, if the damages have been assessed in respect of the Western portion only, then they are clearly in my opinion out of all proportion to the injury.

On the objection taken ninthly to the verdict, we need only repeat here what we announced on the argument. We see nothing in the affidavit filed, or in the notes of the Judge, to induce us to believe that the juror alluded to was actuated by prejudice, or was likely to have misled or prejudiced his brethren.

The seventh and eighth grounds of motion, as has been already noticed, were disposed of by a written judgment in August last. The only remaining objections, therefore, are the fourth, fifth, and sixth; to which we now proceed.… [Left out of this extract because this section of the hearing is long winded and (for me) does not add to William's story]

We now come to the sixth objection. The counsel for the defendants [Charles Humphrey and Another] offered in evidence a crown grant to John Eales, under whom the defendants [Charles Humphrey and Another] claimed, comprising a portion of the land in controversy. We think that the evidence was rightly rejected, according to the rule of this court of the 12th April, 1856, which provides that the plea of not possessed, or that the close [run] was not the plaintiff's [William Nowland's] close [run], shall put in issue only the fact that the plaintiff [William Nowland] had exclusive possession when the defendant [Charles Humphrey and Another] entered, but not any circumstances which made the entry lawful…

William Won the Case in Terms of Damages but Not in Terms of Exclusive Possession

The Chief Justice of the Supreme Court of New South Wales, Sir Alfred Stephen (1844–1873) determined that William was entitled to the damages (£2150) judged to be his (in *Nowland v Humphrey and Another* held in August 1858) based on Stephen's view 'Humphrey and Another' had trespassed on land deemed to be in the 'exclusive possession' of William.

Again, William had won the case without full acknowledgement of Wallalla Station and its boundaries. The only land recognised as William's was the land 'Humphrey and Another' trespassed upon. Wallalla, and its 87,040 acres was ignored. The £2150 offered by the court was not good enough for William; he had spent 21 years improving the pastures at Wallalla Station and his work, effort, and licence needed to be recognised, by the courts.

For William, he needed a comprehensive and final judgment in his favour that entitled him to sell the whole of Wallalla Station; all 87,040 acres! Otherwise, William would be left with nowhere to graze his cattle on the Liverpool Plains and possibly forfeit access to any other land on the Liverpool Plains, if Robinson's proposed land tenure legislation was passed by both houses of Parliament (Legislative Assembly and Legislative Council) in NSW.[349]

William Took his Case for Exclusive Possession of Wallalla Station to the Privy Council

William was at an impasse and took his case to the Privy Council in London, paying security of £2500. See the account that follows.

SYDNEY NEWS.
SUPREME COURT-FRIDAY.
(From the S. M. Herald [10 March 1860, page 4])
Special Sittings in Banco. –
Before Chief Justice Dickinson and Mr. Justice Milford.
APPEAL TO THE PRIVY COUNCIL – NOWLAND V HUMPHREY

The Court, after hearing Mr. Stephen for the appellant, and Mr. Martin, Q.C., for the respondent, granted leave to appeal to the Privy Council, but directed that the plaintiff [William Nowland] should, in the interim, recover the fruits of his judgment in the original court hearing [£2150 on the 17 August, 1858] in giving security to the extent or £2500, for the restitution or the damages, If necessary, and for costs.

To take his case to the Privy Council, William needed to provide £2500 in security to the Supreme Court. A large sum of money that William probably did not have and could not raise; given what we know of his financial status. One can assume to cover the cost of this final hearing in London's halls of established officialdom, he gave the Supreme Court the money he had received in damages from 'Humphrey and Another' (£2150) and added in another £350 of his own, to make up the difference. William was not prepared to walk away. He presumably, saw the money as a means of gaining a fair and impartial judgement (in his favour) far away from the systemic bias he had endured in the colonial court system. All he wanted was official recognition of the boundaries of Wallalla Station (all 87,040 acres of it!). William was obviously convinced the Privy Council decision would be in his favour; he had the documentary evidence and had been the lessee for Wallalla for 20 years. For William, the money would be well spent. He would win, sell his improvements and move on. After nine years in and out of Court, he could not just walk away with the money, even though it was £2150.

CHAPTER 22

MORE FAMILY TRAGEDY FOLLOWED BY GRIT AND DETERMINATION

William's and Mary's Son John

William's decision to take his case to the Privy Council on the 10 March 1860, came nearly two months after the death of his and Mary's son, John (18). John died of epilepsy on the 18 January 1860. He is buried at Camberwell Anglican Church Cemetery beside his parents.[350] The family notice in the local paper read:

> *The Maitland Mercury and Hunter River General Advertiser,*
> *7th February 1860, page 1.*
>
> *DEATH – On the 18th Jan last at the house of his father, at Falbrook, Hunter river, from epilepsy, John, the fifth son of William and Mary Ann Nowland, aged 18 years; his parents and eight brothers, live to mourn his loss.*

How devastating for William sr., Mary and John's brothers.

William Consistently Selling Stock

Soon after John's death, William advertised the sale of '100 Head of Prime Fat Cattle' from the Mooki (presumably from Wallalla Station). The ad read as follows.

> *The Maitland Mercury and Hunter River General Advertiser,*
> *21 January 1860 page 4.*
> FOR SALE, ONE HUNDRED HEAD OF PRIME FAT CATTLE
> *From the Mooki,*
> CAMPBELL'S HILL YARDS,
> ON MONDAY, JANUARY 23rd, 1860.
>
> *ISAAC GORRICK, SENR., has received instructions from Mr. William Nowland, to sell by auction, at the Sale Yards, Campbell's Hill, on MONDAY, January 23, 1860, at Twelve o'clock, 100 Head of Prime FAT CATTLE, from the Mooki, Liverpool Plains.*

The above lot are nearly all Bullocks and are for positive and unreserved sale.

Terms Cash

Around three weeks later, William is selling '300 breeding sheep'.[351] See below.

The Maitland Mercury and Hunter River General Advertiser,
14 February 1860, page 1
FOR SALE or to LET on the HALVES [352]
about three hundred (300) BREEDING SHEEP.
Apply to WILLIAM NOWLAND,
Falbrook, near Singleton.
February 10, 1860.

Do these two ads and the money gained from the sale of '100 head of prime fat cattle and 300 breeding sheep' have anything to do with William's decision to appeal to the Privy Council in London about the disputed boundaries of Wallalla Station? Maybe. As told in the previous chapter, just over three weeks later, on the 10th March 1860 William decided to take the case of Wallalla Station once again to the Supreme Court and this time he won the right to a very costly appeal to the Privy Council in London; with security of £2500 required. We know he had £2150 in damages from 'Humphrey and Another' and he needed to raise the difference £350. Did the sale of this stock assist him in this matter? Most likely.

Later in the year (June 1860) William was selling stock again; 'horses for sale' and the sale or exchange of his 'forty colts and fillies'. See below.

The Maitland Mercury and Hunter River General Advertiser,
16 June 1860, page 3.
HORSES FOR SALE.

FORTY COLTS and FILLIES, from one year old up
to two years, or will exchange for young horned
cattle or sheep. Apply to

WILLIAM NOWLAND

Camberwell.

June 2, 1860.

Wallalla Station is not Displayed on Reuss and Browne (1860) Map of Pastoral Land

In the same year (1860), Reuss and Browne published a map of the pastoral lands within the two developing colonies of New South Wales and Queensland. Today, this map provides us with the location of all of William's runs on the Liverpool Plains and New England Tablelands (past and present); except for Wallalla Station. Walhollow Station is displayed on the part of the map where according to the descriptors in the *Government Gazette* and the court cases Wallalla Station once stood. (See Figure 25.)

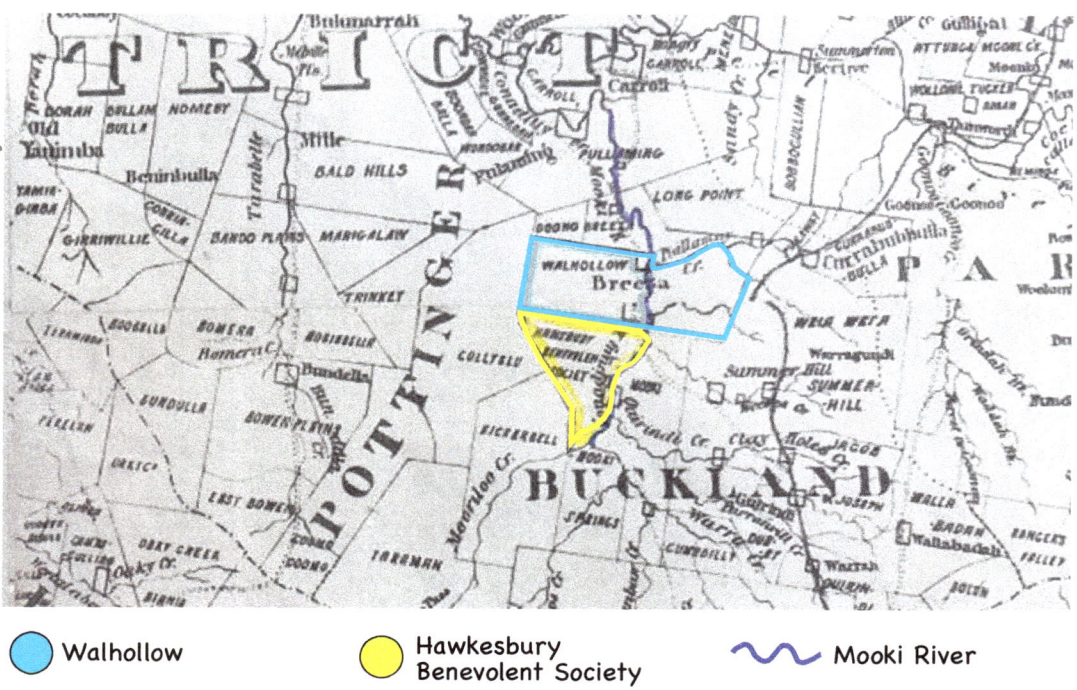

Figure 25: Walhollow, HBS and Mooki River.

By the time the Reuss and Browne map was published Wallalla Station was nowhere to be seen, it had been consumed by Eales' Walhollow.

Chas Marries Ann (Annie) Susan Squire

The year 1860 was also a year of celebration for William (56) and Mary (47). Their fourth eldest son, Charles ('Chas', 20) married Ann Susan Squire ('Annie', 19) at Patrick Plains [Singleton] and Chas and Annie's first son (William's and Mary's first male grandchild (born in 1862) was named 'John James Nowland'; most likely after Chas' deceased siblings, James and John.[353]

Chas and Annie lived initially on the New England Tablelands, near Armidale, and then moved to Warrah Ridge.[354]

After Chas' and Annie's marriage, William sr. and Mary still had five sons at home, some relatively young: Robert (24); Alex (14); George (12); Alfred (9); and Henry (7). Their two eldest sons, William jr. (28) and Michael (26) were probably spending most of their time at Ward's Mistake, and maybe Chas and Annie had joined them there, given their first two children, twins John James and Ada, born in 1862, were registered at Armidale.

Back in Camberwell

William sr. still busied himself with the promotion of Camberwell. In 1860, William's responsibilities included the local church and school. In the article that follows, William is described as 'the lessee of the Church [St Clement's] and the Schools Lands for twenty-one years' [1839–1860].

Sydney Mail, 22 September 1860, page 8.
NOWLAND V. REYNOLDS[355]

In this case an application for special injunction had been made on the part of the plaintiff [William Nowland] to restrain the defendant [Reynolds] from cutting timber. The plaintiff [William Nowland] who was a lessee of Church [St Clement's] and School Lands for twenty-one years [1839–1860], and the defendant [Reynolds] a tenant under him [William Nowland].

Mr. Gordon appeared for the plaintiff [William Nowland], and Mr. Butler for the defendant [Reynolds]. A number of arguments were advanced, and authorities cited as to the nature and extent question was, whether the defendant [Reynolds] ought to be restrained from cutting timber for fencing. The defendant [Reynolds] having come into possession through the plaintiff [William Nowland], and other questions in the suit as to title, remaining still open HIS Honor granted the injunction, the costs to be costs in the cause.

More About William's Character

The above article reaffirms what we already know about William's character. William warning others about trespassing on his station, notifying others of impounded stock that could only be retrieved at a price and of course the various court hearings and appeals. For me, William did not hesitate, he would call out what he believed to be wrong and then while things were being sorted out or settled, he just got on with what he needed to do to make a living.

William, the eternal opportunist took advantage of any change in land tenure policy as quickly as possible as demonstrated by: his land grant in 1824; his on-going purchase of allotments to expand Rosedale in the 20s, 30s and 40s; being one of the first onto the Liverpool Plains as a squatter (c.1826) and again in 1837, at Dridool Station along the Namoi River; and, moving onto the New England Tablelands, maybe with his brother Henry, as early as 1836, at Guy Fawkes; and, claiming a run of his own there, Ward's Mistake, in 1842.

William provided a living for himself and sustained himself and his family, as a squatter, pastoralist and later, as a grazier.[356]

John Robertson's Proposed Changes to Land Tenure

In the 1840s, William positioned himself as a pastoralist under Governor FitzRoy's Order in Council (1847) and all the security of tenure it offered for those who leased crown land, despite the challenges he faced at Wallalla Station. William's leases for Ward's Mistake and Wallalla (despite the disputes) were secure with no rumours of change, until 1856, when John Robertson, a supporter of the squatters in the past, entered parliament and set about developing a new land tenure policy aimed at reducing the squatters' dominance on the pastoral lands of NSW.[357]

Three years later, in September 1859 Robertson presented three Bills to the Legislative Assembly on land tenure: 'crown land sales', 'crown land occupation' and 'leased land occupation'. The first two Bills were successful and the last one failed (27-30).[358]

So, William renewed his licence for Ward's Mistake as required by the Order in Council and as he had done for the last 13 years (1847–1860).[359]

William Renewed His Licence for Ward's Mistake

The newspaper article that follows shows William's renewed licence for Ward's Mistake. The article also references in the preamble, Robinson's failed Bills (in September 1859) and his continued advocacy for free selection.[360]

Empire, 4th December 1860, page 4.
THE SQUATTING DISTRICTS AND THE RESERVES.
NEW ENGLAND AND MACLEAY.

THE following is a list of runs in the above district, with the names of their proprietors, according to a parliamentary return ordered by the Legislative Assembly to be printed, 21st September, 1859. The rent paid for those 7,123,580 acres is £4285 15s., or about half a farthing per acre per year. The amount of reserved land which would have been thrown open to free selection in this district, if Mr. Robertson's Bill had passed, amounted to about 165,000 acres.

A list of the different reserves, with the number of acres in each, is given at foot.

There are a few "indefeasible reserves" not included in the following list, but as they are devoted to public purposes they would not have been available for free selection if the Land Bill had become law. We have no means of ascertaining what portion of the reserves has been taken up under the leaseholders' pre-emptive right, but it is believed that this right has not been availed of to any considerable extent. We give these particulars of the New England and Macleay district in preference to those of others, as it is probable that should a liberal Land Bill be passed in the coming session, a good many persons, in taking advantage of free selection, will turn their attention to that district, from the well-known adaptability of its soil and climate to the purposes of agriculture.

STATIONS AND OWNERS Acres

…Ward's Mistake, William Nowland 81,920

[Rent based on the above data was 1/8 penny per acre, and based on this figure the cost of William licence for Ward's Mistake was approximately £102. 8s.]

The licence for Ward's Mistake was renewed throughout the rest of William's life and as told earlier, after William's death the station was purchased by his son William jr. and remained in the family until 1901.[361]

William's Letter to the SMH (in 1861) was More Than a Letter of Reminiscence

As we know, after William renewed his licence for Ward's Mistake in December 1860, he sat down to write a letter to the Editor of the SMH about his life as a squatter. We have already covered most of this letter that informs us about William's various runs; Warrah (c.1826), Dridool (1837), Wallalla (1839), Boonanga (1840) and Ward's Mistake (1842). In coming back to the letter, the detail at the end, informs us of the case William wished to put forward for the *'original squatters'* if John Robertson's proposal for *'free selection'* was approved by both houses of Parliament. William tells us, it would have been better if the Commissioners were never appointed, because without them, there would have been one-third the lawsuits. William also expresses his concerns about *'free selection'*. He advocates if the selectors were given free access to crown land, they may choose the best land along the river front and block entry to the waterways for the *'original squatters'*. Then, if this was the case, the squatters (now known, as pastoralists) would probably abandon their stations, and the government would lose a substantial source of revenue.

For William, the amount of money the squatters had paid in licence fees and taxes for stock over the last 25 years (c.1836–1861) for the less fertile land on their stations (away from the river front) should be acknowledged in any new land tenure policy, by offering the squatters from time to time the first opportunity to purchase the river frontage of their stations.

William suggested *free selectors* should be directed to other areas of land closer to settlement. For William, there were thousands of acres near settlement where the land was cheaper (as low as, five shillings per acre) and the small freehold farmer given the cheaper price would readily purchase such land. William reinforced this point, by putting forward the case, if the selectors were located closer to settlement a new source of revenue would be created for the government, and within this more densely settled area selectors would have ready access to the knowledge of other graziers and would quickly learn about the best way to farm in the harsh conditions of a 'sunburnt country'.

William ends his narration on free selection by commenting on the respect that should be shown to the *'original squatters';* given their contribution to the colony. For William, squatters were the ones who facilitated the formation of all the towns beyond the boundaries of settlement, and for him, without the adventurous nature of the squatters everyone would have stayed in Sydney and the gold in the interior wouldn't have been discovered; William is a bit far-fetched here.

This last part of William's Letter to the Editor of the SMH follows.

> *The Sydney Morning Herald, 23rd Jan 1861, page 3. [continued]*
>
> *…It would have been much better for the government and squatters if there had been no commissioners appointed; and there would not have been one-third of the lawsuits in the Supreme Court about stations. In many cases the commissioners have been the means of the lawsuits.*
>
> *It is reported that the Government will allow free selections on the frontage of the squatters' runs. If ever that is allowed, it will do away with squatting altogether, for the majority of runs in New South Wales have but the one run of water for the stock to drink at; for it is well known there are huts, fences, foot passengers, and dogs, all along the frontage of the run, that bush cattle will not go and drink—they would rather perish on the back ground.*
>
> *If the free selector is allowed, to purchase the frontage, the Government will then lose the heavy assessment and rental that the original occupier paid. As the squatters are paying a heavy assessment and rental for the back ground (sic) of their station, and agreeable to continue, I think they ought to be allowed from time to time to purchase the frontage of their runs.*
>
> *As there is no market for farmers produce so far off water carriage or railroads, if the Government were, for the first five years, to have free selection after survey within a hundred miles of water carriage and railroads, as they have thousands of acres within that distance.*

A few days ago, I heard some free selectors conversing together; they said they knew of plenty of land within twenty miles of the present railroad, and if they could purchase it at five shillings per acre they would, and pay the cash down, although not the best land, rather than go into the interior. It is admitted by most persons that good land is worth one pound per acre, and the back land from 2s.6d. to 5s; and if sold by the Government would create a large revenue and population, within one hundred miles of water carriage and railroads.

Any "free selector" that may require a station can procure it at the present time, within forty miles of the Barwin River. I think that it would be more honourable than wishing to cut up the original squatter's station; and it would also enable them to find out with what ease the "squatters make their fortunes." There is nothing like experience.

The original squatters were the means of the first formation of all the towns beyond the boundaries of the colony; also, the road side towns, leading to the above. But for squatters, the people would have staid [sic] in Sydney until they were smoke-dried, and there would have been no gold found.

WILLIAM NOWLAND

January 21st.

For William, free selectors should be offered small freehold farms, on cheaper land close to settlement, and the original squatter (now pastoralists) who had established large runs (now known as stations) in the interior, should from time to time, be given the opportunity to purchase the water frontage of their stations.

PART FOUR

The Changes in Land Tenure

William was quick to respond to the changes in land tenure

CHAPTER 23

JOHN ROBERTSON'S PROPOSED CHANGES TO LAND TENURE POLICY

Success at Last

John Robertson envisaged a more flexible and practical land tenure policy and convinced parliament of his intentions, eight months after William's (January 1861) Letter to the Editor of the SMH.

Both Houses of Parliament, the Lower House (Legislative Assembly) and the Upper House (Legislative Council) passed Robertson's two new Bills on land tenure policy on the 16th October 1861 and two new Acts came into effect: the *Crown Lands Alienation Act 1861*, and the *Crown Lands Occupation Act 1861*.

The Crown Lands Alienation Act 1861

The *Crown Lands Alienation Act* made the 'nineteen counties of location' (set by Governor Darling, in 1826) redundant, and replaced the land tenure policy implemented by Governor FitzRoy in 1847; as instructed in the Order in Council.

Under the new Act, all town and suburban land (throughout NSW) would be sold through auction, and the leased Crown land of the original squatters now pastoralists would be opened to competition through the process of 'selection and sale'. New conditions were required if pastoralists were to retain their lease/s. They would need to build a homestead, demonstrate they lived on the leased station, have a documented viable farm (stock would be assessed for this purpose) and show their commitment by progressively purchasing sections of the station (as designated by them) at the cost of £1 per 640 acres.

As part of their pre-emptive lease, the existing pastoralist had the first right of purchase and could readily choose which parts of their station/s they wished to progressively purchase. Though if they didn't start to purchase their station/s in this way, free selectors had the right to come onto their station/s and take up the land they were interested in (selection before survey) and then apply to the Crown to purchase the land they had chosen. In this way, this first Act enabled all Crown land (leased and available for purchase) to be opened to 'free-selection before survey' with the only Crown land excepted from 'free-selection' being the Crown land reserves.[362]

Under Robertson's *Crown Land Alienation Act* any interested party could choose a small allotment of land just as before when William and his brothers went to Glennies Creek (Falbrook) circa 1823; but there was a difference. There were conditions for purchase (known as 'conditional purchase') that include the requirement for the selector to reside on the land. See below.

The purchase was conditional on:

* *the area being limited to 40 to 320 acres at £1 per acre*

* *paying a deposit of one quarter of the purchase price [after survey]*

* *adding improvements to the value of £1 per acre*

* *the selector residing on the land, and occupying the land for three years*

* *after three years the balance of the purchase had to be paid to the Colonial Treasurer together with a declaration that improvements had been undertaken on the land*

* *payments could be made from year to year. In practice the balance of the purchase price, with interest [5%], could be paid over an extended period. It was not unusual for 20 or 30 years to pass before freehold title was eventually granted.*

Where more than one purchaser selected the same land, the Act provided mechanisms including arbitration to settle ownership. Crown Land bought by conditional purchase and abandoned in less than three years after purchase was declared forfeited in the Government Gazette and sold at auction.

While 'selection claims' could be lodged at local Land Offices, the administration of the Lands Department was centralised in Sydney. Land selections were processed slowly with long delays due to backlogs, distance, inaccurate survey maps, partial decisions, and reappraisals.[363]

The Crown Lands Occupation Act 1861

The second Act, the *Crown Lands Occupation Act 1861* covered 'leased' Crown land within the newly defined boundaries of settlement (that is, within town land, suburban land, first class settled districts, second class settled districts and unsettled districts). The Act targeted the pastoralists with their large expansive stations; the squatters of the past who originally set up runs beyond the boundaries of settlement, and who had (since c.1836) leased their 'now' stations (sometimes, still called runs) from the Crown.[364]

Under the 'Occupation Act' leased pastoral Crown land was let at the minimum size of 640 acres for one year in settled districts, and for five years in second class settled districts, and unsettled districts. The pastoralist could lease a further 640 acres (without competition) and up to three times their own purchased or granted land subject to the land being available and the lease not inhibiting access to the water supply (usually the rivers) for adjoining stations.

Through the 'Occupation Act' Robertson sought to curtail the on-going disputes about boundaries that had played out in the courts for years: with appeals, counter appeals, and indecision that went on for decades for pastoralists, like William. Any disputes would now be settled through arbitration; there would no longer be a judge, jury, and inconsistent and conflicting accounts from witnesses.[365]

Any pre-emptive lease (where the pastoralists wished to purchase leased Crown land) was required to be gazetted within two months of the lease, and the cost of purchase at a maximum was £1 per 640 acres. If not purchased, a lease could be renewed once they expired, if the land was not required for sale (free selection) or for any other government purpose.[366]

As before, and since Governor Bourke's 1836 Act, stock was still assessed as part of the lease, with a new requirement of a minimum amount of stock on each station, based on the acreage of the station, for the purpose of ensuring the maximum use and viability of Crown land.

Robertson envisaged greater diversity and opportunity for farmers with two main types of farms: small freehold farms mainly producing agricultural products and grain crops; and large stations with their expansive pastures and livestock. In theory, both the *Crown Lands Alienation Act 1861* (that facilitated small freehold farms) and the *Crown Lands Occupation Act 1861* (that regulated leased Crown land) enabled a government managed and controlled land tenure policy. No longer were the pastoralists (former squatters) free to do what they were partial to and expand their properties in an ad hoc manner based on the loudest voice in the courts. The pastoralists on leased Crown land would be regulated, subject to rigorous assessment of the productive value of their stock and required to purchase their station/s over time if they were to avoid competition from free selection. In concert, the *Crown Lands Alienation Act 1861*, would provide new small freehold farms (40–320 acres in size) throughout the colony and enable a greater spread of settlement, grain and other forms of farm produce.

Though both Acts were well grounded and designed to work in unison and provoke change, those under the Alienation Act (small lease holders purchasing Crown land) and those under the Occupation Act (pastoralists on leased Crown land) inevitably came into conflict, as the free selectors spread into the interior and competed with the original squatters for Crown land. As noted below.

After responsible government was established in 1855, the NSW Parliament passed legislation with the aim of unlocking land occupied by squatters. The Crown

Lands Alienation Act 1861 allowed a person to select for purchase between 40 and 320 acres of Crown land outside town boundaries; a deposit of 25% was payable with the balance payable three years and three months later... Leased land was open to selection and sale at any time. The principle of free selection was greatly abused by free selectors and squatters and led to a bitter struggle between them.[367]

The new Alienation Act enabled pastoralists, like William, to purchase small allotments of Crown land throughout NSW, as long as they adhered to the requirements of conditional purchase, and the restrictions placed on land set aside for land reserves.

William and his fellow pastoralists (the original squatters) could also, through the Occupation Act, retain their large leased holdings in the interior, provided they complied with the new regulations, and competed successfully through purchase, when their leased land was challenged by free-selectors.

The Aboriginal People and their Nations were Ignored

The Government's policy of *terra nullius* formalised by Governor Bourke (in 1835) was entrenched and implicit. Nowhere in the Alienation Act or the Occupation Act is there reference to First Nations people.[368]

On the boundaries of settlement, the frontier wars continued in places like the New England Tablelands. In concert, the Native Police positioned themselves on the margins of settlement for the purpose of moving Indigenous peoples off Country, usually with force, violence and massacre. The dispossession and destruction of Country spread as the settlers moved further north and over the border into the newly emerging colonial state of Queensland.[369]

In stark contrast to First Nations people, William's life was stable and certain. He was building on what he had at Rosedale and Ward's Mistake and waiting on a decision from the Privy Council.

CHAPTER 24

THE PRIVY COUNCIL'S DECISION ON WALLALLA STATION

Just over two years after William's appeal to the Privy Council, a summary of his case appeared once again in the SMH, and several other local papers, with no avail. Their Lordships in London had deferred their judgment. See below.

> *The Sydney Morning Herald, Monday 21 April 1862, page 8.*
> *THE PRIVY COUNCIL.*
> *AUSTRALIAN APPEAL CASES*
>
> *Trial appeal from a judgment of the Supreme Court of New South Wales, in the case of "Humphery and Christian v. Nowland" has been heard before the Judicial Committee of the Privy Council; present, Lord Chelmsford, Lord Justice Knight Bruce, Lord Justice Turner, and Mr. J. T. Coleridge.*[370]
>
> *The arguments commenced on the 4th February and concluded on the 7th. The following is a report of the case: – The appeal is from a decision in a case that is termed in Australia a "squatting" action; that means a question between settlers who claim the right of occupancy of a tract of land acknowledged by both parties to be the property of the Crown. The present respondent was plaintiff [William Nowland] in an action of trespass to land, comprising a very extensive tract of country, lying on both sides east and west of the River Mooki, at the Liverpool Plains, New South Wales.*
>
> *It appeared, from the evidence adduced at the trial, that the present respondent [Humphrey and Christian], and also the appellant [William Nowland] with their respective servants and flocks, had been on the locus together for several years. Each party claimed the land, as being the last of a chain of occupiers…*
>
> *[The previous iteration of the case put by both William Nowland and Humphrey and Christian, not included here, followed. Then the summary of the judgement, as told below].*
>
> *…The respondent (plaintiff in the action) [William Nowland] obtained a verdict in the court below-when £2150 damages were awarded for the trespass [of*

Humphrey and Christian]. The defendants [Humphrey and Christian] moved for a new trial, on the grounds of the damages given being excessive, and the improper admission and rejection of evidence.

The application for a new trial was refused by the Supreme Court of New South Wales, and against that decision the present appeal was brought. ... [Additional information here: The large sum of money (£2150 damages) was not good enough for William. He went back to the Supreme Court once again and asked for a new trial to clarify the boundaries of Wallalla, as detailed in his lease, and then based on the Supreme Courts, refusal, William took his case to the Privy Council. Though they couldn't decide]

... Their lordships deferred giving judgement.

Just over three weeks later, a final decision from the Privy Council appeared in the SMH, and again in several local papers, including the *Albury Banner and Wodonga Express*, who entitled their articles, 'Important Squatting Case' and 'The Great Squatting Appeal Case'.[371]

The final summary of the judgment that follows, ended a 20-year saga for William (1842–1862). Another long read, but worth it; the judgment measured and aimed at satisfying both parties. Humphrey and Christian, required to pay the court costs and William denied exclusive possession of Wallalla Station.

The Sydney Morning Herald, 15 May 1862, page 5.

THE PRIVY COUNCIL

Judgement of the Lords of the Judicial Committee of the Privy Council, on the appeal of Humphrey v. Nowland, from the Supreme Court of New South Wales, delivered 6th March, 1862. Present: Lord Chelmsford, Lord Justice-Knight Bruce, Sir Edward Ryan, Lord Justice Turner. Their Lordships think that it would not be satisfactory that the rights of the parties should be finally determined by the verdict given in this case. Upon its delivery the Chief Justice who tried the cause expressed his condemnation of it in very strong terms, stating that he believed it to be "utterly wrong". This opinion he seems never to have abandoned; and although he delivered the judgment refusing a new trial, and so far concurred with the majority of the Court, yet in various parts of it he intimates his own unaltered impression of the unsatisfactory nature of the verdict. It is evident that he was unable to satisfy himself whether the jury thought that the exclusive possession of the plaintiff [William Nowland] extended to the – whole of the land; or was confined to that part which lay on the western side of the river Mooki. But he thought the verdict erroneous, whichever way it was taken, and he expresses this opinion very decidedly and pointedly in the following passage of the judgment:

"If the jury have in fact assessed damages for the entire station, it follows that, according, to my view of the matter, the damages are assessed wrongly. On the other hand, if the damages had been assessed-in respect of the western portion only, then they are clearly, in my opinion, out of all proportion to the injury."

If, on consideration of the evidence, their Lordships had been fully and clearly satisfied that the jury were warranted in the conclusion to which they came, they would of course not have felt themselves bound to yield to the opinion of the Judge who presided at the trial, notwithstanding the advantages he possessed from having; had the opportunity of seeing the witnesses under examination, and of forming an accurate judgment upon the case; but their Lordships would not venture to differ from the opinion of the presiding Judge, except upon clear and satisfactory grounds, and, upon a careful consideration of the whole of the evidence, they cannot help concurring in the view taken by the learned Judge of the impropriety of the verdict, whether it is to be applied to the whole or only to a part of the land in dispute.

It clearly appears that for upwards of twenty years before the present action was commenced there had been a concurrent possession of portions of the land by the predecessors of both parties; if there had not been almost an exclusive possession on the defendant's [Humphrey's and Christian's] part of the land on the eastern side [western side?] of the river. It is not an immaterial circumstance in this contest that the defendants [Humphery and Christian] and those who used the run before them, appear not to have depastured the land with cattle, but only with sheep, while the plaintiff [William Nowland] and his predecessors turned on no sheep, or at least, only a very few, but depastured principally, if not solely, with cattle; as it seems that horned cattle will not graze on spots were sheep are depasturing. These facts tend strongly to prove that the possession by the defendants [Humphery and Christian] and their predecessors must have interfered very materially with any right which the plaintiff [William Nowland] may at any time have acquired by reason of the previous possession either of himself or those who preceded him.

The plaintiff [William Nowland] or his predecessors may occasionally have denied the right of the defendants [Humphery and Christian], or of those whom they succeeded to the use of the land, and there may have been instances of a more forcible assertion of claim in the plaintiff's [William Nowland's] line of possession by acts of impounding (though these acts are not confined to one side only), but the plaintiff [William Nowland] never asserted his right to an exclusive possession by proceedings at law before the year 1852, when he brought an action against Eales, the immediate predecessor of the defendants [Humphery and Christian] in the use of the land.

The result of this action was not of a nature to afford much countenance to the plaintiff's [William Nowland's] present proceeding; for although the jury were in his favour as to a hut, of the pulling down of which he complained, they found that the land itself was held in common by him and Eales. Now the circumstances under which the land was used from the time the defendants [Humphrey and Christian] began to depasture it with their sheep till the action against him, were not different from those which had previously taken place.

A succession of occupiers on both sides had been permitting one another to continue undisturbed in the use of the land, and each fresh occupant at the commencement of his occupation found that he was not to be the sole possessor unless he could remove some other person who was exercising a right upon the land similar to that which he claimed.

The plaintiff [William Nowland], upon this state of things, asserts his right to the exclusive possession of the land against the defendants, on the ground that the first possessor in his line was upon the land before any one of the predecessors of the defendants [Humphrey and Christian]; and he [William Nowland] shapes his case in this manner:- He says that the first lawful occupier was Parrott, who transmitted his legal possession through different persons to him [William Nowland]; that the first person who entered, upon the land while Parrott was in possession was a trespasser; that all who followed this original trespasser were themselves also trespassers; and that although they continued undisturbed for whatever length of time by those who represented the first lawful possessor, the illegal character of their original possession never changed; and that at the end of fifty years a person who had obtained possession in the line of the first possessor might maintain trespass against a successor of the original trespasser who continued to use the land.

If this view of the law is correct, it would utterly exclude the well known and important doctrine of acquiescence upon which rights of every description have been constantly decided. The plaintiff, [William Nowland] however, asserts that this mode of presenting the case is justified by a course of decisions in New South Wales upon similar questions applicable to waste lands in the colony. Their Lordships have not been informed of the exact nature and extent of those decisions. They are referred to in the judgment given upon the 7th and 8th objections raised upon the motion of the defendants [Humphrey and Christian] for a new trial, but all the cases mentioned in that judgment are decisions of the Courts in this country. It does not appear clearly, from the expressions used in the judgment, that the Judges meant to proceed as far in the protection of an original possessor of waste land and his successors as the argument of the respondent [Humphrey and Christian] asserts, although their language is perhaps not sufficiently guarded upon this point. At the same time, if there are decisions in the colony applicable to a species of interest or possession of a very peculiar character, and entirely distinct from any state of things which could possibly exist in England, their Lordships would be very reluctant to try these decisions solely by the test of English authorities. But acquiescence is a principle which must be universally applicable, and especially, as it would seem, to such a species of possession as that which was in controversy in the present action.

Now, it appears to their Lordships that very insufficient weight was given to the facts which established an uninterrupted continuance of the same state of things for a very long course of years. The non-interference of the possession, which may be described as represented by the defendants [Humphrey and Christian], was not only important in its bearing on the exclusive possession claimed by the plaintiff [William Nowland], but it reflected back upon the original possession, and gave a character to the very origin of the title which was the foundation of the plaintiff's [William Nowland's] claim. If Parrott and those who succeeded Parrott suffered patiently the intrusion of other persons upon the land, an exclusive right to which is now claimed upon the footing of his [William Nowland's] original possession, it is surely very strong evidence either that Parrott did not possess the sole right, or that he [Parrott] was willing to permit others to share the use of the land with him, and surrendered the possession to his successors only to the extent to which he himself enjoyed it.

Their Lordships, in considering the whole case, cannot forbear from also expressing an opinion that due weight was not given upon the trial to the effect of the plaintiff's [William Nowland's] schedule under his insolvency. It certainly is a most important document, bearing not only upon the question of damages, but upon the right itself which was involved in the action. It scarcely seems credible that if the plaintiff [William Nowland] had such a valuable possession as to entitle him to a sum of £2000 as damages for the intrusion upon it for four years, it should have been altogether omitted from his schedule or that his creditors should have been ignorant of this available item of property, and should not have compelled him to give them the benefit of it. And if it was of the value which it has assumed in the action, and the plaintiff [William Nowland] had not cattle enough to stock the land (which appears to have been the case), it is still more unaccountable that he should have retained the precarious use of it, constantly liable to disturbance as it was from his inability thoroughly to use it, and should not have availed himself of the profit which he might have acquired by the transfer of his possession.

Their Lordships forbear from any further remark upon the evidence in the case, as there must be a new trial, the result of which they desire not to anticipate. Of course, upon such trial care will be taken to distinguish the evidence applicable respectively to the eastern and western sides of the river, to which very different considerations appear to attach; and the attention of the jury will, of course, be called to the difference between these two portions of the disputed land, in order that the important question of acquiescence may be distinctly applied to each, and that if damages should be given, it may be known to what they were applied, and how they were estimated.

Their Lordships will recommend to her Majesty that the judgment appealed from be reversed, and a new trial granted; and that the costs of the rule in the Court below abide the event of the cause, and the costs of this appeal be paid by the respondent [Humphrey and Christian].

The Privy Council agreed to a new trial if 'Humphrey and Christian' wanted to pursue the matter, and were reluctant to rule on possession, given the distinct and contrasting character of possession in the colony compared to England; though they agreed 'exclusive possession' by William could be challenged. For them, Parrott may not have had possession of all the land he offered William when William purchased the improvement from Parrott and Ross, in 1839.

The Privy Council then questioned William on two other grounds: firstly, if Wallalla was his, why had he not declared his licence for the Station (or the assets he had on this land) in his schedule, when he was declared insolvent in 1849; and, secondly, in *Nowland v Humphrey and Another* (held on the 17th August 1858) 'for them' William did not have enough cattle on Wallalla Station to justify damages of £2150 (stated as £2000 in the above summary of the case).

In William's favour the Privy Council determined that Humphrey and Christian were required to pay the cost of the appeal and hopefully, based on this decision, the monies William paid as security (£2500 in March 1860) to enable the appeal to go ahead, were returned to him.

After the judgment, the case quickly became redundant. William had already sold the improvements he had made on Wallalla Station to John Eales (c.1860) and Humphrey and Christian, never opted for a further appeal.[372]

CHAPTER 25

WILLIAM AND HIS BOYS PURCHASE ALLOTMENTS AT WARRAH RIDGE

William always stayed ahead of the game. Well before the Privy Council's judgment (in May 1862) he knew he had to move on and repositioned himself; and that is just what he did! As soon as the Robertson Acts came into effect in October 1862, William (now 58) and his eldest sons, William jr. (30), Michael (28), Robert (26), Charles (22), Alex (16) and George (15) each purchased a pre-emptive lease at Warrah Ridge on the Liverpool Plains; one of the locations set aside by the Department of Lands for selection before survey.

The Nowlands moved quickly, and purchased as best they could adjacent allotments, to ensure an expanse of pasture. Then when William sr. and the older boys were away Mary (now 49) and the youngest two sons Alfred (11) and Henry (9) probably managed and maintained Rosedale with their staff (most likely, a farm servant [house maid] and farmhand).

There would have been plenty of exuberant talk around the kitchen table. Just like before, when William and his three brothers (Michael, Henry, and Edward) had gone to Glennies Creek (c.1823) to get in first and each stake their claim on small adjoining allotments. William and six of his sons (nearly 40 years later) were now doing the same, this time at Warrah Ridge.[373]

Robert's Logbook

Robert (27) kept a logbook of the family's farm activities at Warrah Ridge; some extracts from 'June 1863 to December 1868' follow.[374]

Robert Nowland, Warrah Ridge

Arrived at Kangaroo Park on 1st July 1863 in company of C. Nowland [Chas], W. Nowland Senior, ['our' William sr.] H. Ranyard, Tallent, Coughlan, Gilmour and wife, Fanny.

Paid £80 deposit for 320 acres in Warrah Ridge called Kangaroo Park on the 25 of June, 1863.[375]

Frank bottomed the well July 27, 1863.

A Nowland [Alex] block of land was taken August 6, 1863.[376]

R. Nowland [Robert] started a mail bag on Saturday 10 Oct. 1863.

R. Nowland [Robert] arrived at Warrah Ridge on Sunday the 30 July 1864 with 1020 ewes bought off James Sevil at ten shillings and six pence per head.

H. Nowland [Henry] and G.N. [George Nowland] arrived at Warrah Ridge with 1160 sheep from Glennies Creek [most likely, Rosedale] on the 27 October 1864.[377]

Alexander Nowland, G. Nowland [George] and Frank Squires started to New England on Thursday 10th of November 1864. [Probably going to Ward's Mistake]

W. Nowland Sen^R, Alex Nowland, G. Nowland [George] and T. Dunn started from Warrah Ridge to New England to gather 500 bullocks sold to Christian at £2.0.0 per head. Started on 16 September 1865.[378]

Arrived at Warrah Ridge on the 16 March 1866 with 2200 wethers.[379]

Sold 1000 wethers to J. Sevil at 13/6 per head [13 shillings and 6 pence per head] on 26 March 1866 to be taken away in two months and a fortnight from the above date.

W. Nowland, [most likely, William jr.] H. Nowland [Henry] and W. Bates started down to Glennies Creek [Rosedale] with 154 ewes on Tuesday the 10 July 1866.

Warrah Ridge

18 August 1866.

Received from R. Nowland [Robert] the sum of two pounds £2.0.0. on account of fencing done for William Nowland [presumably William jr].[380]

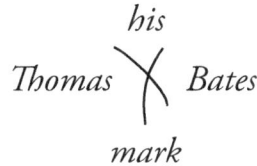

witness

Alexander Nowland

Henry Mercer arrived at Warrah Ridge on Sunday 6th December 1868….

The Farming Practices of the Nowlands

Robert's logbook provides us with a glimpse into the farming practices of the Nowlands at Warrah Ridge. The Nowlands established themselves on their small allotments: grazed sheep, and cattle; employed farm labour and stockmen for the various jobs around the farm, such as, sinking wells, providing fencing, shepherding and shearing sheep (these last two activities are elsewhere in Robert's logbook and not included above); and, moved with their stock between New England (presumably Ward's Mistake), Warrah Ridge, and Glennies Creek (Rosedale). Robert's logbook also provides us with accounts of the sale of their stock and the price received.

During the next two decades (1860s and 70s) William sr. and his boys, established new farms on their allotments at Warrah Ridge; and for William sr. two additional allotments in the adjoining Parish of Telford (detailed later in the chapter).

The Nowland Allotments and the AACo

Ironically, the Nowland allotments were located directly above the AACo's Warrah Station that had consumed William's first squatter's run on the Liverpool Plains (also named 'Warrah') along with several others, in and around 1833. Twenty-eight years later, William returned (with some of his sons) and claimed several allotments at Warrah Ridge, just north of the AACo under a new Act: the *Crown Lands Alienation Act 1861*.

The three maps that follow show the relative position of the AACo's Warrah Station and the Nowland allotments. The extract from the first map (a very informative historical map) shows the relative locations of the AACo's Warrah Station and the allotments at Warrah Ridge (under the *Crown Lands Alienation Act 1861*), as well as the approximate locations of Telford and Quirindi. (See Figure 26.)[381]

The proximity of the Nowland allotments, at Warrah Ridge, to the AACo is also evident in the second map, from the NSW Land Registry Services 'Historical Maps – Buckland County, Parish of Warrah, 1885'. (See Figure 27.)

A third map of all the Nowland allotments in Warrah Ridge and Telford (in 1885) is included next, to gain a sense of the amount of land William sr. and his boys had strategically accumulated (in adjoining allotments) over a period of around 23 years (1862–1885). (See Figure 28.)[382] Note, the shaded area in this third map dates from 1862 and shows three generations of Nowland allotments.[383]

William died in April 1884 and passed on his allotments at Warrah Ridge and Telford to his sons and grandchildren (detailed in the last chapter of the story).

As told earlier, when the Nowlands moved to Warrah Ridge (c.1862) their allotments were very close to the land where William had claimed his first run some forty years earlier, as a squatter; his Warrah on the Liverpool Plains. Now William and his sons each had a deed of entitlement for each of their allotments (either a

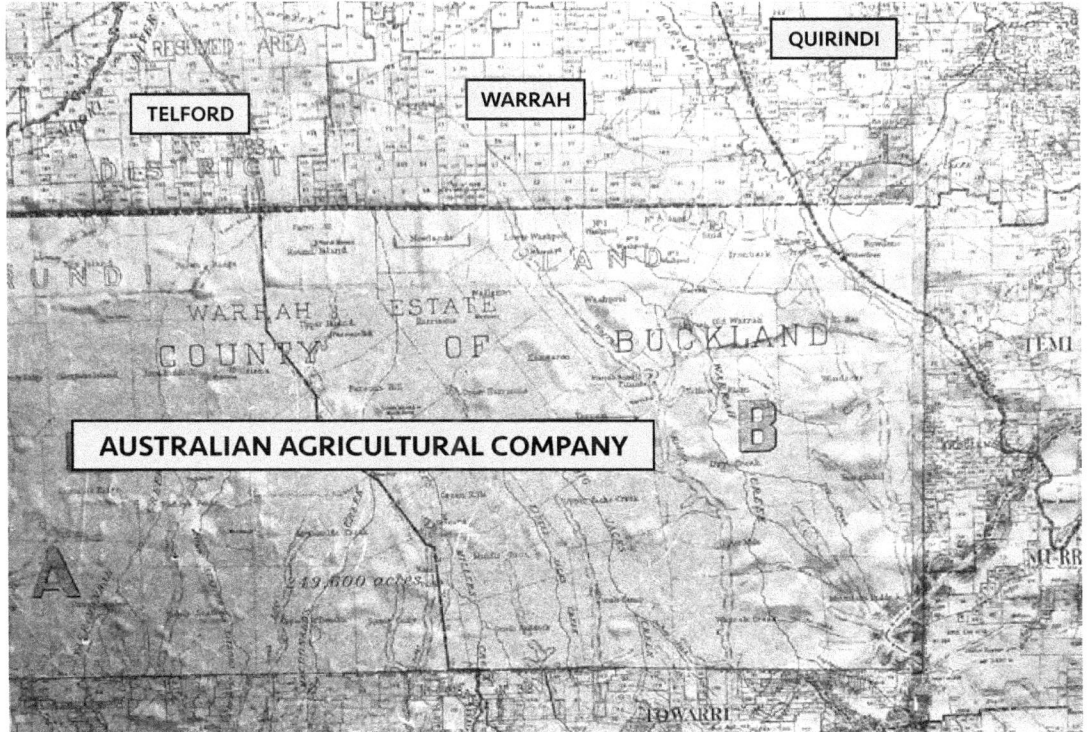

Figure 26: Relative Locations: Warrah Estate (AACo), Telford, Warrah Ridge and Quirindi (Map One)

pre-emptive lease or a title of purchase) and classified as graziers under the *Crown Lands Alienation Act 1861*. The only former run (now known as a station) William still had was managed by his eldest son, William jr.; Ward's Mistake on New England Tablelands. William had leased this reasonably large station (40,960 acres in 1842 and 81,920 acres in 1860) for over 20 years and under the *Crown Lands Occupation Act 1861*, he was required to purchase part of the station (a minimum 640 acres for £1) to keep the free selectors at bay.

A Retrospective on the Nowlands at Warrah Ridge

A generation later (in April 1930), a retrospective on the Nowlands at Warrah Ridge is provided below in John James Nowland's obituary, in 1930. As told earlier, John James Nowland (born in 1862) was Chas and Annie's eldest son and William's and Mary's first male grandchild.

Sydney Morning Herald – 10th April 1930, page 13.
OBITUARY.
MR. J. J. NOWLAND.

The death has occurred after a long illness of Mr. John James Nowland, a member of one of the oldest families In New South Wales, and one who played

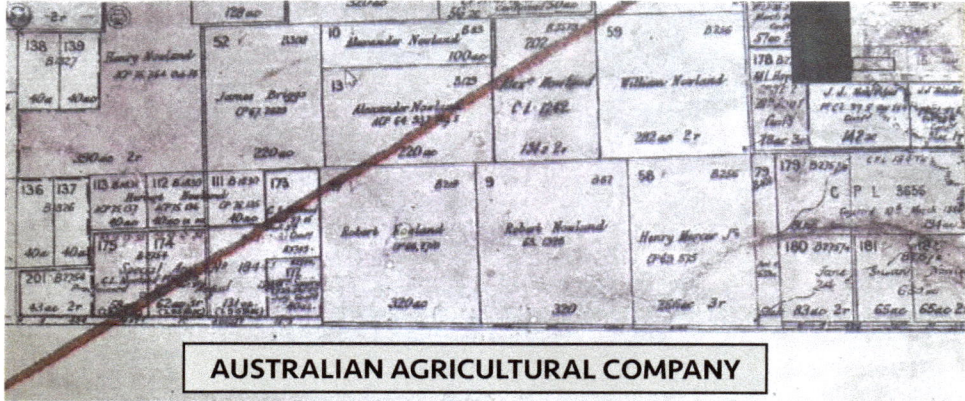

Figure 27: Location of Some of the Nowland Allotments (all adjoining) at Warrah Ridge Relative to the AACo's Warrah Estate (Map Two)

a prominent part in opening up the New England and north-west districts. His great-grandfather, Michael Nowland, came to Australia with Governor Gidley King, the two being personal friends, and was appointed Superintendent of Convicts.[384] *A son, Mr. William Nowland, took up country near Armidale, and later the family owned a station on Liverpool Plains and the greater portion of Warrah Ridge. Mr. William Nowland was the first man to drive a vehicle over the Liverpool Range, a feat of no mean achievement in view of the fact that a track had to be cut for a great part of the way. After disposing of his interest in Warrah Ridge, Mr. J. J. Nowland followed pastoral pursuits in Queensland until he was overtaken by the illness which led to his death. In 1883 he married Miss Emily Smith, a daughter of Mr. and Mrs. W. A. Smith, of Dungog. Mrs. Nowland and four sons and three daughters survive.*

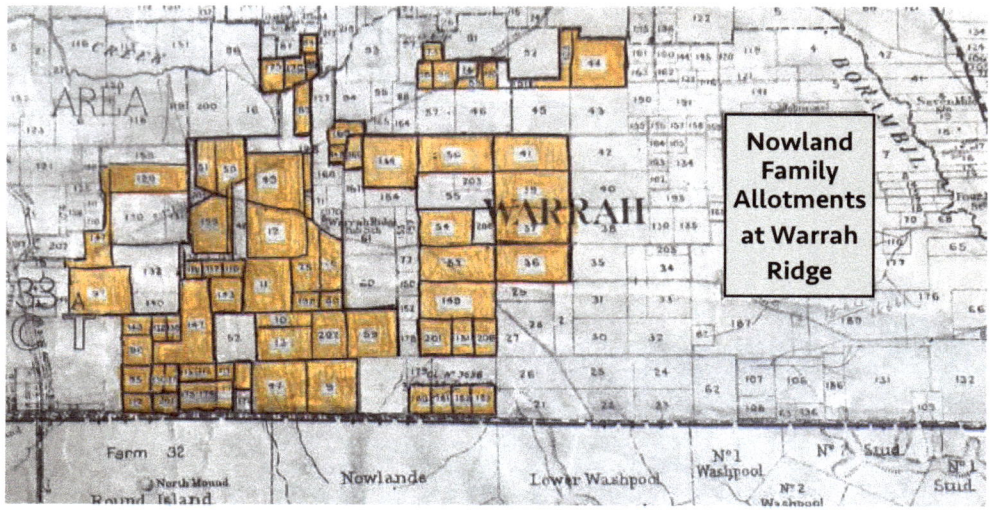

Figure 28: Nowland Allotments: County of Buckland, Parish of Warrah and Parish of Telford (1885) (Map Three)

Chapter 26

Changing Family Dynamics in the 1860s

By 1863, William and Mary, had eight surviving sons. Two of their boys were married, Chas to Annie Squire, in 1860, and Michael to Martha Squire, in 1862 (most likely, sisters). The rest of the boys (except for William jr.) still lived at home with the older ones (Robert 27, Alexander 17 and George 16) away a lot because they needed to travel regularly between Rosedale and the family allotments at Warrah Ridge; and sometimes they went on to Ward's Mistake.

The Loss of William's Brother Henry (66)

All the family were busy establishing themselves at Warrah Ridge when tragedy struck, once again, William's older brother Henry died on the 10th February 1863. The family notice in the paper read.

> *The Maitland Mercury and Hunter River General Advertiser,*
> *19 February 1863, page 1.*
> DEATHS.
>
> *At his residence, Royal Hotel, Muscle Brook, [sic] on the evening of Tuesday, the 10th instant, Mr. Henry Nowland, aged 66 years; deeply regretted by a large circle of relatives and friends.*

Henry was as ambitious as William: an innkeeper, local councillor, mail contractor, coachman, and pastoralist. Today, he is best known for his coaching services and his Nowland's Coach.

As told earlier, Henry had a coach building and blacksmith business in Hunter Terrace, Muswellbrook (from the mid-1840s to 1863). He built his own coaches, purchased, and bred his own horses, and had several contracts to transport mail and passenger in his Nowland's Coach: initially within the region, and later from Maitland to Moreton Bay.[385]

After Henry's death (February 1863) his coaching business was taken over by his eldest son, Robert John Nowland.[386]

A photograph of a Nowland's Coach in storage after the business was discontinued, with presumably Nowland children on it, can be seen in Figure 29.

Figure 29: The Nowland Coach

William the Only Nowland Brother Left

After Henry's death in February 1863, William sr. (59) was the only brother left; forty years after the Nowland Brothers came to Glennies Creek, circa 1823.

All three Farlow sisters who came later (one after the other from the mid to late 1830s) still lived within the region; William's wife, Mary (50) at Rosedale, Edward's wife, Christian (52) at Gunnedah, and Henry's wife, Harriet (58) at Muswellbrook.

William and Mary's Children Followed in Their Footsteps

William sr. and Mary had always made a living from farming and each of their children followed in their footsteps. How young, William and Mary's children were, when they started to help their parents around the family farm at Rosedale is unknown and assumed to be around 5 or 6. They were fast learners; riding horses and droving with their father at a very young age. Henry was eleven when he drove sheep with George from Rosedale to Warrah Ridge some 88 miles (141.6 km).[387]

All the boys now busied themselves droving, advertising and selling stock. The following ad appeared in the *Maitland Mercury* in 1862; Alex 16.

> *The Maitland Mercury and Hunter River General Advertiser,*
> *14th February 1862, page 3*
>
> STORE CATTLE
>
> FOR SALE, about FIVE HUNDRED HEAD of quite well-bred STORE CATTLE, of equal sexes, from one to six years old. They are now on their way from New England to the Mooki River, Liverpool Plains, and will arrive there in about nine or ten days.
>
> ALEXANDER NOWLAND, Glennies Creek, Camberwell.

Followed by:

> *The Maitland Mercury and Hunter River General Advertiser,*
> *8th October 1864, page 1*
>
> NOTICE
> *All Whom it May Concern*
>
> I HEREBY GIVE NOTICE that I intend starting with a FLOCK OF SHEEP on or about the 13th of October, to TRAVEL from Falbrook to Liverpool Plains via Muswellbrook, Scone and Murrurindi. The sheep will be branded: [-N]
>
> ALEXANDER NOWLAND,
>
> Falbrook, Oct 6th 1864.

And in 1865; Alex 19, selling store cattle, once again. See below.

> *The Maitland Mercury and Hunter River General Advertiser,*
> *7th February 1865, page 1*
>
> STORE CATTLE
>
> FOR SALE, about SIX HUNDRED HEAD of quite well-bred STORE CATTLE, of equal sexes, from one to six years old. They are now being gathered in New England, forty miles north of Armidale, and can be delivered on the station, or anywhere between there and the Mooki River, Liverpool Plains.
>
> Apply to:
>
> ALEXANDER NOWLAND
>
> Glennies Creek Camberwell.
>
> January 31, 1865
>
> [the same ad. appeared again in the paper on the 11th Feb. 1865]

Alex's younger brother, George 18, was also involved in the sale of store cattle. See the ad that follows.

> *The Maitland Mercury and Hunter River General Advertiser,*
> *18th February 1865, page 3*
> STORE CATTLE
>
> *FOR SALE, about 500 Head of Quite Well-bred STORE CATTLE, of Equal Sexes, from one to six years old. They are now on their way from New England to Warrah Ridge, "Liverpool Plains", and will arrive there next Wednesday, and will remain there till they are sold. Parties wishing to purchase could either have part or the whole.*
>
> *Apply to ALEXANDER NOWLAND, Glennies Creek, Camberwell; or to GEORGE NOWLAND, Warrah Ridge, Quirindi, near the A. A. Company's Station, Warrah. February 13, 1865.*

William and Mary Now With Grandchildren

By the end of 1865, William sr. (61) and Mary (52) had four surviving grandchildren: Chas' (24) and Annie's (24) three children (John and Ada, twins, born in 1862, and Mina, born in 1864); and, Michael's (30) and Martha's (23) child (Clara, born in 1862). Michael's and Martha's other child, (William, born in 1864, died in 1865).[388]

By the Mid-1860s, Family Life Had Changed

By the mid-1860, six of William sr.'s and Mary's boys had moved out of home and all were graziers.[389] William jr. (33) lived at Ward's Mistake and was already well established as a grazier; Michael (31), Charles (25), and their families, lived permanently at their own homesteads (Michael at Borambil, Charles at Warrah Ridge); and, Robert (29), Alex (19), and George (18) (though all unmarried, and returning to Rosedale, as needed) were probably spending more and more time on their own allotments, at Warrah Ridge. While William sr.'s and Mary's two youngest boys, Alfred (14) and Henry (12) were most likely doing the opposite; spending more time at Rosedale and moving to Warrah Ridge as required.

William sr. also needed to spend a fair amount of time away from home given the conditions of purchase for his allotments at Warrah Ridge and Telford. The *Crown Land Alienation Act 1861* required evidence of the establishment and development of a pre-emptive lease. The occupant was required to be there. William could no longer come and go as he wished or stay away from his allotments for long periods of time.

The distance William travelled also added to his time away from home. As told earlier, it was at least 88 miles (141.6 km) between Rosedale and Warrah Ridge. Though presumably, William was away from home far less than before, given his age (61) and the availability of the boys to look after William's interests at Warrah Ridge, Telford and Ward's Mistake.

PART FIVE

Changes in Transport and Family Life

The dramatic, remarkable and devastating changes to Country within such a short period of time

Forty-six years after the first settlers entered Wonnarau Koori Country via the Bulga Track

CHAPTER 27

THE ROADS THE NOWLANDS TRAVELLED & THE PADDLE STEAMERS THEY TOOK SOUTH

The roads the Nowlands travelled were difficult to navigate, be it by horse, buggy, or coach. For forty years (c.1825–1865) William had travelled north along the 'Great Northern Road' (initially a track carved out by the drovers) to his various stations on the Liverpool Plains, and since the late 1830s, he had followed the same so-called road up onto the New England Tablelands on what only could be described as an arduous and challenging journey.

For a lesser time, around 30 years (c.1823–1853), William had also travelled south along the notorious Bulga Track to the Windsor and Sydney markets.[390] This track was the preferred route of the drovers, despite the demands, obstacles and problems they faced. The shorter route south along the more substantial 'Great North Road', post-1836, had too many steep sections, no permanent waterholes, and very few grazing areas for stock.[391]

Those who travelled the roads north and south from the Hunter, went through hundreds of kilometres of enormous potholes, mud, slush, and sometimes, swollen rivers. The newspaper article that follows (written in 1870) gives us a glimpse into what it was like along the Great Northern Road, and the difficulties travellers faced.

The Sydney Morning Herald, 23 August 1870, page 3.
THE GREAT NORTHERN ROAD[392]
TO THE EDITOR OF THE HERALD

Sirs – I know that your columns are usually open to all matters of public interest, and am sure that you will readily acknowledge that the state of the roads is a subject of vital importance to the commercial interest of the colony. Having within this month travelled over the whole Northern from Muswellbrook to Tenterfield, I am in a position to state that it is impossible for the merchant and importers of Sydney to conceive that one of the main thoroughfare of this colony should be in its present disgraceful and dangerous state commencing at Guest's Hotel, Willow Tree some fifteen miles north of Murrurundi, there commences a succession of creeks, gullies, and wide yawning chasms with abrupt and rotten sides and bed, and a loaded dray once, in it is literally smothered, and the poor bullock driver may lash the last ounce of flesh on his unfortunate cattle without the least effect, and nothing is left for him but to sit down in the mud and bless the impolitic Government under which it is his misfortune to live.

Nearly the whole way to Tamworth the bed of the road is one mass of slime and mud. "Jessie's Gap" is really in a most dangerous state. The mail coachman, Wilkinson, who has driven for 13 years, and is one of the best drivers on the road, dare not face it, but waited three hours for daylight, thus delaying the whole Northern mails.

From Tamworth to Uralla the road is as bad, and from Armidale to Glen Innes a great deal worse. In Tamworth there is at present not one case of kerosene, and few candles. The large hall, for a meeting last night, had to be lighted with six tallow dips. A large stores stock of sugar consists of 24 lbs., very neatly done up in six paper bags.

At Uralla a storekeeper told me his stock of winter boots had been more than four months on the road, and the bill due before they have come to hand; at Armidale the same complaints. If the people on the Northern Road will not, by united voice and action, demand that something shall be done, to all the merchants and importers quietly see their trade paralyzed and stocks accumulating rather than request the Government at once, by a judicious expenditure of £10,000 or £12,000, to render the roads practicable for dray to travel.

On a fair calculation, there are as least goods to the amount of £40,000 now in the stores or fast in the mud which ought to have been delivered and sold. The loss to the storekeepers of the Northern districts is at least £10,000 profit, and to Sydney a return of at least £50,000.

COMMERCIAL

In the 1860s, dubious roads like the one described above (The Great Northern Road) were the only option for the Nowlands when they left Rosedale, unless they decided to go to Sydney via paddle steamer.

The Paddle Steamers

In the 1830s, William and Mary had two choices of paddle steamer: the *Sophia Jane* (from 1831) or *William the Fourth* (from 1832).

Sophia Jane

The *Sophia Jane* (1831–1846) was the first paddle steamer in NSW. It was built in England as a sailing ship and was converted to a paddle steamer on arrival at Sydney Cove, in May 1831. On her maiden voyage as a paddle steamer, the *Sophia Jane* transversed the coastal waters of the colony between Sydney Cove and Queens Wharf, Morpeth, on the Hunter River; a journey of 11 hours and 36 minutes with the return journey, two hours and 23 minutes longer. As told in the following article.

The Sydney Monitor, Saturday, 25th June 1831, page 4
THE SOPHIA JANE

This fine steam-vessel returned to port, from the maiden trip to Hunter's River on Wednesday evening, having accomplished her task in the most gratifying manner. She left Sydney cove on Sunday morning, [19th June] at 10 minutes past 7, and arrived at Newcastle at 13 minutes past 3, [in 8 hrs. and 3 mins] having been delayed for a short time by taking the cutter Emma in tow, about three miles from the entrance.

On [the following] Monday morning, at 11 o'clock, she started for the Green Hills [Queens Wharf, Morpeth], which she reached in 3 hours and 33 minutes,

Figure 30: Paddle Steamer – *Sophia Jane*

Figure 31: P.S. *Rose*

although, in crossing the shallows in Limeburners' Bay, the power of the engine was necessarily slackened. At a quarter past 1 on Tuesday, she left the Green Hills, and full power being given to her paddles, she would have reached Newcastle in three hours, had she not got entangled amongst the shallows, by which she was delayed a full hour. On Wednesday she left the harbour of Newcastle at 20 minutes past 11, and entered the Heads of Port Jackson at 7 [in 5 hrs. and 40 mins]. The wind was adverse both going and returning, and consequently the sails were seldom used.

A painting of the *Sophia Jane* is depicted in Figure 30 and shows a wooden sailing ship with two wooden paddle boxes, one on each side of the vessel, positioned opposite each other, and halfway down the ship.

William the Fourth

In the same year the *Sophia Jane* arrived in Sydney Harbour (1831), Marshall and Lowe, who were local shipwrights, completed a similar ocean-going paddle steamer at the Deptford Shipyards, Williams River, Clarence Town (26 km north of present-day Raymond Terrace) that they named *William the Fourth* (1831–1863). This second paddle steamer's maiden voyage went from the Deptford Shipyards to Sydney Cove in November 1831.[393]

Both the *Sophia Jane* and *William the Fourth* competed for patronage between

Sydney Cove and Morpeth from 1832.³⁹⁴ Then, in 1841, a new type of paddle steamer, the 'iron paddle steamer' started to contest the same route.

The first iron paddle steamer to compete for custom along this route was the *Rose* (see Figure 31). It was built in London and arrived in Sydney unannounced, at night; it was found by the locals anchored in Darling Harbour on the 8th April 1841.³⁹⁵ The maiden voyage of this faster and lighter vessel from Sydney to Morpeth on the 15th April 1841 took around six hours; travelling 81.80 nautical miles at 14 knots per hour.³⁹⁶

By the 1840s, the journey from Morpeth to Sydney by iron paddle steamer took around six hours while the alternative route via the Great North Road, with its steep gradient and inhospitable environment took up to four days. The other route from Sydney, as told earlier was the Bulga Track (later known as the Putty Road); a long and arduous trek mainly used by drovers.³⁹⁷

Travelling from Rosedale to Sydney by Road and then Steamer

Between 1831and 1863, passengers who wished to go to and from the Hunter to Sydney by paddle steamer usually came to Queens Wharf at Morpeth, by road. While from 1858, the locals from Maitland and its surrounds had an alternative. They could travel from Maitland to East Maitland for 2.7 miles (4.4 km) by steam train and then walk to the Queens Wharf, Morpeth along the road for a further 2.8 miles (4.5 km).³⁹⁸

When William, Mary and/or their boys decided to go to Sydney by paddle steamer (prior to May 1863) they travelled by road from Camberwell to the Queens Wharf, Morpeth for some 50.2 miles (80.8 km).³⁹⁹ Given William had lots of buggies (detailed in his will) the family probably travelled by buggy, until Henry provided them with the option of going on his Nowland's Coach to the wharf (c.1842).

On other occasions, when William sr. and/or the boys were going to Sydney either together or alone by paddle steamer (for business or to see family) they most likely initially travelled by horse to Morpeth (and stabled their horses there, until they returned) and then once Henry had his coaches (c.1842) they probably travelled in the Nowland's Coach.

Prior to 1852, on arrival in Sydney by paddle steamer the Nowlands had two choices if they wanted to go on to Windsor or Wilberforce. They could travel the 26.5 miles (42.7 km) to Windsor by coach, or travel by paddle steamer as far as Parramatta Wharf (the first, 14.9 miles) and then catch a coach from there to Windsor (11.5 miles/18.6 km).

See Figure 32 for a photo of a typical paddle steamer servicing Sydney Harbour and Parramatta River; the *Black Swan* (c.1844).

Figure 32: P.S. *Black Swan*, c.1844, stopping at a wharf on Sydney Harbour

CHAPTER 28

THE STEAM TRAINS

In 1852 a new railway line was opened between Sydney and Parramatta (today's Granville Station) and gave the Nowlands another option of going by steam train to Parramatta and then by coach to Windsor. Twelve years later in 1864, the railway line west from Sydney went all the way to Windsor, and the Nowlands could disembark from the paddle steamer in Sydney Cove and board a steam train to Windsor.[400]

At the Hunter end of the journey, Singleton Railway Station was opened on 7th May 1863 and from that date on, the Nowlands no longer needed to go by road to the Queens Wharf, Morpheth. They could catch a steam train from Singleton to Newcastle and board a paddle steamer at Kings Wharf, Newcastle (near present day, Queens Wharf Newcastle). At the start of their journey from Rosedale they needed to travel by road from Camberwell to Singleton (9.3 miles) before boarding the steam train to Newcastle Station; and most likely from there, they walked the last 486 yards (444.3 metres) to the Kings Wharf, Newcastle.

The introduction of the steam trains (in 1863) into this part of the interior made the journey to Sydney for the Nowlands (and the other travellers) more comfortable, quicker and easier.

It had been 40 years since the first settlers came up the Bulga Track by horse and dray and invaded Wonnaura Koori Country. Now, the steam trains had arrived to further undermine Country, and in juxtaposition facilitate extraordinary growth and development across the interior.

An excellent cartographic map follows that displays the progressive development of the railway line north from Sydney and the eventual link between Sydney and the Hunter, in 1889. (See Figure 33.)

The Very Small Village of Camberwell

The coming of the railways stymied William's dream of a township at Camberwell and his vision of a well-recognised town, supported by the local community and anyone who stopped in while travelling north or south along the Great Northern Road.

Camberwell was just too close to Singleton. A traveller, in September 1865 tells us of this reality as he travelled north along the Great Northern Road, and passed through Singleton, Camberwell, and the Chain of Ponds, at Liddell. See the article that follows (p.220).

THE STEAM TRAINS

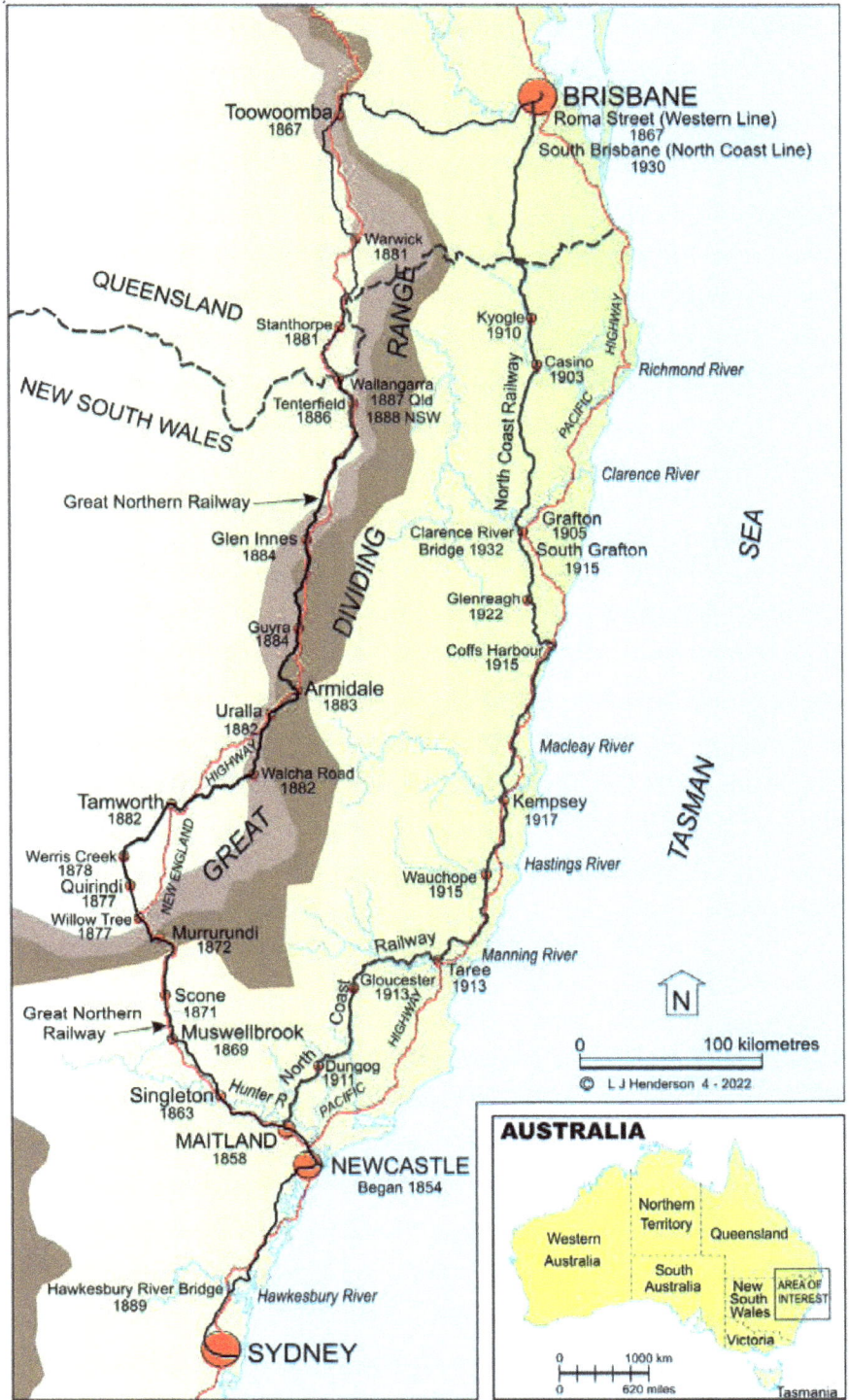

Figure 33: Map showing the Great Northern Railway's link to Brisbane and to the North Coast Railway as well as the dates of the openings of each station
(Cartography: Lawrence Henderson)

The Maitland Mercury and Hunter River General Advertiser, 7 September 1865, page 2.
NOTES OF A TRIP THROUGH THE NORTHERN DISTRICT.
BY AN EX-REPORTER.

... Directly after crossing the river at Singleton you commence to ascend a long and rather steep hill, from the top of this eminence a capital view of Singleton is obtained. I was disappointed, however, in the extent of the town as seen from this hill, it does not appear nearly so large as, after riding through George-street, one would naturally expect...

... The drive from this hill to Rix's Creek [on the way to Camberwell] is a splendid one, the road being remarkably good, and there being a gentle slope all the way. The distance from Singleton is variously estimated at from three and-a half to five miles, judging by the time it took me to travel it, I reckon about four miles to be the correct thing. At Rix's Creek there is a good substantial brick public house, and one or two huts near, that is all the population to be seen from the road. Back in the bush, I believe, there are a few settlers.

From this stage to Glennies Creek, or Camberwell as it is now called, is five miles, there is nothing on the way calling for special remark, with the exception perhaps at one rather good prospect from the summit of the first hill after leaving the Auckland Hotel, at Rix's Creek.

The township of Camberwell is very prettily situated on a series of gentle declivities, rising up from each side of the creek known as "Glennie's (sic) Creek". The most prominent feature in the whole township is the English church, which appears to be large enough to accommodate at least twice as many people as the entire village at the present time contains. It is a large, very substantial looking, stone structure. On making enquiry, I learnt that it was erected many years ago, in the early history of the colony, [first service, 1844] at which time there were located in the neighbourhood of Camberwell a great many Government men. [Someone had 'big-noted' Camberwell, to this traveller. Was it William?]

This accounts for the erection of so large a building [St Clement's] in so small a space. Another object which strikes a stranger is the bridge across the creek, which is one of the best for so insignificant a place that I have seen.

Formerly, before the construction of this Bridge, every fresh or flood of any height interrupted traffic, now, however, the mail, and of course teams, can pass even when the creek is bank high. One very noticeable thing in connection with this structure is the unusual strength of the railing. It would be well if every bridge that is built were protected in a similar way, instead of being left, as many of them are, with a railing of so flimsy a nature as to afford no real barrier against a restive horse.

The Rev. W. W. Dove, I should have mentioned above, officiates at Glennies Creek at stated intervals. The congregation varies in number from five to fifty. The township of Camberwell is supported principally by the traffic on the road, which of course is considerable. There is, however, a little land round about (sic) under cultivation. Besides the church, the place contains a national school, at a very low ebb-two public houses, one store, and a post office. The Great Northern Railway crosses the road here, and for a distance of some two miles or so is on the left of the road going towards Muswellbrook.

Between Glennies Creek and the Chain of Ponds the country is more open, and the drive on that account more pleasant. For the information of persons who like myself may have often wondered, when looking at the map, where "Liddell" is, I may mention that Liddell and the Chain of Ponds are the same thing. Liddell is the name of a township laid out by the Government: no township however has been formed, and the public house and store, and a few huts round about, retain the original name of Chain of Ponds. To be explicit, there is no township here at all. ...

The writer of the above article described Singleton as a 'reasonably large town', Camberwell as a 'small village' and Liddell as a 'staging post' with just a public house (Chain of Ponds) and a store.

Despite the size of Camberwell, the residents still lobbied for a station (William, presumably amongst them) and although they got their station, it was not within the village and closed a few years later. As told below.

The local railway opened on the 1st January 1866 and was called Camberwell Station and was four miles [6.4 km] from the village. Within a few years Camberwell station was scrapped and a new station was built at Glennies Creek, with a Mr. Jim Mayer as station master on a salary of £150 per year. Another station was built farther on at Ravensworth.[401]

These three local railway stations near Camberwell were sequentially demolished, though Ravensworth Railway Station survived until 1975.[402]

From the start (post-1st January 1866) those travelling north-west by train from Newcastle more frequently alighted at Singleton (rather than Camberwell) given Singleton was a much larger settlement.

The road that once passed through Camberwell had also been realigned and diverted away from the village, over a new bridge at Falbrook Creek (c.1860). In searching for a document on this bridge to ascertain the date of completion (most likely late 1860) I came across the following two articles that are worthy of mentioning because 'a person or persons' tried to blow up this new more elaborate bridge. *Who was laying down all the dynamite, probably in the dead of night, in an attempt to blow up, the new Falbrook Creek Bridge? We can only speculate. See below.*

New South Wales Government Gazette,
5 November 1861, Issue no. 2024, page 2342
Department of Public Works,
Sydney, 8th October, 1861.
ONE HUNDBED POUNDS REWARD.

WHEREAS some evil disposed person or persons did, on the night of the 6th instant, attempt to blow up the Falbrook Bridge, near Singleton, with gunpowder, and succeeded thereby in doing it great injury: Notice is hereby given, that a reward of One Hundred Pounds will be paid by the Government to any person, not being one of the offenders, who shall have such information as shall lead to the apprehension and conviction of the guilty party or parties.

W. M. ARNOLD.

And then a traveller complaining about the width of the new bridge. See below.

The Sydney Morning Herald, 1 November 1861, page 8.
THE FALBROOK BRIDGE EXPLOSION.
To the Editor of the Herald.

Sir, Observing that a reward of £100 is offered by the Secretary for Public Works for the discovery of the party who recently damaged the above bridge, I have been induced to enquire where the said bridge is, and I find that it is better known as the New Bridge," at Glennie's (sic) Creek, nine miles beyond Singleton.

Now, Sir, as I happen to know something of said bridge, I beg, with your permission, through your columns, to say a few words to the public on the subject. Some months ago my business required my taking a journey on the Northern Road, and on enquiring of a party of bullock drivers of the state of the roads, they replied that they had greater cause to complain of the new bridge in question than of the roads.

The complaint is, that it is too narrow, and that they can't walk alongside of their teams without much danger from the cattle kicking out at and knocking them down, and the possibility of the wheel passing over them before they could get out of the way. I shortly reached the bridge myself, and I must say that I do not wonder at some one trying to get rid of a cause of daily irritation.

To the best of my recollection, it is about forty yards long, and only from nine to eleven feet wide, in which space it is impossible for a man to take proper care of his team while crossing the bridge.

The only expense of making the bridge a few feet wider would be in the flooring, which would be a more trifle compared to the cost of the whole structure, which might have been good for traffic for twenty or thirty years who is chargeable with the defect complained of, I know not but it is most discreditable to any Government to permit the money of the public to be expended under such inefficient supervision.

TRAVELLER.

Sydney, October 30.

The bridge survived and along with the forementioned factors (the size of Singleton and the railway line) stymied William's dream of Camberwell becoming a large bustling town that everyone popped into as they journeyed to and from the interior.

However, there is no doubt the pretty little village of Camberwell remained a haven for William, his family and all those who cherished it.

CHAPTER 29

ROSEDALE AND THE DISPERSAL OF FAMILY

Camberwell a 'very prettily [rural village] situated on a series of gentle declivities, rising up from each side of the creek known as Glennies Creek' sustained William and Mary for the rest of their lives, and Rosedale, remained in the family until the 1920s.[403]

The extract below from a newspaper article on Rosedale, in September 1904 when William sr.'s second youngest son Alfred (53) was running the estate is informative and tells us a little of Rosedale's history.

> *The Maitland Daily Mercury – 9 September 1904, page 2.*

The name "Rosedale" is, I am sure, familiar to a large number of the 'Mercury' readers. It is quite a household word throughout the length and breadth of this district. The estate, which is situated on the left bank of Glennies Creek, a short distance from the junction of this stream with the Hunter river. The property was acquired in the good old days by Mr. W. Nowland, some time (sic) deceased, [1884] and who was one of the old pioneers of the north. Mr. Nowland left the property to his two sons, Messrs. Alfred and Henry. The latter, however, disposed of his share of the property to Mr. Haling at a satisfactory price. The remaining part is still held by Mr. Alfred Nowland, a gentleman worthy of the name of his good old father. The homestead over looks (sic) an extensive magnificent, alluvial flat, which, just at present, a very nice natural picture. — clad with a luxuriant coat of lucerne, wheat and barley. The picturesque verdant garb is heightened to a considerable degree by the approximate fruit trees bursting into bud and bloom.

Convenient, to the homestead in various positions, stand elaborate haystacks which, in themselves, speak for the productiveness and richness of the soil. Here, I may mention that Mr. Nowland [Alfred] had the ill-luck to lose about 20 tons of hay a few weeks ago through the interior part of the stack heating to such an extent as to cause a general conflagration of the whole, fortunately, the night was calm, otherwise more serious damage may have resulted.

Extensive piggeries[404] have been erected under the supervision of one of Mr. Nowland's sons (one of them Vivian). They are so constructed that in the transformant (sic) of pigs from one yard to another no trouble can be experienced, swinging gates ingeniously and systematically facilitating all movements. The loading and unloading of animals are also made easy by a contrivance similar to that observed at railway stations for the trucking of stock; the fencing is so arranged that the youngest pig cannot escape. Splendid shelving sheds are also provided for each sty. The whole reflects the greatest credit on its ingenious designer, Mr. V. Nowland. And judging from the fine sample of breeding sows, exclusive of a large number of other young animals, Mr. Nowland will certainly make the undertaking a success, particularly as he has started on such a fine systematical line.

Mr. Nowland [Alfred] has also an extensive apiary, and in this line he is thoroughly versed. He has been busily engaged for some days past preparing the honey for exhibition at Singleton Show this week, and from what I have seen I feel certain that the display will prove a cynosure to visitors on the ground… I wish Mr. Nowland [Alfred] success with his exhibits at the coming show, as he has a considerable number of entries, and has gone to much trouble and expense in getting them up.

Rosedale was still in the family in 1904, and Alfred and his son Vivian still contributing to the local community.[405]

Robert Marries Jane Susan Mercer

Going back to 1867. Alfred was 16 and his older brother Robert (31) was getting married. Robert married Jane Susan Mercer (birth year unknown), and their marriage was registered at Patrick Plains (Singleton).[406]

In the 1860s, William, Mary, their children and their extended family were yet to face the tragic death of Robert (as told in the previous note, 406.) At this stage of William's and Mary's lives (1867) three of the older boys were married (Chas 1860, Michael 1862, and Robert 1867) and all three lived at Warrah Ridge.[407]

The Nowlands Were Still Working Together

The Nowland boys and their father (William) were all buying and selling stock and moving cattle and sheep between Ward's Mistake, Warrah Ridge, Rosedale and the local stock yards (markets). An example of Alex (now 21) advertising for store sheep follows.

> *The Maitland Mercury and Hunter River General Advertiser,*
> *13th June 1868, page 1*
> **STORE SHEEP**
> **AUCTIONEERS AND OTHERS**
>
> WANTED TO PURCHASE, about 1,500 STORE SHEEP – one-half Wethers, and the other half Ewes – from two to four years old. Apply to.
>
> ALEXANDER NOWLAND
>
> *Glennies Creek, Camberwell, 13th June 1868* [408]

By 1869, Chas (29) and Annie (28) had seven children,[409] Michael (35) and Martha (27) had three surviving children,[410] and Robert (33) and Jane (age unknown) had two children.[411] Their local town was Quirindi; 12.6 miles (20.4 km) away. Their brothers, Alex (23), George (22), Alfred (19) and Henry (16) still travelled between their allotments at Warrah Ridge and Rosedale, while home for their eldest brother, William jr. (37), was at Ward's Mistake; still quite a remote area with the local township of Armidale 30 miles (48.2 km) away.[412]

The Nowland Boys Actively Participated in Their Local Communities

Two articles were found where the Nowland boys are attending a sporting event where everyone is celebrating: in the first article, the foundation of the colony (81 years earlier) and in the second, Queen Victoria's birthday. Both provide an insight into the sporting events of the time and the competitive nature of the Nowland boys. The first article follows; the 'Grand Athletics Sports Carnival' at Armidale with Messrs. Nowland competing in two events: High Jump and Pole Vault.

> *The Armidale Express and New England General Advertiser,*
> *30 January 1869, page 2.*
> *Grand Athletic Sports*
>
> *...the prospect which has excited much interest at Armidale for several weeks past came off on the race course (sic) reserve on Tuesday last 20th instant, being the anniversary of the foundation of the colony.*[413]
>
> *We believe that the credit of initiating a series of sports that have proved so attractive here is chiefly due to Lord Bertrand Gordon, whose practical knowledge on the matter has been of much service with reference to the preliminary arrangements, and also in carrying them out in an effective manner... We estimated the number of persons on the ground at nearly 400, and no doubt – it being a very general holiday – there would have been considerably more but for some horse racing at*

Uralla, which attracted a number of our residents who prefer that pastime to the feats of athletes. Many carriages and other vehicles were on the course during the athletic sports, and a considerable number of ladies were present. The music of Mr. Ashton's circus band was freely contributed during the great part of the day.

The arrangements made by the officers were very good, considering the short time they had to attending to them. A sufficient area was roped in, and reserved for the officers, and the competitors for each sport, while the track for running and walking, matches, &c., was marked by flag and the officers were distinguished by having ribbons and carrying small flags. The police aided them in preserving order, which, with a trifling exception during the last sport, was well kept.

There were two innkeepers' booths at hand, and from the great heat they appeared to be well patronised. A number of fruit stalls and the like were also frequently visited. The heat was intense, and until late in the afternoon a pretty strong wind made the course very disagreeable, clouds of fine dust continuously sweeping over it and almost hiding those who occupied the more exposed position. The dust raised by the horsemen who-followed or went parallel with the runners and walkers in the matches was also a serious annoyance to the latter. However, everything that could be done to mitigate inconvenience and ensure a good view to the spectators, that was possible under the circumstances was done by the officers having charge of the sports, and we have no doubt that by next anniversary day, with the course paled (sic) in and otherwise improved, athletic sports then will prove increasingly attractive.

In such weather as there was on Tuesday, it was surprising that the entrances were so numerous, and probably there is no race save the Anglo-Saxon one that would brave sultry heat and the inconveniences of hard and dusty ground from which the grass has been burnt up, in carrying out sports requiring great energy and under such circumstances. The officers have reason to be proud of their success in introducing so extensive a series of athletic sports on anniversary day, and we trust that their intention of having similar sports annually will be well supported by the public. Towards evening there were a few drops of rain, insufficient to lay the dust, but from the wind falling, and some shade from clouds, the ground became less disagreeable to those present.

First Youths race – 75 yards for all youths 14 years and under, Prize, £1…

… Sixth—Running High Jump Prize. £2, with sweep of 2s. 6d. added. 1

The competitors were Messrs. Nowland (1), C. Coventry (2), Saddler, and Lord B. Gordon. Won easily by Nowland who jumped over a pole 5 feet 3 inches from the ground…

> ... Tenth—Pole Vaulting Prize, £1.10s.
>
> The competitors were Lord B. Gordon (1), and Messrs. Nowland (2), Wm. Gordon (3), Saddler, Larnach, and H. Scholes. This was a most excellent contest, and it lasted a considerable time, each of the unsuccessful competitors gradually falling off as the pole was raised (to rest lightly on pegs in two posts) beyond his mark. Mr. Wm. Gordon stuck to his work with on extraordinary amount of perseverance, and it was surprising to see such vaulting from a man of his firm-set frame mid weight. But at length Lord B. Gordon and Mr. Nowland were left, and the interest of the contest redoubled. Mr. N. [Mr. Nowland] struggled manfully, but eventually succumbed to the superior vaulting of Lord Gordon, whose, winning-leap with the pole at a height of 8 feet 6 Inches was beautifully done, and elicited great applause. During this lengthy contest, the last event of the day, the spectators cheered vigorously every neat leap. The severe nature of the work was shown by the baiting steps of the competitors...

It is unknown who the Messrs. Nowlands were at the Grand Athletic Sports held at Armidale on anniversary day; they may have been William sr.'s sons or possibly his nephews. While the next account is explicit. Alex 23, and his younger brother, George 22, on opposite teams playing cricket at the newly formed Warrah Ridge Cricket Club.

> *The Maitland and Hunter River General Advertiser,*
> *1st June 1869*
> *DISTRICT NEWS*
> *MURRURINDI*
> *(from our correspondent)*
>
> CRICKET AT WARRAH RIDGE – A club has been newly formed at Warrah Ridge, and a match was played on 24th May, in honor of her Majesty's Birthday, between two elevens of the club. Although it was late in the season, everything passed off satisfactorily, and everyone present seemed to enjoy themselves. Mr. Alexander Nowland won the choice of innings, and he sent Mr. George Nowland's team to the wickets. The batting of Mr. G. Nowland was praiseworthy... The first eleven, Mr. George Nowland's [team] made 37 in their first innings, and 51 in their second, total 88. The second eleven, Mr. Alexander Nowland's made 47 in their first innings, and 11 in their second, total 58. The first eleven therefore won by 30 runs.

George's team was better on the day, winning by 30 runs.

Kamilaroi Country Consumed and Shattered

A lot had changed since William sr. and his fellow squatters first went up onto the Liverpool Plains, 44 years earlier (c.1826). The settlers had changed the entire landscape and consumed Kamilaroi Country. Towns, roads, settlement, farm allotments (with fences) and a colonial way of life divorced from First Nations people was all encompassing and pervasive. The settlers had taken over completely, and the Country William sr. first saw had largely gone.

Family Life For William and Mary Had Also Changed

By the end of the 1860s, William sr.'s (66) and Mary's (57) children were all independent and capable of looking after themselves. As told earlier, three of the boys were married, Michael (36), Robert (34), and Charles (30) and lived at Warrah Ridge. William sr.'s and Mary's eldest child, William jr. (37) managed Ward's Mistake, and the younger boys Alex (24), George (23), Alfred (19) and Henry (16) were often away from home and on the road, droving the family's stock between Warrah Ridge and Rosedale (and sometimes going as far as Ward's Mistake). All the boys, managed their own allotments, helped their parents at Rosedale when needed, sold and purchased stock at the local stock yards and possibly, still drove theirs and their father's stock to the Hawkesbury and/or Sydney markets. William sr. and Mary were also grandparents with 12 grandchildren; aged between 8 and around 1.

In looking back through the events of William sr.'s life in the 1860s, he had moved from a pastoralist fighting for the recognition of Wallalla Station to the ownership of several pre-emptive leases at Warrah Ridge (along with his sons) ironically just above William's first squat (c.1826) that he had called Warrah. All seemed more settled for William and his family, even though Camberwell had not become the large prosperous town that William had sought.

CHAPTER 30

CAMBERWELL IN 1869

In 1869, another informative article appeared in the local press on why Camberwell never grew beyond a small village. The account draws on factors such as: the new expensive bridge (Falbrook Bridge) on the Great Northern Road had diverted traffic away from Camberwell; the Post Office (and its Post Office Hotel and Store) which was located at Ashton, on the opposite side of the road to the main village; the local church, St Clement's appearance that looked like a ruin on its western side (because it had never been completed); the church services were unreliable; mail deliveries were less frequent; and Camberwell station was positioned at a distance from the village and rumoured to be relocated even further away (and, as we know, at Ravensworth).

All told in the colourful and revealing narration that follows:[414]

> *The Maitland Mercury and Hunter River General Advertiser,*
> *18 December 1869, page 4*
> ***DISTRICT NEWS***
>
> *In this colony with few exceptions, every town, nay every village, no matter how remote or insignificant, has its correspondent. It is remarkable that these gentlemen, paint everything couleur du rose. Judging from their descriptions you would imagine their almost deserted hamlets were emporiums of trade and commerce, their dry and sandy waterways were flowing, their patched and arid plains were valleys teeming with vegetation, their rocky and embrowned ridges were "hills with verdure clad." In this respect Camberwell has not been so fortunate and I purpose giving you a few items concerning it which may not be uninteresting: –*
>
> *The village of Camberwell is situated on the Falbrook or Gennie's Creek just where the Great N. Road [Great Northern Road] crosses it. At best it was but a small village, still, what with the traffic and local trade, there was a good share of business done, sufficient to support two inns and a good sized store. Some years since, however, the Government altered the road from the old crossing place to the site of the present new bridge, this naturally turned the traffic and with it the trade, thereby rendering the houses and the old line valueless.*
>
> *As an instance of the depreciation of the value of property which this alteration caused. I may mention that the Victoria Inn, a first-class building, particularly well adapted for business, and which cost £2000 odd in building alone was some time since sold for £290, together with 70 acres or thereabouts of alluvial land adjoining.*[415]

All other properties, have of course, equally decreased in value from the same cause-strangely enough, the Camberwell post office is at Ashton on the opposite side of the creek; here also are the Post Office Hotel and store. There is also a good Public School at Camberwell, under the conduct of a lady who is, I am informed, very successful in teaching the young idea (sic) "how to shoot". As the traffic gradually deceases or perhaps ceases, I presume Camberwell will experience the same fate as the village so truthfully and feelingly described by Goldsmith, without sharing the charm and interest which we always attach to "Sweet Auburn".

I may state that Falbrook takes a raise in the Mount Royal Range and after a picturesque course of 30 miles, discharges itself into the Hunter at Archerfield, the seat of G. Bowman Esq. jnr., the Falbrook except in times of extreme drought, never ceases running, its water is marvelously bright and pure. The alluvial flats on its banks are very rich, only requiring seasonable rain to ensure remunerative crops-unfortunately we have to contend with many seasons of drought.

Our Church of St. Clements is situated on the Ashton side, opposite to the village, and is built on land given by the late Dr. Bowman. It is of stone, and, I think, the Gothic style of architecture, and has a substantial and imposing appearance. The Western end is still unfinished and tends to give to the passer-by the idea of ruins. Our present minister is permanently appointed to two other parishes, in addition to that of St Clements. He resides at Jerry's Plains. According to the present arrangement we have service once a month, but if owing to floods or any other cause, he cannot come on the day appointed, he does not attend until the next month, and thus we have service sometimes not more than once in two months. Now this in a rather populous neighbourhood, near the centre of civilisation, does not say much for the watchful care of our Bishop, or else shows a scarcity of clergyman of our persuasion. True, the audiences are very poor at times, but this is owing in a great measure to the uncertainty in the services. People grow tired of riding seven or eight miles only to be disappointed.

Apropos of railways. It is admitted on all hands that we are going into debt at railway speed, and as I presume all portions of this country will have to pay their fair proportion or at least the interest on the money borrowed to carry said railways forward, it is but reasonable they should participate in the benefits and conveniences said to accompany the introduction of the 'iron horse'. In the days of coaches and horses, we usually received five mails each way per week; now, with wondrously increased facilities of carriage, we only receive three – Tamworth and Armidale – and latter towns 200 miles from here, have their five mails weekly, what have we done that we should be cut so short? There are a considerable number of country people who go to Camberwell for their letters &c. This inconvenience can surely be remedied by making up a mail for Camberwell, instead of Singleton, as at present. Again, considerable annoyance is felt because the Commissioner for Works has chosen to place a goods shed and siding at Bowman's Creek, instead of here. In this case I think we have been slighted, and our just claims ignored, by the powers that be; and I feel sure that any unbiassed person, knowing the localities, would be of the same opinion. If studying the convenience of the greatest number is to be any guide in the matter, there can be no two opinions about which is the more suitable site. Now there is a great man who has charge of a large estate, not 100 miles from this favored site at Bowman's Creek, and the inhabitants in their simplicity think it is to suit his convenience that the siding, &c., is to be there.[416]

To be sure he has a great many bales of wool and casks of tallow to go down per train; but of course this is only bosh, and not to be thought of for a moment. Why there are not more than forty persons to avail themselves of the train at Bowman's Creek, while at Falbrook it is no exaggeration to say they amount to hundreds.

Fancy, Mr. Editor, one of your West Maitland farmers wishing to send some hay to Lochinvar per train, and having to go three or four miles towards Morpeth to a station, before he could put it on the trucks. This supposition correctly represents present our position here. It is to be hoped the Minister for works will remedy this inconvenience by placing a siding where it was originally intended it should be-viz., near where the pariah road to Camberwell crosses the railway line.

Dec 8.

As told above, 'every small village no matter how remote or insignificant, has its correspondent'. William, in Camberwell's case, was probably one of the correspondents. Throughout his life, William most likely wrote to the local paper regularly to foster the interests of his very small village, despite its size and lack of patronage. Though we will never know because it was customary for the correspondent not to sign their name.

The correspondent from Camberwell in the early 1870s also wrote to the local paper advocating for a railway station in Camberwell.[417] Again as above, the correspondent was most likely 'our' William.

Later (in 1876) William's second youngest son Alfred (at 25) took up the same cause for a railway station in Camberwell, along with the need for a Post Office, as detailed in the next chapter.

PART SIX

The Dynasty William Believed He Had Created

William orchestrated in his Will how the Nowland farming practices he believed he had put in place should continue for generations to come –
How wrong he was

CHAPTER 31

THE NOWLAND FAMILY AND THEIR FARMS

The 1870s opened with William's and Mary's fourth surviving son Chas (30) before the Supreme Court of New South Wales for insolvency. Chas (unlike his father at the beginning of the 1850s) confronted only one hearing; Chas owed his creditors less than £100 and agreed to pay.[418]

George Marries Alice Blanche Aldwell

In June 1871, William and Mary's sixth surviving child, George (24) married Alice Blanche Aldwell (23) at St Clement's Camberwell.[419] The family notice in the local paper read:

> *The Maitland Mercury and Hunter River General Advertiser*
> *17 June 1871, page 1.*
> *MARRIAGES.*
> *On the 3rd instant, by special licence, at St. Clement's Church, Camberwell, by the Reverend T. H. Shaw, B.A., George, sixth son of William Nowland, Esq., of Rosedale Estate, Camberwell, to Alice Blanche, third daughter of the late William Montgomery Aldwell, of Brompton Row, London.*[420]

George's and Alice's first three children were born at Rosedale.[421] The birthplace of their other children suggests they moved around a little, though that was not the case.[422] George and Alice lived at Warrah Ridge for most of their lives where they built their 'Hazel Cottage' and established a life for their children on the allotments George purchased under the Alienation Act of 1861. For around 45 years (c.1862 to c.1907) they were both active participants in the Quirindi community.[423]

Some of the Traits of William sr. Were Mirrored in His Sons

George was very much like his father; striving for his local community and walking through every door that opened in pursuit of his interests. Both, William's and Mary's lives were long enough to see some of George's achievements; George became a J.P. and a magistrate within William sr.'s lifetime.

The voices of Robert and Alfred, like their father are portrayed in their letters to the editor of the local papers. It was common practice for community members to write to their local paper to draw attention to a coming event, matters of interest, and at other times, matters of concern, and Robert and Alfred were amongst them.

Robert like his father aired his grievances in the local paper. In 1873, Robert (now 37) wrote to the paper and complained about not receiving his newspaper in the post. What followed was a small flurry of articles on the matter. The incident started with the following account.

The Maitland Mercury and Hunter River General Advertiser,
14 August 1873, page 3.
ORIGINAL CORRESPONDENCE.
NON DELIVERY OF NEWSPAPERS.
(To the Editor of the Maitland Mercury.)

Sir, – I would like to be informed of the reason of the non-arrival of my newspapers, which are addressed to the Quirindi Post-office. The Mercury of 31st ultimo has not reached me; but I would not take the trouble to mention the loss of that, were it not that I have been deprived of some score or more previously, and I think it is high time that I should make a complaint about it. As I feel confident that the papers are posted from your office, I imagine that the fault rests with some post-office official.

I am, sir, yours respectfully,

ROBERT NOWLAND,

Warrah Ridge, Qurindi. 1st August, 1873.

In response, to Robert's complaint as well as another from a Mr. Chas Whittaker, the Secretary to the Post-Office General, Sydney (S. H. Lambton) wrote to the *Maitland Mercury* to clarify what had happened to the missing mail; that he believed had now arrived at both residences, as told in the following article.

The Maitland Mercury and Hunter River General Advertiser,
13 September 1873, page 2.
NON-DELIVERY OF NEWSPAPERS.

We have the pleasure of laying before our readers a gratifying proof of the prompt completeness with which all complaints of non-delivery of newspapers (or letters), are enquired into by the Postmaster General. We received on Thursday the following official reply from the Secretary to the Post-office –

General Post-office, Sydney, Sept 10, 1873.

Gentlemen – Adverting to your communications of the 14th and 20th ultimo, I have now the honor to inform you, that enquiries have been made at the several post offices at West Maitland, Murrurundi and Quirindi respecting the issues of the Maitland Mercury of the 29th and 31st July last, respectively addressed "Mr. Chas Whittaker, Holmwood, near Quirindi and Mr. Robert Nowland, Warrah Ridge, Quirindi," and reported not to have reached their destinations.

It has proved impossible to elicit any explanation of the non-receipt of these papers in due course, but I learn from the Postmaster at Quirindi that both newspapers have now reached the addresses, though that for Mr. Nowland did not arrive for three weeks after that gentleman's report.

I have to add that instructions have been given to the Postmaster named, which by being observed will enable the Department to discover where these delays occur in future and thus prevent similar complaints as far as possible – I have the honor, &c.,

S.H. LAMBTON, Secretary.

Though this was not the case for Robert. He was yet to receive his mail, so he wrote to the local paper once again. See below.

The Maitland Mercury and Hunter River General Advertiser,
20 September 1873, page 2.
NON-DELIVERY OF NEWSPAPERS AND LETTERS.

We have been rather surprised by the receipt on Thursday of the following letter –

(To the Editor of the Maitland Mercury)

SIR – I wish to draw your attention to a statement contained in a letter from the Postmaster General to you, which appeared in your last Saturday's issue. The Postmaster General states that be was Informed by the Quirindi postmaster that my missing paper reached me three weeks after my report such, however, is not the case, for the paper in question has not up to the present time come to hand.

It may not be out of place to mention here that since I complained of the loss of my newspaper three letters sent to me – one from Mr. F W Darbys Cattie Creek, another from Mr. J. Mettams Black Creek, and the third from Gunnedah, by the Rev. Mr. Gough – all addressed to Warrah Ridge, Quirindi have not reached me yet.

I am sir, your obedient servant.

ROBERT NOWLAND,

Warrah Ridge, Quirindi, ser. 16th 1873

In the end Robert must have received his paper and letters because no more complaints were found on the matter in Trove.

William sr.'s second youngest son, Alfred (25) also wrote to the local newspaper in 1876, defending Camberwell Railway Station, and the Camberwell Post Office.[424]

William sr. Also Penned Some New and Informative Articles

In 1873, William sr. wrote to the *Maitland Mercury* warning others of a noxious yellow weed that had killed 55 herd of his cattle. William was concerned for the stock of other graziers. He collected a sample of the weed, gave it to the editor of the *Maitland Mercury* and then wrote the following letter to the paper.

The Maitland Mercury, April 26, 1873, page 2
CATTLE POISONING.

WE received, the other day, from a correspondent, a statement reporting the death of a number of cattle belonging to Mr. W. Nowland, through eating some poisonous herb that grew on the line of road along which they were travelling. Mr. Nowland has since sent us the following letter, which will be of service as placing more clearly beyond doubt the true cause of the death of these cattle, and as helping stockowners and persons in charge of travelling stock to identify the plant which has done the mischief, and to guard as far as possible against incurring similar losses:

Sir—As the following facts may be of some service as a warning to drovers and others who have cattle to travel between Breeza and Merriwa, I would feel obliged if you will insert them in the Mercury :— I had a mob of cattle, numbering 600 head, started from my "Ward's Mistake" station, in New England, and brought to Warrah Ridge, at which place they were drafted into two lots, the one of 400 bullocks (which I had sold at £4 4s. per head, to be delivered at Edinglassie) were taken down the cattle road, and had just reached that road on the reserve near the Round Island, where the cattle grazed for half-an-hour. When it was discovered that they were eating the poison weed they were moved on immediately, and soon began to show the same symptoms of poisoning that a dog would that bad had a dose of strychnine: some of them would stagger, fall, and become convulsed, and never rise again; others would fall and rise again several times, but not one that had once fallen with it ever recovered.

I lost fifty-five head in this manner, fifteen of them died within eight hours, and thirty six more next day, the remaining four lingered and died afterwards. The poison weed may be known by those who are not acquainted with it as a plant with spreading leaves, which resemble sage leaves, and with a narrow stalk about a foot long, at the top of which is a hard yellow flower, almost round in shape; it grows only in damp places. Cattle bred on the plains seldom eat it, but strange cattle, horses, and sheep [not bred on the plains] will eat it ravenously. It is a powerful poison, and I think that one-half of the various reports of the breaking out of diseases in stock are owing to the destruction caused by this weed. I may mention as a proof that it was not pleuro-pneumonia, or any other such disease, that killed my bullocks, that the 200 head that were drafted off from the other lot were taken down the road via Murrurundi to Musclebrook (sic), and not one died, nor showed any symptoms of disease of any kind, although they were running with the other lot on the day previous to their being poisoned. I may add that, upon examination of some of them after they died, it was discovered that their lungs were perfectly healthy.

A desire to prevent loss of property to many of your readers is my excuse for trespassing thus far on your space.

I am, sir, &c,

WILLIAM NOWLAND,

Rosedale, Camberwell.

24th April, 1873.

In the above Letter to the Editor, William tells us a lot about himself. At the age of 69, he still drove cattle up and down the Great Northern Road, some 46 years after he first entered the Hunter. On this occasion, William was taking his stock to market with 400 bullocks amongst them. Presumably, his own breeding stock, 32 years after he first purchased a pure-bred young bull from James Bowman (in 1841) and took it up onto the Liverpool Plains and put it amongst the Hawkesbury Benevolent Society's cattle at Mooki Station.[425]

William's 'warning to others of a noxious yellow weed that looked like sage' found at Round Island, on the Liverpool Plains, was received with a barrage of negative commentary. The first response in the newspapers came from Jules Joubert (the Secretary of the Australian Agricultural Society) based on advice from William Woolls (a botanist from Parramatta).[426] See the newspaper article that follows.

> *The Maitland Mercury and Hunter River General Advertiser,*
> *7 June 1873, page 5.*
> ## THE LIVERPOOL PLAINS POISON PLANT.
>
> *We are favoured by Mr. Jules Joubert with the following letter, relative to the specimen of the Liverpool Plains poison plant recently sent us (sic) by Mr. William Nowland, of Camberwell. As we reported at the time, Mr. Nowland believes this plant to be the one which killed 25 of his cattle, [55 according to William] when passing over Liverpool Plains, near Round Island. But Mr. Jules Joubert, to whom we forwarded part of the specimen, for more scientific report, has, as will be seen, kindly submitted it to Mr. Woolls, of Parramatta, the well-known botanist; and Mr. Woolls is not satisfied that eating this plant alone could have killed the cattle… Sydney, June 8, 1873.*

Jules Joubert was then supported in the papers by a local resident who lived in Murrurindi; W. H. Gordon.[427] As told below.

> *The Sydney Morning Herald, 11 June 1873, page 31*
> ## CRASPEDIA CHRYSANTHA.
> ## TO THE EDITOR OF THE HERALD
>
> *SIR-The following letter received this morning from, Mr. W. H. Gordon, Murrurundi, will set at rest the question raised as to the poisonous qualities of the "Craspedia Chrysantha" as it is of some importance to stockowners I beg to send it to you for publication.*
>
> *Yours,*
>
> *JULES JOUBERT,*
>
> *Secretary Agricultural Society N.S.W.*
>
> *227, George-street, June 10.*
>
> *Murrurundi, June 9, 1873.*
>
> *Dear Sir, Much doubt, having existed in my mind regarding the reported properties of plants growing very profusely some twenty-six miles from here, said to have killed Mr. Nowland's and other persons' cattle, I determined to try its effects, so as to fully satisfy myself whether the plant was as baneful as reported to be. On Wednesday last I obtained from the neighbourhood of the Round Island, Liverpool Plains, a bag of the plant known to the residents and others as the poison weed (in my opinion the Craspedia Chrysantha, of this I may be mistaken) the contents of the bag had been carefully gathered and weighed 30lbs. I have a very quiet milking cow which on Friday afternoon I shut up without any food, on*

Saturday about midday I put her into the bail for milking. Then placed before her 15 lbs. of the poison weed, but she would only eat a few of the yellow flowers. I then sprinkled a few handfuls of lucerne with it, and in a very short time she had eaten the whole. I then took her out of the bail after milking, and kept her without food until 5 p.m., then gave her the remaining 24 lbs. of the poison weed and some lucerne at 9 o'clock, when I saw her the whole was eaten: the next morning I turned her out as well as usual. The poison weed did not in any way affect her. I may also mention that she had no water from the time she first had the poison plant until at least ten hours after it was all eaten. Should any person interested wish to try any experiments I will with pleasure, in a few days' notice, obtain as much of the poison weed as may be required for the purpose, but I am certain that this is not the plant that has poisoned the cattle. I almost think that this plant is one of the daisy tribe. I have taken the liberty to forward you this, thinking you might wish to make it known.

Yours, &c.,

W. H. GORDON

J. Joubert, Sydney.

William sr. then followed, with a rejoinder that questioned the validity of Gordon's experiment. See below.

The Maitland Mercury and Hunter River General Advertiser,
17 June 1873, page 3.
ORIGINAL CORRESPONDENCE.
(To the Editor of the Maitland Mercury)

SIR, "Fools rush in where angels fear to tread" is exemplified in some of the opinions that have been tendered relative to the poisonous properties of the plant a sample of which I sent to your office. It is to be regretted that the persons who are so ready to offer their opinions on the subject are not owners of livestock, who have had some experience amongst cattle and sheep. The absence of correspondence on the part of persons who could reasonably be expected to have some knowledge of the affair is attributable, no doubt, to the fact that such persons fear to be too positive on the subject, since doubt has been raised; but at the same time are fully convinced in their own minds that the weed in question is the one that poisoned my cattle, and others on Liverpool Plains; such at least is the position I take, and I shall not depart from it until I am convinced to the contrary. My reason for suspecting this particular weed is because all the cases of cattle poisoning that I have noticed for the past seventeen years have occurred where it grew plentifully, and after travelling cattle eating it.

That "cock and bull" story of Mr. W. H. Gordon's, which you copied from the Herald, *will of course be taken for what it is worth (at any rate it will about Murrurundi and Liverpool Plains). For example: After a cow's refusing to eat a certain plant, just fancy her being made to eat 39 lb. of it, not mentioning a quantity of lucerne, which was given to increase her appetite and make the other taste better, no doubt. Mr. Editor, I would like you to weigh 39 lb. of the weed, and then you would be able to judge of the capacity of that old "milker's" stomach.*

I remain, sir, yours respectfully,

WILLIAM NOWLAND,

Rosedale, Camberwell.

14th June, 1873.

W. H. Gordon responded with a retort telling the editor of the *Maitland Mercury* 'William's letter was rude, insulting and unkind, and he was not about to get into a paper war'. For William Gordon his intentions were honourable and explained in length in the letter that follows. For him, his reputation was at stake.

The Maitland Mercury and Hunter River General Advertiser,
19 June 1873, page 1.
(To the Editor of the Maitland Mercury)

SIR – In your issue of to day (sic), Tuesday, a letter appears signed William Nowland, certainly as rude, insulting, and unkind a production as could be penned by any person, and I think especially by Mr. Nowland, as will be seen by this letter. I have no intention to have a paper war with the writer of the letter alluded to but beg for space to state briefly a few circumstances in connection with the matter alluded to.

About three weeks past I was asked to procure, if I could, for a gentleman residing some distance from here, specimens of the plant called by drovers the cattle poison weed, from the locality of the Round Island, Liverpool Plains. I did this in due course, and forwarded it with such particulars as I could, and had years ago gleaned at different times relative to its reported poisonous qualities. Some very important information was given by a person, a resident of this district, who has for many years travelled with cattle the locality where the plant grows. He states that seven or eight years ago he had a drove of cattle on route for Sydney, and having received a very important message be camped his cattle in and about the place where the poison plant grows but did not know it until afterwards. He stayed there an entire night, a whole day, and part of a day, and none of the cattle suffered. He further states about two years afterwards he passed over the same ground with cattle, from New England, that they travelled at the usual pace, but made no halt in the locality; and yet during the day he bad three head of the cattle die and yet he does not believe the poison plant killed them.

I have heard from other persons, also drovers of cattle and sheep: some say they think the plant poisonous because they have always heard so, and do not believe it is. I forwarded in due course the specimens as requested, and the persons who examined it do not believe it to be poisonous (one a most competent judge, whose report upon the matter will shortly be published).

A few days after hearing the opinion given two gentlemen called upon me, and asked if I could direct them (they had been advised to call upon me) to the place where the plant in question grew. They rested a night with me, and I accompanied them to the locality of the Round Island, where the plant grows, although there are numbers of other places known to me where it is also. With assistance a quantity of the plant was gathered, and brought to my house, and from the opinion given by one of the gentlemen and others during our trip, I felt certain it could be given to my cow very safely, although I was promised payment for it, if required, should it die.

The result has been published, and will be certified publicly presently. May I ask Mr. Nowland what I gained by all the trouble and expense? If Mr. Nowland had a number of his cattle die, through eating some plant, whether the poison weed or not, I think he should be thankful to any person who endeavoured to unravel the mystery by moving in the matter, at any rate; common decency should have prevented him from publicly insulting them. There are gentlemen who reside near, and have great flocks and herds daily running over this Upas ground.[428]

Will any person who reads this believe if there was the poison in the weed there, lately sent forth to the world, by the reported death of Mr. Nowland's cattle, – that they would not have the ground avoided as past land, and even have notices put up by way of caution to the unwary persons who might come there with passing stock.

During the seventeen years I have resided here I have given a helping hand in every good work and undertaking for the public weal [interest] of the district; and can also say, without fear of contradiction, that I have spent more money and time in scientific researches (sic) than any resident in the district during that period.

In conclusion, I beg to state that in a few days a quantity of the poison plant will be sent to Sydney, and experiments will also take place here, of which notice will be given, so that any person interested may judge for themselves as to the poisonous properties of the plant, which has already caused me much trouble, expense, and great annoyance.

I am, sir, your obedient servant,

W. H. GORDON.

Murrurundi, June 17th, 1873.

This was not good enough for William, he responds once more.

> *The Maitland Mercury and Hunter River General Advertiser,*
> *21 June 1873, page 3.*
> ORIGINAL CORRESPONDENCE.
> *(To the Editor of the Maitland Mercury)*

Sir—If you will kindly allow me space to reply to a few remarks contained in Mr. W. H. Gordon's letter, which appears in to-day's Mercury, I shall feel obliged.

Mr. Gordon says that my last letter was "rude and insulting" to him; but I can assure that gentleman that I did not write it for the purpose of insulting him or any person, but merely as a warning to any of the public who may be interested, not to be led astray by representations made by persons who are quite ignorant on the subject.

Mr. Gordon's letter continues by saying that "If Mr. Nowland had a number of his cattle die through eating some plant, whether the poison weed or not, I think he should be thankful to any person who endeavoured to unravel the mystery by moving in the matter, at any rate." The "if" is quite unnecessary.

As to Mr. Gordon's endeavouring to unravel the mystery, I think he was doing quite the contrary by stating that the weed was not poisonous, which would have closed all enquiries if the statement had been generally believed. I was very anxious and am still so, that the subject should be well ventilated; but at the same time I wish it to be investigated by gentlemen whose statements can be relied upon, and who are botanists.

I am pleased to see that one person in the district acknowledges the good works of Mr. Gordon, and that one himself: perhaps he has forgotten the old saying about self-praise.

I remain, sir, yours respectfully,

WILLIAM NOWLAND,

Rosedale, Camberwell.

19th June, 1873

Over the coming week the articles from William and W. H. Gordon about the noxious weed (or maybe it was the Upas ground, see note 439) were copied to several other papers, with a further rejoinder that follows from the Riverina, that reiterated Joubert and Gordon's view.

> *Australian Town and Country Journal,*
> *21 June 1873, page 11*
> *To the Editor*
>
> *Sir; In your issue of the 7th inst. I see that Mr. Nowland has forwarded you a species of plant, which he asserts has poisoned some fifty-five head of cattle on the Liverpool Plains. The same sort of plant grows in profusion on the arid plains of Riverina (sic), and I can assure you that I have seen numbers of cattle eat this plant in great quantities in the Murrumbidgee; but however they did not show any symptoms of being poisoned when I saw them several days afterwards ...I am fully confident that the plant is perfectly free from much poisonous qualities; so therefore I hope Mr. Nowland will now be convinced that the said plant in not of a poisonous nature and he no doubt still believes it is. Hoping you will give space to this and oblige.*
>
> *I am yours &c.,*
>
> *B.A.R.*

This was the last article found on the subject, after all the back and forth, 'argy-bargy' and the added opinion from the Murrumbidgee. It appears, William had no more to say; he stated his case and left it at that.

Alfred Married Lauretta Annette Aldwell

Two years later (in 1875) there was another reason to celebrate; Alfred (24) married Lauretta Annette Aldwell (21) at St. James' Church, Sydney. The family notice read:

> *The Singleton Argus and Upper Hunter General Advocate,*
> *12 May 1875, page 2.*
>
> *Married May 6th, at St James' church, Sydney, by the Rev. G.C. Bode, ALFRE, the seventh son of W. Nowland, Esq., of Rosedale, Camberwell, N.S.W., to LAURETTA ANNETTE, fourth daughter of the late Mr. William Montogomery Aldwell, of Brompton Row, London.*

Alfred and Lauretta had 13 surviving children between 1876 and 1900.[429]

Alex Married Naomi Simpson

The following year (1876) my ancestor and possibly yours, Alex Nowland (30) married Naomi Simpson (19) at St Clement's Church, Camberwell. The family notice follows.

> *The Sydney Morning Herald, 2nd Feb 1876, page 1.*
> *Family Notice*
>
> NOWLAND-SIMPSON – *January 26th at St Clement's Church, Falbrook, by Rev. E. Huband-Smith, B.A. Trinity College, Dublin, Alexander, fifth son of William Nowland, Esq., of Rosedale, Camberwell to Naomi Kate, eldest daughter of the late Mr. John Percy Simpson, formerly compositor of Limerick, Ireland.*

Alex and Naomi had six surviving children between 1877–1891.[430]

How Did George, Alfred and Alex Meet Their Respective Wives?

George's, Alfred's, and Alex's wives (Alice, Lauretta, and Naomi, respectively) all lived in Sydney before they were married, and Alice and Lauretta were sisters. How the couples met is unknown. My view, based on conjecture, follows. William sr.'s sister Sarah, her husband William Adnum, and their eight children lived in George Street, Sydney. Maybe, over the years, the Nowland boys (initially with their parents) visited Sarah, William and their children (William Adnum died in 1861 and Sarah in 1878). Then as they got older the Nowland boys attended social gatherings in Sydney (at the local Anglican church, in the Sydney Botanical Gardens, and/or at big event, such as, the Australia Day Regatta) and it is on one of these occasions, they each met their prospective partners.

A Time of Mixed Feelings

The mid-1870s was also a period of mixed feelings for William sr., Mary and their extended family. From a positive perspective, Michael (42), Robert (40), Chas (36), Alex (30), George (29) and Alfred (25) were all pastoralists (graziers) and married with homesteads of their own. By 1876, William sr. and Mary also had a growing number of grandchildren: 7 from Michael and Martha; 10 from Chas and Annie; 6 from Robert and Jane; 3 from George and Alice; and, 1 from Alfred and Lauretta – 27 in total, and ranging in age from 14 (Chas' and Annie's twins 'John James' and 'Ada' and Michael's and Martha's, 'Clara') to a baby (Alfred and Lauretta's, 'Alfred jr.'). Yet not all was well. Four deaths occurred in the family: Robert's and Jane's 'Gertrude' (1877–1877); Chas' and Annie's 'Ernest' (1877–1877); Alex's and Naomi's 'Mary' (1877–1878); and, Alfred's and Lauretta's 'Arthur' (1877–1877).

Four infants in the extended family died (three in 1877, one in 1878) and only one of them with a known cause of death; Alfred's and Lauretta's 'Arthur' who was stillborn.

In searching through the newspapers (in Trove) between the years 1877 and 1878 (to find if the other children could have died from an epidemic) several articles appeared warning of the prevalence of smallpox, scarlet fever and whooping cough in various places, both within the state and interstate, with whooping cough found locally. An article in the *Clarence and Richmond Examiner and New England Advertiser* cautioned readers about an outbreak of 'throat disease' (whooping cough) amongst juveniles in 1877. See the article that follows.

Clarence and Richmond Examiner and New England Advertiser, 8 September 1877, page 2.

Juvenile Epidemic. – The throat disease which has carried off so many young children within the past few months is exciting great anxiety in the minds of parents. Its nature seems to baffle all the medical men in town, and it has proved we regret to state, fatal in many instances. The latest victim to its ravages was a fine little boy of six… As there is good reason to believe that this disease is infectious, we urge parents to use every caution.[431]

After the death of Alex and Naomi's child 'Mary' in April 1878,[432] William sr. lost two of his sisters; Elizabeth Nowland Rochester (75 yrs. on the 18th May 1878) and Sarah Nowland Adnum (64 yrs. on the 26th June 1878)[433] and Mary lost her sister, Christian (67 yrs. on the 24th July 1878).[434] This would have been a very difficult time for William sr., Mary, their boys, their families, and the extended family.

CHAPTER 32

THE NOWLAND VOICES IN THE PAPERS

In piecing together, the rest of William sr.'s story the newspapers of the time continue to provide a wealth of information. An engaging example is a report in the *Evening News* (Sydney) where Chas attempts to help a boy, named Tommy, 'who was bitten by a snake on the Messrs. Nowlands' property'.[435]

The descriptors in the article about the incident, provide an interesting and somewhat amusing explanation of some of the home remedies used to extract the snake's venom from Tommy. You can almost hear the discussions around the dinner table from those who read the article: *'Now listen here! No playing with sticks around snakes, like Tommy with the black snake at Warrah Ridge'*.

What happened follows: all dramatised by the journalist.

> *Evening News, 28 April 1876, page 2.*
> *Successful Treatment of Snake Bite*
>
> *The Warrah Ridge correspondent of the Singleton Argus reports the following case of successful treatment of snake bite. It appears that on the afternoon of Friday, the 31st ultimo, about an hour before sunset, a little boy of about seven summers, named Thomas Graham, son of a shepherd in the employ of the Messrs. Nowland, of Warrah Ridge was amusing himself after the fashion of boys of his age by ploughing the ground with a stick, on the margin of the plain about a mile from his mother's residence. According to his statement he was quite ignorant of the fact of impending danger, unfit he felt and saw, to his surprise and horror, a black snake four feet long attached to the point of the fourth finger of his left hand. To run backward and shake the reptile off was but the work of a moment, and his next thought was to run to the nearest house, about half a mile distant.*
>
> *Lucidly before he had proceeded far, he met his brother Sam, a little fellow some two or three years older than himself [9 or 10] who had the presence of mind (brave and thoughtful little fellow that he was) to tie a piece of twine tightly round the finger near the knuckle joint. By this time another brother rode up, who, upon learning the facts, started off at a gallop, and returned in a few minutes with a pair of scissors, with which he quickly snipped the piece out, and he sucked the*

wound for a minute or two, but soon had to desist as he experienced great dizziness and inclination to vomit, which he did freely.

This brother, who is about fifteen, describes the finger as being quite black and having marks on it similar to those that would be produced by running thorns into the finger. The little fellow was then brought on as quickly as the horse could carry him and his eldest brother to the residence of Mr. C. Nowland [Chas]. Mr. Nowland sucked the wound for fully half-an-hour, until he could no longer draw any blood from it, frequently washing his mouth out with cold water during that time. He described the dizziness he felt precisely as young Graham did after sucking the wound, only more severely as it did not leave him for a whole day afterwards.

Luckily a bottle of Wolfe's Aromatic Schiedam Schnapps was procurable in the neighbourhood, and frequent doses of it mixed with water were taken internally by little Tommy, and it was not until he had taken fully half a pint of the fiery spirit, and that within the abort space of fifteen minutes, that it began to show any intoxicating effects, and then only to a very slight extent.

In the meantime, some spirits of ammonia was applied to the wounded part, but this had apparently, no effect, and, as far as bystanders could judge, acted like the veritable "chip in porridge." The little fellow felt very drowsy at times, but he was kept awake and moving about pretty constantly, and by degrees the effects of the poison wore off. The boy is as well now as ever be was, and, it is to be hoped, has been taught a lesson for life to beware of snakes in the grass. It is added that the youngsters had noticed the publication of the treatment resorted to in a previous snake poisoning case and acted literally up to the directions then given.

After this experience, there probably was a lot of talk amongst the Nowland children in the weeks that followed about Chas, Tommy and the black snake.

William Selected as One of the Trustees of the Camberwell Common

Five months later, William sr. became one of the Trustees of the Temporary Common at Camberwell. As told in the article that follows.

New South Wales Government Gazette,
25 September 1877, page 3677.
Colonial Secretary's Office
Sydney, 24th. September, 1877.

HIS "Excellency the Governor, with the advice of the Executive Council, has been pleased to nominate the undermentioned gentlemen as Trustees of the Temporary Common at Camberwell, to hold office until the next (General Election of Trustees of Commons, to be held in January, 1880, viz. :—Messieurs William Nowland, Thomas Baldock, Thomas Hassall, Thomas Bates, and John Deane.

JOHN ROBERTSON[436]

William Purchased More Allotments at Warrah Ridge

According to William's Will (detailed in the last chapter) in the 1870s he purchased the following allotments at Warrah Ridge : Lot 85, 120 acres, on the 6th June 1872; Lot 127, 122 acres, 15th April 1875; Lot 125, 65 acres, 10th June 1875; Lot 84, 80 acres 19 August 1875, and Lot 129, 46 acres 16th January 1879 (433 acres in total). All the allotments next to and/or mixed in with his sons' allotments.

Fearful Drought Plagues Australia

In the latter part of the 1870s, Australia was in drought and William and his sons (like others) relied on the common grazing land along the stock routes to fatten their stock.[437]

For many months in the early part of 1878, William and his boys moved a mob of 6,500 sheep from place to place in search of food. By May, they had successfully fattened the sheep for market and were 30 kilometres southwest Tamworth when the sheep foraged amongst a purple weed (Paterson's Curse?) and 800 of the sheep died.[438]

The Nowlands (most likely penned by William sr.) wrote to the local paper about their experience and the article was copied to several local, state, and interstate papers, in Brisbane, Cooma, Geelong, Melbourne, Adelaide, and Mount Gambier. 'The Week' (a Brisbane newspaper) provided a comprehensive account. See below.

The Week (Brisbane, Qld), 18 May 1878 page 6.
A POISON PLANT

The Muswellbrook Times states that a mob of 6,500 of Messrs. Nowland's sheep were (after travelling for many months in search of feed during the drought) on their downward journey, in a marketable and fat condition. The lot had reached a spot near the crossing of the new line extension, something under a mile from Currabubula [30 km south-west of Tamworth] having travelled without feed for five miles beyond Tamworth, a total distance of about 30 miles.

On reaching a knob the site of the AA company mishap,[439] *the flock at once set to work ravenously to demolish a species of common weed that occupied the place of grass there abouts. It seems that the entire flock, in their hunger, had commenced to graze in a body, and almost directly afterwards some of their number 'furwelted' (for the information of the uninitiated i.e. turned on their backs) and died at once in great pain.*

Upon seeing what was going on the drovers at once set the dogs to round up the mob; but within a short space of five minutes, so quickly had the poison sap spread its influence, fully 300 herd were defunct. The drovers having quickly run the mob to safer quarters, about half a mile further on, a muster was made, when 360 herd were found to have dropped dead at the first halting place, and about 400 at the next – in all fully 800.

The weed has a slim 'stalky' appearance, bearing a unique purple flower, and is well known for its slight seed pods and absence of foliage. [Paterson's Curse?] Having heard of the AA Company's mishap, order has been issued by Mr. Nowland that the drovers should particularly guard against a common weed – the one so well known, bearing a yellow flower – and thus the sheep had unluckily been permitted to take their fill upon a poisonous one.

The sheep were in fine condition, and, being about the best of the flock, were fairly estimated at 10s per head, a total loss to Messrs. Nowland of 400 pounds sterling. It is believed that the animals fed but sparingly on the weed, no ill result would have followed, as sheep seem to be especially fond of the plant in question. A few years ago these gentleman lost some 50 herd of bullocks from the same cause. [Reported by William sr. in 1873 and that time it was a yellow sage like weed].

During the late 1870s, several other pastoralists also wrote to their local paper about their stock being poisoned by a mysterious weed. In the end, incident after incident occurred and a collection of supposed introduced mysterious weeds were reported in several papers both within the state, interstate and as far away as Western Australia.[440]

The Official Response

The official response came from a botanist 'Dr. Woolls'; the same botanist who dismissed William's 'yellow sage like weed' five years earlier (in June 1873). Woolls still believed William's yellow sage weed was not a source of poison and denoted it (in the summary that follows) as 'Caltrops (*Tribulus terrestris*)'.[441] Woolls collected a variety of supposed noxious weeds from the places that graziers had identified, tested them and found most to be harmless.[442] To reassure the graziers, Woolls advocated poisoning may occur if the stock were grazed where the weeds were in a 'wild state' (too many in the one spot) or after being furiously driven for some time, the stock ravenous when rested, over grazed too plentifully on weeds, to satisfy their hunger. A summary of Woolls' finding as reported in the *Daily Mail*, follows.

The Sydney Mail and New South Wales Advertiser, 16 November 1878, page 781. Plants Supposed to be Poisonous

It will be remembered that last year several reports were received of heavy losses to graziers through cattle eating certain plants. The flats around Dubbo especially were dreaded by drovers, but there was a feeling of uncertainty regarding the causes of death among the mobs of travelling stock.

The Rev. Dr. Woolls, who has ere [until] now exercised his skill in botany to benefit his fellow colonists, has lately received from the Macquarie, and also the Namoi, specimens of several plants which are supposed to be injurious to cattle. One of them, the Maltese thistle (Centaurea melitensis), which appears to have spread far inland, is not indigenous, and, as far as known in other countries, does not possess any poisonous properties. The flower heads are yellow and thorny, but the leaves are not prickly. This plant has been suspected by drovers, but apparently without cause.

With regard to the species of Swainsona, on the Macquarie (S. galegifolia and S. luteola), is probably that in seasons when grass is scarce, they are noxious, for they are nearly allied to the Darling pea, which has been known to have a deleterious effect on stock. In different parts of Australia, there are upwards of twenty species of Swainsona, and many of them are popularly termed Indigo.

It was suggested some time since by Baron Mueller, that the seeds of these plants should be subjected to a rigorous toxicological and chemical examination; but very little has yet been done in that direction, and with the exception of some experiments made upon sheep by giving them large quantities of S. Greyana, scarcely anything is known of the different species, so far as their poisonous qualities are concerned. It is stated that the Darling pea, were cultivated, is not injurious to sheep, though there can be no doubt that in a wild state it produces extraordinary effects on horses.

Observing persons have remarked that, in good seasons, when other pasture abounds, the difference species of Swainsona are eaten with impunity, and that it is only in bad seasons, unfavourable results may be looked for. Datura Tatula or Stramonium, the seeds of which are decidedly poisonous, has found its way far into the interior, and Solanumnigrum, which may certainly be suspected, occurs very frequently on stations, but there is no evidence to prove that they are eaten by sheep and cattle, and indeed the former is so nauseous in taste, that it is not at all likely to be eaten by them.

It appears that not only the seeds but the leaves of Stramonium are poisonous, for Dr. Barton mentions the cases of two British soldiers who ate them by mistake for those of another plant, and he states that the one became furious and ran about like a madman, whilst the other died with all the symptons of tetanus. On two occasions, specimens of Caltrops (Tribulus terrestris) have been sent to Dr. Woolls from the Namoi and Mooki, and the drovers say that the plant has killed cattle. Caltrops, which is common to Europe, Africa, and Asia, as well as Australia, is a prostrate plant with small yellow flowers, pinnate leaves, and prickly seeds, but, so far as the experience of other countries shows, it is eaten with impunity, and does no injury, except sometimes to the feet of cattle when they tread on the seeds.

In cases of supposed poisoning from plants, the carcases of the beasts should be subjected to a post-mortem examination and the contents of the stomach analysed, for without a careful investigation, the cause of death is mere conjecture.

Furious driving, feeding too plentifully (especially on such species as Medicago denticulata, a kind of Trefoil), and sudden atmospheric changes sometimes prove as injurious as the so-called poisonous plant.

Figure 34: Liverpool Plains Circa 1866

The Destructive Nature of Settlement

Woolls' commentary on all the various weeds that had spread through Country provides a further insight into the destructive nature of settlement. A lot had changed in the natural environment of the Hunter, Liverpool Plains, and the New England Tablelands since William, his brothers and all the other settlers had taken Country. It had been just over 50 years (1826–1878) since the settlers had entered the Hunter and taken Wonnaura Koori Country; followed by the progressive destruction of Kamilaroi Country on the Liverpool Plains (post-1826) and Anēwan and Bānbay Country on the New England Tablelands (post-1832).

The settlers had essentially destroyed the natural environment with their towns, roads, railways, farms and their introduced stock, weeds, and animal species (most notably, rabbits). The changes were phenomenal and challenged the original inhabitants. Each Aboriginal Nation demonstrated profound resilience, despite the murders, massacres and containment in government reserves. Each Nation survived to tell their story and remarkably each retained their culture, despite the obstacles, and with resilience, passed down their heritage to each new generation. Today they share their voices so we can all be enriched through their knowledge, language, ways of living and truth telling.

In contrast to the afflictions Indigenous peoples faced, settlers like William sr. and Mary benefited from settlement and the changes they had made to Country. Like the other settlers, William's and Mary's lives were entirely different and diametrically opposed to First Nations people. The image of a stockman with his cattle on the Liverpool Plains is indicative (see Figure 34). The landscape below bare and denuded of trees with introduced pastoral lands instead of native scrubland, trees and grasses.

The extract below of a retrospective on the Liverpool Plains (1907) demonstrates the commonly held view of the settlers: the land was there for the taking in a society and people driven by financial gain. Settlement, possession of land and the assets that came with ownership were symbols for them of status and progress.

The Sydney Morning Herald, 3 January 1907, page 5
THE OLD LIVERPOOL PLAINS.

"Of those who were squatting on the Liverpool Plains of 50 years ago [1857], I think there are only about three of us left," said Mr Charles W. Lloyd, of Double Bay, in course of a conversation with a "Herald" representative yesterday…

Mr. Lloyd… came out to Australia in 1854, and went direct to the Liverpool Plains…his brother, John Charles Lloyd, was one of the pioneers…

We were all 'squatters,' and a 'squatter' in these days was just like the squatter of England, who sits down on a piece of a common and is liable to ejectment at any time. I think I am correct in saying that no one had any really fixed right whatever to the lands they squatted on in those days, as no one exercised their preemptive right of purchase of land round the homesteads until the early sixties, and about the time of the Robertson Free Selection Act, which was so ruinous in its consequences to most of the pioneers…[443]

I think I am correct in saying that there were no recognised rights until Sir George Gipps's time, when Orders-in-Council were first promulgated. Very few people have seen the Orders-in-Council of those days in regard to land, but it seems to be beyond dispute that they evidenced a wisdom and foresight that much subsequent legislation dealing with the same matters has lacked.

At the time Mr Lloyd first went to the Plains [1854] there were no railways in Australia. Travellers from Sydney landed at Morpeth, the distance thence to the Namoi was about 200 miles, and this had to be done on horseback, or by private vehicle. Mr Lloyd did the Journey in five days, at that time considered good travelling. To-day [1907] the Journey can be accomplished in eight or nine hours.

"Yes, everything was done in a very primitive fashion those days" said Mr Lloyd in reply to a question "There was no fencing for stock. The latter were all shepherded. The first big wire fence was erected on Burburgate station (Lloyd Brothers) in 1856. I superintended the erection of the first ten miles myself. All our neighbours thought It a wild scheme, and nobody followed our example to any great extent until 15 years after. Before we started [fencing] you could have driven from Darling Downs to Broken Hill without striking a fence, and now from one end of the State to the other I don't know a single station that Isn't fenced in".

In 1862 "I don't think the Australian Agricultural Company had put £500 worth of Improvements on Warrah which is one of the finest runs in the district, and one which Is now [1907], I understand turning in about £30,000 or £40 000 per annum…"

"It is curious to look now at the towns of Gunnedah, Narrabri, Manilla and Boggabri," continued Mr Lloyd, "and think that at the time I am speaking of [1854] none of them existed…"

There was little or no agriculture carried on around Gunnedah, Boggabri, or Narrabri until about 1870. Prior to that I don't think there were more than 1000 acres under cultivation [for example cultivation of corn] …

[The following paragraph the most telling]

The contrast that the county presents to-day compared with the old days is wonderful. Travelling from Maitland to Tamworth there used to be scarcely any open country excepting patch's here and there on the Hunter. It was a dismal and uninteresting

Journey, mostly on bush tracks through box forests. With the clearing that has taken place you now see the most beautiful bits of scenery and in the Peel Valley particularly some of the finest wheat crops imaginable. Goonoo Goonoo now looks magnificent with its wheatfields and its good grazing land, where as aforetime it was woefully uninteresting, and the Piallaway country between Goonoo Goonoo and Duri station, which we used to regard as very inferior land even for grazing, is now a magnificent extent of alternating pastoral and agricultural country...

"It is a pity, said Mr Lloyd in conclusion, that there is no record of what the old pioneers of this country really did to pave the way for all this prosperity that Is now so apparent. People nowadays however are only interested in the men who have made money and they are mostly the men who had the way marked out for them by those hardy ones of 60 years back who, as it proved In all too many cases, simply sowed for others to reap".

[We know from William Nowland's story that he was one of these 'pioneers.']

The Great Northern Railway Comes to Quirindi

The coming of the railway was a decisive ingredient in the changes the settlers imposed on First Nations people and Country. By 1877, the railway line north had been built as far as Quirindi and the original landscape in the vicinity of settlement was forever changed.

The descriptors in the *Maitland Mercury* of the journey on the first steam train from Murrurundi to Quirindi on the 13th August 1877 give us an insight into the countryside William and Mary travelled through as they went to visit their children and grandchildren at Warrah Ridge; leaving from Singleton or more likely, from Ravensworth Station.[444] See below.

> *The Sydney Morning Herald, 16 August 1877, page 6*
> OPENING OF THE RAILWAY TO QUIRINDI
> *(From Tuesday's Maitland Mercury)*

On Monday the additional twenty-four miles of the Great Northern Railway, which have at last been completed out of the contract for the extension to Tamworth, were opened for public traffic. The extension begins at the Murrurundi station, and proceeds for about three miles along the valley of the Page and then taking a somewhat sharp curve, crosses the river over a substantial timber bridge.

The lines then carried along the side of the Liverpool Range, crossing from spur to spur over some very heavy embankments. Glimpses are gained, far below, of the valley and the picturesque town of Murrurundi, nestling in the shadow of the great mountain; and from the point of junction of the railway with the coach road over the Gap, and up to the tunnel mouth, the sight is a very pretty one indeed. This point, we fancy, will be a favourite one with travellers, as the view from it will add a pleasure to the journey, joined to the pleasure of breathing pure mountain air.

A little further on the tunnel begins, and continues for 528 yards. The line emerges into Doughboy Hollow, on old camping place for teams, and a small village. Then, for some miles, there is broken country, and the first station is reached, fourteen miles from Murrurundi, at Warrah.[445] *This station is some distance from, but in sight of, a very old road-side hostelry, the Willow Tree Inn. There is a goods shed here also.*

Leaving Warrah, the line traverses a tract at first undulating, but gradually getting more flat, (sic) and giving glimpses of cultivated land and views of beautiful grazing plains. At twenty-four miles from Murrurundi is the present terminus at Quirindi, this is a pretty little village, surrounded by country pleasantly diversified by hill and valley.

At Quirindi, both because it is to be the terminus for some time, and because it will receive a great deal of the wool and other traffic from Liverpool Plains, there is a goods station. The total length of the line now open from Newcastle to Quirindi is 114 miles [183.5 km].

This extension has been under way for some years. The Murrurundi length was opened in April, 1872, and the contract for the extension to Tamworth was taken in April, 1874. And, now, after all the delay, twenty-four miles only have been finished rather less than five miles a year. Truly remarkable progress! It is fair to the contractor, however, to state that the length just completed is the most difficult part of his work, and that he has had great drawbacks in every respect.

At Murrurundi yesterday morning holiday was kept, and the two trains which left for Quirindi in the afternoon were well patronized. Mr. Rae, the Commissioner for Railways; Mr. Whitton, the Engineer-in-Chief; Mr. Higgs, traffic manager and Messrs. W. C. Browne, Hanley Bennett, and Scholey, with other gentlemen, formed the official party for the opening. They came to Quirindi in advance of the mail train from Newcastle.

Quirindi was making holiday with flags, and there was a large concourse of people about the station who cheered lustily as the train came in. The weather was lovely. On the arrival of the mail train, Mr. Rae was welcomed by Mr. C. P. Gruggen, J.P., chairman of the local committee, and he proceeded to declare the line open... Much cheering followed the announcement, and the ceremony of opening was concluded in that way.

... The banquet was held in the goods shed of the new station ... The shed was very well and tastefully decorated with evergreens and flags, and a plentiful supply of

creature comforts was upon the tables. About 160 gentlemen were present.

After the toasts of "The Queen" and "The Prince of Wales" had been duly honoured, the chairman gave "His Excellency the Governor," who, he said, had written expressing his regret that previous engagements would prevent his being present on the occasion… Mr. Abbott, of Murrurundi, … [gave] a humorous speech … Mr. Rae, in responding, referred at large to the railway systems of the colony, the manner in which they were started, and subsequently taken over by the Government, and to the advantages likely to accrue from the junction of our lines with those of the other colonies, in promoting a uniformity of duties, and also furthering confederation.

Several other toasts were given and responded to, and the proceedings terminated about 3 o'clock. A number of the visitors remained for the ball which was to be given at the goods shed in the evening, others returning to Newcastle by a train leaving Quirindi at 6 o'clock.

The steam train north from Singleton to Quirindi provided a faster and more comfortable way to travel. No more bouncing up and down in a coach or buggy for hours on end when William and Mary went north to see family at Warrah Ridge.

William Joined the Debate About a Railway Line South

The railway line south between the Hunter and Sydney was yet to be built and William decided to share his thoughts on the matter. He wrote to the Singleton *Argus* in support of the proposed railway between Singleton and Sydney and describes the route he would take based on his knowledge of the area. He described every nook and cranny, farm and creek along the way, and told the editor it had been 25 years since he had travelled any of the roads south of the Hunter and maybe some of the names of the places had changed.

William's account conjures up images of William's travels south as a younger man. He probably passed the time of day with the graziers he met on the way; he certainly knew them.

'How's the weather been fairing John? Dry up our way.'

'Good to see aye Patrick, nearly there, the cattle have found it difficult this time. How about you? Any news?'

The Singleton Argus and Upper Hunter General Advocate,
19 June 1878, page 2.
THE PROPOSED RAILWAY TO SYDNEY.
(To the Editor of the Singleton Argus.)

Sir,—Considering the importance of the above subject at the present time, I do not think it out of place to offer a few remarks regarding the route to be followed by the proposed railroad. Having travelled for many years between the Hunter and the several towns south of it, and by several routes, I would like to point out the route which I consider would pay the country best, and benefit the greatest possible number of persons. To begin at the northern end, I will take Singleton as the starting point. I would then proceed to Broke, and thence follow the valley of Wollombi Brook up to Wollombi Township (this can be done by crossing the creek once only); thence along the main Wiseman's Ferry Road to Laguna, at which point I would leave that road on my left hand and proceed up a valley, and along Paddy McAlise's road to a place culled the Common, which leads me down to the McDonald River. I would cross that river near the Church, and proceed over a small range of easy ascent to "Webbe's Creek near Mr John Rose's farm; thence up a valley which heads on a ridge dividing the waters of Colo from Webbe's Creek; thence down a valley to Mr. Patrick Burn's farm, and cross the Colo River immediately below the junction of Weeney Creek; thence up a valley which bends on the main ridge dividing the waters of Colo from Phil Roberts' Swamp, and cross that swamp and Currency Creek; thence across the Hawkesbury River to join the Richmond line at Mulgrave, Windsor; or any other suitable point.

As it is upwards of twenty-five years since I travelled any of the roads south of the Hunter, some of the places I have mentioned may not be known now by the names I have given. The route I have sketched would be as direct as any other that I can remember, and has the advantage, of passing through the best agricultural land between the Hunter and Hawkesbury. There would be no great engineering difficulties to contend against, no deep water to cross; and it has the additional advantage of having an inexhaustible supply of good timber suitable for sleepers, bridges, and in short, for all the purposes required for making the line. Between Colo and Webbe's Creek alone more than sufficient timber could be found for the whole extension.

I have made these few remarks in the hope that some person whose acquaintance with the locality is of more recent date than mine, may take up the subject.

Trusting that you may find space for this in your journal.

I remain,

Your most obedient servant

WILLIAM NOWLAND

Rosedale. June 18, 1878.

[We insert Mr. Nowland's letter with pleasure, and are sure that the advocates of the Singleton-Sydney railway scheme will feel indebted to him for the valuable information he has given. We invite further correspondence on the subject.—ED.]

William's suggestions on the best way to transverse the rugged land south from Singleton to the Hawkesbury provides us with a further insight into William as a person and the life he led. He had travelled along the Bulga Track (and other tracks south) for around 30 years (1823–1853); first with his brothers and later with his sons. Then 25 years later, William thought his views would still be useful to those who had started to survey the area (in 1878) for the proposed railway line between Singleton and the Hawkesbury.

William was not the only one, there was plenty of discussion in the local and Sydney papers about how to join the Sydney Railway line to the Newcastle/Singleton line, or whether it was needed at all; for some, the paddle steamers were the best form of transport between Newcastle and Sydney. Those who supported a railway line fell into two camps: the Newcastle residents who wanted the railway line to go from Newcastle down the coast and cross the Hawkesbury River at Cogra Bay, and then from Brooklyn via Hornsby to Sydney; and the Singleton constituents (like William) who proposed the railway line transgress the rugged and less settled areas south between Singleton to Windsor and cross the Hawkesbury River at Windsor, and from there join the Richmond line to Sydney.

Given the topography, one cannot image today that the Singleton to Windsor route was ever considered or taken seriously. It is interesting to explore this part of William's story from this aspect alone. The advocates for the Singleton to Windsor route were taken seriously, and for a while they thought they had a chance. The discussion in the newspapers is fascinating and full of politics, self-interest and positioning. The extracts below from some of the key articles (in 1878) provide a sense of the heightened concerns of the two conflicting camps: both passionate in their opinions and canvassing for government support.

'An opinion was then expressed that the scheme of a railway from Sydney to Singleton was too absurd for any Ministry to entertain…'

'We, the undersigned, residents of the city of Newcastle, request you will call a public meeting of the citizens to protest against the expenditure of the public funds in the construction of a railway from Singleton to Sydney…'

'There could be no doubt that a railway for the Great Northern Line to Sydney would damage the port of Newcastle…'

'We have it on excellent authority (reports the Singleton Argus) that four surveyors are at present employed on the survey on the railway line from Sydney to the Great Northern Line. It is proposed to start the line from Riverstone station, 28 miles from Sydney. – Progress reports have been sent in but some time will necessarily elapse before anything definite is decided upon. Meanwhile the public meeting, the holding of which we suggested some time since, remains one of the things of the future…'

'TO THE HONOURABLE THE MINISTERS FOR PUBLIC WORKS, NEW SOUTH WALES. The memorial of the inhabitants of the city and port of Newcastle in public meeting assembled humbly showeth that your memorialists view with considerable surprise an attempt now being made by certain individuals in several localities acting in concert with others in the metropolis for the purpose of promoting a scheme having for its object the formation of a branch line of railway to tap the Great Northern at or somewhere near Singleton and from thence to Sydney…'

'It would be an absurdity to take passengers on route from Newcastle to Sydney, as far as Singleton before they started!…' 'the inhabitants of Newcastle would be caused to make an unnecessary detour of about 100 miles.

'Singleton – Sydney Railway. At last steps are about to be taken in this city [Newcastle] to prevent the carrying out of the proposal, lately put forward with a flourish of trumpets at Singleton, for a railway between that town and the metropolis [Sydney]. A requisition to the Mayor, asking him to call a public meeting to protest against the project, is being signed. It is to be hoped that the characteristic apathy in regard to such matters will be absent on this occasion, and that every effort will be made to upset a scheme that has for its object the destruction of the best interests of this city [Newcastle] and district…'

'The good people of Singleton have come to the front this time in real earnest, to see what can be done to elevate their town into something like political and social importance. However unpleasant may be the reflection, it is doubtless a fact that Singleton does not enjoy that celebrity…'

A very largely attended and unanimous meeting was held at Gosford on Saturday, to consider the many reasons in favour of constructing a railway through the Brisbane Water district, and to connect the Northern with the Western and Southern railway…'

A resolution affirming that the best route, and the one possessing the most general *benefits, is from Newcastle, passing through Brisbane Water, and terminating on the north shore of Port Jackson … protest against the expenditure of the public funds in the construction of a railway from Singleton to Sydney…'* [446]

Amongst all this flurry of correspondence (in 1878) William only wrote to the paper once about his views on the best route south for a railway line. Though this would not last long. William hadn't given up on a route from Singleton to Sydney via the Hawkesbury as will be detailed soon.

The Demise of Falbrook National School at Camberwell

For now, the demise of Camberwell's National School was probably at the forefront of William's mind. The school was worse for wear and the government was not willing to spend money on it. See the extract below from recent research (2009) that covered amongst other things the history of the Camberwell area.

> *In 1879, the 30' x 50' building was described by the Clerk of Works as 'a very inferior building from the very first and its present condition, which is of general decay, is not worth spending any money on'.* [447]

William Starts to Reflect on His Life

William was relatively old in 1879 (75 years) and started to reflect on his life.[448] He penned a letter to his nephew Alex to tell him all about his life as a squatter on the Liverpool Plains. Alex was impressed, and in turn, wrote to William's local newspaper.[449] Alex's letter follows.

> *The Singleton Argus and Upper Hunter General Advocate,*
> *23 July 1879, page 2*
> *Early "Recollections of Liverpool Plains.*
> *To the Editor of the Tamworth Observer.*

DEAR SIR, —I enclose a letter signed 'W. Nowland,' which you will perceive was written in 1861, giving an account of that gentleman's squatting experiences in 1827.—I am pleased to state the old gentlemen [William 75 yrs.] is still in the land of the living, and residing on his 'Camberwell Estate' [Rosedale] near Singleton. I received a letter this week from him, in which he states that Messrs. Onus, Williams, Singleton, and Baldwin, formed stations on Liverpool Plains early in 1827, a few months previous to his taking up country.[450] These names will be familiar to most of your readers, and I have no doubt Mr. Nowland's letter will be interesting to them also. The station taken up by all those gentlemen now forms part of the 'Warrah Estate' the property of the A.A. Company.

Yours obediently,
Alex. Johnson. [Johnston]
Tamworth, 10th July, 1870 (sic).

[given William's age and the date of the article, the last date in the above article should read 10th July, 1879].

Nothing further was found in the papers about William's life as a squatter, until after his death; detailed towards the end of the story.

Family Life at the End of the 1870s

By the end of the 1870s, all the Nowland boys were married (except for William jr. and Henry) and four of the boys lived permanently at Warrah Ridge (Robert, Chas, George, Alfred) with Michael nearby at Borambil. William and Mary had numerous grandchildren, 36 in total, ranging in age from four babies, all born in 1879,[451] to the three eldest grandchildren, all born in 1862, and now 17.[452]

There was plenty of family to visit in and around Warrah Ridge. Family, Mary would only see occasionally prior to the construction of the railway line north as far as Quirindi (in 1877). While for William, circumstances had always allowed him to see family, more often. William travelled on a regular basis between Rosedale and Warrah Ridge as a grazier and probably often stayed with family. William and their boys worked together, helped each other out, drove their cattle and sheep together between their various homesteads (when needed) and sold their stock (sometimes together) within the local regional markets.[453]

Over the years, William and Mary had lost several of their siblings. For William, all his siblings were deceased, except for Mary (his sister and the wife of the now deceased Alex Johnston). William's sister, Mary was 70 and still lived in Scone. While for William's wife, Mary, four of her siblings were still alive; Harriet (74) at Muswellbrook, Ann (72) at Wilberforce, Elizabeth (64) at Windsor, and James (59) at Wilberforce.[454]

Death of Mary's Sister Harriet Farlow Nowland

In the first year of the following decade (August 1880) Mary's sister Harriet (75) died. The family notice that follows said very little.

The Maitland Mercury and Hunter River General Advertiser,
28 August 1880, page 1.
Family Notices

At her residence, near Muswellbrook, on August 20th, 1880, Mrs. Harriet Nowland, relict of the late Mr. Henry Nowland, of Muswellbrook; aged 75 years.[455]

Death of William's Remaining Sibling Mary

Then in 1881 William (76) lost his remaining sibling; Mary Johnston (née Nowland). No family notice was found in the papers for Mary (72) who died on the 24 December 1881.[456]

The death of William's sister Mary was a significant loss. Fifty-seven years earlier (c.1823) William and his three brothers Michael jr., Henry, and Edward had entered the Hunter. Followed by the Farlow sisters progressively in the 1830s and William's sister, Mary and her husband Alex Johnston in 1842. Now, only William (76) and his wife, Mary (68) remained from amongst these mainly first-generation colonial Australians (the Nowland siblings and Farlow sisters) who had come to a very different Hunter; the pristine Country of the Wonnarua Koori.

CHAPTER 33

WILLIAM STILL AN ADVOCATE FOR CAMBERWELL

In the 1880s, William and Mary were still adjusting, improving and enriching their lives at Camberwell. Rosedale was their family home and Camberwell was their very small village. Camberwell, a place of importance to them, despite its size. The correspondent (most likely, William) always 'big noted' Camberwell and rose once again to its defence, as detailed in the following article.

> *The Maitland Mercury and Hunter River General Advertiser,*
> *5 June 1880, page 7.*
> ### *CAMBERWELL*
>
> *Why is Camberwell unrepresented in the columns of your various issues? This question has often entered my mind, but as often have I been at a loss to solve it. Well, if you will accept my humble services, I shall experience much pleasure in acting as correspondent for the neglected little village.*
>
> *Camberwell, — better known by the name of Glennies Creek, is situated on the Great Northern Road, nine miles [14.5 km] from Singleton. It was once a stirring place, but since the iron horse [railway] has passed through and wended his way onwards, things have assumed a different feature, both in the line of business and amusements.*
>
> *Times have changed and so has Camberwell. The external appearance of some of the present buildings seem to say "we have seen better times." There were, I believe, three public houses in full operation, doing a "roaring" trade, some years back, but there is only one to be seen now, and that one is quite sufficient for the present demand of the inebriant fluid.*
>
> *Besides this public house there is one wine shop, whose business is very limited. There are also two Churches (English and Scotch), a various number of private residences, and a Public school, which is badly in need of repairs. The accommodation is inadequate to the attendance, viz., 41, on the roll. The attendance was very small for some time previous to the new teacher's arrival (Mr. John Shanahan), but he seems to be gradually regaining the deserters.*
>
> *The greatest area of the land about Camberwell is used for pastoral purposes, for which it is well adapted, as the grass is noted for its fattening properties. There are a few farms along the creek, which produce very fair crops.*

In the 1880s, Camberwell had just enough to sustain itself; probably, a small general store and possibly a blacksmith, and as mentioned above, a public house, a wine shop, two churches, a highly respected school teacher and a small public school. It was also picturesque and productive with its winding creek, rolling pastures and yellow fields of crops, such as, wheat, bailey, maize (for fodder) and tobacco.[457]

Despite William's expectations, Camberwell never grew to be large enough to be designated as a town. There were too many competing forces that restricted its growth; it was too close to Singleton, and by the 1880s, the Great Northern Road and Northern Railway bypassed this very small settlement.

Nearly 40 years after Camberwell had officially been declared as a site for a township (18th November 1840) Camberwell was described as a village under the *Crown Lands Alienation Act 1861*, as detailed next.

New South Wales Government Gazette, 30 August 1880, page 4439
Department of Lands,
Sydney, 30th August, 1880.
SITE FOR THE VILLAGE OF CAMBERWELL.

HIS Excellency the Governor, with the advice of the Executive Council, directs it to be notified, that in pursuance of the provisions of the Crown Lands Alienation Act of 1861, the following portions of Crown Lands are declared to be set apart as sites for the village of Camberwell, and of suburban lands to be attached thereto…

Around 8 months later, in February 1881, the correspondent for Camberwell wrote once again to the local paper about this 'forgotten village'. This time to the *Singleton Argus*. As detailed below.

Singleton Argus, 2 February 1881, page 2.
Camberwell
(From our Correspondent)

WHY cannot Camberwell claim a representative in the columns of your journal as well as other parts of the district? This question I have often weighed in my leisure thoughts, but as often have I been at a loss to arrive at a solution. Since her ungrateful children have left her almost buried in oblivion, I, although merely a stranger on her stage, will, by kind permission, raise my voice in (sic) Camberwell's behalf.[458]

Before entering into local occurrences, it may not be out of place to give a few introductory remarks hearing on the above named township.[459] *No doubt a great many of your readers are personally acquainted with Camberwell, and equally as many, if not more, know it merely by name, and probably some do not know it either one way or the other.*

Well, it stands on a beautifully pellucid stream of permanent water, highly prized for its wholesomeness and purity, called after, I believe, that upright, honorable, Dr. Glennie, whose remains are now sleeping in a narrow bed of clay.[460]

The distance from Singleton, along the Great Northern Road, is about nine miles [14.5 km]. The external appearance of the buildings, which are now somewhat dilapidated, seem to say "we have seen better times." But alas! those times are vanished, whether they will return again must be left to the future to prove.

The cruel iron horse, they say, has been the cause of this great change, which has wrought similar changes in a great many other small towns along the Northern line… The Post-office is conducted by Mr. Batt, a very careful postmaster. We have a pound, kept by Mr. P. Traynor… There are two wineshops belonging, respectively, to Mr. Drane and Mr. Langford. There are two churches—a Church of England and a Presbyterian. There is also a Roman Catholic Church convenient to Glennies Creek platform, which is about two miles from the village. The Public School, I must reluctantly admit, is not creditable to the Educational Department. It is, at present, undergoing repairs. A good attendance has been obtained in this school since the recent appointment of the present teacher, Mr. Shanahan. It is, I believe, classified as an eighth-class school.

On the bank of the creek stands a large brick building, once a publichouse [Queen Victoria Inn], the property of Mr. Nowland [William]. It is now tenanted by Mr. J. Irwin and Mr. S. Paul…[461]

…We have no policeman stationed here, the people being too good to require the services of such an officer. [Sounds like William, based on his signature style of writing previously to the papers].

Camberwell, I am positive, is the seat of a very extensive field of coal. Ledges of coal may be seen, in various parts of the creek, projecting from the banks; likewise large blocks have been discovered a short distance from the surface, by men digging post-holes. It is a wonder some enterprising gentleman does not open a coal pit in the locality, as it affords every facility for the purpose.[462]

The greater part of the land approximate to the creek is well adapted for agriculture, and the various herbage which it produces is noted for its fattening properties… The wheat crops have turned out to be very good in the locality this time. The young corn is commencing to assume a sere and hopeless aspect from the effects of the suffocating winds and the great heat, which we have been experiencing recently.

Athletic sports were held at Mr. Boyle's, Clarefield, on last Wednesday, … I have been informed that the amusements were well patronised and everything went off quietly.

Health is very good amongst us just now, considering the unfavourable weather we have been experiencing recently. A thunderstorm seems looming in the distance this morning, as black clouds are thick in the west, and an occasional rumbling of thunder is heard.

January 28th, 1881.

As told earlier, it was common practice for the correspondent of a locality (town or village) to write to the papers (usually the local ones) about what was happening in their vicinity; the weather, critical incidences, their achievements, advancements, events, festivities, etc. Though the correspondent rarely if ever signed their name and because of this expected custom we will never know if William was the correspondent for Camberwell. However, there is a lot in William's story that suggests he was the voice of Camberwell in the local papers either personally or through someone he encouraged to write to the papers about Camberwell's achievements; either someone else that lived in the village or someone who was interested and just passing by.

Would a Railway Line Between Singleton and Sydney Help Camberwell?

We know that William did sign his name as an advocate for a railway line between Singleton to Sydney. When the first route William suggested (in 1878) was rejected, he wrote once again to the *Singleton Argus* (in 1880) to present some alternatives. A precis of William's letter was included in the *Singleton Argus* on the 19th March 1880 and a month later printed in full in the same newspaper. William this time, suggested two alternative routes: one via Parramatta and the other via Pitt Town. William's letter read as follows.

The Singleton Argus and Upper Hunter General Advocate,
21 April 1880, page 2.
(To the Editor of the Singleton Argus)

SIR, —As the proposed railway from Singleton to Sydney via. Broke seems to be disapproved of, I should, now suggest the following route:— Let Singleton be the starting point; thence through Messrs. Dangar and Mackay's estate to estate to Millfield; thence to Laguna; thence cross to the right of Wiseman's Road; then along McAlise's Road to Richard Judd's farm on the Macdonald River; thence cross the river, passing the church and over a small ridge to John Rose's farm at Webb's Creek; thence up a small ridge which divides Colo River from Webb's Creek, where abundance of timber may be had. (If Parramatta should be chosen as the point of junction, here, at the east end of this ridge, is a most suitable spot for a bridge, as the banks are high and not far apart.)

From this proceed to Burn's old farm, and cross the Colo River immediately below the junction of Weeney Creek; thence up a valley which heads on the main, ridge, dividing the waters of Weeney Creek from Phillip Robert's swamp, crossing that swamp and Currency Creek; thence to avoid the low lands (sic) of Wilberforce, cross to David Brown's farm now in the possession of Mrs. Burdekin; thence cross the Hawkesbury River, passing, through Mr. George Hall's farm to Pitt Town, where a bridge would not cost much, as the land is high on both sides of the river; thence to McGrath's Hill, about 1¼ mile south of Windsor, and thence either to, Mulgrave or Blacktown.

I remain your obedient servant,

WILLIAM NOWLAND

Rosedale, Camberwell, 19th April, 1880.

William's descriptors of his suggested alternative routes for the railway line between Singleton and Sydney are a valuable addition to his story. William must have travelled these byways, numerous times with his stock, pre-1853. He appears to know (as mentioned earlier and based on memory) every nook, cranny, creek, farm and farmer along the way.

Tracing William's Sons Lives Through Articles in the Local Papers

William's sons are readily found in the local papers in the 1880s. Of note, at this stage of William's story is the report in the local paper of Alfred's active participation in the Camberwell community. See below.

The Maitland Mercury and Hunter River General Advertiser,
22 February 1883, page 5.

Commons' Trustees – The Gazette of Feb. 16 says the following commons trustees had been elected: Camberwell: Messrs. George Bates, Edward Langford, Alfred Nowland, George Vick Pearse, and Frederick William Puxly.

On this occasion, Alfred (32) rather than William sr. was elected as one of the Trustees for the Camberwell Common. Why was this the case, given Alfred, Lauretta and their children lived at Warrah Ridge? Probably, because Alfred's father William sr. was experiencing regular bouts of chest pain, shortness of breath and fatigue and Alfred had returned to Camberwell to help his brother (Henry 30) run Rosedale.[463]

Alfred Returned to Live Permanently at Rosedale

From circa 1883, Rosedale became the family home of Alfred (32), Lauretta (29) and their children (Alfred jr. 7, William 6, Vivian 4, Edwin 3, Cecil 1 and Millicent, a baby). As told earlier, Alfred and Lauretta spent most of the rest of their lives at Rosedale; some 42 years between circa 1883 and 1925. While their children progressively left home (Rosedale) once they became old enough to do so; just as most of their uncles (William sr.'s and Mary's sons) had done before them.

During this part of their lives (1883 to 1925), Alfred and Lauretta were both active and well-respected members of the Camberwell community.[464]

Some examples of Alfred's participation in the local community in 1883 are included next. In the first account, Alfred with other community members successfully gained the direct exchange of mails between the Mail Guard's North and Camberwell.

Singleton Argus, 28 March 1883, page 2.
CAMBERWELL MAILS.

The following letter has been handed to us for publication:—

General Post Office.

Sydney, 22nd March, 1883.

SIR,—Referring to your letter of the 17th instant, accompanying a petition signed by Messrs. Alfred Nowland, Arthur Bowman, George V. Pearce, and other residents of

Camberwell, asking for a direct exchange of mails between the Mail Guard's North, and Camberwell. I am directed to inform you that the desire has been acceded to.

I have, &c.,

S. H. LAMBTON.

Secretary.

Around two months later, Alfred is the convener of a meeting to erect a railway station at Glennies Creek, and Henry is one of Alfred's supporters. See the article that follows.

Singleton Argus, 23 May 1883, page 2.
Railway Accommodation at Glennies Creek.

A WELL-ATTENDED meeting of residents of the district was held at Mr. Drane's at Camberwell on Saturday afternoon, to consider what steps should be taken to induce the Government to erect station buildings at Glennies Creek...

Mr. A. Nowland, [Alfred] the convener of the meeting, said that this matter had been the subject of conversation amongst the people there for some time, but of course those little debates generally ended in nothing, but a week or so ago it was decided to call a meeting to urge the necessity of having increased railway accommodation at Glennies Creek...

Mr. Henry Nowland supported the resolution. He did not think a goods-shed and porter in charge would be sufficient to meet the requirements of that important district. Nothing short of a station should satisfy them...

The following month (June 1883) Alfred's attention (along with other members of the Camberwell community) turned to the proposed railway station at Glennies Creek (that we know went ahead) and the opening of the New School at Camberwell. Alfred is praised and well regarded in the account, and Lauretta is mentioned as one of the ladies that assists with the day. See below.

Singleton Argus, 2 June 1883, page 2.
Opening of the New School at Camberwell

"God Save the Queen" was then sung by the whole assembly, after which three hearty cheers were given for Her Majesty [Queen Victoria]; Mr. Gould and Mrs. Gould, and Mr. Alfred Nowland... The toast was drunk with enthusiasm and with musical honors.

...He [Mr. Pearce, another member of the Camberwell community] knew they were thinking of a railway station for Glennies Creek. He was pleased to see Mr. A. Nowland [Alfred] had taken action in the matter, and everyone would confess that since Mr. Nowland's return to the district [from Warrah Ridge] that gentleman had stirred up the people. Hearing of the meeting lately held there, he wrote to Mr. Nowland, saying that it would be better to have a porter in charge instead of asking for a station house. He did not write in that strain without giving the matter considerable thought. He knew the difficulty there was in inducing the railway authorities to erect a railway station without very strong reasons being shown.

... The health of Mr. Fletcher [presumably Camberwell community member] proposed by Mr. H. Nowland, [Henry] was warmly received and responded to. "The School Opening Celebration Committee,"... To Mr. A. Nowland, [Alfred] the energetic secretary, praise was especially due. Mr. Nowland would keep the people there moving, and he would advise them all to back him up. He hoped they would have many more such pleasant reunions. The name of Mr. A. Nowland, [Alfred] was coupled with the toast, which was drunk with musical honors.

Mr. Nowland, [Alfred] in replying, asked the visitors to overlook any shortcomings they may have noticed. ["You have done first-rate."] They had done the best they could. (Applause)

…The ladies of Camberwell deserve great credit for their efforts in making the day such an enjoyable one.[465] *Foremost among the other workers were Messrs. A. Nowland, [Lauretta] J. Drane and G. V. Pearce …*

In the fourth account (that follows) in July 1883, Alfred and Henry are part of a deputation to the Minister of Works for a railway station to be placed at Glennies Creek.

Evening News (Sydney), 6 July 1883, page 3
STATION AT GLENNIES CREEK
Messrs. Gould and H. Levien introduced a deputation to the Minister of Works [Francis Wright][466] *consisting of Messrs. A. Bowman, A. Nowland [Alfred], H. Nowland (Henry) and John Drane. Their object was to have a station placed at Glennies Creek…*

And lastly (September 1883), Alfred writes to the General Post Office Sydney about the reduction in tenders for the mail between Glennies Creek and Camberwell.

Singleton Argus, 22nd September 1883, page 2
Camberwell Post Office
General Post Office Sydney, 17th September 1883 Sir – with reference to your letter of the 12th instant enclosing one from Mr. A. Nowland (Camberwell) complaining that tenders for the mail between Glennie's (sic) Creek and Camberwell are being call for twice or thrice instead of six times per week…

William sr.'s and Mary's third youngest son George (36) was also evident in the papers at Warrah Ridge with the notification of Georges appointment as a magistrate, in August 1883.[467] While, Henry appeared in the paper as part of the Camberwell Cricket team in 1884.[468]

Henry the Last to Marry

Eighteen eighty-three (1883) was another year of celebration. On the 7th November 1883, Henry (30) married Martha Elizabeth Clark (25) at Elizabeth's parents' residence in Oban; their marriage registered at Armidale.[469] The family notice in the local paper read:

The Armidale Express and New England General Advertiser,
4 December 1883, page 3
At the residence of the bride's parents, on November 7th, by the Rev. Thomas Johnstone, Henry, youngest son of William Nowland, Esq., Sen., of Rosedale, Camberwell, to Martha Elizabeth, eldest daughter of Thomas P. Clark, Esq., of Oban.[470]

The Marriage of William's and Mary's Eldest Grandson 'John James Nowland'

Just over two weeks after Henry and Martha married, William sr.'s and Mary's eldest grandson (Chas and Annie's son) John James (21) married Emily Lydia Smith at South Grafton. The family notice in the local paper read.

Clarence and Richmond Examiner and New England Advertiser,
1 December 1883, page 4.
MARRIAGE

NOWLAND-SMITH – On November 24th, at South Grafton, by the Rev. J. L. Bosworth, JOHN JAMES, son of CHARLES NOWLAND, Warrah Ridge, Quirindi, and Queensland, grazier to EMILY LYDIA, daughter of WILLIAM A. SMITH, Esq., J.P. (late of the Williams River), grazier, South Grafton.

Death of William's and Mary's Third Son Robert

The year 1883 was also a time of immense tragedy and shock for William sr., Mary, their surviving sons, and extended family. William sr. and Mary's third eldest son, Robert (47) died on the 19th April 1883, at Warrah Ridge, most likely from a heart attack. The family notice in the local paper read.

Singleton Argus, 8 May 1883, page 2.
DEATH.

On 19th April, 1883, at his late residence, Warrah Ridge, of disease of the heart, Robert, third beloved son of WILLIAM NOWLAND, of Rosedale, Camberwell, in his 47th year, leaving a wife and ten children to mourn his loss.

As told earlier, George (36) and Henry (30) were the executors of Robert's Will and Robert's estate was worth £2105.[471]

In the same year (1883) Robert and Jane lost their baby son Henry.[472] It is not known if Robert was alive when their youngest child (Henry) died; no family notice was found.

William Decided To Write His Will

Just over three months after Robert's death in April 1883 William sr. finalised his own Will, on the 20th July 1883. Most likely prompted by the sudden and unexpected death of his son from heart disease. A condition that had plagued William since the late 1870s (c.1878).[473] He too could die of heart disease without warning.

WILL OF WILLIAM NOWLAND
Dated 20 July, 1883

(Ref. 10186 Ser.3 S.A.O.)

To his wife MARY ANN – All my household goods and effects, my horses, buggies, carts, horses and farming implements usually used in and around my residence at Camberwell. Also all that flock of sheep at present or at the time of decease depastured in the County of Durham. Also all that mob of cattle at present depasturing at Warrah Ridge or at time of decease depastured in the County of Durham. All my six allotments of land at Musswellbrook.

To my eldest son William and his heirs, those three several portions of land situate in the Parrish of Warrah, County Buckland respectively containing 320 acres, 60 acres and 40 acres of land being portions 49, 77 and 78 provided he grant transfer and convey within — months after my decease or earlier if practicable all those 142 acres at present in the name of the said WILLIAM NOWLAND situate in Parish Aukland County Durham Unto and to the use of my two younger sons ALFRED NOWLAND and HENRY NOWLAND, their heirs and assigns as tenants in common provided the said ALFRED and his wife and said HENRY do severally and respectively within the like period or earlier if practicable grant, transfer and convey the hereditaments hereinafter mentioned in and to the persons hereinafter named.

I devise unto my Trustees hereinafter named their heirs and assigns all those five several parcels of land situate in the Parrish Warrah and County Buckland respectively containing 320 acres, 318 acres, 165 ½ acres, 167 acres, and a conditional purchase of 46 acres of 16 Jan. 1879 being portions 12, 60, 75, 76 and 129. To hold same to the use of my son CHARLES NOWLAND for the term of his natural life and from and immediately after his decease to the use of all the children of my said son CHARLES begotten or to be begotten on the body of his present wife who may have attained the age of 21 years their heirs and assigns as Tennants in common.

I devise to my son ALEXANDER and his heirs ALL that parcel of land situate in the Parish of Warrah, County Buckland containing 282 ½ acres portion 59.

I devise to my son GEORGE and his heirs those six several parcels of land situate Parish of Warrah, County Buckland containing 98 acres and 40 acres freeholds and conditional purchases 80 acres 19 Aug. 1875, 120 acres 6 June 1872 (?) 65 acres 10 June 1875 and 122 acres 15 Apr 1875 being portions 89, 148, 84 and 85, 125, 126 and 127.

I devise to my sons ALFRED and HENRY and their heirs as Tennants in common all those three several parcels of land situate in Parish Aukland, CountyDurham respectively containing 276 acres and 316 acres freeholds and a conditional purchase of 312 acres of 12 Mar 1874 being portion 123 and also all those two several parcels of land situate Parish Darlington County Durham respectively containing 90 acres freehold and a conditional purchase of 13 Sept. 1877 of 178 acres being portion 137 and all that parcel of land situate in the village of Camberwell containing 2 acres on which is erected the old Queen Victoria Hotel being a grant by purchase from the Crown and also of that and singular those several parcels of land situate in the village of Camberwell being lots 1 to 9 inclusive of Section 5 respectively containing 1 Rood 11 perches, 1 Rood 20 perches, 1 Rood 24 perches, 1 Rood 22 perches, 1 Rood 39 perches, 1 Rood 37 perches and three of 1 Rood 36 perches each 1 to

Figure 35 Transcript of the 'Will of William Nowland dated 20 July 1883' [p. 1]

20 inclusive of Section 6 respectively containing 2 Roods each. Lots 11 to 14 inclusive of Section 8 respectively containing 2 Roods each. Lots 5 to 11 inclusive of Section 10 respectively containing 2 Roods each. Lots 5 to 7 and 10 to 12 inclusive of Section 11 respectively containing 2 Roods each and Lots 1 to 4 inclusive of Section 12 respectively containing 1 Rood 32 perches, 1 Rood 29 perches, 1 Rood 27 perches and 1 Rood 28 perches PROVIDED the said ALFRED grant, transfer and convey within 3 months after my decease or earlier if practicable all those two several conditional purchases of 254 acres 4 Feb. 1875 and 171 ½ acres 25 Apr 1878 situate in the Parish Telford County Buckland being Portions 129 and 147 at present held by and standing in the name of said ALFRED NOWLAND to my Trustees hereinafter named, their heirs and assigns To hold the same to the use of my son CHARLES NOWLAND for the term of his natural life and from and immediately after his decease to the use of all the children of my said son CHARLES begotten or to be begotten on the body of his present wife who have attained or may there after attain the age of 21 years their heirs and assigns as tenants in common And provided further that the said ALFRED NOWLAND grant transfer and convey within the like period of 3 months after my decease or earlier if practicable all that parcel of land containing 120 acres being portion 51 and also all that conditional purchase of 7 Feb. 1867 containing 193 acres being portion 50 both situated in Parish Warrah County Buckland at present held by and standing in the name of the said ALFRED Unto and to the use of the said GEORGE NOWLAND, his heirs and assigns for ever And provided further that the said Alfred and his wife also grant, transfer and convey within the like period of 3 months after my decease or earlier if practicable all that conditional purchase of 15 Apr 1875 containing 320 acres of land being portion 128 (?) in the Parish Warrah County Buckland at present held by and standing in the (maiden) name of the wife of the said Alfred Nowland to the use of the said GEORGE Nowland his heirs and assigns for ever And provided further that the said HENRY NOWLAND also grant transfer and convey within the like period of 3 months etc. all that conditional purchase of 11 July 1867 containing 320 acres of land being portion 37 in the Parish of Warrah County Buckland at present held by and standing in the name of the said HENRY NOWLAND Unto and to the use of WILLIAM NOWLAND the younger his heirs and assigns for ever and I declare that my Trustees shall during the minority of any grandchildren of me entitled in expectancy or otherwise to any share of interest in any real estate under this my Will enter into and remain in possession on receipt of the rents and profits of each share or interest in any such real estate and premises and apply the same as is in manner herein after directed in respect of any grandchild of me in expectancy to share under this my Will. I devise bequeath unto my Trustees hereinafter named their heirs executors and administrators and the survivors or the survivor of them or the heirs executors or administrators of such survivor or other Trustees or Trustee for the time being of this my Will hereinafter referred to as my Trustees or Trustee all and singular my Run or Station known as Ward's Mistake situate in the District of New England in the said Colony together with all and singular the horses, cattle, sheep, plant, goods chattels and effects thereto belonging and usually held used and enjoyed therewith and thereon and also all and singular the freehold land thereunder and thereto belonging consisting of two separate parcels of land respectively containing 50 acres and 100 acres being Portions Nos. 1 and 12 situate in the Parish of Seeley (?) County of Clarke in the said Colony and also one other parcel of land containing 640 acres Portion No. 1 in the Parish of Ward's Mistake county of Clarke aforesaid together with the preleases and all rights and appurtenances thereunto respectively belonging hereinafter referred to as my Station property upon Trust to superintend conduct manage and carry on my business as a grazier in the best and most profitable manner and as such grazing estates are usually superintended conducted managed and carried on and with full power to employ and expend such portion of the profits as may arise therefrom in the purchase or selection of all or any

Figure 35 Transcript of the 'Will of William Nowland dated 20 July 1883' [p. 2]

such parcels of land as may to them or the majority of them seem desirable upon and in connection with the management protection and efficient conduct of the said Run and I direct that my Trustees shall at the expiration of each and every six months cause an estimate to be made of the receipts and expenses in connection with the working and management of such Station and after putting aside such sum or sums of money as may to them or a majority of them seem desirable for the management of the said Station and as a provision for contingencies stand possessed of the profits during the preceding 6 months upon Trust to pay one eighth part or share thereof to each of my sons William Nowland, Alexander Nowland, Alfred Nowland and Henry Nowland and upon Trust as to one other eighth part of share thereof in trust to pay to my son MICHAEL NOWLAND for the term of his natural life and from and immediately after his decease in trust for all the children of the said Michael Nowland begotten or to be begotten on the body of his present wife who may then have attained or may thereafter attain the age of 21 years or being a female that age or marry in trust for that child and upon trust as to one other eighth part or share in trust for such of the children of my late son ROBERT NOWLAND now deceased as may have or may thereafter attain the age of 21 years or being a female that age or marry in equal shares and if there be but one such child then the whole to be in trust for that one child and upon trust as to one other eighth part or share thereof to retain in the first place therefrom the sum of £675 in trust as to the sum of £450 portion thereof to meet the sum in some or one of the modes of investment hereinafter authorised and to hold the sum and the investments for the time being representing the sum in trust for such of the children of my son MICHAEL NOWLAND as may have then attained or may thereafter attain the age of 21 years or being a female that age or marry in equal shares and if there be only one such child then the whole to be in trust for that one child and in trust as to the sum of £225 for my son the said ALEXANDER NOWLAND and after the said sum of £675 shall have been so retained then upon trust as to such eighth part or share of the said income to pay the sum to my said son CHARLES NOWLAND during the term of his natural life and from and immediately after his decease in trust for all the children of the said CHARLES NOWLAND begotten etc. who may have attained or may thereafter attain the age of 21 years in equal shares and if there be but one child then the whole to be in trust for that one child and upon trust as to the remaining eighth part or share thereof to retain in the first place therefrom the sum of £450 in trust for such of the children of my late son ROBERT NOWLAND now deceased as may have or may thereafter attain the age of 21 years or if a female that age or marry in equal shares and if there be only one such child etc. and after the said sum of £450 shall have been so retained then upon trust as to such eighth part or share of the said income to pay the same to my said son GEORGE NOWLAND and I hereby declare that my Trustees if unanimous may from time to time mortgage my Station property or any part thereof or give Liens on wool (?) if in their opinion the same may be necessary for the payment of my funeral and testamentary expenses and my other and remaining debts and also for the purpose of being expended and used in and for the improvement and protection and more efficient management of my Station Property such mortgages and liens to contain all usual and ordinary covenants conditions and agreements including powers of sale in default of payment an further that my Trustees or Trustee if unanimous may also sell and dispose of the whole of my said Station Property or any part thereof by public auction or private contract or partly in one way and partly in another under and subject to such conditions and stipulations as to all acts and deeds which they may deem necessary for affectuating any such mortgage lien or sale of my Station Property as aforesaid and after payment of all expenses attendant thereupon and all liabilities incurred in the management and conduct of my Station Property to stand possessed of the monies arising therefrom upon the like trusts as are herein contained in respect of the income to arise from the management thereof and I hereby declare that it shall be lawful for

Figure 35 Transcript of the 'Will of William Nowland dated 20 July 1883' [p. 3]

my Trustees from time to time to allow to each one of them for their individual management care and attention in the conduct superintendence and management of the said Station Property such sum or sums of money as would reasonably be paid to any stranger for the like conduct superintendence and management and I declare that if any grandchild of me entitled in expectancy to a share under this my will shall be under age of 21 years and being a female shall be unmarried then and in every such case my Trustees may apply the whole or any part of the income of the expectant share of such minor for or towards his or her maintenance and education with liberty to pay the same to the guardian of such minor without being liable to see to the application thereof and shall invest the residue (if any) of the said income and the resulting income thereof to the intent that such accumulation shall be added to the principal share from which the same shall have arisen and follow the destination thereof but my Trustees or Trustee may at any time resort to the accumulation of any preceding year or years and apply the same for or towards the maintenance or education of any person for the time being presumptively entitled thereto and I declare that all monies liable to be invested under this my will may be invested in NSW Government Debentures or dividend paying bank shares doing business in the Colony of NSW or at fixed or other deposits in any such Bank or in Government Savings Banks at interest or upon real securities in NSW but not elsewhere and I hereby appoint my sons William Nowland George Nowland Alfred Nowland and Henry Nowland Trustees and Executors of this my Will and I declare that all Trusts and powers herein reposed and vested in my Trustees or Trustee my be exercised by the survivor of them or other trustees for the time being of this my Will and I direct that my Trustees shall whenever a vacancy may occur in their number while my Station Property may remain unsold forthwith proceed to the filling of such vacancy it being my desire that the number of my Trustees shall not at any time be less than nor more than four.

I devise all estates vested in me as Trustee or Mortgage unto my said Trustees subject to the charges and equities affecting the same but so that money received by any mortgage shall form part of my personal estate and I direct that if by the time I am deceased there may not be sufficient money the property of my estate to pay all my funeral and testamentary expenses duties and liabilities that the balance shall be the first charge upon and paid out of my station property and I hereby devise and bequeath the rest residue and remainder of my estate and effects unto my dear wife Mary Ann Nowland her heirs executors and administrators and I declare that every interest under this my Will to be taken by any female shall be for her sole and separate use and benefit free from the duties and engagements of any husband so that her receipt alone shall be sufficient for any money matter or thing therein acknowledged to have been received and I hereby revoke and make void all former and other Wills Codicils and testary writings by me at any time theretofore made etc.

                           Signed William Nowland
                     Witnessed Albert J. Gould, Solicitor Singleton
                          Sm. W. Robinson, Managing Clerk.

CODICIL - Whereas I have directed payment of the income arising from the care and management of the property referred to in the shares and proportions therein mentioned now it is my will and desire and I direct that the whole of the nett profits arising from my station property after making such payments and allowances as are in my said will directed shall be paid to my said wife Mary Ann Nowland for the term of her natural life and that from and immediately after her decease the same income shall be divided and paid as directed by my

Figure 35 Transcript of the 'Will of William Nowland dated 20 July 1883' [p. 4]

said above written Will and subject to such direction I ratify and confirm my said Will. In witness whereof I have set my hand this 20th day of July in the year of our lord 1883.

30th July 1884 probate granted to William Nowland, George Nowland, Henry Nowland and Alfred Nowland the trustees and executors. Testator died 28 April 1884. Estate sworn at £4500.

Donated by Jim & Mel (Nowland) Baker

Figure 35 Transcript of the 'Will of William Nowland dated 20 July 1883' [p. 5]

CHAPTER 34

WILLIAM'S LAST WILL AND TESTIMONY

Based on the preceding document, a table that identifies each inheritor and what each received, follows.

INHERITOR	INHERITANCE
MARY ANN NOWLAND	– *All my household goods and effects, my horses, buggies, carts and farming implements usually used in and around my residence at Camberwell.* [Rosedale] – *All that flock of sheep at present or at the time of decease depastured in the County of Durham* [Rosedale] – *All that mob of cattle at present depasturing at Warrah Ridge or at time of decease depasturing in the County of Durham* [Rosedale] – *All my six allotments of land at Muswellbrook.*[474] – The *rest residue and remainder* of William sr.'s estate and effects to Mary Ann Nowland: after the funeral expenses and the other inheritances Mary's sons received as listed in the Will. For example, Alfred and Henry inherited 1295 acres at Rosedale and Mary inherited the rest; most likely Mary inherited the land surrounding the homestead and at least 262 acres. [Rosedale was 1557 acres in 1857]. – At Ward's Mistake – *after making 'all other payments and allowances' as specified in the Will all* and *any other nett (sic) profit will be paid to my said wife Mary Ann Nowland for the term of her natural life.*

INHERITOR	INHERITANCE
WILLIAM NOWLAND JR. AND HIS HEIRS	– *Those three several portions of land situate in the Parish of Warrah* [Warrah Ridge] portions: 49 (320 acres); 77 (60 acres); 78 (40 acres) provided here transfer his 142 acres at [Rosedale] to Alfred and Henry Nowland. – 420 acres in total [+ the transfer of 320 acres from Henry, detailed under Henry's inheritance]
CHARLES NOWLAND AND HIS HEIRS	– Five parcels of land [Warrah Ridge] portions: 12 (320 acres); 60 (318 acres); 75 (165.5 acres); 76 (167 acres); 129 (46 acres) – 1,016.5 acres in total [+ the transfer of 425.5 acres from Alfred – detailed under Alfred's inheritance]
ALEXANDER NOWLAND AND HIS HEIRS	– Portion 59 [Warrah Ridge] 282.5 acres in total
GEORGE NOWLAND AND HIS HEIRS	– Six parcels of land [Warrah Ridge] portions: 89 (98 acres); 148 (40 acres); 84 (80 acres); 85 (120 acres); 125 (65 acres); 126 (122 acres).[also listed 127 with no acres recorded] –525 acres in total [+ lot 127 and the transfer of 633 acres from Alfred – detailed under Alfred's inheritance]
ALFRED AND HENRY NOWLAND AND THEIR HEIRS	– Tenants in Common Rosedale 1295 acres of the Rosedale Estate – In the village of Camberwell: Queen Victoria Hotel + 2 acres of land; Village allotments, Lots 1–14 – Provided Alfred Nowland transfers allotments at Telford to Charles Nowland: 129 (254 acres) and

INHERITOR	INHERITANCE
ALFRED AND HENRY NOWLAND AND THEIR HEIRS, cont.	147 (171.5 acres) and transfer allotments at Warrah Ridge to George Nowland: 51 (120acre); 50 (193 acres) and 128 (320 acres) – Provided Henry Nowland transfer allotments at Warrah Ridge to William Nowland jr.: 37 (320 acres) – With the transfers: Charles would receive an additional 425.5 acres; George an additional 633 acres; and, William jr. 320 acres.
TRUSTEES (EXECUTORS) OF THE WILL – WILLIAM NOWLAND JR. – GEORGE NOWLAND – ALFRED NOWLAND – HENRY NOWLAND	Responsible to: – Insure, William sr.'s grandchildren *'share upon this Will.'* – *'Superintend, conduct, and manage and carry on my business as a grazier at Run or Station Ward's Mistake, horses, sheep, plant, goods, chattels and effects' on leased and freehold portions.'* Freehold land portions: 1 (50 acres), 12 (100 acres) Parish of Seeley, County of Clarke, and portion: 1 (640 acres) Parish of Ward's Mistake, County of Clarke. – 'Each and every six months' the Trustees were required to 'estimate' monies needed to continue the family business at Ward's Mistake and then any money above this amount was to be distributed in two ways: [1] amongst William sr.'s surviving sons (William jr. Michael, Charles, Alexander, George, Alfred, and Henry) and the children of Robert (deceased). Each to receive a one eighth share. [2] A specified amount of money to be placed in a Trust for the

INHERITOR	INHERITANCE
TRUSTEES (EXECUTORS) OF THE WILL – WILLIAM NOWLAND JR. – GEORGE NOWLAND – ALFRED NOWLAND – HENRY NOWLAND, cont.	grandchildren on each branch of the family.[475] The amount specified for each branch of the family varied; Robert's children to receive the most (£675 +£450), followed by Charles (£675), then George (£450) and lastly Michael and Alexander whose children to receive the same amount (£225). – From time to time, each Trustee by 'arrangements between them' to 'individually manage' Ward's Mistake. – William sr. also tells the Trustees where to invest their monies: NSW Government Debentures and Government Savings Banks. – If for any reason the Trustees nominated changed after William sr.'s death the vacancy/vacancies should be filled, and the Trustees remain as four. – All remaining net profit at Ward's Mistake to be paid to Mary Nowland.

William's Will is a product of the times. The first thing that stands out is the language and structure. Besides being convoluted, the patriarchal society is evident from the start with statements such as, *'begotten or to be begotten on the body of his present wife'* a statement repeated each time a new married son is introduced into the Will.

The Will also demonstrates (like other men) William was aware of the status of women in society. To safeguard the interests of his wife/granddaughters as benefactors, the following statement is included *'I declare that every interest under this my Will to be taken by any female shall be for her sole and separate use and benefit free from the duties and engagements of any husband'*…

In contrast, the final statement in the Will reflects the subordinate status of women; *'… and that from and immediately after her decease [Mary Ann Nowland] the same income [her income from Ward's Mistake] shall be divided and paid as directed by my said written Will'*…

Besides the phraseology of the Will, the other factors that stands out include: Mary (William's wife) received very little; the inheritance for each of William's sons was differentiated; and, the amount of money directed to be paid into a Trust for each of the grandchildren varied, and based on each child's parentage (who was their father).

William sr. had his favourite sons or maybe these sons were the ones William felt were more compliant and/or more capable of carrying out his wishes after his death, and they needed to be wooed/rewarded with a larger inheritance. These sons included: William jr. (who predominately managed Ward's Mistake); George (who was a J.P. and magistrate in Quirindi); Alfred (who had returned to Rosedale and showed his dedication to the homestead and the small village of Camberwell) and Henry (yet to be married and also demonstrating an interest in Rosedale and the Camberwell community).

These four sons, as Executors of the Will were responsible for the probate and the ongoing management of Ward's Mistake. William instructed in his Will that any future profits from Ward's Mistake were to be distributed every six months in the following way. Firstly an unspecified amount of money was to be set aside for ongoing management, maintenance and investment, secondly another unspecified amount of profit in equal portions (one-eighth each) was to go to each of William sr.'s seven surviving sons (William jr., Michael, Chas, Alex, George, Alfred, and Henry) and the children of Robert (with this last lot of money in equal portions placed in a Trust for each child until they turned 21) and finally, after these and some other commitments (specified in the next paragraph of William's story) were accounted for, any left over net profit (every six months) was to be given to their mother Mary. In essence, the responsibility for the actual amount of money to go to each of these categories (based on the profits every six months) was up to these four sons: the Executors of the Will.

William also prescribed, given Robert was deceased, his children would receive an immediate amount of £675 to be shared equally amongst them, and placed in Trust for each, until the age of 21. In addition, some of the on-going profits from Ward's Mistake were to be placed in a Trust for each of William's grandchildren. Each grandchild to receive a specified amount based on their parentage (father). Chas' children, an equal share from £675; Robert's children, an equal share from £450; Michael's children, an equal share from £450; George's children, an equal share from £450; Alex's child (and later, if other children) an equal share of £225. While, Alfred's and Henry's children were excluded from these arrangements, probably because they would inherit Rosedale.

William also stipulated what would happen after the death of each son. If one of the Executors of the Will died another son would step in (unspecified) to ensure there would always be four sons carrying out William's wishes regarding Ward's Mistake. Furthermore, on the death of each son their children would inherit their father's share of the net profit from Ward's Mistake.[476]

William sr. also differentiated the inheritance for each son. In terms of freehold acreage, they would inherit: Chas would inherit the most; 1,016.5 acres at Telford and Warrah Ridge (from William sr.) and 425.5 acres (transferred from Alfred). While Alex (mine and possibly your ancestor) received the least (282.5 acres at Warrah Ridge).[477]

Reading back once again through William's Will one can readily see most of the Will was redundant. It depended on the collective response of William's sons to his prescriptive directions well into the future and as it will be shown soon, it just didn't happen. The only legitimate possessions William had to offer were, his freehold land, the transfer of his leases to his sons, his stock, homesteads, and all his goods and chattels. Anything else in the Will that required his sons input to obtain, was superfluous.

William was prescriptive to the end and believed he could orchestrate what should happen well after he had gone. For me, William sr. (a proud man) died believing he had created a dynasty that would continue for generations on his freehold land at Rosedale, Warrah Ridge and Telford, and, on his mainly leasehold land at Ward's Mistake.[478]

The Life Journeys of William's Children

The lived experiences of William sr.'s children and their descendants were very different to what William sr. had envisaged. William jr. took over the management of Ward's Mistake and sold it in 1901.[479] Michael, Chas, Alex, and George, remained at Warrah Ridge on their own allotments until they either died (Michael jr. and Chas) or their lives took them elsewhere (Alex and George).[480] Some of William sr.'s grandchildren remained at Warrah Ridge, while for the rest of the grandchildren, their lives also took them elsewhere. William's vision was lost, and within three generations, the Nowland name was no longer synonymous with Warrah Ridge.

The outcome for Rosedale was similar. Rosedale remained in the Nowland name for another 41 years. Henry sold his share of Rosedale in 1889 and moved to Guya. While Alfred lived at Rosedale, most likely until 1924, and then sold Rosedale to John Reid Skinner.[481] The Skinners then sold Rosedale to the Bowmans, sometime in the 1950s (date unknown).[482]

In 1957, after the marriage of Mick and Wendy Bowman, Rosedale became their property.[483] The photography that follows of 'Wendy Bowman's Rosedale' (Figure 36) shows part of the original homestead (although most likely renovated and updated).

William assumed his Will would assure the longevity of the three things he valued: Rosedale; his allotments at Warrah Ridge; and, his station at Ward's Mistake. He envisaged each would be handed down from one generation to the next. Yet this

Figure 36: Wendy Bowman's Rosedale

was not to be the case. The aspirations and ambitions of William's children were based on their own experiences and objectives. Each followed their own and varied pathways through life. Though William's sons stayed local for most of their lives, their children (William's grandchildren) either moved to Queensland or elsewhere in northern NSW as graziers or moved to a town or city as urban dwellers in places such as Singleton, Sydney, and Brisbane.

William's Obituary

William sr. died nine months and one week after he signed his Will. The notice of William sr.'s death in the local paper follows.

Singleton Argus, 30th April 1884, p. 2.
Death of Mr. W. Nowland

Another of the old pioneers has just gone to his rest. Mr. William Nowland of Rosedale Camberwell who was the first to take a dray over the Liverpool Range – if indeed, he was not the first discover of the route since adopted – by way of what is known as "The Gap" died on Monday night his 80th year. During the afternoon Mr. Nowland, who has for six years past been troubled with heart disease, experienced a sudden attack and before medical help could be obtained the old gentleman passed away, having been ill about six hours. Mr. Nowland was greatly respected in the district. We hope to be able to glean some further particulars of his life for publication in the future issue. We are informed that the deceased was a native of the colony, having been born in Windsor [Castle Hill] in September 1804. [The future issue of the 'Singleton Argus' featured William's 1861 Letter to the Editor of the SMH 'A Squatter' as detailed earlier in this story].

Another account reads:

> *Australian Town and Country Journal, 7 June 1884, p. 44.*

THE OLD TIMES. – In a recent letter I mentioned the death of Mr. W. Nowland at an advanced age. Mr. George Nowland, J.P., of Quirindi, is one of his sons. The late Mr. Nowland's career was a most remarkable and adventurous one. As far back as 1827, [most likely, 1826] when the Liverpool Plains were a terra incognita, he formed a station on Warrah Creek. There were only two stations formed before his in the district, Messrs. Singleton's and Baldwin's at Yarramindah, and Messrs. Onus and Williams's at Onus Creek.

At that time, the only track over the Liverpool Range, which separates the Liverpool Plains from the coast (and then the rest of the inhabited part of the colony) was so steep as to be almost impassable even to stock and horsemen. All supplies had to be carried over with incredible difficulty on pack-horses.

After three months' travelling in the mountains, accompanied only by a stockman, and with a quantity of rations carried on pack-horses, after being greatly harassed by the blacks, Mr. Nowland discovered the gap in the range between Doughboy Hollow and what is now Murrurundi, and through which the Great Northern Rail way now passes.

Mr. Nowland loaded a dray at Patrick's Plains, as Singleton was then called, and safely brought it to Warrah by the new route, alone which he had made a marked tree line. This was the first dray that ever crossed the Liverpool Range, and forms a memorable epoch in Australian history.

Soon afterwards numbers of persons travelled over the new track, forming stations on the Mooki, Namoi, Gwydir, McIntyre, Barwon, and Balonne rivers, in the order named; also on New England, Darling Downs, &c. Once the key was found to unlock the door, it was easy enough to pass through. However, Mr. Nowland was but ill repaid for his enterprise, for the Home Government gave his station to the A. A. Company, without recompense or redress.

In 1832 Mr. Nowland formed a run for the Hawkesbury Benevolent Society on Phillip's Creek, which was also given over to the A. A. Company,[484] and in 1837 he formed Drildole [Dridool] on the Namoi, then the ultima of civilisation, and where he was greatly troubled by the blacks, who speared both stock and stockmen whenever they had the chance. After losing 300 head of cattle thus Mr. Nowland sold his run for a trifle and bought Walhollow station, which is 10 miles from where Quirindi now stands, from Messrs. Parrott and Ross in the year 1833.

At Walhollow Mr. Nowland was environed by trouble, and became involved in a lawsuit which lasted 20 years, the biggest pastoral cause celebre known in these colonies, the details of which must be fresh in the recollections of the older residents of this district. His stock losses while he held Walhollow mounted to no less than 8000 head of cattle. [Incredible number]

Among the other pastoral runs formed by Mr. Nowland were Ward's Mistake and Boonanga, on the McIntyre River, near the Queensland border. These are a few episodes in the life of one of the leading squatting pioneers of Australia.

At the end of William's life, he had 44, and possibly 46 grandchildren, ranging in age from 22 (John James, Ada and Clara) to one year old Warwick (my grandfather and possibly yours) born in 1883. William may have known of two other grandchildren, Veronica and Harrie (both born in 1884, the year William died). An unimaginable number of grandchildren, for most in Australia today, yet common at the time.

Thirty-three years later (in 1917) William's youngest son Henry (64) wrote a letter to the local paper about how his father came to name 'Doughboy Hollow'; (today's Ardglen) a brook where William camped, when he crossed over the Liverpool Range and descended to the present day, Murrurundi. The topographic map that follows shows the relative place of the gap in the Liverpool Plains that William found, Nowlands Gap, and Ardglen, the replacement name for William's Doughboy Hollow (Figure 37).

The letter Henry wrote to his local paper about his father's Doughboy Hollow

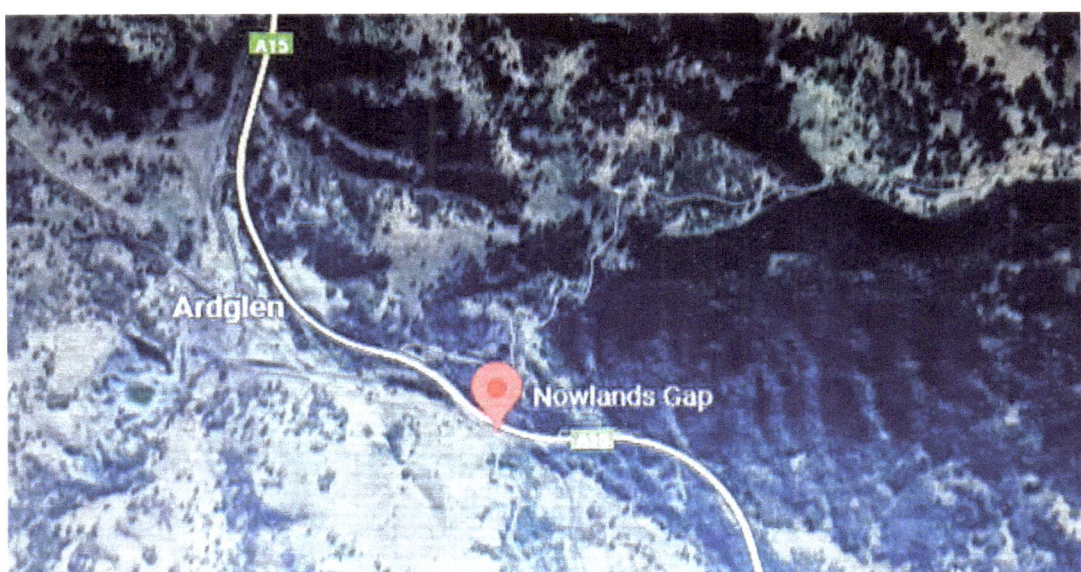

Figure 37: Topographic Map of Nowlands Gap and Ardglen

was copied to several other local, state, and interstate papers, in 1917, including:

- Cressy & Lismore Pioneer
- Camperdown Chronicle
- Gundagai Times
- King Island News
- Lachlan and Condobolin Recorder
- Mortlake Dispatch
- Omeo Standard
- Port Fairy Gazette
- The Newcastle Sun
- The Northern Champion
- The Ramsey Examiner
- The Sunbury News
- The World News
- The Yackandandah Times

Henry's letter read:

The World News (Sydney), 24 February 1917, p. 18.

Henry Nowland of Yarraman Creek, Queensland, writes: -

"My father (the late William Nowland, of Camberwell, near Singleton, N.S.W.) was one of the pioneers of Liverpool Plains, and in crossing over the range followed the tracks of the three or four men who were before him, and these led over a very steep part of the range near the head of Dartbrook.

He first settled at Warrah, afterwards granted by the British Government to the Australian Agricultural Company, and started from that side to look for a better road over the range. "Taking a stockman with him, he soon found the low gap through which the train now passes, and, going on down the range to the river (Page's River), he formed the opinion that by climbing Murulla (frequently called 'Murlo') Mountain, which overlooks Murrurundi, he would be able to see the downs at Scone. He climbed the mountain, and saw the downs as expected. He then returned to Warrah, satisfied that he had found a better road by way of the low gap and the low part of Warland's Range.

"As it was necessary to procure a supply of rations, etc., he returned to the Hunter, loaded a bullock dray at Patrick's Plains (now Singleton), and, with a man or two, made a start to try the new road. The weather was mostly wet on this trip, with the result that the wheels made a good track from Scone right across, and blazed the track (so to speak) for the people who followed after. He crossed Warland's Range, not where the present road is, but very near, if not the actual track since taken by the railway.

"And now I am coming to what I started to tell you. After negotiating the low gap in the main range the little band camped (to us Mr. Abbott's words) 'in the grassy little bay with a rivulet running round it,' and as they were out of bread, and it *was then raining (conditions not favorable to baking), they made doughboys, and while eating these my father said, 'We will call this place Doughboy Hollow.'* [485]

That bullock dray was the first that ever crossed the range in that part of the country, "I am glad to learn that Mr. Abbott protests against the changing of those original—I might say historic—names. To me it appears almost a crime. If the Railway Department had dropped the word 'Hollow,' and called the place 'Doughboy,' it might have been a fair compromise."

An important part of William's story was told once again in the local paper (in 1917) and was of enough interest to be copied to several other papers, 33 years after William sr.'s death.

We will never know the exact location where William camped, alongside a babbling brook he named 'Doughboy Hollow'. The photo that follows is a likely spot where the head waters of the Pages River flows like a brook just on the outskirts of Ardglen. (See Figure 38).

William's Burial Place

William is buried at St Clement's Cemetery, Camberwell; next to his son John and wife Mary Ann Nowland (née Farlow). See the photograph of his resting place and the inscription on his Obelisk that follows (see Figure 39).

The inscription on the front of the Obelisk for William, reads:

> In Loving Memory of WILLIAM NOWLAND
> WHO DEPARTED THIS LIFE ON
> 28TH April 1884
> 79 YEARS, 7 MONTHS
> Earth to earth and dust to dust
> Calmly now the words we say
> Leaving him to sleep, in trust
> Till the resurrection day
> Father, in thy gracious keeping
> Leave we now thy servant sleeping [486]

Though hard to read in print, the inscription at the bottom of the obelisk on the plaque on William's gravestone when cleaned and viewed in person is legible.

Figure 38: A Possible Spot for William's Doughboy Hollow

Figure 39: Memorial Obelisk of William and
Mary Nowland (née Farlow) and Tomb on the left
their son's, 'John' (1841–1860)

More recently (18 November 1990),[487] a small gold plaque for William was placed at the base of his Obelisk in memory of his discovery of a gap in the Liverpool Plains now known as Nowlands Gap. The plaque reads as follows.

TRIBUTE TO

THE LATE WILLIAM NOWLAND
OF CAMBERWELL
WHO IN 1827 EXPLORED AND CLEARED
THE FIRST ACCESSIBLE TRACK OVER THE
LIVERPOOL RANGE AT MURRURUNDI

As told at the beginning of this story, William Nowland birth year is not recorded on his plaque. While his age and the date of his death is and reads:

> …'*William Nowland who departed this life on the 28th April 1884, 79 years, 7 months…*'

The age on William's plaque is taken as his 'true age' and gives him a birthdate and year of the 28th September 1804. It is this year (1804) that is used throughout William's story in positioning him amongst his siblings and calculating his age at the time of each of the significant events in the story.[488]

What a character. For all his life, William strived to be more and more successful as squatter, pastoralist and grazier. He was a role model to all his boys, especially those who grew up to learn and know his farming practice (James died at 4 and John at 18). While William was alive, the whole family were invested in his farming interests at Camberwell, Warrah Ridge and Ward's Mistake. From William perspective, he had fostered three generations of farmers, and structured a Will, to sustain his children, and their children, well into the future.

Figure 40: Mary's and their children's inscription for William at the bottom of the Obelisk

Epilogue

William Nowland was born into an agricultural settlement at Castle Hill sixteen years after the First Fleet entered Eora Country on Gadigal land. As a first generation colonial Australian, William lived through a period of turbulent and profound change as settlers left Sydney town and moved into the interior.

When William was two his family moved to a small, leased farm at Wilberforce on Dharug Country. It is here that William learned the colonial life skills he took with him as a young man of nineteen, into Wonnarau Koori Country (Hunter Valley).

The rapid migration of settlers, like William, into Wonnarau Koori Country (Hunter Valley, c.1823), Kamilaroi Country (Liverpool Plains, c.1826) and Ambēyang, Anēwan and Bānbay Country (New England Tablelands, c.1831) altered and consumed Country. Each advancement, cut a swathe through the interior, interfered with the traditional food sources of First Nations people and brought diseases, death and massacre. In William's story, three deplorable massacres are noted: Waterloo Massacre – Slaughter House Creek, 26th January 1838; the Myall Creek Massacre, 10th June 1838; and, the Darkie Point Massacre, Ebor, May 1841.

Though the impact of the invasion was shattering, these First Nations people remained resilient and engaged in guerrilla warfare in defence of Country for a considerable time as evident in William Nowland's account at Ward's Mistake in 1861. They were resolute and their endurance continues today.

It is hard to believe in the space of 80 years when William was alive (1804–1884) the natural, social and political environment was so transformed, with the genesis of change grounded in the British colonists' arrogant disrespect for First Nations people and their conceited belief that they had discovered a new land. A contemptuous view, formalised 47 years later in Governor Bourke's Proclamation of 'Terra Nullius' ('nobody's land') in October 1835.

The transformation of the natural environment, started in Sydney, radiated out and spread into areas such as the farming community of Wilberforce where William spent his informative years. Each successive Governor subdivided the land into small agricultural allotments, within the areas of expansion, in a rather ad hoc manner. Emancipates and free settlers (both with assigned convict labour) cultivated the allotments for subsistence and the provision of surplus production to the Government Stores (Commissariat, from 1809).

This improvised approach to settlement proliferated for the first 36 years (1788–1824) and blossomed under Governor Macquarie (1810–1821).

A different way to proceed was seeded when John Bigge returned to London (1821), lobbied for change and prepared and presented three Reports (1824) to the British Parliament. For Bigge there were too many small marginal farm allotments focused on subsistence and very limited, if any, encouragement of commercial enterprise and trade.

In 1826, Governor Darling started to implement Bigge's recommendations – most notably in William's story with an offer of a very large land grant of one million acres to the Australian Agricultural Company. Darling also lured wealthy landowners from Britain with a similar, though smaller, guarantee of a land grant on arrival in the colony; all for the purpose of diversifying land use, improving production and increasing exports in products such as, wool, tobacco, flax and grain.

In concert with Darling's aspirations for the wealthier classes, adventurers and settlers of small means started to move into the interior with each new discovery of land beyond the confines of Sydney. In this story, the Hunter Valley was flooded with settlers (c.1824) soon after Howe gained knowledge from his Aboriginal guides of how to navigate the steep and arduous landscape on the northern side of the Hawkesbury River. Convicts, emancipated convicts and first-generation colonial Australians (like William and his brothers) went into the interior in large numbers each to claim a small allotment for themselves; 160 acres each for William and his brothers.

The discovery of the Dartbook Pass onto the Liverpool Plains by Henry Dangar (October 1824) encouraged the most adventurous amongst them to move further north. Singleton and Baldwin went to 'Yarramunba', Onus and Williams to 'Onus Creek', and William Nowland to 'Warrah' (for William, c.1826). Each took their stock up the steep and difficult Dartbrook Pass, erected a hut, placed their cattle on the land and staked their claim across thousands of acres. Others soon followed in large numbers (c. May 1827) after William Nowland found and marked out an easier route onto the Liverpool Plains just above Murrurundi at the headwaters of the Pages River, that is today signposted on the New England Highway, as Nowlands Gap.

These settlers on the Liverpool Plains were officially denoted as squatters because they had moved outside the boundaries of settlement without the Governor's approval. They spread across the interior and consolidated their runs with their huts and stock just before the Australian Agricultural Company, and other affluent favoured settlers and immigrants, arrived with the authority from the Governor to choose, in some cases, the same land as the squatters had claimed.

The deluge of indentured convict labour, emancipated convicts and first-generation colonial Australians into the interior was not just happening on the Liverpool Plains. The flood of squatters outside the boundaries of official settlement was occurring throughout the colony and now extended in a broad arc north, south and west from Sydney, for hundreds of kilometres.

The next Governor, Governor Bourke (in 1834) proclaimed the squatters (and the pastoralists amongst them) were on Crown Land and each run required a licence.

Ten years later (in 1844) Governor Gipps proposed several changes to the licensing arrangement that, if implemented, would make each run exorbitantly expensive to lease, and hopefully from Gipps' perspective force the squatters off their runs. The squatters and pastoralists rallied and voiced their indignation to Gipps, the Legislative Council and the British Government. This unsettled the Establishment and Gipps' proposed changes were postponed (December 1845).

Fifteen months later, Governor FitzRoy (in 1847) offered instead a new set of land regulations as instructed by the British Government in the *Order in Council* of March 1847. This delighted the pastoralists and squatters. The existing lease arrangements remained and were guaranteed for at least the next 14 years with the option for renewal, and the right of pre-emptive purchase once the runs were surveyed. This new legislation however was never fully implemented, because of the pressure and distraction of the surge of immigrants with the Gold Rush.

Nine years later (in 1856) John Robertson, as a member of the Legislative Assembly, started to advocate for further change. For Robertson, the present arrangements of land tenure would not suffice because the squatters were crowding out land opportunities for everyone else: the wealthy landholders who had initially been wooed by grants (since the 1830s) and wished to expand on their assets; those who had come as part of the Bounty Scheme (1835–1841) or through assisted immigration (1837–1850); and, the influx of migrants who had come to the colony during the Gold Rush (post-1852).

Robertson was determined to introduce a new land tenure policy that would cater for all the above groups as well as the squatters and pastoralists. After initial failure, Robertson succeeded, and his vision was implemented through the *Crown Lands Occupation Act 1861* and the *Crown Lands Alienation Act 1861*. This land tenure policy would continue for the rest of William Nowland's life and be replaced by the *Crown Lands Act 1884*.

William lived through all these changes and was a player in each of them: a small landholder at Falbrook; a squatter on the Liverpool Plains and the New England Tablelands; and, a grazier at Warrah Ridge. William showed true grit, determination and an awareness of change that held him in good stead. He was one of the first to stake a small claim (160 acres) at Glennies Creek, Falbrook, in 1824 and over the next 17 years (1824–1841), he purchased adjoining allotments when the opportunity arose, until his and Mary's property (Rosedale) grew to 1,557 acres. As we know, William was also one of the first to go up onto the Liverpool Plains through the Dartbrook Pass where he claimed a large expanse of land as a squatter; Warrah (c.1826). It is here six years later (c.1832) that William had his first encounter with a new type of landholder, the AACo who showed complete disregard for William's cattle and placed its sheep amongst his stock. William was furious but powerless to do anything. Squatters like William were forced off their runs and compelled to move north, where William and his brother Edward claimed a new run for William's and the HBS's stock along the Mooki River.

Around five years later (c.1837), William moved further north to the outer boundaries of the Liverpool Plains adjacent to the Namoi River and claimed a new run (Dridool). By this time, the 'free for all' approach of the squatters to land acquisition was starting to be reined in by Governor Bourke (post-1836) and William needed a licence for this run. Then two years later, the Commissioner arrived (c.1839) to survey the runs along the Namoi River. In William's case, Dridool was divided up between Willliam and the Commissioner's 'favourites' (according to William) and William was left with too small a run to be viable.

This imposition did not deter William. He sold the improvements he had made to Dridool and travelled hundreds of kilometres south with his stock to Edward's (his brother's) HBS's Mooki Station and purchased from Ross and Parrott (in 1839) the improvement to a run, just north of Mooki Station. This new run of William's called Wallalla straddled the Mooki River just below Breeza and became a vein of continuous contention for William in the courts over the next 20 years (1842–1862).

The conflict over the possession of Wallalla between William and several different wealthy landholders was richly documented in the newspapers and tells of hearing after hearing in the Supreme Court, until William finally decided to take his case to the Privy Council, in London, in March 1860.

As we know, William waited two years for the Privy Council's decision in May 1862; a decision that did not all go in his favour. The Privy Council agreed to a new trial based on their judgement that William's claim of 'exclusive possession' of the western side of Wallalla Station could be challenged. In William's favour however, the Council determined that Humphrey and Christian (the respondents in the case) were required to pay the cost of the appeal (£2000) which most likely made William's payment of £2500 as security in March 1860 'null and void' and hopefully this amount of money was returned to him. Subsequently, there were no more court hearings because William had already sold the improvements on Wallalla Station (the quality of the pasture et cetera) to John Eales, circa 1860.

At this stage of William's story, the summary of the Privy Council's decision in the papers (May 1862) is of note because it provides a glimpse into the 'power' positions of the various stakeholders in the case. William had very little, if any, power or influence. William was the son of emancipated convicts, one of the original squatters on the Liverpool Plains and probably spoke with an Irish lilt. While Christian as the 'Another' in 'Humphrey and Another' was a wealthy, privileged and well-connected landowner. The Privy Council's judgement most likely was influenced by the relative social positions of William Nowland and W.B. Christian, along with their probable awareness of the broad and ongoing entrenched conflict and squabbles between squatters in general and the potential for their judgement to act as a precedent and provoke further claims and counter claims between squatters and wealthy pastoralists.

William's other encounter (according to him) with those who were well connected and networked with the Establishment was at Boonanga. William obtained a licence for his Boonanga run in 1840 on the McIntyre River, near Wayland, and held the run for nearly 10 years (1840–1849). Then, when the Commissioner arrived and favoured others, William was so compromised by the boundaries set by the Commissioner he decided to sell his improvements for *"a mere twenty-five pounds".*

After all these quests for land acquisition in the interior, the only run that remained in William's possession from the time that he gained a licence for it (1842) to the end of his life (1884) was Ward's Mistake. This was William's most successful run/station (81,920 acres) and it stayed in the family until circa 1900. While William's other lifetime farming successes included the family homestead of Rosedale, and after 1862, the allotments that William and his family acquired at Warrah Ridge.

Throughout his life, William remained resolute. In his letter to the Editor of the SMH (January 1861) he demonstrates his proactive approach to each rumoured change in land tenure. This is especially evident towards the end of the letter where he gives his opinion of what should happen under John Robertson's proposed new land tenure policy of 'free selection'. Then, once the *Crown Lands Alienation Act 1861* was enacted (October 1861), William and his sons were amongst the first to claim adjoining allotments and secure pre-emptive leases at Warrah Ridge. From 1862 on William and his sons strategically purchased adjoining allotments and continued this practice over the next three generations and until the Nowland name become synonymous with Warrah Ridge.

William's letter to the editor of the SMH also gives us some insight into William's views on his encounters with some of the Aboriginal clans on the Liverpool Plains and New England Tablelands. Initially, William tells the reader while searching for an easy route onto the Liverpool Plains (most likely in the first few months of 1827) he and his stockman *"[endangered their] lives, with the blacks for the space of three months"*. Then at Warrah (c.1829–c.1832) he informs the reader he had been *"tormented by the blacks for about three years"*. Then he provides an extensive account at Dridool (1837–1839)

…was troubled with the aboriginals for two years and a half, continually making attacks upon the men in the huts; and when riding after the cattle, they often made a practice of lying in wait for the men. A stockman of mine was pinned to his saddle by a spear; but fortunately, it went through his clothes, and just at the time they formed a half-moon round him, and then threw spears and boomerangs at him. The man luckily turned his horse and escaped with the spear still sticking in his clothes. Between the drought and the blacks, I lost three hundred head of cattle on the run…

Then at Boonanga (1840–c.1850) *"… The blacks slaughtered about three hundred head of my cattle, and I had one man killed…* and lastly a detailed account at Ward's

Mistake (April 1842–January 1861).

In April 1842, I formed a station on the table lands (sic) of New England, called Ward's Mistake. For the ten years [over 18 years] I held it the aboriginals were slaughtering my cattle right and left, and disturbing them off their run, and, to this day, slaughtering a few of them whenever they want them, I am convinced that from 1842 to this date [23rd January 1861] I have lost five hundred head of cattle by the aboriginals. My station is bounded by the waterfall of the tributaries of the Clarence River, where there is a great shelter for blacks, and the border police have never visited my station for the whole time…

Each of these incidents occurred because William had positioned himself along with other squatters at the forefront of the squatter movement, and the Aboriginal Nations responded with raids and guerrilla warfare, in defence of Country. At Ward's Mistake the Bānbay (most likely in conjunction with the Anēwan, and the Gumbaynggirr) had the added advantage of the topography of the landscape with its gorges and gullies where they could hide and come out at night to disturb and kill stock. As William tells the reader the guerrilla warfare tactics used by the Bānbay were persistent and successful over a period of 20 years.

Only one other account of Aboriginal warriors raiding a Nowland station was found during William's lifetime. Again, on the New England Tablelands (April 1842) and because William does not mention this encounter, it may have been on Henry Nowland's run, Guy Fawkes. The most disturbing element of the article (for me) is the presence of the Mounted Police on a Nowland property; a notorious police force who killed Aboriginal peoples under the guise of protecting the squatters.

One is alerted to any evidence of a relative or family member being directly involved in the killing or massacre of First Nations people. In William's case the research reveals he saw the presence of Aboriginal clans on his runs as an annoyance. For William, they were troublemakers who potentially could endanger his life (while searching for the Pages River Gap), or his stockmen while managing his runs. His views were dismissive of Aboriginal clans and their Nations and typical of the colonial population who saw the land as 'theirs for the taking'. For me, William would have always had his muskets ready, given the norm and values he shared with the colonial settlers and his own experience of raids and guerrilla warfare on his runs/stations.

William lived through a period of dramatic and rapid change in transportation. In William's earliest years (1804–1832) the only way to get around was by walking, riding a horse, horse and cart/dray, or by buggy or coach. Then when travelling along or across the Hawkesbury one would go by boat or punt: and for William, on his father's punt.

Up until 1822, those who wished to travel north from the Hawkesbury needed to go via Sydney town, because the north side of the Hawkesbury was isolated from the interior by a very steep escarpments and dense eucalyptus forest that extended as far as the eyes could see up and down the valleys, gorges and various escarpments. As we know, Singleton and Howe were stymied by the thick scrub when they attempted to find a route north through this forbidding and rugged landscape, and it was only when two Aboriginal guides, Mioram (Myles) and Whirle assisted Howe (in 1820) that a way through was found, and the Bulga Track became a reality (c.1822).

This ill-constructed and dangerous track, with its narrow and steep embankments, became the major route north into the interior. William travelled this notorious route for around 30 years (1823–1853). The only other inland route into the Hunter from the Hawkesbury came later, with the completion of the Great North Road in 1836, after 10 years of arduous work by indentured convict labour. This alternative route took travellers, for at least four days, along very steep pathways and through isolated and rugged areas where there was very limited access to water and waterholes, and very few places to pitch a tent.

The Bulga Track became the predominate stock route and the Great North Road an alternative route that attracted only the most adventurous, such as families heading north in search of a new life, the curious traveller and any correspondent eager to report on new developments in the interior.

A third route by sea on the paddle steamers (from 1831) competed successfully with the roads into the interior, when people were travelling north for leisure, business or to catch up with friends and family. Those amongst them who had decided to permanently move into the interior (possibly the wives and small children of the Nowland brothers) may have sent their goods and chattels by road and travelled themselves more conveniently by paddle steamer. The journey by paddle steamer was easier and quicker – taking less than 10 hours from Sydney Cove to Newcastle.

With the introduction and extension of the railways from Singleton to Newcastle (1863) and Sydney to Windsor (1864) many a traveller between Sydney and the Hunter Valley (including the Nowlands) could travel more comfortably and in a much shorter time by combining travel by steam train and paddle steamer.

The roads within the Hunter Valley also took a long time to be developed into anything that could be called a road. When William entered the Hunter Valley (c.1823) the so-called road was a largely rough and ready track made by the drovers, while the steep slopes of the Liverpool Range acted as a barrier and prohibited any exploration northwest. After William discovered the easier route further north at the headwater of the Pages River, in April 1827 a new drover's trail formed and progressively, as settlement expanded, a rudimentary road was built. Descriptors of this road, the Great Northern Road (now known as the New England Highway) are available in the colony papers (cited between 1860–1880) with many of the articles portraying a road that was as times perilous, always unpredictable, difficult to navigate, especially in times of flood, and at the very least, an uncomfortable journey by coach, buggy or dray.

When William and his family headed north from Rosedale there was no alternative to this problematic road until the railway line was built parallel to the Great Northern Road, from Singleton to Muswellbrook in 1865, and then through what is now known as the 'Nowlands Gap' and onto Quirindi by 1877, and as far as Glen Innes, in 1884: the year of William's death.

William also lived through a period of momentous change in governance. During William's boyhood, youth and early adult life, NSW was a penal colony (1804–1841) managed by each successive Governors and steered at times by influential voices, such as John Macarthur, John Thomas Bigge and William Wentworth. Other notable officials also played their part including, Francis Forbes (Chief Justice), Frederick Goulburn (Colonial Secretary), William Stewart (Lieutenant Governor), John Oxley (Surveyor General) and James Bowman (Principal Surgeon) after being nominated by the British Parliament to form the first Legislative Council of NSW in 1823, with the first meeting held in August 1824.

In the 1830s, other influential settlers such as wealthy townsfolk and pastoralists lobbied for representation on the Legislative Council and by 1842 they had succeeded. Legislation was passed that facilitated their right to elect 24 of the 36 members of the Legislative Council (*NSW Constitutional Act 1842* (UK)).

Thirteen years later, in July 1855 the *NSW Constitutional Act 1842* was revised to enable responsible government within the colony. Two legislative chambers were established: the Legislative Council with nominated members and the Legislative Assembly with elected members. The first sitting of these two chambers occurred just over 10 months later, in May 1856. Those eligible to vote for the elected members of the Legislative Assembly included all males 21 years and older (such as William) who had at least £10 in property assets (as urban dwellers) or £100 in land assets (as a grazier). Four years later, in 1859, male suffrage was extended to include all males 21 years and older, regardless of their financial status.

This change in governance from a penal colony to responsible government, with every male having the right to vote, occurred in conjunction with the separation of Port Phillip from NSW and the creation of two separate colonies: NSW and Victoria in July 1851. Then, eight years later in June 1859, another colony was created, Queensland; with all the borders between these three colonies still the same today.

William's personal life was also deeply affected by change. William had three older 'surviving' siblings, Michael jr., Henry and Elizabeth jr. and three younger siblings, Edward, Mary and Sarah; he outlived them all. William and his wife (Mary Ann Nowland née Farlow) had 10 sons between 1832 and 1851, three of whom died within William's lifetime (James, John and Robert). All of Mary's and William's boys married except for James, who died in infancy and John who died at the age of eighteen. The boys were all brought up on the family farm at Camberwell (Rosedale) and once old enough (around 5 or 6) worked with their father at Rosedale and then (around 12) on their father's stations (Wallalla and Ward's Mistake). Once married, most of the boys (along with their father) established farms of their own at Warrah Ridge.

At the end of William's life (79 years) he had 44, and possibly 46 grandchildren, ranging in age from 22 (John James, Ada and Clara) to one (Warwick, my grandfather and possibly the reader's ancestor, born in 1883). Possibly, William was aware of two more grandchildren; Veronica and Harrie, both born in 1884, the year William died.

With all these children and grandchildren, William believed he had created a dynasty, though that was not the case. Within three generations most of the family had left the region and moved on.

On reflection, William's family (like all families) faced their challenges. William was the patriarch who had his favourite sons and Mary (his wife) the glue that held the family together. William and Mary both lived through a unique period in Australia's history (from a penal colony to self-governance) and the changes they experienced in the social, economic and political landscape were extraordinary.

Throughout his life William's voice can be found in the papers. It is both loud and clear on a variety of topics and his story is told in newspaper summaries of the minutes of the meetings of the HBS and the Legislative Assembly, and in numerous Court hearings between 1842 and 1862. For me, William was a savvy determined man, who was optimistic, confident and assertive, stood his ground, and made the most of every opportunity.

A life well lived and worthy of note.

Endnotes

CHAPTER 1
The Formative Years

1. William Nowland's birth year is registered in 'NSW Registry of Births, Deaths and Marriages NSW' (BDM, NSW) as '1808, district CC' (Church of England, Windsor)'. In 'Find a Grave' William Nowland's birthdate and year is stated as the 14th April 1808, www.findagrave.com. 'Camberwell Anglican Cemetery, William Nowland'. This data though consistent is different to William Nowland's birth date and year on some genealogical sites and in generic online commentary that claims William was born in 1804 at Castle Hill. Further investigation revealed the following 'primary source' on William Nowland's gravestone confirmed his birth year – 'In loving memory of William Nowland who departed this life 28th April 1884, 79 years and 7 months'. In calculating, William's birthdate from this primary data William was born on the 28th September 1804 (Roots Web, www.agecalculatorrootweb.com).
2. William's parents Michael and Elizabeth Nowland (née Richards) moved from the Rocks, Sydney, to Castle Hill, when Governor King appointed Michael to the position of Superintendent of Convicts 'Castle Hill Public Agricultural Settlement' in September 1802, with an income of 50 pounds per year. https://convictrecords.contributions and Colonial Secretary Index 1788–1825 (Colonial Office) Reel 6037, SZ991, p.102.
3. Findagrave, Norfolk Island Cemetery, Kingston, Norfolk Island, 'William Nowland 1792', www.findagrave.com.
4. Michael was initially assigned to the convict ship *Mercury* that sailed up the Thames on the 2nd April 1784 bound for Georgia, North America. While on the Thames, the convicts mutinied, and Michael managed to escape. Michael was later recaptured and sent to Bath County Goal where he escaped once again. A short time later, Michael was recaptured, placed in a hulk on the Thames and years later he was transported to Port Jackson. See Flynn Michael (1993), *The Second Fleet: Britain's grim convict armada of 1790*, pp.461-462; Gillard Dick (August 2020), pp.13–15, Hawkesbury Historical Society, Newsletter, 140; Nowland Ian (1995), pp.42-64, *Michael and Elizabeth Nowland*.
5. England had entered the industrial age and as people migrated to the cities in search of work (where pay and working conditions were poor and uncertain) an underclass and working poor developed. For many, the only way to get by was to engage in 'petty crime'. Then once arrested, sentenced, and found guilty, these 'petty criminals' were initially sent to England's overcrowded and disreputable goals, where they awaited transportation to Britain's latest colony; the death penalty for such crimes had been abolished and these petty criminals supplied a steady source of 'indentured labour' for colonies like NSW. (Shoemaker Robert (c.2017), 'Punishments, 1780–1925'/The Digital Panopticon https://www.digitalpanopticon.org).
6. Michael Nowland, Old Bailey transcript 26th February 1783. www.oldbaileyonline.org
7. Elizabeth Richards 4th August 1787, Summer Assizes, Warwick, Warwick Record Office – Jopson's Coventry Mercury, 13th August 1787, No. 24840 cited in Nowland Ian, (1995) *Michael and Elizabeth Nowland*, p.69.
8. Flynn Michael (1993) *The Second Fleet* Chs.3,4 and 8, pp. 461-2 and 497; Hughes Robert (1987) *The Fatal Shore* pp.145-6.
9. *People Australia, Michael Nowland (c.1758–1828) National Centre of Biography, Australian National University*. www.peopleaustralia.anu.edu.au/michaelnowland
10. P. J. King Letter Book 1, 1788/99 pp. 251-271, 292, 302, 322 and Mitchell Library C187 cited in Nowland Ian (1995), op. cit. p.103.
11. Births registry, BDM, NSW for Sarah; other siblings, family document and https://australianroyality.net.au.
12. 'People Australia', Michael Nowland (c.1758–1828) op. cit.
13. Old Register Book 1, p.117, no. 679 cited in Nowland Ian (1995), op. cit. p.117.
14. 'People Australia', 'Michael Nowland (c.1758–1828)'op. cit.
15. Hawkesbury Visitors Information, 'Macquarie Trail' (p.6) 'Wilberforce – Nowland Cottage c.1810–1816' https://www.discoverthehawkesbury.com.au.
16. Family document; https://australianroyality.net.au; and, subsequent data in the story.
17. Historian Grace Karskens, in collaboration with Darug Traditional Owners and researchers, Leanne Watson, Erin Wilkins, Jasmine Seymour and Rhiannon Wright (19 May 2021) 'Reconciliation Australia 'A Deep Human History: Remapping Darug Place Names and Culture on Dyarubbin, The Hawkesbury River'. www.reconciliation.org.au. Dharug is spelt Darug in this article. Also see Connor John (2002) *The Australian Frontier Wars 1788–1838,* Chapter 3 'The Hawkesbury-Nepean River 1795–1816'.
18. *Sydney Gazette and New South Wales Advertiser* 17 June 1804, p.2, 'Natives'; and later, the *Sydney Gazette and New South Wales Advertiser* 18 May 1816, p.1. 'Proclamation by His Excellency Lachlan Macquarie'.

19. Connor John (2002) op. cit. Ch. 3; Grenville Kate (2005) *The Secret River;* Ryan Lyndall Untangling Aboriginal Resistance and the settlers' punitive expedition: the Hawkesbury River frontier in New South Wales, 1794–1810' *Journal of Genocide Research* (2013), Vol 15, No.2. pp.219-232 https://dx.doc.org; Reynolds Henry (2013) *Forgotten Wars,* especially, pp.25-48, pp.53-68, pp.62-68 and pp.73-75; *The Australian War*s, SBS, September 2022; Karskens Grace (2022) *People of the River,* Part 11 Frontiers, Ch. 5

20. Possum Venessa (on behalf of the Dharug Ngurra Aboriginal Corporation DNAC) (21 October 2020) 'Our Community' https://www.dharugngurra.org.au.

21. Hawkesbury City Council (2021) 'Hawkesbury Local LGA Aboriginal Cultural Heritage Study' https://www.hawkesbury.nsw.gov.au; Hawkesbury and Nepean Wars' Wikipedia (2021) https://en.wikipedia.org.

22. Gill J.C.H. (1969), 'The Hawkesbury River Floods of 1801,1806 and 1809' The University of Queensland https://espace.library.uq.edu.au; *Sydney Gazette and New South Wales Advertiser*, 30 March 1806, p.2, 'Hawkesbury March 27' and 4 June 1809, p.2 'Flood at Hawkesbury; NSW Government (2020)' Rising Waters – Thompson Square' https://thompsonsquare.com.au. Also see, 'Biggs John Thomas (13 March 1823) The State of Agriculture and Trade in the Colony of New South Wales', Report 3, p.11 which notes 'The most considerable inundations of the river took place in the month of March 1806, in the same period of the years 1808 and 1811, in the month of June 1816, in March 1817, in the month of February 1819, and in the month of October 1820.' https://guides.sl.nsw.gov.au.

23. *Sydney Monitor* 6 September 1828, p.5 'Jupiter Hall' "The crops on Hunter River, notwithstanding the strength of the new alluvial soils there, are fast giving way to the severity of the drought" and *The Monitor,* 3 September 1827, p.3, 'Domestic Intelligence' "… Liverpool Plains which are stated to be extensively dry from drought…"

24. General Muster, 12th August 1806, cited in, Nowland Ian (1995), op. cit. p.182.

25. The Government stores, later the Commissariat (1809), provided the means of rations when needed and exchange of local and imported goods. It acted as a 'clearing house' giving 'credits' or 'bills of exchange' for produce and goods received up until 1813, when Governor Macquarie introduced a monetary currency; the 'Holey Dollar'. The Dictionary of Sydney, 'Commissariat Stores' https://dictionaryofsydney.org.).

26. Gill J. C. H. (1869) op. cit. pp.732-735.

27. cited in Nowland Ian (1995), op. cit. p.198.

28. Michael Nowland ran a very successful piggery on Norfolk Island that supplied the government stores and enabled his recognition by Governor King and his subsequent increase in status in the colony. Told as part of Michael's story, in this set of Nowland stories within a family genealogical book written by myself (Lucie Crawford) entitled *By Chance.*

29. W.F. Morrison, *The Aldine Centennial History of NSW* cited in Nowland Ian (1995), op. cit. p.219 e-book https://www.bda-online.org.au.

30. *Architecture Australia Magazine* (April/May 1976, Retrospective) – 'Michael Nowland'. https://architectureau.com/mazines/archite/australia).

31. Lands Titles Australia, Lands Titles Office [L.T.O.], Old Register Book 1, p.143, No 1107, Book 4, p. Nos 1336 cited in Nowland Ian (1995), op. cit. p.183.

32. *Sydney Gazette and New South Wales Advertiser,* 25th April 1812, p.1. *Michael Nowland.*

33. School was voluntary and provided at the local Church's schoolhouse. In the patriarchal culture of the time, boys were more likely to attend, and received an elementary education in reading, writing, arithmetic, history, and geography. Most girls were illiterate and if they did attend school, they were more likely taught the domestic skills of cooking, cleaning and sewing.

34. The settlement of Green Hills was established c. 1791, and its name changed to Windsor on the 8th December 1810 when it was officially proclaimed a town by Governor Macquarie on the 15th December 1810. 'State Archives & Records NSW' www.records.nsw.gov.au

35. The schoolhouse also operated as the local church given religion for most of the community was the focal point of a child's education.

36. It is not known when the photo of Windsor Schoolhouse was taken. The first photo in Sydney was of Bridge Street by a French sea captain Auguste Lucas on the 13th May 1841 www.sl.nsw.gov.au.

37. William's father, Michael Nowland held the status of No. '19' in the colony when he was Superintendent of Convicts at Castle Hill, with Governor King being No. '1'. (Scone Historical Society, Betty Pinkerton 'Nowland Research Folder').

38. *Sydney Gazette and New South Wales Advertiser,* 20th May 1820, p.1.

39. CWAB – Thompson Square and Windsor's First School'. www.cawb.com.au.

40. Elizabeth Nowland (née Richards) Wilberforce Cemetery. https://www.findagrave.com).

41. Told in my story of Elizabeth Nowland (née Richards) in the family book called *By Chance.*

42. Jessica Brian (8 Aug 2019) 'The Victorian Workhouse' traces the Workhouse back to the *Poor Law Act of 1388.* https://www.historic-uk.com.

43. Weebly (2020), 'Warwick Goal – JOHN COLLINS-CHARTIST' https://www.chartistcollins.com.

44. Elizabeth Richards' and Hannah Bolton's names are on the Lent Calendar (March-May) 1789 for Warwick County Gaol. https://www.findmypast.com.au.

45. This arduous work was typically 'women's work' in County goals. Lennox Suzie (2025) 'The Tedious Job of Oakum Picking in a Victorian Prison' My Macabre Road trip https://mymacabreroadtrip.com/oakum-picking; Wicklow Goal (23 June, 2014), 'Work and Chores-Wicklow's Historic Goal https://ww.wicklowshistoricgoal.com.

46 The *Lady Juliana* was the first 'all' female convict ship and was commissioned to provide women to increase the gender mix in the mainly male colony of NSW. (Edwell Penny (2016) *Lady Juliana*, Dictionary of Sydney, www.dictionaryofsydney.org).
47 Sian Rees (2001), *The Floating Brothel*.
48 Michael Flynn (1993), *The Second Fleet*, p.20.
49 Penny Edwell (2016) *Lady Juliana*, op. cit. https://dictionaryofsydney; South Australian Maritime Museum 'History Trust of South Australian Passenger in History' https://passengers,history.sa.gov.au. In comparison, the ship Elizabeth's 'husband to be' Michael Nowland arrived on, the *Scarborough* that lost 73 convict men at sea. ('Second Fleet' www.wikipedia.com; which provides a comparative table of the deaths on all the Second Fleet convict ships).
50 The *Lady Juliana* arrived on the 3rd June 1790, but poor weather delayed the ship's entry into the harbour for three days.
51 There had been no contact with Britain since the First Fleet left England on the 13th May 1787 and the colony was nearing starvation. (Michael Flynn (1993), op. cit. p.19.).
52 Penny Edwell (2016) *Surprize,* Dictionary of Sydney' https://dictionaryofsydney.org. Nowland Ian (1995), op. cit. p.94 cites a slightly higher number of convicts, 47 males and 157 females and Michael Flynn (1993), ibid. provides another variation on the numbers 37 men and 157 women. There were many more women on the *Surprize* because there were already 191 males and 100 female convicts on Norfolk Island (Willetts Jen 'Norfolk Island – Convict Ships and Notes' https://www.freesettlerorfelon.com/norfolk_island.
53 David S. Macmillan (2006) Australian Dictionary of Biography – 'Robert Ross' https://adb.anu.edu.au cited in Nowland Ian (1995), op. cit. p.96; Margaret Hazzard, 'Convicts and Commandants of Norfolk Island' cited in Nowland Ian (1995), op. cit. p.97.
54 William in 1792 and Ann at the age of 18 in 1819. (William's death not registered, Deaths registry, BDM NSW for 'Ann'.
55 Births registry, BDM, NSW 'Sarah Jane Nowland 1814' at the Church of England, Windsor.
56 Marriages registry, BDM, NSW 'Elizabeth Nowland and Henry Richardson 1814'.
57 Elizabeth jr. and Henry Richardson had three children between 1815–1820. Their marriage did not last. Elizabeth jr. left Henry and had '9 more children' with James Rochester between 1824–1843 (Births registry, BDM, NSW for 6 of the children, the rest from a Nowland tree Ancestry.com). Elizabeth jr. and James, married in 1850, the year Elizabeth's first husband, Henry Richardson, died. (Deaths registry, BDMs, NSW) Elizabeth jr. lived at Windsor and died on 18 May 1878, aged 80. ('Elizabeth Nowland Rochester' St. Matthews Anglican Cemetery Windsor www.findagrave.com.au; Obituary 'Cumberland Newspaper' 25 May 1878, p.5.).
58 One of Michael Nowland's major creditors, Edward Wills, died in 1811. Edward Wills' wife Sarah, remarried in 1812 and was prompt by her new husband, George Howe to settle her previous husband's estate. Sarah responded in 1817 and called in her previous husbands' creditors, one of them being William's father, Michael Nowland. (Australian Royalty, 'Edward Wills' https://australianroyalty.com; Ian Nowland, op. cit., p.211).
59 No BDM, NSW; source; gravestone Wilberforce cemetery https://www.findagrave.com; family document; and https://australianroyality.net.au . Ann is buried between her parents at Wilberforce Cemetery.
60 *Sydney Gazette and New South Wales Advertiser*, 20th May 1820, p.1 'Government and General Orders'.

CHAPTER 2
Venturing into the Hunter Valley

61 John Thomas Bigge, (Judge and Royal Commissioner) "was commissioned in 1819 to report on the Macquarie administration [in NSW] for the Colonial Office and investigate every detail of life in NSW" (NSW Government: The Bigge report – Australian Joint Copy Project (AJCP) (6 January, 2025) https://www.guides.sl.nsw.gov.au; J.M. Bennett (2006), 'John Thomas Bigge' (1780–1843) Australian Dictionary of Biography https://adb.anu.edu.au.
62 John Thomas Bigge, Report of the Commissioner of Inquiry of the state of Agriculture and Trade in the Colony of New South Wales, 4 July 1823, p.12. https://guides.sl.nsw.gov.au/ajcp/colonial_office_bigge_report.
63 Oct/Nov – the month varies depending on the source.
64 Major General Lachlan Macquarie was the Governor of NSW from 1810–1821.
65 Parr, Journal (1817) SRNSW Fiche 3271, 2/3623; Macqueen (2004) pp.63-79, cited in *Brokers and Boundaries,* ANU Press (2016), Chapter 4, Mark Dunn 'Aboriginal Guides in the Hunter Valley, New South Wales', p.66. https://press.anu.edu.au.
66 Singleton's Journal (5 May 1818) SRNSW Reel 6047, 4/1740: 212 cited in *Brokers and Boundaries*, ANU Press (2016), ibid. p.66. Mark Dunn on pp.66-68, also provides an informative account of the party's reluctance to continue given the large group of Aboriginal men who challenged them. https://press.anu.edu.au.
67 William Paterson, soldier, and explorer (1755–1810) discovered the Hunter River in 1801, by sea. (David S. Macmillan (2006), 'William Paterson (1755–1810)', Australian Dictionary of Biography https://adb.anu.edu.au. 'Newcastle was the site of the first secondary penal establishment in the colony. In 1801 Governor King authorised the establishment of a small settlement of soldiers and convicts to be employed in coal mining at Newcastle, but due to unfavourable factors they were recalled in 1802. The settlement was again established in March 1804. Initially it was intended to accommodate the Irish convicts who had staged the uprising at Castle Hill [of interest to Michael Nowland's story who was the Superintendent of Convicts at Castle Hill during the Rebellion]. By 1818 there were over 1000 convicts at the Newcastle Penal Settlement. In 1820 Governor Macquarie proposed to England that the convicts should be removed from Newcastle and the district

	be opened up to free settlement.' (Research Data Australia, 'AGY-2111-Newcastle Penal Establishment' https://www.researchdata.edu.au.)
68	The Darkinjung name for Murphy is unknown, as is the case for the other Aboriginal guides and each is referred to in this account (with respect) by the only known names; English pseudonyms.
69	University of Sydney (2010-2013), A History of Aboriginal Sydney' www.ahistoryofaboriginalsydney.edu.au; *Brokers and Boundaries*, ANU Press (2016), op. cit. p.61. In this account, Mark Dunn refers to the guides as Myles, Mullaboy, Murphy, Whirle and Bandagran. ANU Press https://press.anu.edu.au.
70	Wonnaura Nation Aboriginal Corporation (2021/06) 'Boundaries of the Hunter Valley Aboriginal People – Wonnaura Kooris https://wonnarua.org.au.
71	*Brokers and Boundaries,* ANU Press (2016), Mark Dunn op. cit. pp.68-69. https://press.anu.edu.au.
72	Ibid. pp.70-71.
73	Ibid. p.71.
74	Aboriginal people believed that this invasion was temporary because they couldn't imagine anyone would leave their homeland forever.
75	*Brokers and Boundaries,* Mark Dunn op. cit. pp.71-72. A statement in 'Boundaries of the Hunter Valley Aboriginal People – Wonnaura Kooris' informs us that one of the Aboriginal guides from the Darkinjung people who showed Howe the upper reaches of the best route [now the Putty Road] was later killed by his clan. https://wonnarua.org.au. Based on *Brokers and Boundaries,* Mark Dunn op. cit. chapter 4, this Aboriginal guide may have been Whirle or Bangagran.
76	Wikipedia 'Bulga Track'. www.miragenews.com.hawkesbury.
77	*Sydney Gazette and New South Wales Advertiser,* 'Michael Nowland jr.', 4th March 1820, p.2, and 29 Sep. 1821, p.2. As told earlier, the separation of Elizabeth jr. and Henry Richardson also had a profound impact on the family's Punt (Nowland Punt) with the Deeds of title transferred to John Howe (the explorer in the previous account). Henry Richardson before he separated from Elizabeth jr. worked on the Nowland Punt with Michael jr. and Michael sr. and was one of the creditors. Then once Elizabeth jr. and Henry Richardson separated these arrangements ceased and Michael sr. finances went awry. All detailed in Michael sr. story in the family book *By Chance*.
78	'The present month of February makes the fourth month of continued drought this season …the maize is in a terrible condition that sown in and about Windsor and its vicinity …upon closer inspection turns out to be mostly all stalk and leaves, – hardly any cob…' (*Hobart Town Gazette and Van Diemen's Land Advertiser*, Saturday 23 February 1822, p.2 'Sydney Intelligence').
79	Allan Wood (1972) 'Dawn in the Valley: The Early History of the Hunter Valley Settlement,' p.16 cited in Griffiths John (2010) *Industry & Perseverance – A History of David Brown (1750–1836) and Family*. National Library of Australia https://nla.gov.au.
80	There is a large, grassed amphitheatre at Coolah Tops National Park that overlooks the Liverpool Plains.
81	The name of this overland route into the Hunter (disclosed by John Howe's Aboriginal guides) varies depending on the time frame. It was also known as Parson's Rd and Putty Road. The earliest account found in the newspapers under the name 'Putty Road' is in *The Australian* on the 10th August 1827.
82	Mark Dunn (2015) Thesis PhD (UNSW) 'A Valley in a Valley: Colonial Struggles over land and resources in the Hunter Valley, NSW 1820–1850', p.144, '… the word of his [John Howe, 1820] successful expedition spread amongst the families settled along the Hawkesbury River and some soon followed his lead without permission.'
83	Perry T. M. (1963*) Australia's First Frontier*, p.41 tells us, 'In 1822 the settlement of the Hunter Valley began with the survey and allocation of blocks, and during 1823 a steady stream of settlers began to arrive in the district to select sites for their farms.'
84	Mark Dunn (2015) op. cit. p.163, '…the passes were issued in Sydney, with the particulars of travellers, what stock or animals they had with them, where they were travelling to and for what purpose… The passes were valid for between 7 and 21 days, depending on how far into the Hunter the group was travelling and whether they were returning to Windsor or not. An estimated four days was needed to get across the mountains via the track.'
85	William and his brothers 'chose the rich alluvial flats around Glennies Creek, Falbrook (Camberwell today) and the size of each of their runs was determined by the amount of money they could afford to pay once the runs were converted into grants. With each grant there was an 'Annual Quit Rent' and a 'Quit Rent Redemption Rate'. The Annual Quit Rent was an annual fee for the lease of the land from the Crown, and the Quit Rent Redemption was the cost of purchasing the land which made the Annual Quit Rate 'null and void'. For each run of 160 acres (four in total for the Nowland brothers, in 1824) they would be required to pay an annual Quit Rent of one pound and four shillings and Quit Rent Redemption of 24 pounds once they were converted into grants. (Henry Dangar (1828), 'Index and Directory to Map the Country Bordering Upon the Hunter River' p.17. (e-book available at: 'Trove Digital Advanced Search'. https://nla.gov.au.)
86	Under the previous Governor (Governor Macquarie 1810–1821) indentured convict labour was available to emancipated convicts, first-generation colonial Australians and free settlers on application. The Nowland children had been brought up on their parents' farm with such labour. Also, in April 1822, under Governor Brisbane (1821–1825) it became mandatory for settlers with grants, to house one indentured convict for each 100 acres of their grant. The settler was also required to provide each convict with food, clothing, and shelter in return for their labour. (Heydon J.D. (2006) 'Sir Thomas Makdougall Brisbane' [Governor Brisbane], Australian Dictionary of Biography https://adb.anu.edu.au.)

87	Dangar Henry (1828), 'Index and Directory to Map the Country Bordering Upon the Hunter River' op. cit. p.17.
88	Campbell J. F. (1 June 1926) 'The Genesis of Rural Settlement on the Hunter', *Journal and Proceedings of the Royal Australian Historical Society*, Vol XII 1926 Part II, p.85. https://hunterlivingstories.com/tag/land-settlement-hunter-region; https://trove.nla.gov.au; Noble Lillian M. (date unknown) *The Glennies Creek Story*, Singleton Historical Society, p.5.
89	Ellis Martin Scott (1799–1829) was a merchant who arrived in Sydney on the *Triton* in 1825. (Vivienne Parsons (2006) 'Ellis Martin Scott (1799–1829)', Australian Dictionary of Biography https://https://adb.anu.edu.au).
90	NSW Land Registry Services, HLRV [Historical Land Record View]. https://www.nswlrs.com.au.
91	A pre-emptive lease is 'a lease where the lessee has the first right of purchase'.
92	Campbell (1 June 1926) op. cit. pp.80, 82 and 85.
93	Ibid. p.85.
94	Michael jr. established himself as a farmer at Wilberforce, became the Constable of Wilberforce in 1840, and returned to the occupation of a Blacksmith, later in his life. There are accounts in Trove Digital Newspapers (www.sl.nsw.gov.au) that tell of each of these parts of his life journey between 1821–1854. At the age of 52, Michael jr. married Jane Greentree in Wilberforce on the 13th October 1846 (Marriages registry, BDM, NSW; family document). Some genealogical sites state Jane's maiden name as Pope, while the Marriages registry, BDM, NSW cites Jane's maiden name as 'Jane Greentree.' Michael's obituary on the 16th Nov. 1854 (*Sydney Morning Herald*, p.8) reads in part "much respected and deservedly regretted … kind and benevolent disposition…" Michael jr. was 61 when he died and is buried next to his parents and sister, Ann, at Wilberforce Cemetery (though his grave is a little further away than their three that all sit together) ('Michael Nowland (1794–1854)' Wilberforce Cemetery, www.findagrave.com).
95	Michael sr. was plunged into financial difficulty with the separation of his daughter Elizabeth jr. and her husband Henry Richardson in 1821 (Henry Richardson one of Michael sr.'s financers). The following year, Michael was dismissed from his position as District Constable and Pound Keeper, Lower Wilberforce for 'repeated Drunkenness' in May 1822, and subsequently decided to sell his land at Toongabbie in March 1824, after which he had only four years left, in a 'complex, confronting and challenging' life. All detailed in the family book entitled *By Chance*.
96	Lillan M. Noble 'The Glennies Creek Story' op. cit. p.1, tells us 'In recent years, descendants of the Wonnarua have expressed the wish to be identified as "Koori". In future references I wish to acknowledge their desire and will use the name "Koori".'
97	'The traditional lands of the Wonnarua Koori are estimated to comprise an area extending across 5,200 square km from the Upper Hunter River above Maitland, west to the Great Dividing Range towards Wollombi.' ('Wonnarua'. Wikipedia https://an.wikipedia.org).
98	T. M. Perry (1963), *Australia's First Frontier* pp.31-35.
99	Extract from James Miller 'Koori: A Will to Win' cited in WNAC [Wonnarua – National Aboriginal Corporation]. https://Wonnarua.org.au.
100	The reader is invited to examine the full content of these articles and the others available in 'Trove Digital Newspapers' (www.sl.gov.au) during 1826/7. For me, most of the articles demonstrate, the self-righteous nature of the settlers who had little or no regard for the Wonnarua Koori.
101	These articles reflect the commonly held view with very few exceptions – for example, an article in The Monitor, 1 September 1826, appears to show some regard though with an air of arrogance and states in part "The blacks deserve better treatment at our hands. Have they not inherited the lands, we have wrested from them, for ages? Is it not reasonable we should, when they wrong us, forbear as much as possible? Are we not infinitely the most powerful? Should we not, therefore, be magnanimous? Cowards only, are revengeful? … The natives after all, are a harmless, inoffensive, though brave race of men; therefore, severity towards them, is much to be deprecated."
102	Governor Brisbane established the Mounted Police on 7th September 1825, with the dual role of rounding up and curtailing the number of escaped convicts and subduing the First Nations people where conflict between them and the colonist occurred. They were first deployed in Bathurst in November 1825, and a detachment was sent to Wallis Plains (Maitland) in February 1826, under the command of Lieutenant Lowe to suppress the Wonnarua Koori. (NSW Mounted Police – Wikipedia; Ketchell Misha 'From Colonial Cavalry to Mounted Police: a short history' https://theconversation.com).
103	Gore Sarah (16 August 2021), 'Protect Wonnarua History from Mining Destruction, O'Brien Criminal & Civil Solicitors. https://obriensolicitors.com.au/protect-wonnarua-history-mining-destruction.
104	Dr Maria Cotter 28th March 2022, Submission to the NSW Government Independent Planning Commission, p.3. https://www.ipcn.nsw.gov.au.
105	Large swathes of Country was seized by the British Crown (via their representative the Governor of the day) with complete disregard for each Aboriginal Nation and Country.
106	James Wilson-Miller (2005) 'Conflict in the Valley: The Triumph of the Wonnarua' pp.5-6 AARE Annual Conference Parramatta 2005. https://www.aare.edu.au/data/publications/2005/wil05317.pdf
107	As James Wilson-Miller tells us in his book 'Koori, "A Will to Win" (1985, p.1) and in the 1987 Documentary of the same name (Screen Australia) *"This is the beginning of a story of triumph for the survivors of those frontier days, who resisted every attempt to destroy them as a separate race and culture."*
108	Ryan et al (2025), 'Colonial Frontier Massacres in Australia 1788-1930' (Glennies Creek, 1st September 1826) https://11c21ch.newcastle.edu.au/colonialmassacres/detail.php?t+570 Emeritus Professor Lyndall Ryan's scholarly work provides an invaluable contribution to an informative understanding of the extent and nature of colonial frontier massacres between 1788 and 1930. Emeritus Professor Lyndall Ryan (14 April 1943-30 April 2024)

109 The Hawkesbury Benevolent Society (HBS) was established on 13 December 1818 to care for the poor. The Society provided 'food handouts' in the form of 'corn, wheat (maize) and meat' from their established farms in the Hawkesbury (c.1819), and later from their runs in the Hunter (est. 1824), and on the Liverpool Plains (est. 1832). (W.M. Walker, 'History of the Hawkesbury Benevolent Society' 1887, pp.3-5. (Available digitally in Trove https://nla.gov.au) Thomas Dargin, the son-in-law of John Howe (who went on the 1820 expedition with Howe to find an overland route into the Hunter Valley) gained the first tender (1824) with the HBS to take the HBS cattle to his (Dargin's) grant in the Hunter (the run claimed by Dargin in 1822) ('Thomas Dargin Australian Royalty'. https://australianroyalty.net.au).

110 ibid. W.M. Walker (1887, p.7). Noted here and explored later.

CHAPTER 3
A Squatter on the Liverpool Plains

111 Bigge's three reports to the House of Commons included: The State of the Colony of New South Wales (19 June 1822); The Judicial Establishments of New South Wales and of Van Diemen's Land (21 February 1823); and The State of Agriculture and Trade in the Colony of New South Wales (13 March 1823). All three reports are available at https://www.sl.nsw.gov.au.

112 Australian Agricultural Company https://www.sl.nsw.gov.au. The founding members of the company included the 'who's who' of the British and Australian establishment. 'A group of about 400 well-connected British investors funded the company with a combined capital of one million pounds…amongst the principal members of the company were the Attorney-General and the Solicitor General of England, 28 members of Parliament…the Governor, Deputy Governor and eight directors of the Bank of England, the Chairman and Deputy Chairman and five Directors of the British East India Company besides many other eminent bankers and merchants of England. There were 41 investors based in NSW which included some of the wealthiest colonists such as the Macarthur Family and Phillip Parker King…' (Wikipedia 'Australian Agricultural Company').

113 Marriages registry, BDM, NSW 'Henry Nowland and Harriet Farlow 1825'. Henry and Harriet had 12 children between 1825 and 1850: Ann (1825), Sarah (1827), James (1829), Henry (1837), Robert (1838), William (1840), Harriet (1842), Archibald (1846), Frederick (1850), and three other children. Births registry, BDM, NSW for Sarah (Wilberforce); Henry (The Hunter); and, William jr. and Harriet jr. (Muswellbrook area). Knowledge of the rest of the children is based on the following documents: Elizabeth S. Parkinson 'Historical Feature: Henry Nowland – The Forgotten Pioneer of Muswellbrook', *Muswellbrook Chronicle*, August 24, 1984, p.10; a family document; a Nowland tree in www.ancestry.com; and, the online genealogical sites including 'Australian Royalty' www.australianroyalty.com

114 Henry and William's occupations cited in the '1828 Muster – Wilberforce'. (A wheelwright is a person who makes and repairs wooden wheels.)

115 In 1834, Henry sold his 640 acres at Glennies Creek, Falbrook to Richard Dines and moved to Muswellbrook where he was the first resident and publican; initially managing a general store (1834), then 'The Golden Fleece Inn' (c.1836), later known as the 'Royal Hotel' (circa 1839). Henry then built a 'Royal Hotel' of his own in Muswellbrook (completed c.1842). Also, in the 1840s, Henry secured several contracts to deliver the mail in the 'Nowland's coach' from Maitland to Moreton Bay (several of these coaches were built by Henry in his business in Hunter Terrace, Muswellbrook). In addition, Henry, built the 'Chain of Ponds Inn' at Liddell (1842, rented by James Watson) as a stopover point for travelers/coaches. Henry also owned several homesteads north of Muswellbrook (Callatoota, Overton and Wallamundi). Henry (66) died on the 19th February 1863, and Harriet (75) on 20th August 1880. James Ryan 'Toby' described Henry (on his visit to Muswellbrook in 1836) in his book 'Reminiscences of Australia (1895) as "a rough diamond and a thorough Australian born celt…would not let anyone pass his place hungry or thirsty if he knew it…he also did many special good turns for his brother settlers. His was a household name wherever you travelled." Other sources for commentary on Henry Nowland include: Elizabeth S. Parkinson (1984) op. cit.p.10; 'Henry Nowland between the dates 1825 and 1863' Trove Digital Newspapers (www.sl.nsw.gov.au); Elizabeth S. 'Liz' Parkinson (c.1990), 'The Pioneering Nowland Brothers' (www.upperhunter.org).; 'Historical Land Grants' State Library of NSW; BDM, NSW; and the commonly used online genealogical sites such as Ancestry, Australian Royalty and Familypedia.

116 Gray Nancy (2006) 'Henry Dangar (1796-1861)' Australian Dictionary of Biography https://adb.anu.edu.au.

117 Rolls Eric (2011), 'A Million Wild Acres' pp.61-62; *The Australian*, 23 December 1824, p.2-3.

118 Ibid. Rolls Eric (2011), p.74, states, that based on the number of cattle on Liverpool Plains recorded in the Australian on the 9 May 1827 the date (April 1827) in William Nowland's account is incorrect and should be earlier (maybe April 1826). This is because when William first entered the Liverpool Plains through the Dartbrook Pass (c.1826) to find and establish 'Warrah' there were only a few other settlers and not many cattle on the Liverpool Plains. Then later (most likely, April 1827), when William showed the settlers the way through a much gentler pass (detailed soon) they came in much larger numbers. As *The Australian* on the 9 May 1827, p.2, tells us, 'Ten thousand head of cattle have already marched to the fertile country called Liverpool Plains'.

119 *Sydney Gazette and New South Wales Advertiser,* 13 September 1826, p.1. 'Government Notice' – 'Boundaries fixed within which Persons who may be allowed to purchase, or to receive Grants.'; The formalisation of the term squatter in NSW comes from this decree as noted in the following account. "In 1826, the limits of location were decreed by Governor Darling and land grants could only be issued within these boundaries… People choosing to settle on unoccupied land outside the

jurisdiction of the Nineteen Counties [determined in 1829 and excluding the Liverpool Plains] were classed as 'squatters'. The term [squatter] (first appearing in 1828) [and later as the colony developed, and squatters gained rights over their land] they came to [be referred] to [as] a person of high social prestige who grazed livestock on a large scale – often having no legal title to the land beyond being the first European to settle on it. Successful squatters were among the wealthiest class of people in the colony and came to be described (in a play on the English aristocracy) as the 'squattocracy'." www.sl.nsw.gov.au

120   Rolls Eric (2011), op. cit. p.71.
121   Professor John Atchison (PhD Thesis, 1973) 'Port Stephens and Goonoo Goonoo -A Review of the early period of the Agricultural Company 1824–1849' provides a map (between pp.47-48) that shows Henry Dangar's 1825 route north from Muswellbrook to Port Macquarie, Commissioned by Governor Brisbane, with the objective of finding new grazing land to the north. According to the map, Dangar went from Muswellbrook to Murrurundi and crossed onto the Liverpool Range where the 'Nowland Gap' now stands. He then travelled north-east, then east (crossed the Peel River) and then went on to Hanging Rock. From here, Dangar explored in a south-easterly direction along the Barnard River through 'unknown land' that included present day, Giro, Bretti and Knoril Flat. Dangar then headed north-east through present day Strathcedar, Central Lanedowne and Lorne until he reached Port Macquarie. (Professor J.F. Atchison thesis is available online) This unsourced map (assumed based on a combination of Dangar's journal and the undated map that Dangar drew for the AACo) is the only found data to support the following view expressed by some in the literature: 'Henry Dangar discovered the "Pages River Gap" and William Nowland revealed it to the settlers'. For example, in Carter H.R. (1974) *The Upper Mooki*, p.13, it is stated, '… it does not seem that he [William Nowland] was aware that Henry Dangar had found and used the same pass in 1825… it is almost beyond doubt that Dangar used the crossing before 1826.' While Eric Rolls (2011), op.cit. p.74, notes, 'For some reason Henry Dangar did not advertise that pass…When William Nowland wrote his letter to the *Sydney Morning Herald* thirty-four years later, he was still unaware anyone had used the pass before him. Indeed no one knew Henry Dangar had discovered it until 1969 when Dr John Atchison who was studying records of the Australian Agricultural Company found an undated map. There was no complementary journal, but John Atchison proved the map from the company records.'
122   Eric Rolls (2011) op. cit. p.74.
123   The settlers followed and by May 1827 the number of cattle on the Liverpool Plains had increased significantly. See footnote 118; ibid. Eric Rolls (2011, p.74))

CHAPTER 4
The Kamilaroi Nation

124   The Kamilaroi – Short Documentary NITV (2019), (National Indigenous TV). Produced by Idemitsu Boggabri Coal 'HOME/The Kamilaroi' (https://www.thekamilaroi.com). This award winning (Community Excellence Award) short documentary (22 mins) celebrates the 'First Nations people' of the Liverpool Plains, the 'Kamilaroi (Gamilaraay, Gomeroi)'. Elsewhere, depending on the article, the Kamilaroi People are denoted as either the Gamilaraay, Gomeroi or Kamilaroi, with some accounts giving preference to Gamilaraay rather than Kamilaroi. Dr. Hiliary Smith (July 2022) 'Kamilaroi, Gamialaraay, or Gomeroi' provides a linguistic interpretation of the various spelling of Kamilaroi and states in part, 'When Europeans first arrived in Australia, they wrote down languages according to what they heard, without understanding how the languages work… In the nineteenth century some Europeans thought they heard "g" at the start of the word Gamilaraay and wrote it down as Gummilroy, while others heard "k" and wrote it down as Kamilaroi… When we speak quickly, we sometimes miss out some of the sounds and the words become shorter… Gamilaraay is spoken quickly it sounds something like Gomeroi or Gummeroi, and some people prefer to use one of those spellings to describe their language group.' (Dr Hiliary Smith (2002), ('Kamilaroi, Gamilaraay or Gomeroi', Winanga-Li Aboriginal Child & Family Centre (on Gamilaraay Country, Gunnedah) https://www.winanga-li.org.au). The variations on 'Kamilaroi' within Aboriginal literature/communities are acknowledged, with respect.
125   A map of Indigenous Australia is available online see Norton David R. (1996) 'The Aiatsis Map of Indigenous Australia', Aboriginal Studies Press, AIATSIS and Auslig/Sinclair, Knight, Merz 1996 https://www.abc.net.au/indigenousmap (on this map the Darkinjung Nation is denoted as 'Darkinung')
126   "Wiradjuri country is the largest in NSW, stretching from the eastern boundary of the Great Dividing Range. Drawing a line from the present towns of Hay and Nyngan approximates the western boundary. While Gunnedah and Albury mark the northern and southern boundaries of Wiradjuri country… Wiradjuri Country borders Kamilaroi Country north-east of Dubbo at Gunnedah." ('The Wiradjuri people' https://www.bathurst.nsw.gov.au).
127   Dhiiyaan Aboriginal Centre (2025), 'Kamilaroi Culture'. Moree Plains Tourism https://www.moreetourism.com.au. The towns in 'Murri' Country include Moree, Inverell, Narrabri and Gunnedah. Another excellent account is provided in Friends of Myall Creek (21 May 2021) 'RECONCILIATION TRAIL – Moree to Myall Creek – Kamilaroi country' https://www.myallcreek.org .
128   Wikipedia, 'Gamilaraay' and 'Wonnarua'
129   Cumbo Gunerah (Red Chief/Red Kangaroo) is revered and respected by the Kamilaori people as the 'Great Warrior Chief'. ('The Kamilaroi – Short Documentary op. cit). Cumbo Gunerah lived from circa 1680 – circa 1745. (O'Rouke Michael (2005), 'Sung for Generation. Tales of Red Kangaroo War Leader of Gunnedah', p.150, e-book https://www.scribd.com)
130   The first record found in Trove Digital Newspapers of the name the 'Warrumbungles' without any reference to the Arbuthnot

Range is in *The Sydney Gazette and New South Wales Advertiser* on the 28th October 1830, p.3, concerning a 'party of bushrangers'. This mountain range that we know today as the 'Warrumbungles' was initially named the Arbuthnot Range by Oxley, but the name did not last long; some 12 years later, the Kamilaroi name was used instead; and maybe earlier by some of the settlers.

131 O'Rourke Michael (2009) 'Pages to the North-West Plains' p.5 states 'Warrumbungle mountains themselves, or at least their western sector, belonged to Wiradjuri-speaking groups. In short, the boundary between Kamilaroi and Wiradjuri fell approximately along a line drawn from Coonabarabran to Coolah' ebook https://www.scribd.com

132 The Deputy Surveyor General George Evans sketched this image. How amazing. Source: Oxley John, *Journal of An Expedition in Australia Part 11* https://gutenberg.net.au/ebooks

133 Cunningham Allan (1832), 'Brief View of the Progress of Interior Discovery in New South Wales', *Journal of the Royal Geographical Society of London,* Vol 2, 1832, p.110. ('Allan Cunningham' https://scholar.archive.org; also see https://www.gutenberg.net.au e-book under the title of the article). As told earlier, Allan Cunningham discovered the Pandora Pass on the 9th June 1823. He also examined the western and northern sides of the Liverpool Plains in May 1825.

134 *The Australian*, Friday 3 May 1833, p.3, 'Hunter's River. Murder by the Aborigines. — A dreadful Murder (sic) has been committed at Mr. Renkin's Station at Liverpool Plains, called the barber's (sic) Stock Yard, the overseer and four assigned servants were found dead in the hut; and from the horrible manner in which their bodies were mangled, there can be no doubt but that the murder was committed by the natives…'; *The Colonist* (Sydney) Thursday 30 June 1836, p.4, 'LIVERPOOL PLAINS. We have received intelligence of a dreadful outrage committed by the blacks at a station belonging to the Messrs. Hall of Pitt Town, situated on the Liverpool Plains on the banks of the River Anglo…'; *The Sydney Monitor*, Friday 27 October 1837, p.2, 'We are sorry to hear that a dreadful murder has been committed by some aboriginal natives in the neighbourhood of Liverpool Plains. According. to the report which reached our office last night, it appears that two stock-keepers have been killed by them. – Colonist.' During this time (post 1828–1837) no account of the settlers killing the Kamilaroi on the Liverpool Plains was found in Trove. A report prepared for the Liverpool Plains Shire Council by Dr Parry Naomi with Christison Ray (December, 2019), 'A Thematic History of Liverpool Plains Shire' (https://naomiparry.net) tells us on p.7, 'Between 1836 and 1838 a series of reprisals resulted in the worst massacres of Aboriginal people in NSW history. In September 1837 up to 20 Aboriginal people were killed by stockmen in reprisal for cattle theft at Yarramanbah. In November 1837 a posse of stockmen avenged the deaths of two of their own by killing 200 Gomeroi over several days in a mountain gorge.' The source for these accounts is cited in ibid. Dr. Parry Naomi (2019) as Lyndall Ryan https://c21ch.newcastle.edu.au/colonialmassacres/detail.php?r=624

135 *Sydney Gazette and New South Wales Advertiser*, 8th October 1831, p.2. 'Small Pox (sic)' 'It appears from a parcel investigation, recently made into the disease resembling the small pox among the natives in the interior…'

136 'In the summer of 1837–38, NSW policeman Major James Nunn and around 30 mounted soldiers and stockmen swept through the Gwydir region on an expedition to "repress" Aboriginal people, writes historian Paul Irish. They committed a series of atrocities in the area. The Waterloo Creek massacre on January 26, 1838, was among the most savage.' (Archibald-Binge Ella and Rhett Wyman Rhett (January 24, 2020), 'Struggle and survival: Three Aboriginal perspectives on Australia Day' *Sydney Morning Herald* https://www.smh.com.au

137 'Police and settlers hunted down Aboriginal families, pursuing them for kilometres across their country, before gunning them down in a creek bed in north-west New South Wales. Official records state at least 40 men, women and children were killed, but other historians suggest hundreds of Aboriginal people died that day.' (Higgins Isabella and Gollard Sarah, 25 January 2020. 'Australia Day: January 26 marks a massacre in NSW. Will a cement plaque really work?' ABC News, Live Blog https://www.abc.net.au). Note the day and month of the 'Waterloo Massacre' 26th January; the same day and month as today's 'Australia Day'.

138 Korff J. (2023) 'Myall Creek Massacre (1838)', Creative Spirits'. https://www.creativespirits.info

139 'About Friends of Myall Creek' https://myallcreek.org

140 The Massacre Story – Friends of Myall Creek https://myallcreek.org/the-massacre-story. The extract in the text of the story is only a partial account. A comprehensive perspective is provided on the 'Friends of Myall Creek website including the following "There is no eyewitness account of the killings but about 800 metres from the huts, the defenseless people were hacked and slashed to death. Only one of the whole clan was spared. John Blake [one of the perpetrators] appears to have selected an Aboriginal woman for himself and so spared her. All of the other Aboriginal people were beheaded and their headless bodies were left where they fell." So disturbing. Another moving account of what happened can be found at the 'Myall Creek Massacre Memorial Stone' site on 27th June 2018, on 'The Feed SBS' (You Tube) 'Reconciliating Murder: The Myall Creek Massacre'.

141 Ryan James T. 'Toby' (1895) *Reminiscences of Australia*, p.57.

142 Withcombe Patricia Mary (2015) 'The Twelfth Man: John Fleming and the Myall Creek Massacre' Honours Thesis, University of Newcastle., Australia. https://docslib.org/doc/6016899/john-henry-flemming-and-the-myall-creek-massacre

143 Marriages registry, BDM, NSW, 'John H. Flemming and Charlotte Dunston, 1840'.

144 'The Wirrayaraay People are one of the clans of the Kamilaroi. 'On 10 June 1838, a gang of stockmen led by a squatter rode into Myall Creek Station and brutally murdered about twenty-eight unarmed women, children and old men. The younger Wirrayaraay men were away cutting bark on a neighbouring station.' Friends of Myall Creek (2025) 'Text of the Myall Creek

Memorial Plagues' [Plague 6] https://myallcreek.org/test.
145   *Sydney Morning Herald*, 15 September 1842, p.2, 'Lower Liverpool Plains It will take us about eight days to travel from thence to our station on the Mooney, where I understand there is plenty of grass and water, the blacks still remaining very quiet in that quarter; but on the Barwin they are killing cattle in all directions, and have also killed some horses.' *Sydney Morning Herald*, Wednesday 26 October 1842, p.2 'October 11 – The blacks have of late been particularly troublesome on the Gwydir and M'lntyrc Rivers. On the latter they have killed four white men within about two months, as well as having hunted Mr Hargrave's men away in sight of the huts and speared his three horses. In fact, unless some such active person as Mr Fry besent (sic) there, who would keep the binds in order without unnecessary severity, the squatters will have to turn out in self-defence. No person wishes to treat the unfortunate wretches with harshness, but it is indispensable that they should be taught to respect property, and at present there is little or no prospect of that being accomplished.' Similar accounts at the time include, *Sydney Morning Herald*, 21 November 1842, p.2 'LIVERPOOL PLAINS – THE BLACKS'; *The Colonial Observer*, 23 November 1842, p.626 'DEPREDATIONS OF THE BLACKS AT LIVERPOOL PLAINS'.
146   Talbott Dolly, op. cit. 'The Kamilaroi – Short Documentary'

CHAPTER 5
A Pastoralist and Squatter

147   Deaths registry, BDM, NSW; Wilberforce Cemetery 'Michael Nowland, 1828'. (www.findagrave.com).
148   After William's father Michael sr. died his mother Elizabeth sr. married Peter Vaughan at St Matthew's Church of England, Windsor, in 1829; part of Elizabeth sr.'s story in the companion book *By Chance*.
149   Marriages registry, BDM, NSW. Mary's husband, Alexander Johnston came to Australia as a convict, he was convicted of treason as part of the Scottish Insurrection of 1820 (a week of strikes and unrest amongst artisan workers, such as, weavers, shoemakers, blacksmiths) that culminated in arrests and trials for treason. (Scotland's People, 'The Radical Rising of 1820' https://www.scotlandspeople.gov.uk). Alexander arrived in Sydney as a convict at the age of 16, on the 'Speke' on the 18 May 1821. (convict ship 'Speke' https://convictrecords.com; 'Alexander Johnston' https://convictrecords.com; 'Alexander Johnston + Mary Nowland https://australianroyalty.net.au). Mary and Alexander had 11 children, between 1828–1853: Gilbert (1828); Alexander jr. (1830); Mary jr. (1832); Elizabeth (1834); Anne (1836); Michael (1839); Sarah (1841); William (1842); John (1845); Alfred (1847); Thomas (1853). (Gilbert, Alexander jr. Michael and Alfred ('Births registry, BDM, NSW'). All of the children noted in, 'Alexander Johnston + Mary Nowland https://australianroyalty.net.au. Initially, Mary and Alexander lived in the Hawkesbury, and then they followed William to Glennies Creek, Falbrook (Camberwell) in 1842. Detailed later in this story.
150   Marriages registry, BDM, NSW 'Edward Nowland and Christian Farlow 1829'. Edward and Christian had 5 children between 1829–1842: Edward (1830) Wilberforce; James (1831) Wilberforce; Christian (1833) Wilberforce; Matilda (1836) registered at Wilberforce in 1843; Robert (1842) also registered at Wilberforce in 1843. (Births registry, BDM, NSW; 'Edward Nowland + Christiana Farlow' https://australianroyalty.net.au.) There is also an unnamed, sixth child in 'our' family document, and in a Nowland Tree Ancestry.com. Christian is sometimes cited as 'Christiana' on some genealogical sites, and both names need to be searched. 'Christian/Christiana' is registered as 'Christian' in the 'Births registry, BDM, NSW' in 1811, in the 'Marriages registry BDM, NSW' in 1829, and denoted as 'Christian' (as the mother), in the registration of each of her children in the 'Births registry BDM, NSW' except for the registration of her last child, Robert (in 1843) where the mother is noted as 'Christiana'. Christian/Christiana is cited as 'Christiana' in our family document and on the genealogical site 'Australian Royalty'. Ian Nowland, as Christian's great-great grandson cites her name as 'Christian' in his publication *The Story of Michael and Elizabeth Nowland* (1996) and this version of Christian's name is used throughout this story. Edward and Christian initially lived in the Hawkesbury and moved to the Liverpool Plains circa 1836. Detailed later in this story.
151   During these years (1823-c.1860) settlers who moved out of Sydney and secured 'official land grants' within the borders of settlement, from the Governor, to graze sheep and/or cattle were mostly called 'pastoralists' regardless of the size of their property. In the second part of the 1800s, the name 'grazier' was the preferred term, and today the generic term 'farmer' is common.
152   The year could have been 1832. Eric Rolls (2011) op. cit. p.105 states, "When Sir Edward Parry, in 1832 inspected the land Henry Dangar chose for the company [on the Liverpool Plains] he wrote down a list of twenty-three squatters who would be affected by the move." [William Nowland, one of them.] Eric Rolls (2011) on p.101 also states "In February 1833 six thousand young sheep spread among William Nowland's cattle on Warrah Creek. William Telfer had charge of them…" Another source states, the AACo did not establish 'Warrah Estate' until 1833. ('Australian Agriculture and Rural Life – Australian Agricultural Company' www.sl.nsw.gov.au). While this data is informative, the AACo may have been on Warrah a year earlier in 1832. The ANU Archives 'Warrah Station deposit' notes, "Warrah was acquired by the Australian Agricultural Company in 1833 and was originally managed by W. Telfer 1832–1836". (The Australian National University, 'Australian Agricultural Company – Archives' https://archivescollection.anu.edu.au).
153   Based on the previous account (ibid.) in the ANU AACo Archives 'Warrah Station deposit', it is assumed the superintendent in charge was W. Telfer. (William Telfer).
154   ANU, 'Australian Agricultural Company – Archives'. https://archivescollection.anu.edu.au.

155 ibid. ANU, AACo Archives.
156 The established approach to 'land settlement and tenure' was exemplified earlier when William and his brothers each claimed an allotment at Glennies Creek, Falbrook (c.1823). Each allotment at Falbrook was 'within the boundaries of settlement' and the occupant (once the land had been surveyed) was entitled through 'custom and practice' to the first pre-emptive lease with the option of first purchase. Squatters, like William, assumed this would be the case 'in the near future' on the Liverpool Plains. They believed they were just ahead of the mob. They had got in first and would soon turn their claim into a pre-emptive lease. Though that was not to be the case. They would remain as squatters with no land rights for more than a decade (1826–1836); detailed later in the story.
157 Parry Ann (2006) 'Sir William Edward Parry (1790–1855)'; Gray Nancy (2006), 'Henry Dangar (1796–1861);' and Saclier M.J. (2006) 'George Boyle White' (1802–1876), Australian Dictionary of Biography https://adb.anu.edu.au.
158 Marriages registry, BDM, NSW 'William Nowland and Mary Farlow 1831'. William and Mary were married at St John's Anglican Church Wilberforce which also functioned as the School House up until 1859, when the Church (as a stand-alone building) was complete. Both historical buildings still stand today at 43-43a Macquarie Road Wilberforce.
159 NSW Land Registry Services, HLRV [Historical Land Record View]. https://www.nswlrs.com.au.
160 Marriages registry, BDM, NSW 'Sarah Jane and William Adnum 1831'. Sarah and William had 8 children (7 surviving) between 1831–1850: Elizabeth (1831); Francis (1833); William jr. (1835); Sarah jr. (1837); Henry (1840); Mary (1842); Edward (1846); Frances (1850). (Births registry, BDM, NSW, district not stated, assumed Sydney). It is assumed given the same name for Frances (1850), Francis (1833) died. Sarah Jane and 'her' William settled in Sydney and lived at 266 George St. (Trove Digital Newspaper under the key words and dates; 'William Adnum 1831–1850'). This part of George Street is Australia Square today. 'This' William was a Coppersmith at 266 George St. Sydney. William Adnum (age unknown) died in 1861, and Sarah (64) in 1878. (Deaths registry, BDM, NSW).
161 As noted earlier, Henry Dangar was the assistant government surveyor, under John Oxley 1821–1827. In 1830, Henry Dangar "was offered, and accepted, an appointment as a surveyor to the company [AACo] under Sir Edward Parry." Dangar worked, in this capacity for the AACo, until 1833. (Nancy Gray (2006) op. cit.).
162 Edward initially managed this run for the Hawkesbury Benevolent Society and then William (in 1843). Detailed later in the story.
163 This extract from the Reuss & Browne's map (1860) shows the extent of the HBS's 'Mooki Station' at 'Breeza' adjacent to the Mooki River some 25 years later and this is why it is more than 1000 acres.
164 'In November 1832, tenders were called for a person to undertake the depasturing [grazing] of the Society's stock at their station (of 1000 acres) and stockyards at Liverpool Plains, from the 1st January 1833, and at a meeting held for that purpose, Mr. Edward Nowland's offer at £69 per annum, was accepted in preference to several others.' (M.W. Walker (1887), op. cit. p.7 https://nla.gov.au) N.B: The year in William's accounts is slightly different to the HBS's; 1832 and 1833, respectively.
165 'On the 8th March 1834, … the president [of the HBS] Captain Brabyn, stated that he had received a report from Mr. Nowland [Edward], the Superintendent of the Society's stock, stating the Australian Agricultural Company had taken possession of the land now held by the Society, and also of that adjoining; at the same time stating that the land was their property, and that the society had no claim on it. A letter was also produced from Mr. Cox stating that he had made application at the offices of the Colonial Secretary and Surveyor-General, and was informed that no land was chartered to the Society, at Phillip's Creek, Liverpool Plains, nor was there any entry of the land at all.' (ibid. M. W. Walker (1887) pp.7-8). From my perspective, Edward and William had chosen the run [as was the practice on the Liverpool Plains] and assumed it would be converted into a grant. Yet this was not to be the case, the AACo and the free settlers with money and the prospect of international trade had negotiated and continued to negotiate with the Colonial Secretary and Surveyor-General for the best the Liverpool Plains could offer.
166 ibid. M.W. Walker (1887), p.8.

CHAPTER 6
The Nowland Brothers and The Farlow Sisters

167 The data that has determined this view includes: the occupation of Henry, (running the general store, Muswellbrook, since 1834) and the birth of Henry and Harriet's third child, Henry jr. registered in the Hunter in 1837; the birth of William and Mary's third child, Robert in 1836 also registered in the Hunter; and, the knowledge of Edward's tender for the HBS at Mooki River in 1835, and, the birth of Edward's and Christian's fourth child, Matilda in 1836 (whose birth wasn't registered until 1843, as detailed later in this story).
168 The large gap between Sarah (1827) and Henry jr. (1837) is unexplained. It is assumed that there were unregistered children who did not survive infancy between Sarah and Henry.
169 Rev. Halcombe J.J. (1868) in 'The Emigrant and the Heathen on Sketches of Missionary Life', p.39, describes Muswellbrook in 1848, 'We drew up … at the Royal Hotel. Nine years before this had been the only building in the place [1839], a mere bush inn, surrounded by forest [Henry and Harriet's general store, now an inn]. And, in spite of its name, it was only a weather-broad cottage, with the royal arms standing, not very conspicuously, against the front, and containing two sitting rooms and two small bedrooms, entered from the verandah, besides those commonly used for the publican's family.' And then on p.41, 'In 1848 Muswell Brook had a population of about 300, including a doctor and a clerk of petty sessions.' (University of Newcastle, e-Book https://downloads.newcastle.edu.au).
170 Noble Lillian M. (date unknown, most likely, 1990s) *The Glennies Creek Story*, pp. 24-26. Singleton Historical Society.

Lillian Noble's book is based on stories handed down from one generation to the next and provides recollections back to the first settlers, circa 1823. Lillian Noble died in 2000 and is buried at Camberwell Anglican Church Cemetery. ('Lillian May Wellard Noble,1907–2000', www.findagrave).

171 Rolls Eric (2011) op. cit. p.101. Colonel Snodgrass was the Commander of the NSW Mounted Police in 1830. (Lea-Scarlett E.J. (2006) 'Kenneth Snodgrass (1784–1853)' Australian Dictionary of Biography https://adb.anu.edu.au. Colonel Snodgrass' appalling actions against the Kamilaroi Nation are detailed in the next chapter of this story.

172 This view is based on Michael Nowland sr.'s employment of indentured labour, the requirement for convict labour on the land grants in the Hunter, and Naomi Nowland's (Mary's future daughter-in-law) employment of a domestic servant (as was typical of the time); detailed in the family book *By Chance* as part of Naomi Nowland's story.

173 Like all of William and Mary's subsequent children, Robert is registered in BDM, NSW but his place of birth is not stated. It is assumed Robert was born in William and Mary's 'log cabin' at Falbrook with the assistance of a female neighbour or two, or maybe one of Mary's sisters. Mary helped deliver many of her own grandchildren at Rosedale, as detailed later in this story. The bravery of women at the time in such remote areas cannot be understated.

174 NSW Land Registry Services, HLRV [Historical Land Record View]. https://www.nswlrs.com.au. Rosedale still stands today. 'Rosedale farm and homestead' the property of Wendy Bowman (1957–2023) is substantially altered, yet there is still evidence of the original homestead. Rosedale only remains today due to the guardianship of Wendy Bowman who fought the mining companies and won. ('Hunter Valley farmer takes on mining company – and wins https://www.nswfarmers.org.au). Wendy Bowman (89 yrs.) died on the 26th July 2023. (Connell Cecilia and Bernasconi Amelia (1 August 2023), 'Award-winning Hunter Valley environmentalist and farmer Wendy Bowman dies aged 89', ABC news https://abc.net.au/news).

CHAPTER 7
William Nowland – the Furthest North

175 Denoted as Dridrool in Reuss & Browne (1860) op. cit. 'Map of New South Wales and part of Queensland…'; Eric Rolls (2011), op. cit. p.115, notes, 'William Nowland, tired of his cattle being disturbed at water on the Mooki by trespassing sheep, sent one herd in March 1837 beyond all others on the Namoi to the western end of a chain of lagoons, swamps and channels known as Dridool.'

176 Rolls Eric (2011), op. cit. p.115.

177 'The Waterloo Creek Massacre site at "3837 Millie Road, Jews Lagoon" was declared a site of state heritage significance as "a place of frontier conflict" and listed on the New South Wales State Heritage Register. The site is recognised as a significant place, as a place of memorial for the Aboriginal community that honours the resistance and resilience of their ancestors.' ('Waterloo Creek Massacre' Wikipedia).

178 Again, note the date; 'Australia Day' is the same month and day.

179 Gregoire Paul and Medim Ugur (19 Nov 2021), 'The Frontier Violence Perpetrated by the NSW Mounted Police' https://www.sydneycriminallawyers.com.au/blog.

180 Between 1837 and 1839, NSW (and Australia generally) went through a period of extreme drought, there are several newspaper articles reporting on the drought including a retrospective in *The Queenslander*, Sat 19 Sep. 1885 ' by Mr. N. Bartley who states, '1837, 1838, and 1839 brought a three years' drought, which almost exterminated the sheep and cattle of Australia, and dried up that great "father of waters" the big Murrumbidgee River itself…' and an article in *South Australian Gazette and Colonial Register,* 17 November 1838, p.4, 'DROUGHT IN NEW SOUTH WALES' that gives notification of a 'day of fast' in recognition of the impact of the droughts. The article states, 'By the Sydney papers (to the 27th October) we observe that his Excellency Sir George Gipps had appointed Friday, 2nd November, to be observed as a day of fasting and humiliation throughout New South Wales, on account of the calamitous drought with which that territory had been afflicted. While we deeply regret to perceive by the Accounts from the interior that the losses of cattle and sheep, occasioned by the absence of rain, had been very great…' How bizarre fasting in recognition of the drought. Maybe a social hangover from medieval times.

CHAPTER 8
Governor Bourke's Proclamation

181 As told earlier, Governor Bourke was Governor of NSW from 1831–1837.

182 'In 1835, John Batman declared that he had negotiated a "treaty" to claim the lands of the people of the Kulin Nation (around Port Phillip, near the present site of Melbourne). However, the treaty was not valid under European law or Kulin lore and is now recognised by many in the Victorian Aboriginal community as an attempt to disadvantage the people of the Kulin Nation.' (Deadly Story 'The Batman 'treaty' is signed' Kulin Nation https://deadlystory.com); 'The so-called treaty was declared void on 26 August 1835 by the Governor of New South Wales, Richard Bourke, who asserted that all land within the colony belonged to the Crown and that it [the Crown] had the sole authority to dispose of it.' (Wikipedia, 'Batman Treaty').

183 Government Gazette Notices – *New South Wales Government Gazette*, 12 October 1836, p.761 'Crown Lands'.

184 Campbell (1968), op. cit. p.26.

185 Ibid. Campbell (1968), pp.19-20.

186 NSW State Archives Collection 'Commissioners of Crown Land for Liverpool Plains' https://researchdata.edu.au

187 The Gumbaynggirr people are the traditional owners of Guy Fawkes. The Gumbaynggirr nation stretches from the Nambucca River in the south, to around the Clarence River in the north, up onto the Great Dividing Range in the west and across to the coast at Coffs Harbour. Archaeological evidence indicates that the valley of Guy Fawkes' Gorge was occupied by Aboriginal people for over 10,000 years. Important traffic and trade routes followed the Guy Fawkes and Boyd rivers and linked the tablelands to the coast. The gorges were also where hunting and initiation rituals took place [boras] (Wilderness Australia (Aug 2022) 'Exploring Guy Fawkes' https://www.wildernessaustralia.org.au; 'Map of Indigenous Australia – AIATSIS' https://aiatsis.gov.au/explore/map-indigenous-australia).

CHAPTER 9
Governor Gipps' Response to The Slaughterhouse Creek Massacre and The Myall Creek Massacre

188 Cowlishaw Gillian (1993), 'Roger Milliss (1992) 'Waterloo Creek: The Australian Day Massacre of 1838. George Gipps and the British Conquest of New South Wales', Review Article', *Australian Journal of Anthropology* (1993, p.63) https://www.academia.edu.

189 Stephen Gapps and Mina Murray (28th July 2021) 'From Colonial cavalry to mounted police: a short history of the Australian police horse'. https://theconversation.com.

190 Carpenter Michelle, Colonial History – Kamilaroi – A Nations Identity' https://www.kamilaroianationsidentity.weebly.com.

191 *The Kamilaroi* – Short Documentary, op. cit.

CHAPTER 10
Legal Disputes, Claims and Counter Claims

192 Stone Barry (2019), 'The Squatters. The Story of Australia's Pastoral Pioneers', p.48. provides us with some generic data towards the end of the 1840s, 'By 1848, the number of squatters in New South Wales totaled 1865. They owned 5.5 million sheep and 882,000 cattle and occupied 220,149 square kilometres of pastoral lands – around 29,610 acres per squatter.' Walsh Brian (2020), ''Toil and Trouble from Maitland to Moreton Bay – John Eales' Convicts', p.48, tells us, on the Liverpool Plains' 'The 1840s returns to the Commissioner shows that 1,154 'whites' were living on 130 stations on the Liverpool Plains, comprising 1078 men and a meagre 77 women'.

193 Guilford Elizabeth (2006) Australian Dictionary of Biography,'John Eales (1799–1871) "John Eales (1799–1871) [wealthy] grazier and pioneer pastoralist [arrived in NSW in October 1822 and was given a land] grant of 2,100 acres (850 ha) about four miles (6.4km) from Morpeth [in the Hunter] … in the 1830s he acquired by purchase [based on improvements e.g., pasture and stock] and squattage a number of runs on the Liverpool Plains…" [Including Walhollow, denoted as Walholla in Guilford's account, a run adjacent to and bordering William Nowland's Wallalla and now the land of a 'free settler']. https://adb.anu.edu.au. With this mix of 'cashed-up free settlers and squatters on land adjacent to each other' a notable phenomenon started to emerge in the 1830s on the Liverpool Plains, (as elsewhere): two decisively different groups sometimes adjacent to each other with differentiated land rights; squatters required to have an 'annual licence' for their runs' (as was the case with William's Wallalla) and wealthy pastoralists (such as John Eales at Walhollow) with 'large land holdings' given or purchased with the approval of the Governor of the day.

194 'Free selection before survey' is discussed later in William's story when it is enacted by the *Crown Land Alienation Act, 1861*.

195 Campbell (1968), 'Squatting on Crown Land in New South Wales'p.43 'Supplementary list of Runs in the Liverpool Plains District, government Gazette of NSW 1848, '182. (Lessee) Nowland William (Name of Run) 'Wallalla (Walhollow)' (Approx. Acreage) 87,040, (Frontage River or Creek), Mooki River.

196 Walker M.W. (1887) History of the Benevolent Society, op. cit. p.9, "16th March 1837 – The Committee received a Letter from Mr. Edward Nowland superintendent of stock, dated the 10th February preceding, stating that some parties has (sic) Trespassed upon the Society's land at Mooki, when it was resolved to furnish Mr. Nowland With a copy of the correspondence with the Government on the subject of its selection, to arm him in ejecting the intruders. This appears to be the first of these interruptions which subsequently caused so much trouble and loss to the Society respecting the run,and the Surveyor-General was immediately written to in the subject… The only matter connected with the institution which has created vexation and serious loss is that relating to the Society's run at Mooki, which has been trespassed upon an unwarranted extent by certain parties."

197 Each squatter branded their cattle to differentiate the stock. The HBS used the brand mark of 4D on their cattle, William used the brand mark of WN with an N elsewhere, for example under the rip or shoulder, and Edward is assumed to have branded his cattle in a similar way to William with EN instead of WN.

198 As told in an earlier chapter, Bourke's Proclamation and the 1836 Act required the identification of the boundaries of each run and the determination of the quantity of stock on each run on an annual basis. Then based on these two factors (the boundaries of the run and the quantity of stock) the amount of money owed to the Crown per annum for each run was determined. Under Governor Bourke the cost of the licence for each run was £10 per annum and a halfpenny for every head of stock. Later, Governor Gipps under his tenure, differentiating the fee for stock, based on the stock type (cattle, sheep or horse). Not all the squatters agreed with the Commissioner, or with other squatters/settlers, about their boundaries and/or their stock; thus the subsequent court cases.

199 See, Research Data Australia, 'Commissioner of Crown Lands for Liverpool Plains' NSW. State Archives Collection https://

researchdata.edu.au.
200 William became the Superintendent of the HBS's Mooki Station in 1842 after the death of his brother Edward.
201 The year is probably 1835, given the HBS officially gained the lease for 'Mooki Station on the 24th June 1835.
202 We know this date is wrong given the minutes of the meeting of the Hawkesbury Benevolent Society (see footnotes 163, 164 and 165) and the official possession of Mooki Station by the HBS in June 1835.
203 Assessment was the amount of money each squatter had to pay for each head of stock. As told earlier, under Governor Bourke the fee was 'a halfpenny for each head of stock'. Under Governor Gipps the fee increased dramatically and varied with the type of stock. "I pence per annum for each sheep, 3 pence for each horned cattle and 6 pence for each horse' (Stone Barry (2019) op. cit. p.40 (Governor Bourke's fee) and p.46 (Governor Gipps' new increased fee).
204 This was a common occurrence, because squatters stayed away from their run/s for long periods of time. In my own ancestral history, William and Edward took cattle to the HBS Mooki Station in 1836 and did not return until 1837.

CHAPTER 11
A Pastoralist at Rosedale

205 op. cit. NSW Land Registry Services, HLRV.
206 *Maitland Mercury and Hunter River General Advertiser*, 13 Jun 1889, p.5. 'The Rosedale Estate, Glennie's (sic) Creek.' '… the homestead of Messrs. A. and H. Nowland, Camberwell, about 2 miles from Glennie's Creek…'
207 Births register, BDM, NSW; 'William Nowland 1832'; 'Michael Nowland 1834'; Robert Nowland 1836; James Nowland 1838'; 'Charles Nowland 1840'.
208 op. cit. NSW Land Registry Services, HLRV.
209 ibid. NSW Land Registry Services, HLRV.
210 ibid. William's role in the subsequent development of Camberwell, goes well beyond this decade, and is detailed progressively, in the story, as it occurred, and is also noted by others, including: Yancoal (2009) 'Appendix 14 – European Heritage' https://www.yancoal.com.au, p.12. William was instrumental in the development of Camberwell, initially known as 'Falbrook'; ibid. p.6. 'William Nowland… was influential in the development of Camberwell village aesthetics.' Similar comments are noted in Scone Historical Society 'William Nowland 1804–1884'. https://scone.com.au.
211 Dyster Barrie (1 August 2022), 'The Depression of the 1840s in New South Wales', Australian Dictionary of Biography, National Centre of Biography, Australian National University https://adb.anu.edu.au/essay/29/text40594.
212 'The Queen' was still standing in March 1893 (9 years after William Nowland's death), when Mary Nowland (who died in 1895) and her second youngest child (Alfred), and his family were caught in a flood at Rosedale and had to wade through Glennies Creek to higher ground and Henry's place (Mary's youngest son's, place 'The Queen') ('The *Maitland Mercury* and *Hunter River Advertiser,* 16th March 1893, p.7, 'The Queen').
213 Wikipedia 'Chain of Ponds Inn'; Willetts Jen, 'Lady Mary Fitzroy Inn'. https://www.freesettlersorfelon.com. The Chain of Ponds Inn was built as a stopover for people travelling on the 'Nowland's Coach (Henry's stagecoach business; outlined soon). While William's Inn was built to service the local community and attract travels to stop at the township of Camberwell on their way north.
214 op. cit. NSW Land Registry Services, HLRV.
215 *Sydney Monitor* and *Commercial Advertiser* 13 May 1840, p.2. 'Publican Licences'." … Alexander Johnston Noah's Ark…"
216 Copies of the originals of Alexander Johnston's licences to 'retail fermented and spirituous liquors' at the 'Queen Victoria' Patrick Plains, Camberwell, Fallbrook were cited at the Singleton Historical Society. They are dated: 20th June 1842; July 1843 to 30th June 1844;16th July 1844; and, 15th April 1845 (the licence costing, £30 p.a.). The licence for William's 'Queen Victoria Inn' was then transferred to James Durie on the 3rd December 1845, and the following year Alexander Johnston held the licence for the 'Thorton's Family Hotel' Muswellbrook, dated 25th June 1846. Alex and Mary ran the 'Thorton's Family Hotel' between 1845–1850. ('Alexander Johnston' https://www.jenwilletts). They then moved to Scone, and ran the 'St Albins Arms, Scone' from 1850–1870; renamed the 'Woolpack Inn' 1853 to 1863. (Scone Historical Society, 'Alexander and Mary Johnston (née Nowland) https://www.upperhunter.org/nowlandbrothers). Alex and Mary were amongst the first families in Scone. Alex died on the 21st May 1867 (62 yrs.) and Mary on the 24th December 1881, (73 yrs.), (Deaths register, BDM, NSW). They are buried in the same plot at the Scone Anglican Cemetery. https://www.findagrave 'Scone Anglican Cemetery, Alexander Johnston and Mary Johnston').
217 op. cit. NSW Land Registry Services, HLRV.

CHAPTER 12
Moving Further North as a Squatter

218 Campbell (1968), op. cit. p.20. Campbell cites William Nowland's licence for Boonanga in the year 1840.
219 ibid. Campbell (1856, p.63). In 1849, William Nowland renewed the licence for Boonanga [spelt Boonangar] 46,080 acres.
220 'Map of Indigenous Australia' op. cit. https://aiatsis.gov.au.
221 'Bigambul People' Wikipedia; Bigambul Native Title Aboriginal Corporation, The Bigambul People-Ancestry https://bigambul.org.au.
222 As detailed chronologically in William story the Mounted Police (formed in 1825), the Border Police (formed in 1836) and the Native Police (formed in 1848) engaged in 'despicable, immoral and unacceptable behaviour' against each Aboriginal

223 Nation they came across.

223 Ward's Mistake lies within the lands of the Bānbay People that covers some 6,000 sq kms of the Guyra region and includes present day Ben Lomond, Glencoe, Marowan, Mount Mitchell, Kookabookra and the Boyd River Valley. Bānbay Country adjoins Anēwan Country on the Tablelands and Gumbaynggirr Country on the coast. The Bānbay People are connected to the Anēwan People through a 'shared Totem' (the echidna) and the Gumbaynggirr People through 'language'. (McCrossin's Mill Museum 'Traditional Anaiwan People', 'Uralla Historical Society' https://uhs.org.au/anaiwan and Coffs Coast (2023), 'Yaam Gumbaynggirr Jagun – Here Is Gumbaynggirr Country, City of Coffs Harbour https://www.coffscoast.com.au.) It is assumed that the Bānbay, Anēwan and the Gumbaynggirr Nation came together 'at times' as a resistance force against the squatters on the 'southern and central' New England Tablelands.

224 William transferred this run temporarily to his two eldest sons in 1849, William jr. (17yrs.) Michael (15yrs.) (*Maitland & Hunter River General Advertiser,* 11 August 1849, p.4 'Ward's Mistake').

225 This view is based on research by Callum Clayton-Dixon on the Anēwan (that includes William's run 'Ward's Mistake), detailed soon in this story.

226 Who were these Native Police Callum Clayton-Dixon is commenting on? See Baker Bryce (15 Sept. 2020) 'FROM the VAULT – The Archaeology of the Queensland Native Mounted Police' My Police Museum https://mypolice.qld.gov.au. 'The Queensland Native Mounted Police operated for over 50 years, from 1849 until 1904 [and in other sources as late as 1960s and 70s]. It was organised along paramilitary lines, consisting of detachments of Aboriginal troopers led by white officers. It operated across the whole of Queensland and was explicitly constituted to protect the lives, livelihoods and property of settlers and to prevent (and punish) any Aboriginal aggression or resistance'. From another informative source, Korff Jens 'Massacres: The frontier violence that's hard to accept – Aboriginal people killing aboriginal people'. Creative Spirits. https://www.creativespirits.info/aboriginalculture/history. 'White officers [usually two] commanded groups of about six or seven Aboriginal trackers. The goal was simple to move Aboriginal people off the land the European colonists wanted, often by force and often violently, and to protect and support the settlers. [The Aboriginal trackers] were hired from areas far away from the regions where the killings occurred to avoid [any family ties] with their victims, and to prevent them from running away. Some young Aboriginal men volunteered to join possibly to survive or after losing their family and land to the advancing invasion…' Others were recruited at a young age after their family were killed by the advancing settlement, or after being captured and imprisoned, at an early date. Many of the victims of the 'massacres' instigated by the Native Police (that became increasingly prevalent as the settlers advanced into Queensland) were killed, burnt and their bodies disposed of to avoid any record of their deaths.

227 Clayton-Dixon Callum (27th August 2020), 'Where neither white man nor horse could follow – rough country & the Aboriginal resistance'. Medium Indigenous Research https://medium.com/@IndigenousDS.

228 Clayton-Dixon Callum (2020) *Surviving New England: A History of Aboriginal Resistance and Resilience Through the First Forty Years of the Colonial Apocalypse.* Armidale, New South Wales: Anaiwan Language Revival Program.

229 Reynolds Henry (2021), pp. 182-184. *Truth Telling History, Sovereignty and the Uluru Statement*, UNSW Press. Reynolds notes on p.182, 'The warriors were hard to find and were far too canny to be easily tracked down…the only answer seemed to be exact fierce retribution wherever white men or their property was threatened. … As is probably well known now, the instructions given to the force didn't change for forty years [1849 to 1889]. The white officers were directed to "disperse" any large gathering of Aboriginal people. There was never any definition of how many people represented a large gathering, or advice as to whether it mattered if there were men, women or children present, or even if the particular group had been involved in harassing the frontiersmen or their animals. It was an open secret that to disperse was to shoot at. The evidence is incontrovertible. The main purpose of the native police force was to kill Aboriginal people in sufficient numbers to terrorise them into submission and to prevent them from attacking the colonists and their property.'

230 Finney Eldershaw was part of the party that pursued the Bānbay to Darkie Point and their final horrific demise. (Eldershaw F. (1854), *Australia as it really is, in its life, scenery, & adventure : with the character, habits, and customs of its Aboriginal inhabitants, and the prospects and extent of its gold fields*, pp. 65-73, e-book, Trove https://trove.nla.gov.au). Eldershaw's account of 'the Aboriginal massacre at Darkie's Point' and the chapter that follows ('Aboriginal Australians') is not included here because of the 'bigoted and racist' way it is narrated.

231 The derogative title of Judith Wright's poem 'Niggers Leap' sits in stark contrast to her intent as demonstrated in the words of the poem. (See All Poetry, 'Niggers Leap, New England' by Judith Wright' https://allpoetry.com.) Commentary on Judith Wright commends her work, for example, King-Smith Sue (2007) 'Ancestral Echoes: Spectres of the Past in Judith Wright's Poetry', *Journal of the Association for the Study of Australian Literature,* pp.117-129. https://openjournals.test.library.sydney.edu.au. Judith Wright's book *The Cry for the Dead* also provides an account of the decimation of the Aboriginal people on the New England Plateau.

232 Coffs Trails (3 July 2021), 'Major Points, Darkie Point to Point Lookout, New England' https://coffstrails.com. Also see Callum Clayton-Dixon (2020) op. cit. pp.135-139. On these pages, Clayton-Dixon tabulates 42 accounts of '… frontier conflict across the southern half of the New England Tableland region' with each encounter referenced back to the relevant page/s in the book. Another informative online site is the Centre for 21st Century Humanities, University of Newcastle, Ryan Lyndall et al. (2025) 'Colonial Frontier Massacres in Australia, 1788–1930'. https://c21ch.newcastle.edu.au/colonialmassacres. This site provides an interactive map with descriptors of each massacre.

233 Clayton-Dixon Callum (2020), op. cit. Ch.15 'Against all Odds' pp.132-133.

234 Also see the many other accounts online, including 'The Nēwara Aboriginal Corporation' NITV (National Indigenous TV).

https://www.sbs.com.au.

235 New England High Country (1 July 2021), 'History and Heritage in New England High Country, Hamilton Collins Sempill' https://newenglandhighcountry.com.au.

CHAPTER 13
Why 'Ward's Mistake'?

236 William sr.'s eldest son William Nowland jr. was a bachelor for most of his life and moved permanently to 'Ward's Mistake' as an adult (1850 in the above article). William jr. (64 yrs.) married Anna Catherine Clarke (55 yrs.) in Glen Innes in 1896. (Marriages register, BDM, NSW' 'William Nowland and Anna C. Clarke, 1896'). As told, in the above newspaper article (Guyra Argus on the 31st March, 1949) by Mr. H. J. Clark (William jr.'s stepson) William jr. (75yrs.) died at Oban (Guyra) in 1907; with his death registered at Glen Innes. (Deaths register, BDM, NSW 'William Nowland, 1907').

CHAPTER 14
The Challenges and Tragedies in the 1840s

237 James' death is not registered in the Deaths register in BDM, NSW and no family notice was found in the newspapers in Trove. The date of James' death was found in a retrospective in the *Singleton Argus* 1948; detailed soon in this story.

238 John's birth is not registered. John died of epilepsy, aged 18, in 1860, giving John a birth year of 1842. See *Maitland Mercury and Hunter River General Advertiser*, 7th February 1860, p.1. 'Death Notices'.

239 Nowland Ian (1995), op. cit. p.267.

240 Edward's and James' remains were resumed from Rosedale and reinterred at Whittingham Cemetery Singleton (date unknown). www.findagrave 'Whittingham Cemetery Singleton 'Edward Nowland (1805–24 August 1842) and James Nowland (June 1838 – 10 November 1841)'.

241 As Nowland Ian (1995) op. cit. p.267 tells us, '[Christian] wrote many letters (in beautiful handwritten style) to the HBS and others until mid-1843'. William was appointed the next Superintendent for the HBS in the same year (1843); detailed later in the story.

242 Edwin Baldwin was born in the Hawkesbury in 1805, and was convicted of cattle rustling (stealing) in 1831, and sent to Norfolk Island to serve a seven-year sentence (1831–1838). Edwin returned to the Hawkesbury (c.1838) and found that his wife Alice Clark (who Edwin married in 1826, and left with three children to raise when he was sentenced) had had two more children, each from a different man. Initially, Edwin went back to his wife and later they parted ways. Edwin then coinhabited with Christian, and had three children with her between 1847 and 1850: William Baldwin (1847) Elizabeth Baldwin (1848) and Harriett Baldwin (1850). Christian and Edwin both died in Gunnedah: Edwin (1868, 63yrs) and Christian (1878, 67yrs). The births of their children are not registered in BDM, NSW. The above information was found in Nowland Ian (1995), op. cit. p.269; Australian Royalty, 'Edwin Baldwin and Christiana Farlow' https://australianroyalty.net.au and https://www.geni.com. ibid. Nowland Ian (1995) p.269, notes, 'Christian died on the 24 July 1878 from chronic bronchitis and gastritis. She was buried in the name of Baldwin in the Gunnedah Cemetery…; in an unmarked grave.' Today you can find Christian's grave under the name 'Christiana Farlow Baldwin' 17 Apr. 1811–24 Jul 1878 (67yrs)'. (See Findagrave, 'Gunnedah Historical Cemetery' https://www.findagrave.com).

243 Amongst others, *Maitland Mercury and Hunter River General Advertiser*, 7 January 1843, p.2, provides us with some commentary, '…A drought so unusually long…cattle and sheep reduced to mere skeletons.' While, The Australian 27 February 1843, p.3, notes, "…On the Namoi, there has been a fair show of rain, and the grass is as plentiful, …so the drought which has been so destructive to the flocks and herds on that river, may now be…at an end…"

244 The recommendations of the Molesworth Committee, Inquiry into 'Transportation', 1837 (the Molesworth Committee) for the cessation of the transportation of convicts to the colony was enacted by Governor Gipps and "the last convicts were assigned in 1841. "From 1840 to 1843 the number of assigned convicts shrank from 22,000 to slightly more than 4,000." (Hughes Turnbull Lucy (2008) 'The End of Transportation', Dictionary of Sydney https://dictionaryofsydney.org). Later in the decade (c.1846–1850), other convict laden transportation ships arrived in Sydney, this time with convicts who had served part of their sentences in England and agreed to come to Australia rather than serve any more time in England's overcrowded and notorious goals. These convicts were called 'exiles' and on arrival in the colony were granted conditional pardon or a ticket of leave. They were sent to Australia to provide a much-needed labour force, though a growing number of locals did not agree. The anti-transportation movement in NSW, and the majority of the general population objected to the arrival of the exiles because NSW was no longer a penal colony. (Museum of History, NSW 'Convict Transportation to NSW' https://mhnsw.au; *Goulburn Herald and County of Argyle Advertiser*, 21 September 1850, p.4).

245 McQuilton John (9th June 2019) 'Squatters and pastoralists: land, status and Indigenous dispossession.' Australia Explained https://australia-explained.com.au; Fitz-Gibbon Bryan and Gizycki Marianne (October 2001) 'The 1840s Depression'. Reserve Bank of Australia https://www.rba.gov.au/publications; Stuart Iain (1999), pp.62-65 PhD Thesis, 'Squatting Landscapes in South-Western Australia (1820–1895)', University of Sydney (e-copy available online).

246 William was called before the Courts himself, re the boundaries of Wallalla Station, in the early 1850s, and from that time on until 1860 the boundaries of William's Wallalla were challenged over and over again: as detailed later in the story.

CHAPTER 15
Governor Gipps' Proposed New Regulations For Land Tenure

247 Campbell (1868), op. cit. pp.36–66. Most of the hundreds of runs listed in this 'publication of licenced runs' were greater than 12,800 acres (20sq.mls.)

248 ibid. Campbell (1868) p.38, p.43, & p.64.

249 *Maitland Mercury and Hunter River General Advertiser*, 'Hunter River District News', 23 November 1844, p.2. Earlier in the same year, Henry was nominated, won the poll, and gained the position of a Councillor in the township of Muswellbrook. (*Maitland Mercury and Hunter River General Advertiser*, 'Hunter River District News', 18 May 1844, p.3.). Later in the decade, Henry is also noted as a Councillor for Muswellbrook, in the *NSW Government Gazette* in 1847 and again in 1849. (*NSW Government Gazette* 4 June 1847, p.601, and 11 May 1849, p.773). Henry also entertained the next Governor, Governor FitzRoy in 1847. (*Maitland Mercury and Hunter River General Advertiser*, 17 February 1847, p.4 'THE GOVERNOR'S VISIT TO THE HUNTER. MUSWELL BROOK'.

250 *NSW Government Gazette* 28 June 1845 (Issue No.52 [EXTRAORDINARY]) p.666, No.5. 'Dispatch from Sir George Gipps to Lord Stanley'. Also see Launceston Examiner 19 July 1845, p.7 'Sir George Gipps' Squatting Regulations'.

251 Pastoralists and squatters came together to challenge Governor Gipps and formed a united front against his proposals.

252 *The Australian Daily Journal*, April 11, 1844, p.2 'The Pastoral Association of New South Wales; The Australian, 4 May 1844, p.3 'Pastoral Association of NSW'

253 'A Legislative Council had been established by the New South Wales Act 1823, …[that] consisted of nominated members only. … [Then] the 1842 Act [in NSW] established a [larger] Legislative Council consisting of 36 members, 12 of whom, were appointed by the Queen (on the advice of Her Ministers) and the rest elected by the voters in New South Wales. Eligibility to vote was based upon ownership or occupation of property set at a high value.' Museum of Australian Democracy. *NSW Constitution Act 1842* (UK). Documenting Democracy https://www.foundingdocs.gov.au.

254 McCulloch Samuel Clyde (2006) 'Sir George Gipps (1791–1847)' Australian Dictionary of Biography, National Centre of Biography, Australian National University https://adb.anu.edu.au.

255 Hawkesbury Benevolent Society Papers, ML A626 p.485 cited in Carter H.R. (1974), *The Upper Mooki*, p.36.

CHAPTER 16
Camberwell in the Mid to Late 1840s

256 *Singleton Argus*, 5 March 1927, p.6, 'St. Clement's, Camberwell An Old Edifice'. '…on the actual age of St. Clement's little seems to be known…It is said Bishop Broughton preached there in 1844, which was before a floor was put in…'

257 There are several accounts in Trove of Henry and his provision of supplies and mail to the region and later further north into Queensland. Henry was contracted to convey official mail from 'Singleton, Muswellbrook and Scone by two horse mail cart three times a week for £96', in December 1845. (*Sydney Morning Herald*, 3rd December 1845, p.2 'CONVEYANCE OF POST OFFICE MAIL') and in 1847 "furnish supplies of provision and forage to Patrick Plains, Merton and Muswel Brook (sic), Scone and Murrurundi, Cassilis, Liverpool Plains and New England".' (*Maitland Mercury and General Advertiser*, 2nd December 1846, p.4, 'CONTRACTS FOR 1847'). Henry in another interesting account in June 1850 was contracted to 'deliver mail by horseback between Tamworth and Warialda, Warialda and Calendon, and, Tamworth and Wee Waa, once a week for £365'. (*Maitland Mercury and General Advertiser*, 26th January 1850, p.4 'CONVEYANCE OF POST OFFICE MAIL').

258 Births register, BDM, NSW 'Alexander Nowland, 1846'.

CHAPTER 17
Governor FitzRoy's Tenure

259 The Order in Council changed the regulation of Crown land 'beyond the boundaries of settlement'. This new regulation entitled the squatters (on application) to lease each of their runs for up to 14 years with the option for renewal and the first right of purchase (pre-emption) once the runs had been surveyed. The pressure of the squatters and pastoralists on the previous Governor (Gipps) through the Legislative Council had succeeded in obtaining some security for at least the next 14 years. Henry George Grey (3rd Earl Grey and Administrator in the Colonial Office) constructed the Order in Council (in consultation with George Gipps on his return to London). Then with the approval of the British Parliament the Order was implemented by Governor FitzRoy on the 9th March 1847; though it was never fully operationalised because of the detraction and demands of the Gold Rush in the 1850s and the associated flood of emigrants into the colony. (Ward, John M. 'Grey, Henry George (1802–1894)', Australian Dictionary of Biography, National Centre of Biography, Australian National University https://adb.anu.edu.au.) Squatters like William Nowland in principle now had a more certainty, and a secure hold on their runs; at least for the next 14 years.

260 Henry Reynold (2021), op. cit. pp.182–184.

261 Map of Indigenous Australia's AIATSIS, op. cit.

262 Henry Reynold (2021), op. cit. provides an informative and comprehensive account of the devastation. The bigoted attitudes of the day are also portrayed in several articles in Trove under the keywords 'Native Police' including the following: the first

by Frederick Walker (Commandant of the Native Police) outlining his justification for the Native Police, printed in the *Sydney Morning Herald*, 16 June 1852, p.1 and entitled 'Native Police copy of a Letter from the Commandant Of the Native Police to the Colonial Secretary'; the second, an appalling account of murdering Aboriginal people in *The Queenslander*, 14 September 1867, p.7 'The Native Police'; and, lastly in 1880 in *The Brisbane Courier* 14 July 1880, p.5, 'Blacks and Native Police'.

263   *Sydney Morning Herald*, 8th December 1847, p.3, 'Government Gazette, Tuesday December 3, 1847 Liverpool Plains Proclamation'.

264   Births register, BDM, NSW, 'George Nowland 1847'. George (just like his brothers) was probably born at home. Call the mid-wife was the order of the day.

265   *Government Gazette*, 7th August 1849, p.1164. 'Transfer of Runs'; *Sydney Morning Herald*, 7 November 1849, p.3, 'Government Gazette Supplementary List of Claims to Leases of Crown Lands Beyond the Settled Districts'. Though William jr. and Michael were old enough to have a lease in their own name the reason for transferring the leases had more to do with William sr.'s insolvency which becomes apparent in the next chapter.

266   As told earlier, William jr. lived (as a bachelor) at Ward's Mistake for most of his life and married Anna Catherine Clarke (a widow) 11 years before he died. His brother Michael Nowland married Martha Squire in Armidale in 1862 (Marriages register, BDM, NSW). Michael and Martha had 10 children between 1862 and 1883: Clara (1862); William (1864–1865); Amy (1865); Laura (1869); Maud (1871); Minnie (1875); Susan (1875); Mildred (1876); Beatrice (1879); and, Robert (1883). The first three children were registered at Armidale, and the rest of the children at Murrurundi. (Births register, BDM, NSW). Based on the location of the birth of each of their children, Michael and Martha lived on the New England Tablelands, and most likely at Ward's Mistake, until c. 1865, and then moved to the Parish of Borambil adjacent to Warrah Ridge. Michael died (aged 52 yrs.) in Jericho Queensland on the 9th April 1886 (Family Notice, *Brisbane Courier*, 16th April, 1886, p.1.) Why Michael was in Jerricho Queensland is unknown.

267   Extract from Wilson Miller James (2005) 'Conflict in the Valley: The Triumph of the Wonnarua' Paper presented at the Australian Association of Research and Education (AARE) Annual Conference, Parramatta. The full paper is available at https://www.aare.edu.au/publications/2005/.

268   Reconciliation Trail – 'Moree to Myall Creek – Kamilaroi Country'. op. cit. https://docslib.org.

269   'Male initiation is a rite of ceremonial passage from childhood to adulthood and was a highly celebrated process by which surrounding tribes and clans culminate together to celebrate the next phase of life for a young man. Celebrations often lasted weeks and were conducted at sacred sites called "Bora's" within the Kamilaroi nation. The term "Bora" is also referred to as the actual ceremony and can be used intermingled between the 'place' of ceremony or the actual ceremony itself.' Carpenter Michelle (2011) Kamilaroi – A Nation's Identity – Ceremonies https://Kamilaroianationsidentity.weebly.com/ceremonies

270   'Terry Hie Hie Aboriginal Area was once an important ceremonial and gathering place for the traditional Gamilaraay (Kamilaroi, Gomeroi, Gamileroi, Gamileraay) Aboriginal people. Today it's a tranquil spot, scattered in sections around the small town, which is also called Terry Hie Hie.' (NSW National Parks, 'Terry Hie Hie Aboriginal Area NSW Government https://www.nationalparks.nsw.gov.au

271   Ryan Lyndall, et al. (2025), 'Colonial Frontier Massacres in Australia, 1788–1930', Centre for 21st Century Humanities, University of Newcastle https://c21ch.newcastle.edu.au/colonialmassacres. This online interactive tool identifies known massacres of Aboriginal people on the New England Tablelands, that include but are not limited to, Darkie Point, Elbor, Paddy's Lands, New England and Deepwater Station, New England.

272   Clayton-Dixon Callum (2020), op. cit. pp. 110–130.

273   ibid.

274   The Australian Institute of Aboriginal and Torres Strait Islander Studies (AIATSIS), Missions, stations and reserves', https://aiatsis.gov.au.

275   'In 1883, the Aboriginal Protection Board was established to manage the reserves and control the lives of 9,000 Indigenous people estimated to be in NSW at that time. There were two types of reserves. "Managed reserves", also called stations, were usually run by a manager and provided education, rations, and housing. "Unmanaged reserves" were under police control and only provided rations. Most of the reserves were quite small, with scattered housing. As the settlement grew, reserves were created across NSW and [Aboriginal] people were relocated to them.' (Australian Human Rights Commission, 'Bringing them home report 8. History – New South Wales and the Australian Capital Territory' https://humanrights.gov.au)

CHAPTER 18
William Enters the 1850s Insolvent

276   *Sydney Morning Herald*, 9 April 1849, p.2 'Publican Licences'.

277   NSW Government Gazette, 10 February 1846, Issue No. 12, p.203. 'In the Will of Patrick White'.

278   The west side of Wallalla Station was registered as 'west (Walhallow)' and 'extended for 8 miles along the Mooki River with a depth of about 8 miles' (Government Gazette Notices – New South Wales Gazette, 31 October 1849, p.1621).

279   My interpretation here is John Booth is accusing William Nowland of butchering Patrick White's cattle for meat based on the two statements 'conversion' and 'sticking to the cattle', with the latter phrase slang for 'bleeding the cattle for the purpose of slaughter'. Britannica, 'Livestock slaughter procedures-Slaughter' https://britannica.com.

280 At the time of the hearing, the land on which William had his cattle may have also been in drought as told in the Bathurst Free Press, 19 October 1850, p.3 '…A correspondent from Walhallow, Liverpool Plains, [Messrs. Loder] writes … "I do not believe Liverpool Plains were ever in a worse state for want of rain than at present. The Mooki River is studded with dead cattle to the amount of hundreds, and they are now beginning to die all over the Plains; I have been in the neighbourhood for the last six years, and have seen nothing like the present state of things. Maitland Mercury".'

281 The summary of each of the court hearings (several sessions, over two and half years) is available in Trove under the keywords *Booth v Nowland* (dates, November 1949 to June 1852).

282 Boonanga is not included because it is assumed by this time the improvements to Boonanga had been sold by William and the licence transferred to another.

283 The *Booth v Nowland* case has bemused me for some time especially given that William is described in the latter Court hearings as 'William Nowland late of Singleton now of Windsor'. Obviously, these descriptors do not describe 'Our William of Camberwell'. After searching further, and discovering William's relocation from time to time to Windsor during these years (due to the needs of family, discussed in the next chapter) I decided this was 'our' William who obviously didn't want 'William Nowland of Camberwell' all over the papers: thus, the camouflage. In the end William came out largely unscathed (see Trove *Booth v Nowland* 1849–1852).

284 The newspapers reported on Henry's various contractors "Henry Nowland – Singleton, Muswell Brook, and Scone, by three horse coach, three times a week, and from and to Scone and Murrurundi, twice a week for £180.", (*Maitland Mercury and Hunter River General Advertiser*, 26 Jan 1850, p.4.); "Henry Nowland, by four horse coach, licensed to carry five passengers, from and to Singleton, Muswellbrook, and Scone, twice a week, for £320. And 15s. per seat for all places required by Government, including gold and escort. Henry Nowland by four-horse coach, licensed to carry five passengers, from and to Scone, Murrurundi, and Tamworth, twice a week, for £700. And £1 16s. per seat for all places required by the Government, including gold and escort."; (Government Gazette Tenders And Contracts – *New South Wales Government Gazette*, 21 December 1852, p.1840, "CONVEYANCE OF POST OFFICE MAIL"); "From and to East and West Maitland, Lochinvar, and Singleton, daily; and Singleton, Muswellbrook, and Scone, and Scone and Murrurundi three times a week, £1400, Henry Nowland." (*Sydney Morning Herald* – 20 December 1856, p.5 "CONVEYANCE OF POST OFFICE MAIL').

285 Elizabeth S. Parkinson (1984), Historical Feature: Henry Nowland – The Forgotten Pioneer of Muswellbrook', *Muswellbrook Chronicle*, August 24, 1984, p.9.

286 Births register, BDM, NSW, 'Alfred Nowland 1851'.

CHAPTER 19
William, the Courts and Wallala Station

287 The role and function of the Legislative Council changed significantly during the 1850s. 'Eligibility to vote [for members of the Legislative Council] was extended to men (like William) who owned land worth at least £100 or rented or leased property for £10 or more a year [with a secret ballot introduced in 1855, and universal male suffrage for men 21 years and over in 1859].' (National Museum of Australia (4 Oct 2022) 'Secret Ballot Introduced' https://www.nma.gov.au.) At the beginning of the 1850s, the Legislative Council was an advisory body to the Governor (Governor FitzRoy). In 1853, a 'select committee' chaired by William Wentworth began drawing up a constitution for 'responsible self-government' (achieved on 16th July 1855) with two houses of parliament: the Lower House (a fully elected Legislative Assembly with 54 members) and the Upper House (Legislative Council with 21 members, with each member initially given a five-year appointment, followed in the next term by appointment for life). The original members of the Legislative Council met in the Surgeon's wing of the Sydney 'Rum Hospital' in 1829 (todays colonnaded façade of the NSW Parliament House, Macquarie Street, Sydney) then a larger meeting chamber was built in 1843, and the present-day Parliament House extended once again, to accommodate a new chamber for the Upper House, circa 1855. (Parliament of New South Wales, '1843 to 1855 – Towards Responsible Government https://www.parliament.nsw.gov.au.)

288 The geographical area that encompassed the Port Phillip District (1802–1851) and the township of Melbourne (est. 1835), and renamed the 'colony of Victoria' has not changed. Today it encompasses the same geographical area and is known as the State of Victoria.

289 'John Eales (1799–1871) … grazier and pioneer pastoralist [arrived in NSW in October 1822] and was given a [land] grant of 2,100 acres (850 ha) about four miles (6.4km) from Morpeth [in the Hunter] … in the 1830s he acquired by purchase [based on improvements e.g., pasture and stock] and squattage, a number of runs on the Liverpool Plains…'. [Including Walhollow, a run adjacent to and bordering William Nowland's Wallala Station]. (Guilford Elizabeth (2006) op. cit. https://adb.anu.edu.au.)

290 William drove John Eales' sheep to the Mooki pound and impounded them there because William believed the sheep were grazing on his Wallala Station and depasturing the grass that he used for his stock. It was common practice for those who found straying stock or horses to place them in the local pound, and then advertise in the local paper stating where they were, and asking for a fee (usually reasonable) for the time and effort they had taken in rounding up the trespassing stock and taking them to the pound (though it could also be used as a ploy).

291 The initial reason for this, and other disputes may be because the runs overlapped. In Campbell (1868) op. cit. p.20 the entry in the *Government Gazette* on 19 February 1840, reads 'Eales John, "Walhollow" etc. (five others)'. Then, in the

citation of the *Government Gazette* 1848 on p.40, no.64 'Eales John, "Walhollow" 50,000 acres' and for William Nowland (on a supplementary list for the Liverpool Plains) on p.42, no.182 'Nowland William, Wallalla (Walhollow), 87,040 acres'. In investigating further two questions emerged. (1) Were the boundaries of these two runs ever properly surveyed by the Commissioner? (There were lots of changes in the Commissioner for the Liverpool Plains in the 1840s and this may have caused confusion about who had laid claim to what). See Research Data Australia, 'AGY-3497 – Commissioners of Crown Lands for the Liverpool Plains' op. cit. https://researchhdata.edu.au. (2) Were the boundaries between the two runs (Walhallow and Wallalla) in part the same in the survey of each one and this anomaly was never discovered because each station was surveyed and registered (for a licence) at a different time with the survey for each never cross-referenced? Of note here is the 1848 account in the *Government Gazette*, of both stations where Wallalla Station and Walhollow Station shared the name 'Walhollow'. Probably, all very ad-hoc.

292 Edmund Uhr drove a flock of Richard Jones' sheep (300-400) up the Bulga Track into the Hunter, and onto the Liverpool Plains adjacent to the Mooki River in 1835, where he claimed 150,000 acres (a government grant) for Richard Jones (1786–1852; merchant and pastoralist). Uhr's claim included part of William Nowland's Wallalla Station (1839), Samuel Clift's Doona Station (1837), and part of the HBS Breeza Station (circa 1835). (ibid. Campbell (1968); Marr David (2023), 'Killing for Country' pp. 43-49; Rodgers Peter (October 4, 2023), 'Shinning more light on Australia's brutal colonial past'https://www.peter-rodgers.com.au; The Maitland Mercury and Hunter General Advertiser 5 January 1860, p.3 'Nowland vs Humphrey and Another'; all the other summaries of the court hearings in the newspapers of the time where Edmund Uhr is mentioned in relation to Wallalla Station found in Trove (too many to mention here). All found under the keywords 'Samuel Clift, William Nowland, Edward Nowland, and the Hawkesbury Benevolent Society' between the dates '1832–1860'. In the hearings, Uhr is mentioned in the context of 'past possession' and the commentary predate when William first had a licence for Wallalla (circa 1839). William Nowland was not the only squatter confronted with disputed boundaries. Many other Court hearings can be found in Trove from the 1850s–60s, that tell of similar experiences for other squatters: disputed boundaries, the ad hoc way in which the stations evolved, and the contradictory evidence of the witnesses for the plaintiff and defendant when trying to determine who had a licence/land grant and who was the trespasser. The court cases are a quagmire of half-truths and injustices.

293 West (Walhollow) was the area in dispute and most likely overlapped with John Eales' registration of 'Walhollow'.

294 By the time Reuss & Browne's map was draw (1860) Wallalla Station was no longer in existence and Walhallow was on both sides of the Mooki River; William sr. most likely sold Wallalla (c.1860) to John Eales (detailed in chapter 21).

295 Whether William's mother Elizabeth still lived with her second husband Peter Vaughan is unknown.

296 'Elizabeth Richards Nowland' 'Wilberforce Cemetery (1775–1852). https://findagrave.com.

297 Births register, BDM NSW 'Henry Nowland 1853.'

298 Charles Humphrey was the superintendent for John Eales at Walhollow. (Willetts Jan, 'Charles Humphrey' op. cit. https://www.freesettlerorfelon.com); Walsh Brian (2020) op. cit. Ch. 6, 'Beyond the boundaries – no more violence than necessary'. https://patersonhistory.org.au.

299 This is all so confusing. The names of the stations changed depending on who was writing in the newspaper. In most of the summaries of the court hearings the name Walhalla station [instead of Walhallow] is used and this may be because the summary is based on verbal accounts and mistakes were made because the names were very similar. The area denoted and in dispute was always near the river or on the western side of the Mooki River i.e. the western side of Wallalla Station and the contested part of William's Station.

300 Richard Jones (1816–1892) was a journalist, company director and later a politician. In 1843 Richard Jones established the *Maitland Mercury and Hunter River General Advertiser* [William Nowland's local paper]. He was elected to the Legislative Assembly in 1856 and retained his position representing Durham until 1859 (when the County of Durham was replaced with the seat of Hunter). He then represented 'Hunter' until the end of 1860. ('Parliament of NSW, 'Richard Jones 1816–1892' https://www.parliament.nsw.gov.au ; Wikipedia 'Richard Jones (1816–1892)'. This Richard Jones is the second Richard Jones in William's story. The first Richard Jones (1786–1852, introduced earlier) was a merchant and pastoralist who employed Edmund Uhr to take sheep up onto the Liverpool Plains in the vicinity of Walhallow and Wallalla Station.

CHAPTER 20
Camberwell in the 1850s

301 'CAMBERWELL RACES. Glennies Creek, Camberwell, was the scene of much real sport on Wednesday last; and being but a small place, with but few inhabitants, we must give them some praise for the loyalty so "leal [loyal and honest duty to the monarch] and true", evinced by them on the occasion of the Queen's birthday. The "Queen Victoria" (the inn we mean) was gaily decorated with union jacks. The interior was ornamented with neatness'. (*Maitland Mercury and Hunter River General Advertiser*, 31 May 1854, p.2.).

302 School was voluntary and for those who attended, most had left by the age of 12 or 13. (Schoolhouse Museum of Public Education, 'Early School Days 1870s to 1920s' https://www.schoolhousemuseum.org.au)

303 Noble Lillian M. (date unknown, most likely, 1990s), op. cit. p.48.

304 This account of the Camberwell Schoolhouse moving from a one room Church of England Schoolhouse to a National School is no longer available on-line. The source can be found in the references for the following article (available on-line) The Scone Historical Society 'William Nowland 1804–1884' under the heading 'Camberwell', reference 8' 'Heritas

305 Architecture, Appendix 14, 'European Heritage Assessment, Ashton Coal Project, Camberwell, NSW p.12. 2009. www.scone.com.au When I first wrote this part of William's story during COVID in 2020 this reference was still available on-line.

305 The new schoolhouse on William Nowland's allotments was an 'iron house'. (*Maitland Mercury and Hunter River General Advertiser*, 29th July 1854, p.2. '…an iron house is shortly expected for their Better Location). Such iron houses became popular in the 1850s as the colonies population grew exponentially with the gold rush. These iron houses were constructed in Britain, then dismantled, every component labelled then packed in crates and shipped to their destination, unpacked and reassembled in the new location. ('Portable Iron Houses' https://www.nationaltrust.org.au. Images available online).

306 Also see *Maitland Mercury and Hunter River General Advertiser* 11th March, 1854, p.4.

307 All local government schools gained the word 'National' in the title of their school, post new 1848. For Camberwell, circa 1854. This new title denoted the school's adhered to the colonial government's new education policy aimed at improving and standardizing the type of education offered in local schools. ('History of New South Wales Government Schools' https://education.nsw.gov.au.) This NSW National School System (which Church school were required to adhere to, to gain a government subsidy) was modeled on the Irish National School System. ('National Schools https://education.nsw.gov.au). How interesting.

308 Museums of History New South Wales 'School Record Guide' https://mhnsw.au; NSW Government – Education NSW (6 Mar 2023), 'Early History-NSW Education' 'History of NSW Government Schools Department https://education.nsw.gov.au.

309 Governor Denison was also appointed as the Governor General of the 'Australian Colonies' for the purpose of enabling co-operation between the newly emerging states: New South Wales, Van Diemen's Land, Victoria, South Australia, and Western Australia. During Denison's tenure: the first railway line from Sydney to Parramatta (present day Granville) was completed on the 26 September 1855; responsible government (elected members of parliament) was introduced into 'the colony of NSW (the first ministry sworn in, in June 1856 and the Constitution Act passed into law on the 16th July 1856); and NSW and Queensland were separated into two different states on the 6th June 1859 with Denison being instrumental in moving the border between NSW and Qld further north and well beyond the initial purposed border of the New England Tablelands, to where it is positioned today. It is interesting to note Denison also changed the small rocky island in the harbour to a fortification (given the Crimean War 1853–56) and renamed the outcrop after himself, present day Fort Denison. (Currey C.H. (2006) 'Sir William Thomas Denison (1804–1871)' Australian Dictionary of Biography https://adb.anu.edu.au; Wikipedia 'William Denison')

310 Deaths register, BDM, NSW. 'Michael Nowland, 1854' [Michael's parents are not registered in his death notice in BDM; the death notice reads 'Michael jr.'s age, 61']; Wilberforce Cemetery 'Michael Nowland (1794–1854)' https://www.findagrave.com.au. Michael jr. (William's brother) is buried next to his parents and sister Ann: Michael jr. Row 9, Plot 8; Elizabeth Richards Nowland Row 9, Plot 9; Ann Nowland Row 9, Plot 10 and Michael Nowland sr. Row 9, Plot 11. The gravestones were restored for the 1988 'Australian Bicentenary' that marked 200 years since the arrival of the First Fleet in 1788. As told earlier, Michael and Elizabeth Richards Nowland were both convicts and arrived on the Second Fleet on the 28 June, and 6 June 1790, respectively.

311 Another Family Notice in *Maitland Mercury and Hunter River General Advertiser* – 15 November 1854, p.3. read: "Deaths. At Wilberforce, on the 27th of October last, from dropsy [edema], Michael Nowland, aged 60 years [61]. He died in his home of upwards of 50 years, and a numerous connection of kindred and friends will long feel their loss.

312 Most likely, William jr. (23), Michael (21) and maybe at times, Robert (19) and Charles (15).

CHAPTER 21
William Back in Court

313 This person could be, Arthur Dight (1819–1895) a pastoralist and later (in 1869) a politician and the son of Sir John Dight. (Obituaries Australia, 'Arthur Dight (1819–1895)' National Centre of Biography, Australian National University https://oa.anu.edu.au/obituary). William White was 'another brother' of Patrick White. As detailed earlier, Patrick White (and James White by default) had cattle on Wallalla Station, in the *Booth v Nowland* hearing held in the Supreme Court on the 3rd August 1849. Now (June 1855), William was called to court once more on the matter of the third brother's cattle (William White's cattle) and the amount of cattle William White had on Wallalla Station.

314 The 'alleged delinquencies' are unknown and assumed to be related to William's ads warning others who trespassed on the HBS's Mooki Station. If their stock strayed onto Mooki Station, William would round them up, take them to the pound and refuse to release them until he received payment for the damage the stock had caused to the Station's pasture.

315 Richard Reynolds a fellow pastoralist and (former squatter) had a station that adjourned the HBS's Mooki Station.

316 Richard Reynolds (as told earlier) a fellow pastoralist and former squatter whose land adjoined Mooki Station, died in 1860. (Deaths register, BDM, NSW 'Richard Reynolds 1860'). After Richard Reynolds death, his wife (Eliza Reynolds) was given the larger portion of Mooki Station (through arbitration, in 1862) when the Station was divided between the HBS and Mrs. Reynolds. (*Sydney Morning Herald*, 28 November 1862, p.8. 'THE MOOKI RUN'). The acquisition of this land by Eliza Reynolds becomes relevant to William's story in 1857 when rumours about Richard Reynolds intention to claim parts of Mooki Station for himself emerges from the data.

317 It is unknown why Frederick Scott questioned William credibility as a Witness. Though, most likely, it was because William was the Superintendent of Mooki Station and on these grounds he was seen by Frederick Scott to have a vested interest in the Station and therefore, could not be an independent witness.

318 Mixed possession is assumed to refer to the verbal agreement between William and the HBS for William to graze his cattle on Mooki Station.
319 Richard Jones (1816–1892) a journalist, company director and politician.
320 William denoted as a grazier in this account.
321 Sir John Hay (1816–1892) was a pastoralist, politician and elected to the Legislative Assembly representing the Murrumbidgee in 1856. Martin A.W. (2006) 'Sir John Hay (1816–1892)' Australian Dictionary of Biography https://adb.anu.edu.au.
322 Rumoured at this stage and shown to be true in 1862 when Reynolds' widow Eliza Reynolds was given (through arbitration) a large portion of Mooki Station.
323 Andrew Loder (1825–1900) was a member of the Legislative Assembly of New South Wales and a pastoralist on the Liverpool Plains. Loder 'with his brother was the first settler at Quirindi in 1832 and held property near Murrurundi'. Loder's station was near the HBS's Mooki River Station. (Martin A.W. and Wardle P. (1959) p.130, 'Members of the Legislative Assembly of New South Wales 1856–1901 – Biographical Notes', Australian National University, Open Research Library https://openresearch-repository.anu.edu.au).
324 William Walker (1828–1908) was a solicitor and the secretary of the Hawkesbury Benevolent Society (1861–77), and later a Member of NSW Legislative Assembly (1860-69) and the Legislative Council (1887). (Crew Vernon, (2006) 'William Walker (1828–1908)' Australian Dictionary of Biography https://adb.anu.edu.au). As detailed earlier, William Walker was also the author (1887) of 'History of the Benevolent Society'.
325 One must be measured when reviewing these accounts because they are from one person's perspective filtered by their views.
326 This last statement made by John Reynolds reinforces the view that the boundaries of the runs were ad-hoc, unclear and based on interpretation.
327 'Store cattle' are cattle that still needed fattening and not ready for slaughter. (Cows i.e. (9 Dec 2021) 'Understanding cattle terminology' https://www.cow.ie).
328 'Samuel Clift sr. (1791–1862) was one of 170 convicts transported on the ship Neptune in December 1817. He was convicted at Northampton Assizes "for a term of 14 years, with four others, of having in their possession, without lawful excuse, forged bank notes…" Samuel Clift married Ann Duffy (1802–1867) in 1824.' (Australian Royalty' https://australianroyalty.com.au). 'Samuel Clift was granted his "Ticket of Leave" in 1822 and his "Certificate of Freedom" in 1831… He also received his first land grant "by virtue of being married to a respectable female", Ann was the daughter of a crown surveyor…' (Clift Brett (26 June 2014), 'Presentation to the Planning Assessment Commission Hearing Watermark Coal Project Gunnedah LGA' https://www.ipcn.nsw.gov.au). 'In the mid-1830s, he [Samuel Clift] began acquiring runs on the Liverpool Plains: Doona, Mooki River, Breeza, Weia Weia Creek. The consolidated area of these runs totalled 198,300 acres (80,250 ha) and been known as Breeza Station. It stretched from Spring Ridge and Goran Lake in the west to the ranges east of Werris Creek. Samuel Clift did not live on his land on the plains but generally employed assigned or former convicts to establish and work his runs.' (Clift Tony (30 Oct. 2021), 'A Conspicuous Object. The Maitland Hospital. Supporting those Less Fortunate' https://aconspiciousobject.com.au/stories).
329 As told earlier, no map has been found that shows the location of William's Wallalla Station. The locality of the Station can only be inferred based on the descriptors in the Government Gazette and the information gained from the court hearings re Wallalla's boundaries. William had a licence for Wallalla Station from 1840 to circa 1860 yet it is nowhere to be seen on Reuss & Browne map. Wallalla was consumed by Walhallow when Eales bought the improvements to the Station. While all William's other runs (past and present) can be readily found on Reuss & Browne's map because the names of the other runs were never changed by the new owner.
330 Samuel Clift, an emancipated convict with a land grant and a father-in-law who was a crown surveyor, and William Nowland (who probably spoke with a hint of an Irish ascent) a squatter, a first-generation colonial Australian and the child of emancipated convict parents.
331 The Banco Court was located in King St. Sydney (next to the present-day St. James Anglican Church) and predates the present historical Banco Courthouse built in 1895–1896 and located in St James Rd. Sydney. (Betteridge Margaret (2011), 'King St. Courts', State Library of NSW, Dictionary of Sydney https://www.dictionaryofsydney.org; Wikipedia, 'Banco Court (Supreme Court of New South Wales)' https://en.m.wikipedia.org)
332 Charles Humphrey was the superintendent for John Eales at Walhollow Station. (Willetts Jen, 'Charles Humphrey' https://www.freesettlerorfelon.com).
333 Who this probably was and why, will become apparent shortly in the chapter.
334 *Government Gazette* Private Notices, p.1728, 22 October 1858; *Northern Times*, 13th Oct and the 27th October 1858.
335 Rosedale was the family homestead and most likely had all the common means of subsistence: the vegetable garden, the orchard, the grain crops, dairy cows, beef cattle for eating, along with the sheep, and of course, the pigs.
336 According to McLaughlin John Kennedy (2006), 'Sir John Nodes Dickinson (1806–1882)', Australian Dictionary of Biography https://adb.anu.edu.au, 'As a judge of the Supreme Court Dickinson carried out his duties ably and conscientiously, sometimes under difficulties; he once complained that "the necessity of having to consider one day a point of Common Law, another day a point of Insolvency, and another day an Equity suit has been to me a source of the utmost distraction". Yet he was highly competent, and his demeanour and impartiality were universally respected and admired. Dowling, who described him as "an upright, conscientious, learned Judge", recalled that Dickinson exercised great control over his court and was "exceedingly courteous" to the Bar. Dickinson never became a figure of controversy, and was the more acceptable in presiding at the hearing of several contentious cases of outstanding public interest.'

337   From the mid-1830s on, free settlers came to NSW in significant numbers either through the Bounty Scheme (1835–1841); assisted immigration (1837–1850); the gold rush (since 1851); or, through the migration of wealthy young adventurers from aristocratic families (mainly from England, post 1840s) who were ardent to gain land, money and position, and the establishment of a new family dynasty in a new land. The number of free settlers increased most notably with the gold rush (post 1851) and the introduction of responsible government in NSW in 1855. Two new classes of citizen entered the colony of NSW: firstly, well off and wealthy settlers (such as John Eales) who followed the AACo lead and were also given land grants by the Colonial Government to graze sheep and assist in the expansion of the merino sheep industry, and secondly, free settlers with little cash who required small sustainable allotments for their livelihood and contribution to the social fabric of NSW. The land these two groups required was presently occupied by the squatters and there was too little alternative land left to cater for their needs. The squatters had progressively positioned themselves on a vast expansion of land from the time they had first ventured outside the official boundaries of settlement (circa 1826, for William Nowland and his fellow squatters on the Liverpool Plains) and something needed to change. The Robertson Act (1861) targeted this problem and facilitated the carving up of the squatters' massive stations; detailed in chapter 23.

338   There are several accounts in Trove of William's court cases during this time, including and not limited to: *Maitland Mercury and Hunter River General Advertiser*, 21 December 1858, p.3; *Nowland v Clift*; *Sydney Morning Herald*, 27 May 1859, p.3 *Nowland v Humphrey*; and the *Empire*, Monday 1 August 1859, p.5 *Nowland v Humphrey*.

339   There is example after example in Trove under the keywords 'free selection' of the discussion and debate in the press, such as *Maitland Mercury and Hunter River General Advertiser*, 23 April 1859, p.2; *Sydney Morning Herald*, 20 April 1859, p.4; *Maitland Mercury and Hunter River General Advertiser*, 11 June 1859, p.7; *Illawarra Mercury*, 7 July 1859, p.4; and *Armidale Express and New England General Advertiser*, 13 August 1859, p.2.

340   The Land League (a political lobby group on land issues) was formed in NSW after the introduction of Responsible Government in 1855. The league supported Robertson's proposed new land tenure policy of self-selection (detailed soon). The League's view of the squatters were expressed in a public meeting on the 3rd December 1857 at 'Wynard Square' Sydney and include the following remarks: 'The speaker then proceeded to advert to the squatters as men who had retarded the progress of the colony, without effecting any good whatever, and as a class of men who ought to be opposed and depressed in every possible manner.' (*Sydney Morning Herald*, 24 December 1857, p.4 'The Land League'). The situation now for the squatters was very different (given the changing demographic of the colony) to when the squatters and pastoralists came together to defend their runs under Gipps in the 1840s.

341   In June 1859, Governor Denison determined the border between the colony of NSW and the colony of Qld would be located where the present-day border between NSW and Qld is today, with survey work to start in the early 1860s. (Dr Gerard Carney (10th April 2013), 'The Story Behind the Land Borders of the Australian States', Public Lecture Series, High Court of Australia, www.cdn.hcourt.gov.au).

342   John Robertson was appointed the Secretary for Lands in the newly formed Department of Lands on the 30 September 1859 and he was 'charged with managing the alienation [sale] and occupation of all Crown Land' ('AGY-1114 Departments of Lands https://researchdata.edu.au/agy-1114-department-lands-i/164955).

343   'In 1850 William Nowland Junior took over the management of the property and it remained in his possession until it was sold to Messrs. White brothers in 1900–1901…". (*Guyra Argus*, 31 March 1949, p.4 'How Ward's Mistake was named. More Light on the Problem').

344   These retrospectives were the only way of establishing who was in possession of what.

345   William is trying to gain recognition of the boundaries of Wallalla Station and the station is referred to in this summary of the case as Walhalla which could be interpreted as Walhallow. All very confusing. Did William call the west side of Wallalla, Walhallow or is the writer of the article misspelling Wallalla?

346   As told earlier, the land on the Liverpool Plains and beyond had been denoted as Crown Land by Gipps in 1836, and from that time on, you needed a license as a squatter. On application, you could sell the improvements to the land (hut, pasture, stock) etc. to another, as part of the transfer of the licence to them.

347   According to the Government Gazette, detailed earlier, William did have a licence for this run and placed it in his and William jr. name in November 1849.

348   William employed indentured convict labour until the early 1840s, when the transportation of convicts to the colony stopped and this form of labour ceased. By 1855, William and his 'older sons' managed Wallalla Station themselves.

349   Despite the pressure, William stood his ground. On the day of the judgment of the Court (5th January 1860) the following ad from William appeared in *Maitland Mercury and Hunter River General Advertiser*, p.1:
'TWENTY-FIVE POUNDS REWARD. IT has been represented to me that a man was seen driving a lot of FAT CATTLE, from Mooki River, Liverpool Plains, towards the Hanging Rock Diggings, with SEVERAL OF MINE amongst them, branded as follows: WN rump, N ribs near side, W rump, N ribs W R N offside, W/N rump, N ribs near side, R/N near rump, N ribs. The above Reward will be paid to any Person or Persons on conviction of the Thief or Thieves. I have sold no cattle in Liverpool Plains or New England Districts. WILLIAM NOWLAND, Fallbrook, 3rd January, 1860.'

CHAPTER 22
More Family Tragedy Followed by Grit and Determination

350 'John Nowland (1841–1860)' Camberwell Anglican Church Cemetery. https://www.findagrave.com. John's death isn't registered in the online Deaths registry, BDM, NSW.

351 It is not known when William introduced sheep onto his pastures.

352 What is the meaning of 'Let on the Halves'? 'To let' in the terminology of real estate means 'available to rent'. In combining these two phrases ('let on halves' and 'available for rent') William appears to be renting the sheep for half price with presumably 'the renter' able to harvest and sell the wool.

353 It was common custom to name a child after a dead relative; family forenames were handed down from one generation to the next. (Przecha Donna, 'Given Names and Naming Patterns' op. cit.)

354 Based on the registration of the birth of their children, Chas and Annie lived in Armidale (in 1862) and settled in Warrah Ridge (in 1864); a small farming community near the emerging town of Quirindi. Chas and Annie had 12 surviving children between 1860–1878: twins John James and Ada (1862); Mina (1864); Walter (1865); Annie (1866); Eveline (1868); Lilian (1869): Maria (1871); Mabel (1872); Charles (1874); Alexander (1875); Ernest (1877–1877); and William (1878). John James and Ada were registered at Armidale, Eveline, and Maria at Patrick Plains and the rest of the children at Murrurundi. (Births register, BDM, NSW). Both Chas' and Annie's lives were short and tragic. Chas' wife, Annie (43yrs.) died on the 7th June 1884 (Family Notice, 18th June 1884) and Chas (51yrs.) committed suicide in 1891. Chas faced several challenges in his life, the ones found in Trove include: insolvency (1870); a stillborn child (Ernest, 1877); loss of his wife, Annie (1884); bankruptcy (1891); and a severe drought (1891).

355 This is a different Reynolds [first name unknown] to 'Richard Reynolds' in the hearings on Wallalla Station in the 1850s.

356 In writing William's story, the interchange from time to time of the terms 'squatter, pastoralist and grazier' in the literature became evident, and I wondered which one was the most appropriate during each stage of the colony's development (1820s, 30s, 40s etc.). Initially, William and the others with land grants at Glennies Creek appeared to be known as pastoralist (c.1824-c.1860) and as squatter outside of the boundaries of settlement (c.1826–1836). Then once a licence was required by squatters for their runs (in 1836) the terms 'pastoralist and station' starts to creep into the literature; and sometimes the term grazier. Then after the 'Crown Land Acts of 1861 the term grazier becomes strongly associated with 'free-selection' and smaller farms, like Rosedale.

357 John Robertson (1816–1891) arrived in NSW, in January 1822 (aged 6 yrs.) with his parents and five siblings (James 12, Catherine 10, Brisbane 8, Lavalette 4, Sarah 1). His father, (James Robertson) was a watchmaker and Silversmith, and a friend of Governor Brisbane (1821–1825). Governor Brisbane invited John Robinson's father (James) and his family to come to Sydney, where James was given a land grant at Cremorne (85 acres) and the position of 'Superintendent of Government Clocks'. John Robertson and his 'now' seven siblings (the last two, Agnes,1823, and Glen, 1825, born in Sydney) grew up in Cremorne and were well educated. In 1833, John (17) left Australia as a 'paid hand' on the 'Sovereign' and visited England, where he spent a few days with Lord Palmerston. Robertson then went on to Scotland, Ireland, and France. On the return journey (again as a paid hand) Robertson visited Brazil, and other parts of South America. Once back in Sydney (1835) Robertson made his way to his family's property: 'Plashett Station', Hunter River at Jerry's Plains, and became a station manager for his father (now a pastoralist). In 1838, Robertson (22yrs.) represented the Namoi pastoralists and called a meeting at the Royal Hotel Sydney to protest Governor Gipp's prohibition of the expansion of the squatters into the north-west of NSW; successfully squashed by the squatters. Throughout the 1840s, Robertson continued to support the squatters/pastoralist. He joined the rally against Governor Gipp's proposed land tenure policy in 1844, and in 1847, backed the new land tenure policy (Order in Council) that gave squatters/pastoralists security of land tenure on their leased land for up to 14 years. During this time, John Robertson was a squatter come pastoralist himself (his run, Arrarrowme, 20,000 acres from 1840–1848), and had strong connections with the establishment, and a growing interest in politics. As told earlier, during the early 1850, Robertson's views on land tenure were influenced by the changing demographics of NSW. The gold rush had attracted low to moderate income households who wished to purchase small freehold farm and the squatters/pastoralists were crowding them out. Robertson had a plan to solve the problem, and entered parliament (Legislative Assembly) in 1856, as an elected representative of 'eligible male voters' (such as male landholders with property worth £100, males earning a salary of £100 p.a. and males paying lodging of £40p.a). Subsequently, Robertson, drafted a new land tenure policy which he presented to the colonial parliament in 1859. (Nairn Bede (2006) 'Sir John Robertson' (1816–1891)' Australian Dictionary of Biography https://adb.anu.edu.au; Parliament of New South Wales, 'Sir John Robertson' and 'The History of the Legislative Assembly' https://parliament.nsw.gov.au; National Museum of Australia (28 September 2022), 'Robertson Land Acts https://nma.gov.au; 'for Arrarrowme', *NSW Government Gazette* 20 Sept 1848 Issue 103, p.1225 'No. 145; and for genealogy, Jen Willetts, 'John Robertson' and 'James Robertson'; Free Settler or Felon https://www.freesettlerorfelon.com; Births Registry BDM, NSW 'Agnes Robertson 1823 and Glen Robertson 1825).

358 John Robertson then, withdrew all three Bills because he believed all three were needed for an effective change in land tenure policy. From there, he repositioned himself as 'Premier and Secretary of Lands' (a position he held from the 9th March 1860 to the 9th January 1861). This enabled Robertson to gain support for his views on land tenure and from the 10th January 1861 he focused completely on a new approach to land tenure as the 'Secretary of Lands' (from 10 January 1861 to 15 Oct 1863); though Robertson would become Premier again on five other occasions. As 'Secretary of Lands' Robertson

359   drafted two new Bills on land tenure between September 1859 and circa August 1861 and presented them to the Legislative Assembly in October 1861. This time he was successful and land tenure in NSW was fundamentally changed as detailed in chapter 23 (ibid. Nairn Bede (2006) 'Sir John Robertson (1816–1891); ibid. Parliament of New South Wales 'Sir John Robertson (1816–1891)' https://parliament.nsw.gov.au; ibid. National Museum of Australia 'Robertson Land Acts' https://nma.gov.au).

359   It is assumed William did not renew his licence for Wallalla Station; a view that it supported soon in the story.

360   Robinson's policy of 'free selection' (if adopted) would enable the purchase of Crown Land within the areas currently occupied by those who leased Crown Land under the 1847 Order in Council.

361   Glen Innes Historical Society, 'Catalogue cards on Ward's Mistake'; *Guyra Argus*, 31 March, 1949, p.4. 'Ward's Mistake'.

CHAPTER 23
John Robertson's Proposed Changes to Land Tenure Policy

362   'Land reserves included "town and suburban land, proclaimed goldfields, land under lease to another person for mining purposes, or reserves for the site of a town, village or water supply… The majority of requests for reserves, which effectively quarantined the land from purchase, came from pastoralists. Reserves were proclaimed and gazetted before they were marked out and charted." (Museum of History NSW, 'Conditional Purchase of Crown Land' https://www.mhnsw.au).

363   Ibid. Museum of History NSW, 'Conditional Purchase of Crown Land'; Australasian Legal Information Institute (AustLII), *Crown Lands Alienation Act of 1861* no.26a, *Crown Lands Occupation Act 1861 No 27*. https://www.classic.auslii.edu.au/legis/nsw; *Sydney Morning Herald*, 4 November 1861, p.2, 'Regulation of the Crown Lands Occupation Act', as cited in Department of Lands, Sydney; *Government Gazette Proclamations and Legislation*, 1st November 1861, p.2327. https://www.classic.auslii.edu.au/legis.

364   *Crown Lands Occupation Act 1861 No. 27* https://www.classic.auslii.edu.au/legis/nsw; *Sydney Morning Herald*, 4 November 1861, p.2 'Regulation of the *Crown Lands Occupation Act*', as cited in Department of Lands, Sydney; *Government Gazette Proclamations and Legislation*, 1st November 1861, p.2327.

365   *Crown Lands Occupation Act 1861*, Clause 6. 'In cases in which two or more persons entitled to leases under the Orders in Council or under this Act may claim the same land the lease shall be granted to the person whose right thereto may have been or may be established after due inquiry to the satisfaction of the Governor or the Minister and in any such case in which the right of either claimant to a lease of the land in dispute shall not have been so established it shall be lawful for the Minister to require such right to be inquired into and determined by arbitration and the lease may be granted in accordance with the award of such arbitration.' (ibid. *Crown Lands Occupation Act 1861 No 27*).

366   The pastoralists (mostly the former squatters) claimed their right to the land given their current licence, while the 'free selectors' argued for 'selection before survey'. As told earlier, the *Crown Lands Occupation Act* enabled the use of arbitration when disputes arose (ibid. *Crown Lands Occupation Act 1861 No 27*, see Clause 28(1)). However, nothing was straight forward, and land selections were processed slowly at best with long delays occurring because of backlogs, distances, inaccurate survey maps, partial decisions, and reappraisals. (NSW Land Registry Services (January 2013) 'History of Land and Property Information' https://nswlrs.com.au).

367   Roth Lenny (2014) 'Crown Land Management' Parliament of NSW https://www.parliament.nsw.gov.au/researchpapers.

368   *Crown Lands Alienation Act 1861 No 26a*, op. cit; *Crown Lands Occupation Act 1861 No 27*, op. cit.

369   As outlined earlier, Henry Reynold (2021), *Truth Telling History, Sovereignty and the Uluru Statement* provides an informative account of the devastation.

CHAPTER 24
The Privy Council's Decision on Wallalla Station

370   Now we know who 'Another' was in *Humphrey and Another* held in the Supreme court on the 17th August 1858: one of the Christian brothers (J.B., W.B. or W.M.) and most likely, 'W.B. Christian' whose probate was quite substantial when he died in 1876. As told in the *Glen Innes Examiner and General Advertiser*, 2nd August 1876, p.4. 'Walhollow station on Liverpool Plains, and Broadsound station, in Queensland, were sold in Sydney on Wednesday, by the executors to the estate of the late W.B. Christian and realized sum amounting to £232,000'. [A very large amount of money, possibly a typing mistake in the newspaper article]; Brian Walsh (2020) op. cit., pp.48-49, also notes, 'In 1859 or 1860 William Nowland's Wallala [Wallalla] run past into Eales' hands who consolidated it with his Walhallow East and West into a huge holding of 213,000 acres. This took Eales total squatting runs on the Liverpool Plains to some 330,000 acres. About 1866, Eales sold his Liverpool Plains holdings to the Christian Family.' The sale of the improvements to Wallalla Station to John Eales by William Nowland is not documented. As detailed earlier, the data suggests William sold the improvement to John Eales circa 1860.

371   *Albury Banner and Wodonga Express*, 3 May 1862, p.2 and 24 May 1862, p.3

372   In total the money required for the appeal was £2500 (which William put in) and the judgment required Humphrey and Christian to pay the court costs. Whether William retrieved all or part of the money he had put in for the appeal is unknown. How much money William received from John Eales when he sold the improvements to Wallalla Station to Eales is also unknown. All we can assume is William received some monetary gain and with any luck somewhere around the money he put in for the appeal and hopefully a little extra for the improvements to Wallalla Station.

CHAPTER 25
William and His Boys Purchase Allotments at Warrah Ridge

373   The records in the *Government Gazette* for 1862, 1863, 1864 and 1866 tells us this was the case: William, 100 acres in 1862; Robert 320 acres in 1863 and 960 acres in 1866; Alex,100 acres in 1863 and 220 acres in 1864 and 960 acres in 1866; and George 320 acres in 1863 and 960 acres in 1866. A later map of Warrah Ridge (detailed soon) provides us with a visual account of the pastoral lands of the Nowland's at Warrah Ridge for three generations (William, his son's and his son's children).

374   The transcript that follows is a copy of an extracted transcribed from Robert's logbook: sourced at Quirindi Historical Society.

375   The balance of £240 due three years later, on 25th June 1866 (as detailed in *Crown Lands Alienation Act 1861*, 'conditions of purchase') and cited in Callaghan Terry, 'Notes re Conditional Purchase'. https://www.terrycallaghan.com.

376   Alex's 100 acres conditional purchase £25 with a further payment of £75 due on August 6, 1866 (ibid. Terry Callaghan 'Notes re Conditional Purchase').

377   How interesting, George (17) and Henry (11) drove sheep (presumably by themselves) from Rosedale to Warrah Ridge (around 88 miles, or 141.6 km).

378   Warrah Ridge is 169.3 miles (272.5 km) from Wards Mistake. J.B., W.B. and W.M. Christian had pre-emptive allotments adjacent to the Nowland allotments at Warrah Ridge, and we already know W.B. Christian purchased Walhollow Station from John Eales circa 1866. It was a small world one only needs to look at the allotments adjacent to the Nowlands at Warrah Ridge and familiar names appear, such as, Christian, Loder and Dangar.

379   'Wethers sheep' are adult sheep that have been castrated so they cannot breed. Wethers are used for wool production.

380   The *Crown Lands Occupation Act 1861* facilitated 'self-selection' on small allotments and the widespread use of fencing on alienated land (land sold by the Crown). (Pickard John (2005) 'Post and rail fences: Derivation, development, and demise of rural technology in colonial Australia, Faculty of Science and Engineering, Macquarie University https://researchers.mq.edu.au; Pickard John (2007) 'The Transition from Shepherding to Fencing in Colonial Australia' ibid. https://researchers.mq.edu.au

381   The AACo's Warrah Estate includes all the land below the horizontal dark serrated line that runs east to west towards the bottom of the map. Telford and Quirindi are included because they are referred to later in William's story.

382   This third map has been constructed by combining the 'first historical map' (available at the Quirindi Historical Society) that shows the number of each allotment in the Parish of Warrah/Telford, with the numbered and named Nowland allotments, on a second map (available at the NSW Land Registry Services. https://www.nswlrs.com.au. 'Buckland County, Parish of Warrah and Parish of Telford'). The combination of the first and second map enabled the third map; a visual representation of the amount of land the Nowland allotments occupied at Warrah Ridge and Telford, in 1885.

383   William sr.'s son Michael lived close by at an allotment in the adjoining Parish of Borambil; No.188 (640 acres) (Parish & Historical Maps. NSW Land Registry Services. https://www.nswlrs.com.au '1885 map, County Buckland, Parish Borambil'.

384   Most of this account of Michael Nowland (William sr.'s father) is untrue. A family tale, except for Governor Gidley King's appointment of Michael Nowland as Superintendent of Convicts at Castle Hill (1802–1806). The part about 'the two being personal friends' was handed down from one generation to the next because the truth at the time would have been socially demeaning. Michael Nowland was a convict who came to Australia in 1790 on the most debased convict ship of all, the *Scarborough*. Today, we acknowledge Michael Nowland's resilience and achievements especially in the early part of his life when he was a convict. What he went through, and how he survived is amazing, and part of his story, in this series of stories.

CHAPTER 26
Changing Family Dynamics in the 1860s

385   '[Henry] Nowland was one of the earliest Royal Mail contractors and established routes spanning from Maitland to Morpeth, encompassing the Hunter Valley settlements, inland regions like Armidale, and extending all the way to Brisbane.' (NSW Government – Government Environment and Heritage (8 September 2023), 'Extraordinary History of Nowland's Lochinvar Coach House and Setting, recognised with listing on the NSW State Heritage Register' https://www.environment.nsw.gov.au.)

386   The Nowland mail and passenger service was run by Henry eldest son, Robert John Nowland from 1863 to c. 1919. Under Robert John Nowland (R.J.) the Nowland's Coach ran between Gunnedah and Coonabarabran. This coach is on display at the National Museum of Australia, and descriptors and photos are available online at National Museum of Australia, 'OBJECT BIOGRAPHY Nowland's Mail Coach' https://www.nma.gov.au>Nowland_Mail_Coach.pdf. As noted by the National Museum of Australia, 'It is reported that in 1917 R J's son Harvey Nowland introduced a motor car to the route, but in the event of inclement weather, he was still required to use the coach, its proven record and familiarity leading many to consider it the safer option.' ibid. https://www.nma.gov.au>Nowland_Mail_Coach.pdf.

387   See footnote 363.

388   For each of the children see the Births and Deaths registry, BDM, NSW. Martha's age is based on the Births Register for Martha Squires born in 1842, at Camberwell.

389   By this time the term 'pastoralists' (within the data) is starting to be replaced by the term 'grazier'.

CHAPTER 27
The Roads the Nowlands Travelled and The Paddle Steamers They Took South

390. The dates (1823–1853) are based on an article William Nowland wrote (in 1878) to the local paper where he tells the reader he had transversed the tracks south between Camberwell and Windsor up until 1853; detailed in chapter 31.
391. The 'Great North Road' was built by approximately 720 convicts between 1826–1836 and for the length of around 240 kilometers, from Five Dock in the south to Newcastle in the north. Those travelling the road from Sydney, after it was opened in 1836 went west from Five Dock to Dural, and then north to Wiseman's Ferry, and on to Bucketty, Wollombi, Maitland, and finally, Newcastle. Despite all the work that went into the construction of the road (and the convict lives that were lost) this route was not popular north from Wiseman's Ferry because there were too many steep sections, no permanent and few watering holes, and limited places to stop. Today, most of the 'Great North Road' is used for hiking and has in large part been renamed the 'Great North Walk'. There are many points of historical interest on the walk, including the impressive and interesting section known as the 'Convict Trail' at Wiseman Ferry. Today, the only part of the road still called the 'Great North Road' and used by vehicles is the main road between Burwood and Abbotsford; with an historical signpost at Five Dock. (McHardy Cathy and Mc Hardy Nicholas, 'The Great North Road, Wiseman Ferry Hawkesbury History and Location, Hawkesbury People and Places https://www.hawkesbury.org.au; NSW Government 'Australian convict sites – Old Great North Road' NSW Environment and Heritage' https://www.environment.nsw.gov.au).
392. The road described in this newspaper article was called the 'Great Northern Road' until 1928, then the Great Northern Highway, and finally, the New England Highway in 1933. (NSW Government – Transport, Roads and Maritime Services, 'New England Highway Urban Design Framework' History p.4 https://www.transport.nsw.gov.au).
393. Monuments Australia, 'William IV https://monumentsaustralia.org.au.
394. Willetts Jen, 'Hunter River Steamers 1831' Free Settler or Felon https://freesettlersorfelon.com.
395. *Australian Chronicle*, 8th April 1841, p.3 *The Rose* Steamer.
396. *Sydney Morning Herald*, 'Departures' 16th April 1841, p.2; Willetts Jen, 'Hunter River Steamers 1831' op. cit. Two new 'iron paddle steamers' followed: the *Thistle* (1840–1859) and the *Shamrock* (1851–1857) and transversed the same route between Sydney and Morpeth. (J. H. Abbott J.H.M. (1942) op. cit.) The images of these paddle steamers are mostly in choppy waters; you wouldn't want to suffer from seasickness.
397. It is assumed that Mary Farlow Nowland (and her sisters) most likely travelled on the *Sophia Jane* or *William the Fourth* when they originally came to join their respective husbands in the Hunter in the later part of the 1830s, unless all or any of them were willing to go up the Bulga Track (with their small children) for at least four days with their husband and most likely with their stock; as some women did.
398. Based on this knowledge, one can confidently assume one of the major reasons for the location of Henry Nowland's guest house, the 'Lochinvar Coach House' (built in the 1840s) at Lochinvar, 12 km west of Maitland, was because of its proximity to the Queens Wharf Morpeth and the paddle steamer service to Sydney. Abbott J.H.M (1942) op. cit. 'Chapter X' notes, '"Boshy" Nowland [Henry] had the mail contract, and though he was reckoned "a bit of a nailer" there was nothing mean about the way he dragged his coaches up and down the Valley. Cobb and Co. hadn't yet arrived on the old North Road.'
399. The train service from Singleton to East Maitland began on the 7th May 1863; detailed in the next chapter.

CHAPTER 28
The Steam Trains

400. The railway line terminated at Windsor and there was no railway line between Windsor and Newcastle until 1889.
401. Noble Lillian M. (date unknown, most likely, 1990s), op. cit. p.39.
402. Ravensworth Station (the last of the three stations) opened in 1869, initially as Camberwell Station, and then from 1876, as Ravensworth Station. In 1975, (nearly, 100 years later) Ravensworth Station with its island platform (a single platform positioned between two-railway lines, one going north and the other south) was closed to passenger services and demolished. (Wikipedia, 'Disused regional railway stations in New South Wales'; NSWrail.net 'Ravensworth Station' https://www.nswrail.net>locations).

CHAPTER 29
Rosedale and the Dispersal of Family

403. *Maitland Mercury and Hunter River General Advertiser*, 7 September 1865, p.2. 'NOTES OF A TRIP THROUGH THE NORTHERN DISTRICT BY AN EX-REPORTER'.
404. Alfred's piggery brings to mind his grandfather Michael Nowland and his successful piggeries on Norfolk Island, in the 1790s, that helped feed a starving colony. Michael Nowland's story has been documented in Nowland Ian (1996) op. cit. and by myself in a family genealogy book called *By Chance*.
405. William Nowland sr.'s second youngest son Alfred Nowland sold Rosedale circa 1925 and moved with his wife Lauretta to their daughter homestead 'Maison Dieu' (Gertrude's House). Maison Dieu was 9.5 miles (15.4 km) from Camberwell. Gertrude's homestead 'Maison Dieu' is mentioned in an article on Mr. and Mrs. Nowland in the *Singleton Argus*, 18 August 1925, p.2. Alfred and his wife Lauretta sold Rosedale (probably due to age and ill health) to John Reid Skinner (date unknown). The earliest account found in Trove of someone else owning Rosedale is in the *Newcastle Morning Herald*, 20 August 1929, p.9, 'Mrs. J. R. Skinner of Rosedale'.

406 Marriages registry BDM, NSW, 'Robert Nowland and Jane Susan, Mercer, 1867.' It is assumed after they married Robert and Jane moved to their homestead at Warrah Ridge, although the births of their first two children are registered at Patrick Plains [Singleton]. Several of William sr.'s and Mary's grandchildren were born at Rosedale, this may be because Mary acted as the midwife and/or Rosedale was considered a safer place for her daughter in laws to have their first couple of children. This observation emerges from the data in Mary Farlow Nowland's story, in this series of stories. Robert and Jane had 11 children between 1867–1883, 9 surviving: Alice (1867) Patrick Plains; Herbert (1869) Patrick Plains; Percy (1871); Mary (1872); Amelia (1874); Edith (1875); Gertrude (1877–1877); Adeline (1878); Eunice (1879); Robert (1881) Gunnedah; and, Henry (1882–1883) Gunnedah. Alice and Herbert, most likely born at Rosedale, and Robert and Henry born at Gunnedah. The rest of the children most likely born at Robert's and Jane's homestead, Warrah Ridge and registered at Murrurundi. Based on other evidence (detailed later in the story) it is unlikely Robert, Jane, and their children, moved to Gunnedah in the 1880s when Robert jr. and Henry were born. We know Robert's cousin Robert John Nowland (Henry's son) ran a coaching service at Gunnedah and maybe William sr.'s Robert helped his cousin out from time to time in the early 1880s. William sr.'s and Mary's Robert (47) died on the 19th April, 1883 of heart disease. (Family Notice, *Singleton Argus*, 8 May 1883, p.2; Deaths register not found in BDM, NSW). The executors of Robert's Will were his brothers, George and Henry Nowland, and the probate was £2105. (*Sydney Daily Telegraph*, 21 June 1883, p.4.). Jane (age unknown) died in Ashfield, 1923 (Deaths register, BDM, NSW 'Jane S. Nowland' parents, Henry, and Alice Mercer).

407 This was also the year William's younger sister Mary lost her husband Alex Johnston on the 21st May 1867, (62yrs). As told earlier, Alex Johnston is buried (along with his wife Mary) at Scone Anglican Cemetery.

408 'Store sheep (or other meat animal) in good average condition, but not fat. Usually bought by dealers to fatten for resale.' (Wikipedia, 'Glossary of Sheep Husbandry').

409 John James (7), Ada (7), Mina (5), Walter (4), Annie jr. (3), Eveline (1) and Lilian (a baby). (Births register, BDM, NSW).

410 Clara (7), Amy (4) and Laura (a baby). William (1864–1865). (Births register, BDM, NSW).

411 Alice (2) (1867) and Herbert (a baby) (Births register, BDM, NSW).

412 William jr. when advertising for someone to put fencers around 'Ward's Mistake' in 1857 states 'at Ward's Mistake thirty miles from Armidale'. (*Armidale Express and New England General Advertiser*, 22 August 1857, p.1. 'Bushmen').

413 As acknowledged again this was a significant day for Aboriginal people. Despite the challenges Aboriginal people faced they remained resilient. On Country, they ignored the Aboriginal reserves around Armidale and Walcha (created in the 1850s) and maintained their traditional lives. They continued to gather for their customary meetings and ceremonies. Their resilience prevailed despite the settlers who took their ceremonial sites and decimated their traditional foods. Today they continue to maintain and foster their culture, language, and heritage. (Clayton-Dixon Callum (2020), op. cit. pp.110–130).

CHAPTER 30
Camberwell in 1869

414 Is William Nowland sr. the author of this article?

415 William sr. purchased the Queen Victoria Inn ('The Queen') and the surrounding lands (date unknown, most likely in the late 1860s based on these descriptors). Then, William's two youngest sons (Alfred and Henry) inherited 'The Queen' from William when he died in 1884. 'The Queen' is mentioned in *Maitland Mercury & Hunter River General Advertiser*, 16 March 1893, p.7 'Camberwell'. The article informs us of a flood in Camberwell (1893) that forced William's wife Mary along with Alfred, Lauretta and their children to leave Rosedale (where they all lived) and cross Glennies Creek to higher ground, where they sought refuge in Henry and Martha's house 'The Queen'.

416 The large estate is assumed to be the 'Ravensworth Estate and Homestead "once owned by naval surgeon Dr. James Bowman, who was married to a daughter of John and Elizabeth Macarthur, and ran sheep given to the couple as a wedding present". (Domain (26 May 2020), 'One of Australia's oldest homesteads to be relocated' https://www.domain.com.au; Lapham Jake (2021), 'Future of Historic Ravensworth' ABC Upper Hunter,https://www.abc.net.au).

417 *Maitland Mercury and Hunter River General Advertiser*, 8 December 1870, p.3, 'The Platform at Camberwell'; *Maitland Mercury and Hunter River General Advertiser*, 7 November 1871, p.1, 'Camberwell'; *Maitland Mercury and Hunter River General Advertiser,* 12 December 1871, p.3, 'Camberwell'.

CHAPTER 31
The Nowland Family and Their Farms

418 *New South Wales Government Gazette*, 17 June 1870, p.1337. 'Insolvent Estate of Charles Nowland of Warrah Ridge'.

419 Marriages register (BDM, NSW) 'George Nowland and Alice Blanche Aldwell, 1871'. George and Alice's marriage was registered at 'Patrick Plains '(Singleton).

420 It is unknown why George and Alice needed a 'special licence' to marry, though it could simply be that the banns had not been read three weeks before they were to be married.

421 A family notice was placed in the Sydney paper to informs others of the birth of each of their first three children at Rosedale – *Empire* (Sydney) 1 July 1872, p.1; *Evening News* (Sydney, 11 June 1874, p.2; *SMH*, 27 April 1876, p.1.

422 George and Alice had 10 children between 1872 and 1890: Madeline (1872), George (1874), and Alice (1876), all born at Rosedale. Followed by, Ethel (1877), Claude (1880), Eustace (1881–1882), Cyril (1882), Lavina ('Rene') (1886), Louie

('Louis') (1887) and Muriel (1890). Their fourth child, 'Ethel' was born at the family's homestead 'Hazel Cottage' Warrah Ridge (Family Notice, *SMH*, 5th September 1877, p.1). 'Claude and Lavinia' ('Rene') were probably also born at home (in Hazel Cottage) because their births were registered at Murrurundi. While 'Eustace and Cyril' are registered at Gunnedah, and 'Louie ('Louis') and Muriel' are registered at West Maitland. Whether these latter children were born in these townships or at home is unknown; sometimes children were register sometime after their birth and maybe George was on a business trip and registered them where it was convenient.

423   There are several accounts in Trove that tells us of George's participation in the Quirindi community. George became a J.P. and magistrate within William sr.'s lifetime (*Maitland Mercury*, 7 August 1883, p.4). George's obituary provides a summary of his life; "Mr.George Nowland [68], who died at Oakey Valley, Naughton's Gap, on Thursday last of heart failure, was a prominent citizen, at Quirindi for nearly 45 years [1862 to circa 1907] … held in great esteem here. He was chairman of the Quirindi P and A Society, [Pastoral and Agricultural Society] … Chairman of the Licensing Bench, member of the Land Board, and Coroner for a number of years [and] the Returning Officer for Liverpool Plains. He followed pastoral pursuits and was greatly interested in racing, being patron of The Quirindi Jockey Club for a great many years. He leaves a widow [Alice 67] and three sons, Messrs. George (Manager N.S.W. Bank, Walgett), Claude (with Messrs. Wilkinson and Lavender, Moree), and Cyril (dairyfarmer, Casino). The daughters are Mrs. Somerset [Madeline] (wife of the manager of the Commercial Bank, Moruya), Mrs. Blackall [Alice jr.] (wife of Mr. Blackall, dentist, Gilgandra), Mrs. Harry Grieves, jun. [Louis] (Bank of Australasia, Melbourne), Mrs. Norman Richards [Muriel] (wife of Mr. Norman Richards, of Riverstone meatworks), and Misses Ethel and Irene [Lavinia]. (*Richmond River Express and Casino Kyogle Advertiser*, 15 June 1915, p.2). Alice sr. died in 1929 and parts of her obituary (*SMH*, 11 July 1929, p.12) read: The death of Mrs. A. B. Nowland, of Manly, widow of the late Mr. George Nowland, breaks a link with one of the earliest pastoral families in Australia, and one that has played a part in the pastoral development of this country from the time of Governor King. Her husband was a son of Mr. William Nowland, one of the pioneers of the Liverpool Plains and New England districts, and at one time owned Warrah Ridge, one of the largest holdings in the Quirindi district, until it was subdivided and sold some years ago. Born in England, Mrs. Nowland was a daughter of the late William Aldwell, a member of an old English family, and she came to Australia when a young girl. Although she was 81 years of age at the time of her death, Mrs. Nowland had a remarkably good memory, and often recalled stirring events of the early days. She is survived by two sons, Mr. Geo. Nowland, manager of the Bank of New South Wales, Wellington, Mr.Cyril Nowland, Katoomba … and five daughters, Mesdames Somerset [Madeline], Blackall [Alice jr.], Greive [Louis], and Richards [Muriel],and Rene [Lavinia] Nowland." Alice's other children were deceased: Eustace 1881–1882; Ethel 1877–1915; and, Claude 1880–1918 (Claude died from war wounds, WWI). ('Births and Deaths registry' BDM, NSW, for Eustace and Ethel and Trove for Claude *Moree Gwydir Examiner and General Advertiser* 14 February 1919, p.2 'His Duty Nobly Done').

424   *Maitland Mercury and Hunter River General Advertiser*, 25 January 1876, p.3. 'The Attempted Removal of the Camberwell Post-Office'.

425   Hawkesbury Benevolent Society Papers, ML A626, op. cit. p.485 cited in H.R. Carter (1974), op. cit. p.36.

426   Rutledge Martha (2006) 'Jules François de Sales Joubert (1824–1907)', Australian Dictionary of Biography https://adb.anu.edu.au; Cabel K.J. (2006) 'William Woolls' (1814–1893) Australian Dictionary of Biography https://adb.anu.edu.au

427   This W. H. Gordon was possibly the W. H. Gordon who replaced Mr. Johnstone as Chief Constable for Murrurundi, in May 1860. (*Maitland Mercury and Hunter River General Advertiser*, 15 May 1860, p.3 'Murrurundi. Police Exchange').

428   'Upas' means 'a tall tropical Asian tree of the mulberry family with a latex that contains poisonous glycosides used as an arrow poison' (Merriam-Webster 'Upas definition and meaning' https://www.merriam-webster.com). Was the poison coming from the Upas and on the Upas ground?

429   Alfred (1876) Patrick Plains; Arthur (1877–1877) stillborn, birth and death registered at Murrurrindi; William (1877) registered in 1878 at Patrick Plains, also see 'Family Notice' *Singleton Argus*, 11 April 1877, p.2; Vivian (1879) Murrurrindi; Edwin (1880); Cecil (1882); Millicent (1883); Reginald (1885); and Gertrude (1887) all registered at Patrick Plains, followed by Norman (1889); Horbury (1892); Zuriel (1895); Lauretta (1898); and Terence (1900) all registered at Singleton. (Patrick Plains was the original name for Singleton). After they married, Alfred and Lauretta lived at their homestead at Warrah Ridge (circa 1876-circa 1883), though most of the children were born at Rosedale. They returned to live permanently at Rosedale from circa 1883 to 1925. As told earlier, Alfred inherited Rosedale (along with his brother Henry), from their father, William sr. in 1884. Alfred 'like his father before him' was very active in the Camberwell community his obituary reads: ". 'MR ALFRED NOWLAND' A pioneer of the Singleton and Hunter River district, in the person of Mr Alfred Nowland, died at his residence, Maison Dieu, yesterday morning. [At his daughter's 'Gertrude's homestead – 'Maison Dieu' 15.4 km from Camberwell]. He had been in ill health for about three months. The deceased, who was within three weeks of celebrating his 81st. birthday, was born at Camberwell and lived in the district all his life, many years being spent at Rosedale. He was a man of educational attainments, with gentlemanly traits of character, and was a perfect encyclopedia of information upon the early history of the district as well as matters of general interest. His passing will be regretted by many friends. Deceased is survived by Mrs Nowland [Lauretta sr.], eight [9] sons And (sic) two [three] daughters, viz., Messrs Alfred (New Zealand); Vivian, Edwin, Reg. and Cecil (Queensland); Clifford [Horbury] (Singleton); Zuriel (Canberra); and Terence (Ashfield); Mesdames E.J. Hamilton [Millicent] (Denman); and H. J. Kauter [Gertrude] (Maison Dieu). The funeral took place to-day, the remains being interred in the Church of England cemetery at Camberwell…" (*Singleton Argus*, 2 May 1932, p.2). Alfred's and Lauretta's three other children are not mentioned in Alfred's obituary: Lauretta 1898–1976 (Births and Deaths register,

BDM, NSW); Norman 1887–1917 (Deaths register BDM, NSW) Norman died from complications after operation for appendicitis (*Singleton Argus*, 6 February 1917, p.2); and William 1877 – 1918 who died of from the wounds he received in WWI (*Singleton Argus*, 26 September 1918, p.2). Lauretta died in the same year as Alfred, October 1932, also at Gertrude's Homestead, 'Maison Dieu'. (*Singleton Argus*, 18 August 1925, p.2. 'Mr. and Mrs. Nowland'). Lauretta's obituary read: MRS. L.A. NOWLAND. Mrs. Lauretta Annette Nowland, aged 78, relict of Alfred Nowland, died at Maison Dieu near Singleton. Her husband died last May. Mrs. Nowland was born in Sydney, [Births register, BDM, NSW 1854] and since her marriage had lived practically all the time in the Singleton district. She is survived by eight sons and two [3] daughters. The remains were interred in Camberwell Cemetery. (*Newcastle Morning Herald and Miners' Advocate*, 26 October 1932, p.11).

430 Mary Ethel Kate (1877–1878) Patrick Plains; Hilda May (1879) Patrick Plains; Alexander Edgeworth (1882) not registered and most likely, also born at home at Camberwell; Warwick (1883) Tamworth (my grandfather); Veronica Mary (1884) Gunnedah; Mark, 'Dudley' (1886) Quirindi; and, Margery 'Majorie' (1891) Quirindi. The year of Alexander jr.'s birth is based on Alexander's age when he died (54 yrs.) in 1936 (*Muswellbrook Chronicle*, 28 July 1936, p.1, 'Alexander Edgeworth Nowland'). Warwick's birth year and place of birth is taken from his Military Records. After their marriage, Alex and Naomi most likely lived at Camberwell in a property (224 acres) adjoining Rosedale (*Singleton Argus and Upper Hunter General Advocate*, 15th Sept 1877, p.2. 'General Purchase, 13th September 1877'). By 1883, Alex and Naomi had moved with their two surviving children (Hilda 4, and Alex jr. 1) to their homestead at Warrah Ridge (c.1883–1895). The family, moved back to Rosedale during the 'Federation Drought' (1891–1903) and around the time of Alex's mother's death, in 1895 (Mary Nowland née Farlow). Towards the end of Alex's life, he had cancer of the larynx (most likely from smoking) and the family moved to Singleton. Alex (68) died on the 24th September 1914 and his obituary read: A well-known resident of Singleton, named Alexander Nowland, died yesterday morning at his home in Castlereagh Street [Singleton]. He was 68 years of age, and left a wife, and six children. He died of a malignant disease of the larynx. (*Singleton Argus*, 26 September 1914, p.4, 'OBITUARY'). Naomi (93) died 36 years later, on the 31st January 1950, Naomi's obituary read: NOWLAND – Naomi Kate. January 31, 1950, at her daughters, residence, 6 Gibbs St Miranda, widow of the late Alexander Nowland, late of Singleton, beloved mother of Hilda (Mrs. H. Witts), Veronica (Mrs. O Freebody) Marjorie (Mrs. M McCullough) [McCullagh in Marriages register BDM, NSW and on the electoral roll], Alexander (deceased), Warwick (deceased), and Dudley (deceased). Private interment, Woronora Catholic Cemetery February 2, 1950. (*Sydney Morning Herald*, Jan 1-Feb 28 1950. 'Nowland'). Naomi and her children were Catholics. An aspect of Alex's life that becomes relevant in the final chapter of the story.

431 In December 1877, the *Australian Town and Country Journal* provides a lengthy generic article warning about 'Whooping Cough' entitled 'Diseases and their treatment', and another article in the *Clarence and Richmond Examiner and New England Advertiser*, 5 February 1878, p.2 tells of 'the prevalence of whooping cough in Scone'.

432 *Singleton Argus and Upper Hunter General Advocate* 17 April 1878, p.2, 'Family Notice' 'DIED ON the 10th instant, at Camberwell, MARY ETHEL KATE, infant daughter of ALEXANDER and NAOMI KATE NOWLAND, aged six months and two days.'

433 'Elizabeth Nowland Rochester' Saint Matthew's Anglican Church Cemetery Windsor, 'Sarah Nowland Adnum' Saint Jude's Cemetery, Randwick. Findagrave, https://www.findagrave

434 'Christiana Farlow Baldwin' Gunnedah Historical Cemetery, Gunnedah op. cit. As told earlier, Christiana (Christian) was buried in an unmarked grave' and Christiana's burial place confirmed by Gunnedah Council 10th March 2023.

CHAPTER 32
The Nowland Voices in the Papers

435 By 1876, Robert, Chas, George, and Alfred lived permanently at Warrah Ridge and maybe they were the Messrs. Nowland.

436 In September 1877, John Robertson was the Premier of NSW (17 August–17 December). (Parliament of New South Wales 'John Robertson (1816-1891)'. https://parliament.nsw.gov.au).

437 *Sydney Morning Herald*, 29 January 1878, p.6, William Hogan notes, 'The fearful drought of the present and past two years in Australia and India [1876 to the present] has revived amongst scientific men the sun-spot theory and its effects on terrestrial magnetism and its possible influence on temperature and rainfall. Some of the greatest scientists of the day have written exhaustively on this subject, and furnished many valuable ideas, based on personal observation and careful research …'. WILLIAM HOGAN January 26. How interesting scientists were investigating and providing evidence of climate change as far back as the 1870s with scepticism prevailing. See Halburg F, Cornélissen G., Bernhardt K.H., Sampson, M., Schwartzkopff O., Sonntag D. (3 May 2011), 'Egeson's (George's) transtridecadal weather cycling and sunspots', National Centre for Biotechnology Information, National Library of Medicine https://pmc.ncbi.nlm.nih.gov/articles/PMC3086776/ available on line and well worth a read. The opening lines of the Abstract reads: 'In the late 19th century, Charles Egeson, a map compiler at the Sydney Observatory, carried out some of the earliest research on climatic cycles, linking them to about 33-year cycles in solar activity, and predicted that a devastating drought would strike Australia at the turn of the 20th century'.

438 'Paterson's curse is native to Mediterranean Europe and Northern Africa. It was both accidentally and deliberately introduced to Australia in the 1850s and by 1890 it was showing potential as a major weed…'. NSW Government, Department of Primary Industries (2023), 'Paterson's curse (*Echium plantagineum*)– NSW Weed Wise' https://weeds.dpi.nse.gov.au.

439 The Australian Agricultural Company lost 25,000 sheep at Warrah Station during the severe drought of 1877–78. (Australian National University – Archives Library, 'Australian Agricultural Company Records' https://archives.anu.edu.au).

440 Several accounts in the papers of the day are readily available in Trove under the keywords 'Poison Plant'.

441 Today Caltrops (*Tribulus terrestris*) is classed as noxious. 'Caltrops (*Tribulus terrestris*) is toxic to sheep'. (Weeds Australia, Centre for Invasive Species Solutions, 'Caltrop' https://weeds.org.au); 'Pest plant – Caltrop is toxic to stock and can cause nitrate poisoning, photosensitization and staggers' (Government of South Australia – Weed Identification Notes, Animal and Plant Control Commission 'Caltrop' https://data.environment.sa.gov.au/Content/Publications/pests. The second descriptors above on the effect of Caltrops from the Animal and Plant Control Commission, SA are consistent with William's description of the impact of the Caltrop on his cattle in 1873. '…some of them would stagger, fall, and become convulsed, and never rise again; others would fall and rise again several times, but not one that had once fallen with it ever recovered…' (*Maitland Mercury and Hunter Advertiser,* April 26, 1873, 'Cattle Poisoning').

442 The scientific methods of the day were too limited to enable anywhere near what we know today.

443 The conflict between squatters and free selectors with the introduction of Robertson's Crown Land Acts (1861) was systemic and facilitated by the bureaucratic and centralised nature of the Acts, that inherently led to bribery and corruption and the ultimate demise of the Acts. In 1884, both Acts were replaced with *Crown Lands Act 1884* (NSW) that decentralised the administration of land tenure with the introduction of districts and local land boards and a variety of new leasing arrangements. Parliament of NSW, *Crown Lands Act 1884*, Crown Lands Management – Parliament of NSW, https://www.parliament.nsw.gov.au.

444 Other accounts of the same journey include *Newcastle Morning Herald*, 14 August 1877, p.2, 'Opening of the Railway to Quirindi', and the *Maitland Mercury,* 16 August 1877, p.3, 'Opening of the Great Northern Railway Extension to Quirindi'.

445 The route Mary and William travelled to Quirindi Station via Doughboy Hollow and Warrah is the same route William found some 50 years earlier after three months of searching, most likely, between February and April 1827. Today the Main North Railway line and the New England Highway transverse the same route and pass through the gap William found in the Liverpool Ranges (at the headwaters of the Pages River) and denoted (today) on the New England Highway as 'Nowlands Gap'.

446 Extracts from *Newcastle Morning Herald and Miners' Advocate*, 25 June 1878, p.2, 'Singleton to Sydney'; *Newcastle Morning Herald and Miners' Advocate*, 4 July 1878, p.2, 'Proposed Railway from Singleton to Sydney'; *Newcastle Morning Herald and Miners' Advocate*, 26 July 1878, p.2, 'Singleton – Sydney Railway'; *Newcastle Morning Herald and Miners' Advocate'* 2 September 1878, p.3, 'Proposed Railway Line from Sydney to Newcastle via Brisbane Waters'; *Australian Town and Country Journal*, 7 September 1878, p.26, 'Proposed Railway from Sydney to Newcastle'; *Newcastle Morning Herald and Miners' Advocate'*, 14 September 1878, p.3, 'Proposed Railway from Singleton to Sydney Memorial'; *Maitland Mercury and Hunter General Advertiser,* 17 September 1878, p.5, 'The Proposed Railway from Sydney to Singleton. Meeting at Newcastle'; *Sydney Morning Herald*, 26 September 1878, p.3, 'Proposed Railway Via Brisbane Water'. There are also several other articles in Trove.

447 Heritas – Heritage & Conservation, 'Falbrook National School', www.heritas.com.au. The above account of the Falbrook National School is no longer available on-line, and the source can be found via the Scone Historical Society 'William Nowland 1804–1884' under the heading 'Camberwell' as reference 8' 'Heritas Architecture, Appendix 14, 'European Heritage Assessment, Ashton Coal Project, Camberwell, NSW p.12. 2009. (Scone Historical Society, www.scone.com.au).

448 In 1880, life expectancy in Australia in 1880 was 40 years. (O'Neill Aaron (8 Aug 2024), 'Life expectancy (from birth) in Australia, from 1870 to 2020', Statista https://www.statista.com). Based on this data life expectancy seems to be quite low in the 1880 (many of my relatives lived for at least 20 more years) however when looking more deeply this is explained by the large number of deaths at birth and in infancy.

449 The 'Alex Johnson' (surname assumed to be misspelt) who wrote to the *Singleton Argus* in 1879 is most likely William sr.'s and Mary's nephew 'Alex Johnston jr.' (1830–1917) who lived in Tamworth. See *Maitland Mercury and Hunter River General Advertiser,* 26 July 1879, p.7 'Alex Johnston's Report' that states in part, 'Properties – Few transactions to report. I have some very nice properties in and around Tamworth for private sale…', and other similar accounts on Alex's property reports. Also, Alex Johnston jr.'s obituary mentions he lived for many years in Tamworth. (*Maitland Mercury* 9 October 1917, p.4.).

450 The date is earlier (c.1826) based on previous data in the story.

451 Michael's and Martha's 'Beatrice'; Robert's and Jane's 'Eunice'; Alex's and Naomi's 'Hilda'; and, Alfred's and Lauretta's 'Vivian'.

452 Michael's and Martha's 'Clara'; and, Chas' and Annie's twins 'John James' and 'Ada'.

453 Going down the Bulga Track to the Sydney markets was a thing of the past. The growth in the local markets facilitated by the gold rush and subsequent settlement was more than enough to sustain the Nowlands and their interests

454 Altogether, Mary Nowland (née Farlow) had five older siblings Maria (1800–1834), Harriet (1805–1880), Ann (1807–1902), William (1809–1864) and Christian (1811–1878) and three younger siblings Elizabeth (1815–1887), Robert (1817–1867) and James (1820–1888). Australian Royalty 'Mary Ann Farlow'. https://australianroyalty.net.au

455 A later notice in the *Government Gazette* detailed the Executor of Harriet's Will. Harriet lived with her daughter Harriet jr. at Bollibong, near Muswellbrook, and Harriet jr. was the sole executor of Harriet sr.'s Will. (*New South Wales Government Gazette*, 7 September 1880, page, 4640).

456 Mary Johnston (née Nowland) as told earlier is buried at Scone Anglican Cemetery. (Findagrave, 'Mary Johnston' Scone Anglican Cemetery'. www.findagrave).

CHAPTER 33
William Still an Advocate for Camberwell

457   Also see, Glencore Australia 'Heritage Management Plan. Ravensworth Open Cut' (2022, p.16) 'Early Settlement and Exploration'. https://www.glencore.com.au.

458   The statement here 'although a stranger on her stage' suggests the correspondent this time was a newcomer to Camberwell who was prompting the views expressed in the first article in the chapter (*Maitland Mercury*, June 1880). Most likely the writer of the first article was William Nowland and the second (February, 1881) the newcomer who was most likely encouraged by William to take up the cause for Camberwell. All conjecture (though likely) based on what we already know about William's passion for Camberwell, his sons' relocation to Warrah Ridge and William's age and poor health by this time. (William's health detailed soon in the story.).

459   Camberwell's new status as a 'village' ignored.

460   James Glennie (1880–1876) was one of the twelve sons of Dr. William and Mary Glennie (née Gardiner) of Dulwich, Surry. On arrival in Sydney in 1824, James Glennie was given a land grant by Governor Darling of 2,080 acres at Falbrook. Glennie named his estate 'Dulwich' and Falbrook was re-named 'Glennies Creek' in his honour. Circa 1848, James Glennie leased 'Dulwich' and moved further north along the Gwydir River to 'Unumgar Station'. In 1868, James Glennie sold 'Unumgar' and moved to Queensland. He died in 1876 while returning from Church to his station near Gladstone, Queensland. (Willetts Jen, 'James Glennie' Free Settler or Felon https://www.freesettlerorfelon.com).

461   As told earlier, William probably repurchased the 'The Queen' in the late 1860s when property values in Camberwell were low. As detailed in an earlier article on Camberwell: '…the Victoria Inn, a first-class building, particularly well adapted for business, and which cost £2000 odd in building alone was some time since sold for £290, together with 70 acres or thereabouts of alluvial land adjoining…' (*Maitland Mercury and Hunter River General Advertiser*, 18 December 1869, p.4, 'District News Camberwell').

462   Just over 12 months after William sr. death on the 28th April 1884, his two youngest sons Alfred and Henry extracted coal from Rosedale. (*Newcastle Morning Herald and Miners' Advocate*, 21 May 1885, p.4, 'The first coal sent to market from the Rosedale Colliery, Glennies Creek, reached the Singleton station in two trucks on Saturday last.'). Sixteen months later Alfred and Henry had cut a 'coal seam' on their estate. (*Newcastle Morning Herald and Miners' Advocate*, 25 September 1886, p.10, 'OUR COAL MEASURES. SEVERAL months ago, we stated that Messrs. A. and H. Nowland had succeeded in cutting a splendid seam of coal on their Rosedale Estate…'). Appropriately and with knowledge of the destructive nature of coal mines Wendy Bowman (1934–2023) defended Rosedale against Yancoal for 13 years (2010–2023) and won. (Hespe Michelle (8 August, 2023) 'Tribute: a farmer and a fighter', *The Farmer* magazine https://thefarmermagazine.com.au; Sheather Michael (April 2019) 'Hunter Valley farmer takes on mining company and wins', NSW Farmers Association https://www.nswfarmers.org.au/).

463   As told later in William's obituary, for the last six years of his life (1878 to 1884) William sr. suffered from 'heart disease'.

464   One only needs to place Alfred's name in Trove to find his progressive contribution to Camberwell and his achievements at Rosedale between 1883 and 1925. In contrast, Lauretta's name largely escapes the papers. Like many of the women of the time, Lauretta's contribution to the community remained largely unacknowledged. In history and especially at the family level of genealogy a patriarchal approach still dominates. The voices of women are largely silent though there is one example soon in this story in the local newspaper where Lauretta's contribution to the community is mentioned.

465   The journalist acknowledged the contributions of the women, to the gathering to celebrate the opening of the new school at Camberwell. I am sure the women were the key organisers; sending out invitations and arranging speeches (be it officially through their male counterparts), and of course supplying the delicious food and hall decorations.

466   'Francis Augustus Wright (1835–1903)', Parliament of New South Wales https://www.parliament.nsw.gov.au.

467   *Maitland Mercury and Hunter River General Advertiser*, 7 August 1883, p.4 'New Magistrates'.

468   *Singleton Argus*, 12th January 1884, p.1 'Camberwell'. The interest of the other sons in cricket can also be traced through several articles in Trove, under the keywords 'Cricket' and 'Nowland'.

469   Marriages register, BDM, NSW 'Henry Nowland and Martha E Clark 1883', Armidale; Births register, BDM, NSW, 'Martha E Clark 1859', Wellingrove.

470   Henry and Martha had six children (1884–1899): Harrie 'Howard' (1884) Patrick Plains; Henry jr. (1887); Leo H (1892); Doris K.E. (1893); Thelma M (1895); (all registered at Glen Innes and probably born at Martha's parent's home). Martha's parents lived at Oban and Henry, Martha and their children's family home was 'The Queen' (Queen Victoria Inn) on land that became part of Rosedale. (*The Maitland Mercury and Hunter River Advertiser*, 16th March 1893, p.7). Henry's and Martha's last child, Dnalwon Phillip (1899) was registered at Singleton. [What a strange name and a correct one. Dnalwon died tragically in a railway accident on the 6th January 1933]. (*Townsville Daily Bulletin*, 19 January 1933, p.4). Henry and Martha lived at Rosedale from 1883 to c. 1889 in 'The Queen' on the additional 70 acres, William sr. purchased c. 1869. (*Maitland Mercury and Hunter River General Advertiser*, 18 December 1869, p.4). In 1889, Henry and Alfred (who had inherited Rosedale from William sr.) sold Henry's share of Rosedale that under Alfred and Henry's 'kingship' had grown to 2300 acres. (*Maitland Mercury and Hunter River General Advertiser*, 13 June 1889, p.5.) Henry, and Martha moved to Guya c. 1889 and lived there until 1906. They then moved to Queensland (firstly, residing at 'Yarraman' in the Toowoomba Region, Queensland, and later Nambour in the Sunshine Coast Region, Banyo, Brisbane and finally, Sandgate, Brisbane). Henry was a grazier for most of his life, and an active member of all the local communities he lived in. There are several

newspaper articles in the local papers where Henry lived under the keywords 'Henry Nowland' and the dates '1883 to 1941'. Henry's and Martha's places of residence included: Rosedale, then Guya (where Henry was a Magistrate and J.P.), Yarraman, Nambour and finally, Banyo. Henry (88) died on 26th July 1941 and Martha (88) died six years later, on 17 May 1947. Henry and Martha lived at Eagle Terrace, Sandgate when Henry died, and Martha died at Banyo. Henry and Martha are buried at Mount Thompson Memorial Garden and Crematorium Hollard Park, Brisbane. (Findagrave, 'Mount Thompson Memorial Garden' https://findagrave.com.au)

471 *New South Wales Government Gazette*, 8 May 1883, p.2623.
472 Deaths register, BDM, NSW. 'Henry Nowland 1883'.
473 *Singleton Argus*, 30th April 1884, p.2. 'Death of Mr. W. Nowland'; detailed soon.

CHAPTER 34
William's Last Will and Testimony

474 Additional data for this story.
475 **Michael's and Martha's children:** Clara 21; Amy 18; Laura 14, Maud 12; Minnie 8; Susan 8; Mildred 7; Beatrice 4; Robert a baby. **Robert's (deceased) and Jane's children:** Alice 16; Herbert 14; Percy 12; Mary 11; Amelia 9; Edith 8; Adeline 5; Eunice 4; Robert 2. **Chas' and Annie's children:** twins John James and Ada 21; Mina 19; Walter 18; Annie jr.17; Eveline 15; Lilian 14; Maria 12; Mabel 11; Charles jr. 15; Alexander 14; William 13. **Alex's and Naomi's child:** Warwick (my grandfather, a baby). **George's and Alice's children:** Madeline 11; George 13; Alice jr. 11; Ethel 10; Claude 3; Cyril 1. **Alfred and Lauretta's children:** Alfred 7; William 6; Vivian 4; Edwin 3; Cecil 1; Millicent a baby
476 William sr. believed the Nowland's heritage at Ward's Mistake would continue for generations.
477 It is not known why Alex received so little from his father. What is known is Alex's and Naomi's first child 'Warwick' (my ancestor) was baptised as a Catholic on the 4th June 1884 at St Joseph's, Gunnedah and this was the start of the Catholic lineage on my branch of the family tree. Alex's wife was a Catholic and now William's grandson was also a Catholic. Whether this bothered William sr. is unknown. During my own youth in the 1950s and 60s, Catholics were forbidden by the Catholic Church to go to any Protestant church service.
478 According to William's Will, he had 790 acres of 'freehold land' at Ward's Mistake in July 1883.
479 It is assumed the Trust arrangements William sr. prescribed from the profits at Ward's Mistake at best quickly dissipated, if enacted upon at all according to his wishes.
480 As told earlier in this story, Michael died in Jericho in 1886; Chas died at Warrah Ridge in 1891; Alex moved back to Rosedale, circa 1895; and, George left Warrah Ridge, in 1907.
481 As told earlier, Alfred sold Rosedale (probably due to ill health) to John Reid Skinner circa 1925. Two accounts in Trove in 1948 mention J. R. Skinner's ownership of Rosedale. Firstly, the *Singleton Argus*, 19 May 1948, p.2…" Messrs. J.R. Skinner and sons … The Rosedale Property was purchased by J. R. Skinner from the late William Nowland" [actually, Alfred Nowland] and secondly, the *Singleton Argus*, 18 August 1948. 'The late Mr. J. R. Skinner … passed away at his residence Rosedale Camberwell (1924–1948) …"
482 John Reid Skinner (1869–1948) is buried at Camberwell Anglican Church Cemetery, along with his wife Violet Holmes Moore Skinner (1872–1949) and two of their children. (Findagrave, 'Camberwell Anglican Church Cemetery', www.findagrave.com). It is assumed after the death of their parents the children of John and Violet Skinner sold Rosedale to the Bowmans.
483 Michael Sheather (April 2019) op. cit.
484 As told earlier, William's brother Edward was the Superintendent for the Hawkesbury Benevolent Society and William went with Edward to find a run for the Society on the Liverpool Plains (a grant of 1000 acres from Governor Darling). They settled on establishing a run for the Society at Phillip's Creek, a run that was later incorporated into Governor Darling's 249,600 acres land grant for the AACo on the Liverpool Plains.
485 Mr. Abbott was John Henry Macartney Abbott (1874–1953), an Australian novelist and poet, born in Haydonton, Murrurundi. (Wikipedia 'J.H.M. Abbott'). When Henry wrote his letter to the local paper about 'Doughboy Hollow' J.H.M. Abbott's serial 'Castle Vane' published periodically, in the World News had mentioned 'Doughboy Hollow' and the wagons that once camped there. Presumable, Henry decided the story his father had told the papers in 1861 about 'Doughboy Hollow' needed to be retold. Later, J.H.M. Abbott's serial was published as a book ('Castle Vane' 1920) and can be viewed now as an e-book online. In Chapter XX entitled 'Doughboy Hollow' Abbott states: 'Down below was Doughboy Hollow, a little dip, or bay, in the ranges, through which ran a mountain brook" (Abbott J.H.M. (1920) 'Castle Vane' Sydney: Angus and Robertson, Project Gutenberg Australia – eBook – Produced by Maurie Mulcahy https://gutenberg.net.au). 'Castle Vane, by J.H.M. Abbott' was originally publication in the World's News, in serial format commencing on 30th September 1916.
486 Fourth stance of the following Hymn: Ellerton John (1870) 'Now the Laborer's (sic) Task is Over'. 'Hymnary' https://hymnary.org.text.
487 Parkinson, Elizabeth S. (c.1990) 'The Pioneering Nowland Brothers', op. cit.
488 See footnote 1, p.1.

Figures

Figure 1: 'An Indomitable Spirit'. After, 'Australasian Pastoralists Review', 15th March 1897. (Station Life/State Library of NSW https://www.sl.nsw.gov.au). Illustration: Stewart Crawford.

Figure 2: Thompson Square and Windsor's First School. 'Thompson Square and Windsor's First School' Community Action for Windsor Bridge, www.cawb.com.au

Figure 3: Transcript of Character References. Nowland Ian (1996) *The Story of Michael and Elizabeth Nowland*, Attachments J (1). A photo of the original (less legible) letter Attachment J (3)

Figure 4: Transcript of Reply. Ibid. Nowland Ian (1996) Attachment J (2) A photo of the original (less legible) reply Attachment J (4).

Figure 5: The Nowland Family Allotments at Glennies Creek. Extract from Hunter River District Map 1821 to 1825, Campbell J.F. (1 June 1926), Hunter River District Map 1821 to 1825, 'Genesis of Rural Settlement in the Hunter' p.86. https://hunterlivingstories.com/tag/land-settlement-hunter-region

Figure 6: Spread of Settlement – Lower Hunter Valley 1825. Extract from 'Spread of Settlement beyond Cumberland (The Settled Area 1825)', T. M. Perry (1963) *Australia's First Frontier,* Fig. 5, p.35

Figure 7: *The Kamilaroi* – Short Documentary NITV (National Indigenous TV). Produced by Idemitsu Boggabri Coal (2019) 'HOME/The Kamilaroi' https://www.thekamilaroi.com

Figure 8: Map of Oxley's Expedition. 'John Oxley', Thomas Ron & Sydenham Shirley (2022) 'John Oxley' www.kidcyber.com.au

Figure 9: Liverpool Plains. West Prospect from View Hill. Oxley John (1820) *Journal of an Expedition in Australia Part 11* https://gutenberg.net.au/ebooks

Figure 10: AACo's Land Grant and William Nowland's Run Warrah. Robert Dixon, 20th July 1837 (extract from Map F 891), 'The Colony of New South Wales: exhibiting the situation and extent of the appropriated lands…', 'Digital Map' in Trove https://nla.gov.obj-231316713/view.

Figure 11: The Squatters Head North. Reuss & Browne (extract from map NK5928) 1860), 'Map of New South Wales and part of Queensland…' ('Digital Map' in Trove https://nla.gov.au/nla.obj-230694679).

Figure 12: Hawkesbury Benevolent Society's Grant – Mooki Station, ibid. Reuss & Brown (1860)

Figure 13: William Nowland's Dridool Run (1837–1839), ibid. Reuss & Browne (1860)

Figure 14: Distance between Waterloo Creek and Dridool, ibid. Reuss & Browne (1860)

Figure 15: William Nowland's Wallalla Run (approx. location), ibid. Reuss & Browne (1860)

Figure 16: Wendy Bowman's Rosedale (2023). Photo: Stewart Crawford, 2023

Figure 17: Henry Nowland's Chain of Ponds Inn, Liddell. Upper Hunter org. The Pioneering Nowland Brothers. http://www.upperhunter.org/nowlandbrothers

Figure 18: William Nowland's Boonanga Run (1840 – c.1850). Reuss & Browne, (1860) op. cit.

Figure 19: Location of Ward's Mistake and the Gullies and Gorges. Satellite Map of Ward's Mistake. www.maphill.com.

Figure 20: Ward's Mistake (1860). Reuss & Browne, (1860), op. cit.

Figure 21: St Clement's Anglican Church Camberwell. Photo: Stewart Crawford (2023).

Figure 22: Relative Position of Mooki Station, Walhollow Station and Wallalla Station. Reuss & Browne (1860), op. cit.

Figure 23: William Nowland's 30 Town Allotments. Powditch St (10 allots.) and Dawson St (20 allots.). Parish & Historical Maps, NSW Land Registry Services. https://www.nswlrs.com.au

Figure 24: Location of Wallalla Station in Relation to Walhollow Station and Doona Station (spelt Doono on the map). Reuss & Browne, (1860), op. cit.

Figure 25: Walhollow, HBS and Mooki River, ibid. Reuss & Browne (1860).

Figure 26: Relative Locations: Warrah Estate (AACo), Telford, Warrah Ridge and Quirindi (Map One). Quirindi Historical Society (an invaluable historical map).

Figure 27: Location of Some of the Nowland Allotments (all adjoining) at Warrah Ridge relative to the AACo's Warrah Estate (Map Two). NSW Land Registry Services 'Buckland County, Parish of Warrah' https://www.nswlrs.com.au..

Figure 28: Nowland Allotments: County of Buckland, Parish of Warrah and Parish of Telford (1885) (Map Three). A constructed map by combining the information on map one and map two.

Figure 29: The Nowland Coach. Photo: Ancestry.com.

Figure 30: P.S. SOPHIA JANE. From a painting by Dickson Gregory, image No.; 2805501, State Library of Victoria cited in https://www.pittwateronlinenews.com/australias-first-steamers-history

Figure 31: Paddle Steamer – Rose. Abbot J. H. M. (1942) 'The Newcastle Packets and the Hunter Valley' Project Gutenberg Australia (ebook). https://gutenberg.net.au

Figure 32: PS Black Swan, c.1844, Stopping at a Wharf on Sydney Harbour. Alec Smart (6 Nov 2023), 'Sydney's First Ferry Operators' Neighbourhood Media PS https://www.neighbourhoodmedia.com.au.

Figure 33: Map showing the Great Northern Railway's Link to Brisbane and to the North Coast Railway as well as the dates of the openings of each station. Cartography: Lawrence Henderson (1 June 2022), Maitland Our Place, Our Stories, The Maitland District Historical Society, https://maitlandstories.com.au.

Figure 34: Liverpool Plains Circa 1866, Julie Yeomans for Quirindi & District Historical Society: 'C1866 – Liverpool Plains, in the North of New South Wales by Walter George Mason (1820–1866) – Very rare engraving of Liverpool Plains with a herd of cattle being rounded up by a stockman. From the original edition of *The Illustrated Sydney News*. (Photo from Antique Print & Map Room Gallery)'.

Figure 35: Transcript of the 'Will of William Nowland dated 20 July 1883'. Quirindi Historical Society, donated by Jim & Mel (Nowland) Baker.

Figure 36: Wendy Bowman's Rosedale. Photo: David Fanner in Hunt Elle (24 April 2017), 'Honour for environmental activist farmer, 83, surrounded by mines on three sides. https://www.theguardian.com/environment/2017/apr/24/honour-environmental-activist-farmer-83-wendy-bowman.

Figure 37: Topographic Map of Nowlands Gap and Ardglen. Google Maps.

Figure 38: A Possible Spot for William's Doughboy Hollow. Photo: Stewart Crawford, 2023.

Figure 39: Memorial Obelisk of William and Mary Nowland (née Farlow) and Tomb on the left their son's, 'John' (1841–1860). Photo: Stewart Crawford, 2023.

Figure 40: Mary's and their Children's Inscription for William at the Bottom of the Obelisk. Photo: Stewart Crawford, 2023.

BIBLIOGRAPHY

Abbott J.H.M. (1920) *'Castle Vane' Sydney*: Angus and Robertson Project Gutenberg Australia (eBook), Produced by Maurie Mulcahy https://gutenberg.net.au

Abbott J.H.M. (1942) *The Newcastle Packets and the Hunter Valley*, Project Gutenberg Australia (eBook) https://gutenberg.net.au

Archibald-Binge Ella and Rhett Wyman Rhett (24 January 2020), 'Struggle and survival: Three Aboriginal perspectives on Australia Day', *Sydney Morning Herald* https://www.smh.com.au

Architecture Australia Magazine ('April/May 1976), 'Retrospective' – Michael Nowland' https://architectureau.com/mazines/archite/australia.

Atchison John (PhD Thesis, 1973), 'Port Stephens and Goonoo Goonoo – A Review of the early period of the Agricultural Company 1824-1849', Australian National University Open Research Repository https://openresearchrepository.com.edu.au

Australasian Legal Information Institute (AustLII), 'The Crown Lands Alienation Act of 1861 no.26a'; 'The Crown Lands Occupation Act 1861 No 27'; Marriage Act 1855 No. 30 https://www.classic.auslii.edu.au/legis

Australian Government (DCCEEW) (2022), 'Myall Creek Massacre and Memorial Site' https://www.dcceew.gov.au

Australian National University – Archives Library, 'Australian Agricultural Company Records' https://archives.anu.edu.au

Australian Human Rights Commission, 'Bringing them home report 8 History – New South Wales and the Australian Capital Territory' https://humanrights.gov.au

Australian Royalty, https://australianroyalty.net.au; various individuals as detailed in the Endnotes.

Baker Bryce (15 Sep. 2020), 'FROM the VAULT – The Archaeology of the Queensland Native Mounted Police, My Police Museum https://mypolice.qld.gov.au

Bathurst Regional Council, 'The Wiradjuri people' https://www.bathurst.nsw.gov.au

Bennett J.M. (2006), 'John Thomas Bigge' (1780–1843) Australian Dictionary of Biography, National Centre of Biography, Australian National University https://adb.anu.edu.au

Betteridge Margaret (2011), 'King St. Courts', State library of NSW, Dictionary of Sydney, https://www.dictionaryofsydney.org

Bigambul Native Title Aboriginal Corporation (BNTAC), 'The Bigambul People – Ancestry' https://bigambul.org.au

Bigge John Thomas (1823), 'The State of Agriculture and Trade in the Colony of New South Wales (Third Report, 13th March 1823), Parliamentary Paper136/1823, online version – NSW Government https://guides.sl.nsw.gov.au

Brian Jessica (8 Aug 2019), 'The Victorian Workhouse' https://www.historic-uk.com

Britannica 'Livestock slaughter procedures-Slaughter' https://britannica.com

Cabel K.J. (2006) William Woolls (1814-1893) Australian Dictionary of Biography, National Centre of Biography, Australian National University https://adb.anu.edu.au

Callaghan Terry, 'Notes re Conditional Purchase' https://www.terrycallaghan.com.

Campbell J.F. (1 June 1926), 'The Genesis of Rural Settlement on the Hunter', *Journal and Proceedings of the Royal Australian Historical Society*, Vol XII 1926 Part II.) https://hunterlivingstories.com/tag/land-settlement-hunter-region; https://trove.nla.gov.au.

Campbell J. F. (1968), *Squatting on Crown Land in New South Wales*, Royal Australian Historical Society

Capenter Michelle (2011), 'Colonial History – Kamilaroi – A Nations Identity' https://www.kamilaroianationsidentity.weebly.com

Carney Gerard (10th April 2013), 'The Story Behind the Land Borders of the Australian States', Public Lecture Series, High Court of Australia www.cdn.hcourt.gov.au.

Carter H.R. (1974), *The Upper Mooki*, Quirindi: Newspaper Company, Quirindi Centre

Clayton-Dixon Callum (2020), *Surviving New England: A History of Aboriginal Resistance and Resilience Through the First Forty Years of the Colonial Apocalypse*. Armidale, New South Wales: Anaiwan Language Revival Program

Clayton-Dixon Callum (27th August 2020), 'Where neither white man nor horse could follow – rough country & the Aboriginal resistance'. Medium Indigenous Research https://medium.com/@IndigenousDS)

Clift Brett (26 June 2014), 'Presentation to the Planning Assessment Commission Hearing Watermark Coal Project Gunnedah LGA' https://www.ipcn.nsw.gov.au

Clift Tony (30 Oct. 2021), 'A Conspicuous Object. The Maitland Hospital. Supporting those Less Fortunate' https://aconspiciousobject.com.au/stories.

Coffs Coast (2023), 'Yaam Gumbaynggirr Jagun – Here Is Gumbaynggirr Country, City of Coffs Harbour https://www.coffscoast.com.au

Coffs Trails (3 July 2021), 'Major Points, Darkie Point to Point Lookout, New England' https://coffstrails.com

Connell Cecilia and Bernasconi Amelia (1 August 2023), Award-winning Hunter Valley environmentalist and farmer Wendy Bowman dies aged 89' ABC news https://abc.net.au/news.

Connor John (2002), *The Australian Frontier Wars, 1788-1838*, UNSW Press.

Convict Records https://convictrecords.co.au.; various individuals as detailed in the Endnotes.

Cotter Maria (28th March 2022), Submission to the NSW Government Independent Planning Commission https://www.ipcn.nsw.gov.au

Cowlishaw Gillian (1993), 'Roger Milliss (1992) 'Waterloo Creek: The Australian Day Massacre of 1838. George Gipps and the British Conquest of New South Wales', Review Article, *Australian Journal of Anthropology* (1993, p.63), https://www.academia.edu

Cows i.e. (9 Dec 2021), 'Understanding cattle terminology' https://www.cow.ie

Crew Vernon, (2006), 'William Walker (1828-1908)' Australian Dictionary of Biography, National Centre of Biography, Australian National University https://adb.anu.edu.au

Cunningham Allan (1832), 'Brief View of the Progress of Interior Discovery in New South Wales', *Journal of the Royal Geographical Society of London*, Vol 2, 1832, p.110. 'Allan Cunningham' https://scholar.archive.org; e-book, https://www.gutenberg.net.au

Currey C.H. (2006), 'Sir William Thomas Denison (1804–1871)' Australian Dictionary of Biography, National Centre of Biography, Australian National University https://adb.anu.edu.au

CWAB, 'Thompson Square and Windsor's First School'. www.cawb.com.au.

Ellerton John (1870) 'Now the Laborer's (sic) Task is Over'. Hymnary https://hymnary.org.text

Dangar Henry (1828), 'Index and Directory to Map the Country Bordering Upon the Hunter River, London. (e-book available at: 'Trove Digital Advanced Search'. https://nla.gov.au

Deadly Story, 'The Batman 'treaty' is signed', Kulin Nation https://deadlystory.com

Dhiiyaan Aboriginal Centre' (2025), 'Kamilaroi Culture', Moree Plains Artesian Water Country, Moree Plains Tourism https://www.moreetourism.com.au.

BIBLIOGRAPHY

Dunn Mark (2015), Thesis PhD (UNSW) 'A Valley in a Valley: Colonial Struggles over land and resources in the Hunter Valley, NSW 1820–1850' University of New South Wales https://unsworks.unsw.edu.au

Dunn Mark (2016), 'Aboriginal Guides in the Hunter Valley, New South Wales', Chapter 4, *Brokers and Boundaries,* ANU Press (2016) https://press.anu.edu.au

Domain (26 May 2020), 'One of Australia's oldest homesteads to be relocated' https://www.domain.com.au

Dyster Barrie (1 August 2022), 'The Depression of the 1840s in New South Wales', Australian Dictionary of Biography, National Centre of Biography, Australian National University https://adb.anu.edu.au/essay/29/text40594

Eldershaw F. (1854), *Australia As it Really Is. In its life, Scenery, & Adventure: with the character, habits, and customs of its Aboriginal inhabitants, and the prospects and extent of its gold fields,* London: Darton and Co. (e-Book, Trove https://trove.nla.gov.au

Edwell Penny (2016), *Lady Juliana,* State Library of NSW, Dictionary of Sydney, www.dictionaryofsydney.org.

Edwell Penny (2016), *Surprize*, State Library of NSW, Dictionary of Sydney, www.dictionaryofsydney.org.

Find a Grave https://www.findagrave.com; various gravestones as detailed in the Endnotes.

Findmypast, 'Elizabeth Richards and Hannah Bolton Lent Calendar (March–May) 1789 Warwick County Gaol', Warwick Record Office – Jopson's Coventry https://www.findmypast.com.au

Fitz-Gibbon Bryan and Gizycki Marianne (October 2001), 'The 1840s Depression'. Reserve Bank of Australia https://www.rba.gov.au/publications

Flynn Michael (1993), *The Second Fleet: Britain's grim convict armada of 1790*

Friends of Myall Creek (21 May 2021), 'Reconciliation Trail – Moree to Myall Creek – Kamilaroi country' https://myallcreek.org); 'About Friends of Myall Creek' https://myallcreek.org); The Massacre Story' https://myallcreek.org/the-massacre-story ; 'Text of the Myall Creek Memorial Plagues [Plague 6], https://myallcreek.org/test

Gapps Stephen and Murray Mina (28th July 2021), 'From Colonial cavalry to mounted police: a short history of the Australian police horse'. The Conversation https://theconversation.com.

Gray Nancy (2006), 'Henry Dangar (1796-1861)' Australian Dictionary of Biography, National Centre of Biography, Australian National University https://adb.anu.edu.au.

General Muster (12th August 1806), cited in Nowland Ian (1995), p.182 *Michael and Elizabeth Nowland*, Castle Hill Historical Society

Gill J.C.H. (1969), 'The Hawkesbury River Floods of 1801,1806 and 1809', The University of Queensland, https://espace.library.uq.edu.au.

Gillard Dick (August 2020), 'Michael Nowland a Troubled Life,' *Hawkesbury Historical Society Newsletter*, 140 pp.13-15 (Trove Digital Newspapers)

Glencore Australia 'Heritage Management Plan. Ravensworth Open Cut' (2022, p.16) 'Early Settlement and Exploration'. https://www.glencore.com.au.

Gore Sarah (16 August 2021), 'Protect Wonnarua History from Mining Destruction', O'Brien Criminal & Civil Solicitors. https://obriensolicitors.com.au/protect-wonnarua-history-mining-destruction

Government of South Australia – Weed Identification Notes, Animal and Plant Control Commission 'Caltrop', https://data.environment.sa.gov.au/Content/Publications/pests

Gregoire Paul and Medim Ugur (19 Nov 2021), 'The Frontier Violence Perpetrated by the NSW Mounted Police', Sydney Criminal Lawyers https://www.sydneycriminallawyers.com.au/blog

Grenville Kate (2005), *The Secret River,* Canongate Books

Griffiths John (2010), *Industry & Perseverance – A History of David Brown (1750-1836) and family*, National Library of Australia https://nla.gov.au

Guilford Elizabeth (2006), 'John Eales (1799-1871)', Australian Dictionary of Biography, National Centre of Biography, Australian National University https://adb.anu.edu.au

Halburg F, Cornélissen G., Bernhardt K.H., M Sampson, M, O., Schwartzkopff O., Sonntag D. (3 May 2011), 'Egeson's (George's) transtridecadal weather cycling and sunspots', National Centre for Biotechnology Information, National Library of Medicine https://pmc.ncbi.nlm.nih.gov/articles/PMC3086776/

Halcombe J.J. (1868), *The Emigrant and the Heathen; or Sketches of Missionary Life*, London, eBook, University of Newcastle https://downloads.newcastle.edu.au.

Hawkesbury City Council (2021), 'Hawkesbury Local LGA Aboriginal Cultural Heritage Study' https://www.hawkesbury.nsw.gov.au.

Hawkesbury Visitors Information, 'Macquarie Trail' (p.6) 'Wilberforce – Nowland Cottage c.1810-1816' https://www.discoverthehawkesbury.com.au/)

Henderson Lawrence (1 June 2022), 'The railway extends 1863-1932', Maitland Our Place, Our Stories, The Maitland District Historical Society https://maitlandstories.com.au

Hespe Michelle, (8 August, 2023), 'Tribute: a farmer and a fighter', *The Farmer* magazine https://thefarmermagazine.com.au

Heydon J.D. (2006), 'Sir Thomas Makdougall Brisbane', Australian Dictionary of Biography, National Centre of Biography, Australian National University https://adb.anu.edu.au

Higgins Isabella and Gollard Sarah (25 January 2020), 'Australia Day: January 26 marks a massacre in NSW. Will a cement plaque really work?' ABC News, Live Blog. https://www.abc.net.au

Hughes Robert (1987), *The Fatal Shore*, pp.145-46 London: William Collins Sons and Co. Ltd

Hughes Turnbull (2008) 'The End of Transportation' Dictionary of Sydney https://dictionaryofsydney.org

Hunt Elle (24 April 2017), 'Honour for environmental activist farmer, 83, surrounded by mines on three sides.' https://www.theguardian.com/environment/2017/apr/24/honour-environmental-activist-farmer-83-wendy-bowman.

Karskens Grace, Watson Leanne, Wilkins Erin, Seymour Jasmine, and Wright Rhiannon (19 May 2021), Reconciliation Australia, 'A Deep Human History: Remapping Darug Place Names and Culture on Dyarubbin, The Hawkesbury River'. www.reconciliation.org.au

Karskens Grace (2022), *People of the River*, Allen & Unwin

Ketchell Misha (28 July, 2021), 'From colonial cavalry to mounted police: a short history of the Australian police horse' https://theconversation.com

Korff J. (2023), 'Myall Creek Massacre (1838)'; 'Massacres: The frontier violence that's hard to accept – Aboriginal people killing Aboriginal people'. Creative Spirits. https://www.creativespirits.info

King, P.J. 'Letter Book 1', 1788/99 pp. 251-271, 292, 302, 322 and Mitchell Library C187 cited in Nowland Ian (1995), op. cit. p.103.

King-Smith Sue (2007), 'Ancestral Echoes: Spectres of the Past in Judith Wright's Poetry' *Journal of the Association for the Study of Australian Literature*, pp.117-129. https://openjournals.test.library.sydney.edu.au

Lapham Jake (2021), 'Future of Historic Ravensworth' ABC Upper Hunter https://www.abc.net.au

Lands Titles Australia, 'Lands Titles Office [L.T.O.], Old Register Book 1', p. 143, No 1107, Book 4, p. Nos 1336 cited in Nowland Ian (1995), *Michael and Elizabeth Nowland*, p.183.Castle Hill Historical Society

Lea-Scarlett E.J. (2006), 'Kenneth Snodgrass (1784-1853)' Australian Dictionary of Biography, National Centre of Biography, Australian National University https://adb.anu.edu.au.

BIBLIOGRAPHY

Lennox Suzie (2025), 'The Tedious Job of Oakum Picking in a Victorian Prison', My Macabre Road trip https://mymacabreroadtrip.com/oakum-picking.

Macmillan David S. (2006), 'William Paterson (1755-1810)', Australian Dictionary of Biography, National Centre of Biography, Australian National University https://adb.anu.edu.au

Marr David (2023), *Killing for Country*, Black Inc Books

Martin A.W. (2006), 'Sir John Hay (1816-1892)' Australian Dictionary of Biography, National Centre of Biography, Australian National University https://adb.anu.edu.au.

Martin A.W. and P. Wardle P. (1959), 'Members of the Legislative Assembly of New South Wales 1856-1901 – Biographical Notes', Australian National University, Open Research Library https://openresearch-repository.anu.edu.au

McCrossin's Mill Museum, 'Traditional Anaiwan People', Uralla Historical Society https://uhs.org.au/anaiwan

McCulloch Samuel Clyde (2006), 'Sir George Gipps (1791-1847)' Australian Dictionary of Biography, National Centre of Biography, Australian National University https://adb.anu.edu.au

McHardy Cathy and Mc Hardy Nicholas, 'The Great North Road, Wiseman Ferry', Hawkesbury History and Location, Hawkesbury People and Places https://www.hawkesbury.org.au

McLaughlin John Kennedy (2006), 'Sir John Nodes Dickinson (1806 – 1882)', Australian Dictionary of Biography, National Centre of Biography, Australian National University https://adb.anu.edu.au

McQuilton John (9th June 2019), 'Squatters and pastoralists: land, status and Indigenous dispossession.' Australia Explained _ https://australia-explained.com.au

Merriam-Webster, 'Upas definition and Meaning' https://www.merriam-webster.com

Miller James (1985), *Koori, A Will to Win: the heroic resistance, survival & triumph of black Australia*, Angus and Robertson

Miller James Wilson (2005), 'Conflict in the Valley: The Triumph of the Wonnarua' pp.5-6 AARE Annual Conference Parramatta 2005. https://www.aare.edu.au/data/publications/2005/wil05317.pdf)

Monuments Australia, 'William IV' https://monumentsaustralia.org.au.

Morrison W.F. (1888), *The Aldine Centennial History of NSW*, The Alpine Publishing Company, Sydney, 1888, ebook, https://www.bda-online.org.au

Museum of Australian Democracy, 'NSW Constitution Act 1842 (UK)', Documenting Democracy https://www.foundingdocs.gov.au

Museum of History, NSW (MHNSW), 'Convict Transportation to NSW'; 'Conditional Purchase of Crown Land'; 'School Record Guide' https://mhnsw.au

Muster, Wilberforce' (1828), 'Census & Musters Guide' Museums of History NSW https://mhnsw.au

Nairn Bede (2006), 'Sir John Robertson' (1816-1891)' Australian Dictionary of Biography, National Centre of Biography, Australian National University https://adb.anu.edu.au

National Museum of Australia, 'Secret Ballot Introduced'; 'Robertson Land Acts'; 'OBJECT BIOGRAPHY Nowland's Mail Coach' https://nma.gov.au

New England High Country (1 July 2021), 'History and Heritage in New England High Country – Hamilton Collins Sempill' https://newenglandhighcountry.com.au

Noble Lillian M (1998), *The Glennies Creek Story*, Singleton Historical Society

Norton David R (1996), *The Aiatsis Map of Indigenous Australia*, Aboriginal Studies Press, AIATSIS and Auslig/Sinclair, Knight, Merz, 1996. https://aiatsis.gov.au.

Nowland Ian (1995), *Michael and Elizabeth Nowland*, Castle Hill Historical Society

NSW Government (2020), 'Rising Waters-Thompson Square', https://thompsonsquare.com.au

NSW Government, Department of Primary Industries (2023), 'Paterson's curse (Echium plantagineum) – NSW Weed Wise' https://weeds.dpi.nse.gov.au.

NSW Government – Education NSW (6 Mar 2023), 'Early History-NSW Education', History of NSW Government Schools Department https://education.nsw.gov.au.

NSW Government – Government Environment and Heritage (8 September 2023), 'Extraordinary History of Nowland's Lochinvar Coach House and Setting, recognised with listing on the NSW State Heritage Register'; 'Australian convict Sites – Old Great North Road' NSW' https://www.environment.nsw.gov.au

NSW Government – Transport, Roads and Maritime Services, 'New England Highway Urban Design Framework' https://www.transport.nsw.gov.au.

NSW Land Registry Services, 'HLRV [Historical Land Record View], 'History of Land and Property Information'; 'William Nowland' varies land purchases as detailed in the text of the story. https://www.nswlrs.com.au.

NSW National Parks, 'Terry Hie Hie Aboriginal Area', NSW Government https://www.nationalparks.nsw.gov.au.

NSW Registry of Births, Deaths and Marriages, https://www.nsw.gov.au, various births, deaths and marriages as detailed in the Endnotes

NSWrail.net, 'Ravensworth Station' https://www.nswrail.net>locations.

Obituaries Australia, 'Arthur Digit (1819-1895)' National Centre of Biography, Australian National University https://oa.anu.edu.au/obituary

Old Bailey, 'Transcript, 26th February 1783, Michael Nowland'. www.oldbaileyonline.org

Online genealogy sites, including but not limited to Ancestry.com. Findmypast.com; and. Australian Royalty.com. and as detailed in the Endnotes.

Old Register Book 1, p.117, no.679 cited in Nowland Ian (1995), op. cit. p.117

O'Neill Aaron (8 Aug 2024), 'Life expectancy (from birth) in Australia, from 1870 to 2020', Statista, https://www.statista.com

O'Rouke Michael (2005), 'Sung for Generation. Tales of Red Kangaroo War Leader of Gunnedah', e-book, https://www.scribd.com

O'Rourke Michael (2009), 'Pages to the North-West Plains', e-book, https://www.scribd.com

Oxley John (1820), *Journal of An Expedition in Australia Part 11* https://gutenberg.net.au/ebooks.

Parkinson Elizabeth S. 'Liz', (c.1990), 'The Pioneering Nowland Brothers', www.upperhunter.org

Parliament of New South Wales, 'Richard Jones 1816-1892'; '1843 to 1855 – Towards Responsible Government'; 'The History of the Legislative Assembly'; 'The Crown Lands Act 1884'. 'Sir John Robertson'; 'John Robertson (1816-1891)';'Francis Augustus Wright (1835-1903)', https://parliament.nsw.gov.au

Parr, Journal, (1817), SRNSW Fiche 3271, 2/3623; Macqueen (2004) pp.63–79, cited in *Brokers and Boundaries*, ANU Press (2016), Chapter 4, Mark Dunn 'Aboriginal Guides in the Hunter Valley, New South Wales', p.66. https://press.anu.edu.au

Parry Ann (2006), 'Sir William Edward Parry (1790-1855), Australian Dictionary of Biography, National Centre of Biography, Australian National University https://adb.anu.edu.au

Parry Naomi with Christison Ray (December 2019), 'A Thematic History of Liverpool Plains Shire', a report prepared for the Liverpool Plains Shire Council https://naomiparry.net

Parsons Vivienne (2006), 'Ellis Martin Scott (1799-1829)' Australian Dictionary of Biography, National Centre of Biography, Australian National University https://adb.anu.edu.au.

BIBLIOGRAPHY

Perry T. M. (1963), *Australia's First Frontier – The spread of settlement in New South Wales 1788-1829*, Melbourne University Press, The Australian National University https://openresearch-repository.anu.edu.au

People Australia, 'Michael Nowland (c.1758-1828) National Centre of Biography, Australian National University www.peopleaustralia.anu.edu.au/michaelnowland

Pickard John (2005), 'Post and rail fences: Derivation, development, and demise of rural technology in colonial Australia', Faculty of Science and Engineering, Macquarie University https://researchers.mq.edu.au

Pickard John (2007), 'The Transition from Shepherding to Fencing in Colonial Australia', Faculty of Science and Engineering, Macquarie University https://researchers.mq.edu.au.

Possum Venessa (on behalf of the Dharug Ngurra Aboriginal Corporation DNAC) (21October 2020), 'Our Community' https://www.dharugngurra.org.au.

Przecha, Donna, 'The Importance of Names and Naming Patterns, https://www.genealogy.com

Rees Sian (2001), *The Floating Brothel*, Headline

Research Data Australia, 'AGY-2111-Newcastle Penal Establishment'; 'ACY-3497-Commissioner of Crown Lands for Liverpool Plains'; 'John Robertson First Secretary of Lands' AGY-1114 Departments of Lands, NSW State Archives Collection https://researchdata.edu.au.

Reuss F. H. and Browne J.L. (1860), Map of New South Wales and part of Queensland', digital copy. Trove https://www.nla.gov.au

Reynolds Henry (2013), *Forgotten Wars*, UNSW Press

Reynolds Henry (2021), *Truth-Telling: History, Sovereignty and the Uluru Statement*, UNSW Press.

Rodgers Peter (October 4, 2023), 'Shining more light on Australia's brutal colonial past' https://www.peter-rodgers.com.au

Rolls Eric (2011), *A Million Wild Acres: 200 Years of Man and an Australian Forest*, Hale and Iremonger

Roots Web https://home.rootsweb.com used to calculate William Nowland's birth year

Roth Lenny (2014), 'Crown Land Management' Parliament of NSW https://www.parliament.nsw.gov.au/researchpapers

Rutledge Martha (2006) 'Jules François de Sales Joubert (1824–1907)', Australian Dictionary of Biography, National Centre of Biography, Australian National University https://adb.anu.edu.au

Ryan James 'Toby' (1895), *Reminiscences of Australia*, Sydney: George Robertson and Company.

Ryan Lyndall (2013), 'Untangling Aboriginal Resistance and the settlers' punitive expedition: the Hawkesbury River frontier in New South Wales, 1794-1810', *Journal of Genocide Research* (2013), Vol 15, No.2. pp.219-232 https://dx.doc.org

Ryan Lyndall et al. (2025), 'Colonial Frontier Massacres in Australia 1788-1930', (Glennies Creek, 1st September 1826), https://c21ch.newcastle.edu.au/colonialmassacres/detail.php?r=570. The Emerita Professor Lyndall Ryan's (14 April 1943–30 April 2024) scholarly work provides an invaluable contribution to the informative understanding of the extent and nature of the colonial frontier massacres that occurred between 1788–1930.

Saclier M.J. (2006), 'George Boyle White' (1802-1876), Australian Dictionary of Biography, National Centre of Biography, Australian National University https://adb.anu.edu.au.

SBS Australia (September 2022), *The Australian Wars*

SBS The Feed (2019), *Reconciliating Murder: The Myall Creek Massacre*. YouTube

Schoolhouse Museum of Public Education, 'Early School Days 1870s to 1920s' https://www.schoolhousemuseum.org.au.

Scone Historical Society, Betty Pinkerton 'Nowland Research Folder'. 'William Nowland 1804-1884' https://scone.com.au; 'Alexander and Mary Johnston (née Nowland) https://www.upperhunter.org/nowlandbrothers.

Scotland's People, 'The Radical Rising of 1820' https://www.scotlandspeople.gov.uk

Sheather Michael (April 2019), 'Hunter Valley farmer takes on mining company – and wins', NSW Farmers Association https://www.nswfarmers.org.au

Shoemaker Robert (c.2017), 'The Digital Panopticon, 'Punishments, 1780-1925', https://www.digitalpanopticon.org

Singleton's Journal (5 May 1818), SRNSW Reel 6047, 4/1740: 212 cited in *Brokers and Boundaries*, ANU Press (2016), ibid. Chapter 4, Mark Dunn, p.66.

Smart Alec (6 Nov 2023), 'Sydney's First Ferry Operators', Neighbourhood Media https://www.neighbourhoodmedia.com.au.

Smith Hiliary (July 2022), 'Kamilaroi, Gamilaraay, or Gomeroi', Winanga-Li Aboriginal Child & Family Centre https://winanga-li.org.au

South Australian Maritime Museum, 'History Trust of South Australian Passenger in History' https://passengers,history.sa.gov.au

State Archives & Records NSW, www.records.nsw.gov.au; various records detailed in the Endnotes

State Library of NSW, www.sl.nsw.gov.au; various publications as detailed in the Endnotes

State Library of Victoria, 'P.S. SOPHIA JANE' – from a painting by Dickson Gregory, image No.; 2805501, cited in https://www.pittwateronlinenews.com/australias-first-steamers-history

Stone Barry (2019), *The Squatters. The Story of Australia's Pastoral Pioneers,* Allen & Unwin

Stuart Iain (1999), PhD Thesis, 'Squatting Landscapes in South-Western Australia (1820-1895) University of Sydney (e-copy available online).

The Australian Institute of Aboriginal and Torres Strait Islander Studies (AIATSIS), Missions, stations and reserves', https://aiatsis.gov.au.

The Australian National University, 'Australian Agricultural Company – Archives', https://archivescollection.anu.edu.au.

The Dictionary of Sydney (2008), 'Commissariat Stores', staff writer, State Library of NSW, https://dictionaryofsydney.org.)

The Farmer magazine (8 August, 2023) 'Tribute: a farmer and a fighter', https://thefarmermagazine.com.au

The Kamilaroi – Short Documentary (2019), NITV (National Indigenous TV), produced by Idemitsu Boggabri Coal, 'HOME/The Kamilaroi', https://www.thekamilaroi.com

The Nēwara Aboriginal Corporation' NITV (National Indigenous TV), https://www.sbs.com.au.

Talbott Dolly (2019), The Kamilaroi – Short Documentary (2019), NITV (National Indigenous TV). produced by Idemitsu Boggabri Coal, 'HOME/The Kamilaroi' https://www.thekamilaroi.com

Trove Digital Newspapers: *Australian Chronicle; Australian Town and Country Journal; Glen Innes Examiner and General Advertiser; Launceston Examiner; Newcastle Morning Herald and Miners' Advocate; The Illustrated Sydney News; The Albury Banner and Wodonga Express; The Armidale Express and New England General Advertiser; The Australian Daily Journal; The Australian; The Colonial Observer; The Goulburn Herald and County of Argyle Advertiser; The Maitland Mercury and Hunter River Advertiser; The Monitor; The Muswellbrook Chronicle; The Sydney Gazette and New South Wales Advertiser; The Sydney Monitor; The Sydney Morning Herald; Government Gazette and Notices; The Richmond River Express and Casino Kyogle Advertiser; The Week; Singleton Argus; Newcastle Morning Herald; Hobart Town Gazette and Van Diemen's Land Advertiser*, various articles as detailed in the notes

University of Newcastle, 'Plans for St Clement's Church, situated in Camberwell NSW' The University Library Special Collections https://livinghistories.newcastle.edu.au.

University of Sydney (2010 – 2013), 'A History of Aboriginal Sydney' www.ahistoryofaboriginalsydney.edu.au

Walker W.M. (1887), *History of the Hawkesbury Benevolent Society*, Sydney: Turner and Henderson. (Digital copy in Trove, https://nla.gov.au)

Walsh Brian (2020), 'Toil and Trouble from Maitland to Moreton Bay – John Eales' Convicts' Paterson Historical Society https://www.patersonhistory.org.au)

Ward, John M. 'Grey, Henry George (1802–1894)', Australian Dictionary of Biography, National Centre of Biography, Australian National University, https://adb.anu.edu.au

Warwick Record Office – Jopson's Coventry, Mercury 13 August 1787, No. 24840 (Elizabeth Richards 4th August 1787, Summer Assizes) cited in Nowland Ian (1995) op. cit. p.69.

Weebly (2020), 'Warwick Goal – JOHN COLLINS – CHARTIST', https://www.chartistcollins.com)

Weeds Australia, Centre for Invasive Species Solutions, 'Caltrop', https://weeds.org.au

Wicklow Goal (23 June 2014), 'Work and Chores – Wicklow's Historic Goal, https://ww.wicklowshistoricgoal.com

Wilderness Australia (9 Aug 2022), 'Exploring Guy Fawkes', https://www.wildernessaustralia.org.au

Willetts Jen, 'Alexander Johnston'; 'Hunter River Steamers 1831'; 'James Glennie'; 'Norfolk Island – Convict Ships and Notes'; 'Charles Humphrey'; 'John Robertson'; 'James Robertson'; 'Lady Mary Fitzroy Inn (Chain of Ponds)', https://www.freesettlerorfelon.com)

Withcombe Patricia Mary (2015), 'The Twelfth Man: John Fleming and the Myall Creek Massacre' Honours Thesis, University of Newcastle., Australia, https://docslib.org/doc/6016899/john-henry-fleming-and-the-myall-creek-massacre

Wikipedia, various topics as detailed in the Endnotes.

Wonnaura Nation Aboriginal Corporation (June, 2021), 'Boundaries of the Hunter Valley Aboriginal People – Wonnaura Kooris, https://wonnarua.org.au

Wood Allan (1972), 'Dawn in the Valley: The Early History of the Hunter Valley Settlement' Sydney: Wentworth Books

Wright Judith (1981), *The Cry for the Dead*, Melbourne: Oxford University Press

Wright Judith 'Niggers Leap, New England' , All Poetry, https://allpoetry.com

Yancoal (2009), 'Appendix 14 – European Heritage' Aston Coal Project Camberwell NSW, Hertitas Architecture, https://www.yancoal.com.au

About the Author

Lucie Crawford has a passion for new knowledge and research and was drawn into William Nowland's story when William emerged as an interesting and significant person from amongst Lucie's stories on her ancestry. On approaching the local historical societies, it was suggested that William was a significant historical figure within the Hunter region and a comprehensive account of his life would be valuable. Some of William's story was found in historical documents and books held by the local historical societies, from a variety of cognisant sources on the web and most notably, the National Library's Trove with its numerous newspapers that have enriched the story, while other informative aspects of William's life emerged after extensive and rigorous research.

The approach taken is based on grounded theory and reliant on repetitive findings within the data. It draws upon Lucie's scholarship and professional interests and background in teaching, learning and research at a tertiary level.

www.ingramcontent.com/pod-product-compliance
Lightning Source LLC
Chambersburg PA
CBHW061110070526
44583CB00027B/3241